CHOOSE LIFE

ARNOLD TOYNBEE

and

DAISAKU IKEDA

CHOOSE LIFE

A DIALOGUE

Edited by Richard L. Gage

Choose life and then you and
your descendants shall live
Deuteronomy 30: 19

LONDON

OXFORD UNIVERSITY PRESS

KUALA LUMPUR MELBOURNE

Oxford University Press, Ely House, London W.1

OXFORD LONDON GLASGOW NEW YORK
TORONTO MELBOURNE WELLINGTON CAPE TOWN
IBADAN NAIROBI DAR ES SALAAM LUSAKA ADDIS ABABA
KUALA LUMPUR SINGAPORE JAKARTA HONG KONG TOKYO
DELHI BOMBAY CALCUTTA MADRAS KARACHI

ISBN 0 19 215258 0

Choose Life *is the British Commonwealth edition of* The Toynbee-Ikeda Dialogue: Man Himself Must Choose, *first published in 1976 by Kodansha International Ltd., Tokyo, New York & San Francisco.*

PRINTED IN JAPAN

CONTENTS

II

POLITICAL AND INTERNATIONAL LIFE

III

PHILOSOPHICAL AND RELIGIOUS LIFE

PREFACE

The table of contents of this book will tell the reader, at a glance, that the book covers a wide range of topics. These topics have entered into the dialogue because they are matters of personal concern to the two participants. The dialogue is now being published as a book in the hope that the same topics will prove to be matters of general concern for the authors' contemporaries in the English-speaking world, in Japan, and elsewhere.

The dialogue was originally an oral one. The two participants met in London and their conversation lasted for several days. The record of what they said has been rearranged by Mr. Richard L. Gage. His editorial work has been both skillful and arduous. A reader's eye needs a different presentation from the kind that suits a listener's ear, and the two authors of this book are very grateful to Mr. Gage for the service that he has done for them. They believe that their gratitude will be shared by the reader.

The topics discussed in this book are of very diverse kinds. Some of them are of urgent concern at the present time, but some of them are issues of perennial importance that have been pondered and discussed by human beings ever since the unknown date at which our ancestors first awoke to consciousness. It seems probable that these perennial questions will continue to be debated so long as mankind survives in the psychosomatic form in which we exist in our material environment, that is to say, in the biosphere that covers the planet earth.

Daisaku Ikeda is an East Asian; Arnold Toynbee is a Westerner. In the most recent chapter of mankind's history, the West has been taking the lead and has been playing a dominant role. In the present book, Toynbee suggests reasons for expecting that, in the future, the leadership is going to be taken over from the West by Eastern Asia. Mankind has already been united on the technological plane by the worldwide expansion of the West European peoples' activities within the last five hundred years. The authors agree with each other in expecting, and hoping, that, in the next chapter of history, mankind will succeed in unifying politically and spiritually. Ikeda is more hopeful than Toynbee that this great change can be brought about voluntarily, on terms of equality between all sections of the human race, without further domination of one section over others—an evil that, in the past, has all too often been the price of political and spiritual unification on a less than worldwide scale.

Toynbee is, in general, more pessimistic than Ikeda in the sense that he expects that mankind will have to pay a high price for making those profound changes in attitude, objective, and conduct that both authors believe to be indispensable conditions for the survival of humanity. Is Toynbee's comparative pessimism due simply to his age? (It is notorious that in old age people tend to think that the world "is going to the dogs.") Or is it because he is a Westerner who shares, to some extent, Oswald Spengler's belief that, in the twentieth century, we are witnessing the Decline of the West (*der Untergang des Abendlandes*)? Or is it because he is, by vocation, a historian and is therefore particularly (perhaps excessively) conscious of mankind's tragic failure, hitherto, on the political and, still more, on the spiritual plane of human life—a failure that is accentuated by its contrast with the brilliance of mankind's achievements in technology?

Another possible cause of Toynbee's fear that the next chapter of history may be more violent and brutal than Ikeda thinks that it need be is the difference between the religious traditions in which the two authors have been brought up. Toynbee was brought up as a Christian; Ikeda is a Buddhist of the Northern (Mahayana) school. Both Buddhism and Christianity have spread widely (more widely than any nonreligious institution so far), but the means and the consequences of their dissemination have differed. Buddhism, which has spread almost exclusively by peaceful penetration, has been content to coexist amicably with the other religions and philosophies that it has found already present in the regions in which it has been propagated. Buddhism has established a modus vivendi with Taoism and Confucianism in China and with Shinto in Japan. In contrast to Buddhism, Christianity, like its sister-religion Islam, is exclusive minded; in a number of cases Christianity has been imposed by force—for instance, on a majority of the inhabitants of the Roman Empire, on the continental Saxons, and on the pre-Columbian peoples of Mexico and Peru. An awareness of this dark side of the history of Christianity may make a Christian, or ex-Christian, more skeptical than a Buddhist about the possibility of achieving great social changes peaceably.

In spite of the difference between the authors' religious and cultural backgrounds, a remarkable degree of agreement in their outlooks and aims has been brought to light in their dialogue. Their agreement is far-reaching; their

10

points of disagreement are relatively slight. They agree in believing that religion is the mainspring of human life. They agree that a human being ought to be perpetually striving to overcome his innate propensity to try to exploit the rest of the universe and that he ought to be trying, instead, to put himself at the service of the universe so unreservedly that his ego will become identical with an ultimate reality, which for a Buddhist is the Buddha state. They agree in believing that this ultimate reality is not a humanlike divine personality.

They also agree in believing in the reality of karma, a Sanskrit word that literally means "action" but that, in the vocabulary of Buddhism, has acquired the special meaning of an ethical "bank-account" in which the balance is constantly being changed by fresh credit or fresh debit entries during a human being's psychosomatic life on earth. The balance of a human being's karma, at any particular moment, is determined by the plus or minus sum of the previous credit and debit entries; but the karma-bearer can, and will, change the balance, for better or for worse, by his further acts. In fact, he makes his karma for himself and is thus, at least partially, a free agent.

As the authors see it, a human being's perennial spiritual task is to overcome his egotism by expanding his ego until it becomes coextensive with the ultimate reality, from which it is, in truth, inseparable. There is a Hindu saying "*Tat tvam asi*," which means "That (the ultimate reality) is what thou (a human being) art." But a statement of the identity of "thou" and "that" is only a proposition; it must be turned into a practical reality by strenuous spiritual exertion. This spiritual exertion, made by individual human beings, is the only effective means of social change for the better. Changes of institutions are effective only insofar as they are symptoms and consequences of the spiritual self-transformation of the persons whose relations with each other are the network that constitutes a human society.

Thus the agreement between the East Asian and the Western party to the dialogue published in this book is extensive. How is it to be explained? Today, mankind, all round the globe, is being confronted by a number of acute problems. These problems are now besetting all of us, rich and poor, technologically advanced or backward, no matter whether the people's or individual's ancestral religion happens to be of the Indian or of the Judaic school. The universality of these current common problems is a historical consequence of the worldwide network of technological and economic relations that has been created by the expansion of the West European peoples' activities within the last five centuries. Technological and economic relations engender political, ethical, and religious relations. In truth, in our time, we are witnessing the birth of a common worldwide civilization that has originated in a technological framework of Western origin but is now being enriched spiritually by contributions from all the historic regional civilizations. This recent trend in mankind's history may account, in part, for the striking amount of common ground between Daisaku Ikeda's and Arnold Toynbee's Weltanschauungen. It is also possible that, in their exchange of ideas about philosophical and religious life, the authors have delved into the subconscious psychic strata of human nature to a depth at which they have reached elements of human nature that are the same in all human beings, always and everywhere, in virtue of being the offspring of the ultimate common ground of existence that is at the root of all phenomena.

Down to this point, this preface represents both authors of the book, but Toynbee now thanks Ikeda for having taken the initiative in arranging the meetings and for publication of the dialogue as a book. When Toynbee had reached an age at which it had become difficult for him to travel, Ikeda came from Japan to England to meet him. It was also Ikeda who arranged for the translation of his own part of the dialogue from Japanese into English and for the editing of the whole dialogue in a form in which it could be read as a book. This was a formidable task, and Arnold Toynbee is very grateful to Daisaku Ikeda for having taken it upon his younger shoulders.

EDITOR'S NOTE

This preface was written by Mr. Toynbee in the third person on behalf of both authors and in accordance with their wishes appears in this style.

I

PERSONAL

AND

SOCIAL LIFE

THE BASIC HUMAN BEING

1

Some of Our Animal Aspects

IKEDA: Today sex liberation—a worldwide phenomenon, though especially conspicuous in Europe, America, and Japan—is advancing with such speed and force that it threatens to shake the very foundations of modern society. Things once considered embarrassing are now said and done with complete openness.

Naturally sex must be correctly understood; it must not be concealed foolishly, for this only fosters distorted attitudes toward it. On the other hand, I doubt that the current hands-off, permissive approach to sex is, as some people insist, the way to human liberation. Freedom and license are not the same thing, and I am convinced that there is a grave defect in modern sex freedom; something fundamental is missing in this approach to sex.

TOYNBEE: Man finds himself in the awkward and embarrassing situation of being an animal who is also a self-conscious spiritual being. He is aware that the spiritual aspect of his nature gives him a dignity that other animals do not possess, and he feels that he ought to maintain his dignity. Therefore human beings are embarrassed by those physical organs and functions and appetites that are common to them and to nonhuman animals and that therefore impugn human dignity by reminding us of our physiological kinship with brute beasts. Nonhuman animals are not embarrassed by the functioning of their physical nature because they are not self-conscious. Embarrassment caused by the fear of losing dignity, and the humiliation of actually losing it, are specifically human troubles.

The human device for maintaining dignity in spite of the animal aspect of human nature is to distinguish ourselves from nonhuman animals by inventing certain conventions, which animals do not and cannot emulate, for dealing with those animal organs and functions that are part of our built-in, inescapable biological heritage. One human test of cultivation or civilization is the degree to which we differentiate, by artificial conventions, the human way of dealing with the physical organs and functions that are common to all animals.

IKEDA: All civilizations have their own customs and conventions about sex, and these are generally passed from one generation to another. Today sex education is taught as if it were something very special, whereas it has been a part, in one form or another, of all cultures.

TOYNBEE: Certainly most civilizations do have conventions on those subjects and many times these conventions vary. Today, in our culture, we cover our sexual and excretory organs, we do not have sexual intercourse, or obey what are coyly called the calls of nature, in public, and we observe table manners. Table manners vary greatly. They are a delicate index of cultural differences, but they are not the surest index of cultural health or sickness, because eating and drinking are animal functions that human beings are not ashamed of sharing with rats and cows (as long as we do not eat and drink in the rodents' or the ruminants' way). On the other hand, excretion and sexual intercourse are intrinsically embarrassing to all human beings, whatever their style of culture may be, and therefore all human beings observe conventions in the performance of these natural functions.

Sex is particularly embarrassing because the human sexual appetite does not arise until the age of puberty. Therefore, an adolescent human being must be inducted into a knowledge of the sexual facts of life, and this is a tricky piece of education. If his elders make a mystery of sex and delay enlightening the child till the child is overtaken by the ripening of its sexuality, the effect may be to excite the child's curiosity and to arouse resentment over having been kept in the dark. This may result in the child's being obsessed with the thought of sex and being overeager to indulge in sexual intercourse. On the other hand, if parents were to practice sexual intercourse in the child's sight, they would lose their dignity in his estimation. The child might then become sexual minded before becoming physically mature. In sex education it is hard to find a satisfactory middle course between harmfully excessive frankness and permissiveness on the one hand and harmfully excessive secretiveness and restrictiveness on the other hand.

16

IKEDA: You are quite right. This question probably has always been difficult; it is certainly difficult today.

TOYNBEE: The weak point about human dignity is that we have found no better way of maintaining it than an artificial cloaking of our animal organs and functions. If some nonhuman animal could be temporarily equipped with a humanlike intellect and be given an opportunity for making an uncensored inspection of the human way of life, this imaginary observer would surely pronounce that human dignity is a sham maintained by conventional devices for concealing the truth that the human species is really no more dignified than any other species of living creature. Still, man sincerely feels that he does have dignity and that he would sink to a subhuman level if he were to fail to maintain his dignity. I think that this, rather than my imaginary inspector's verdict on human dignity, is the truth. Man's sense of dignity is another name for his recognition that he is a spiritual being besides, and in spite of, being physiologically an animal organism.

IKEDA: Yes, if we claim that man's spiritual activities are lies and fiction, all of the behavioral conventions that man has devised to support his dignity become meaningless. The truth, however, is that man is spiritual and that his spiritual activities occupy a great part of his being. Consequently, the conventions surrounding sex, eating, and other human animal functions have considerable meaning.

TOYNBEE: In imposing on himself rules for governing his animal organs and functions, man is asserting and protecting his humanity. Mankind, so far, has not had universally uniform rules. The rules in force in different human societies have been various. When we compare different sets of rules, we judge that some are better than others. We are constantly modifying our own rules, but no human society has ever, so far as we know, discarded all rules completely. It is hard to see how any society that did do this could remain human. Human beings have greater freedom of action than animals of other kinds. We are free to behave either worse than nonhuman animals or better. If we did not live under rules, we would surely behave worse.

The right criterion for dealing with the problem of sexual intercourse is the maintenance of human dignity, and in this department of human affairs, dignity is a condition sine qua non for the humanization of sexual relations by a spiritual quality that is still more important than dignity, namely love. Human sexual relations divorced from love and from dignity and reduced to being nothing but the satisfaction of an animal appetite become spiritually

17

degrading. In nonhuman animals, the response to the sexual impulse is unself-conscious and is therefore innocent. Moreover, in these animals' sexual lives, sexual intercourse is regulated by built-in natural controls. In human life, sex without dignity and love is not even bestial: it is spiritually and morally lower than the level at which nature holds the sexual intercourse of beasts.

IKEDA: Of course, a society would cease to be human without rules. It would in fact cease to be even close to human, because scientists have observed that all animals with even limited spiritual qualities observe rules. Certain apes, for example, have definite rules of order connected with feeding and sexual intercourse. These rules are punctiliously observed by the members of the ape societies. Man without rules would be socially lower than these apes.

TOYNBEE: Sex rules are the most important, because sex is the most serious part of human nature's animal aspect. The other animal functions affect only an individual human being. Sexual relations affect at least two persons and will affect more if they produce their natural result, the birth of children. Individual human beings can live without having sexual relations. Monks and nuns renounce them. But the human race cannot survive without them, because otherwise it cannot reproduce itself. The regulation of sexual relations makes it possible for the indulgence of the sexual appetite implanted by nature to be accompanied, dignified, and transfigured by love. The love between husband and wife and between parents and children is, as Confucius taught, the heart of human sociality and morality.

IKEDA: Fundamentally I agree, but I suspect that the loss of sexual morality and the absence of love in sex is part of the trend to think of life in terms of material values only: sex is being converted into nothing but a means of pleasure completely divorced from spirituality. I am convinced that until we analyze this trend in the light of its fundamental causes, we will never arrive at a solution.

TOYNBEE: A human society's total set of rules, manners, and customs is a single, interconnected network. There may not be a logical connection between the rules governing different departments of human life, but there is certainly a psychological connection in the sense that permissiveness or restrictiveness in one field tends to extend to the rest. It is surely no accident that, at the present time, permissiveness about sexual relations is accom-

18

panied by permissiveness about drug-taking, dishonesty, and recourse to violence as a shortcut to gaining personal or political ends.

One cause of the recent outbreak of lawlessness in a number of different fields of life is the turning of millions of men into soldiers in the two world wars and in the many local wars that have also been waged since 1914. War is a deliberate reversal of the normal inhibition against taking human life. For a soldier, killing his fellow human beings is a duty instead of being the crime that it is if he commits murder as a civilian. This arbitrary and immoral reversal of a major ethical rule is bewildering and demoralizing in itself. Moreover, a soldier on active service is torn out of his customary social setting and is therefore released from all his customary social restraints. When he is being commanded to kill, it is no wonder that he also ceases to be governed by other normal inhibitions against raping, looting, and drug-taking. The demoralization of the American troops in Vietnam was an extreme case of what always happens to soldiers on campaign.

IKEDA: In all ages, war brings this kind of demoralization.

TOYNBEE: War is evil; the scientific spirit is not. Yet, unintentionally and indirectly, the scientific spirit has, I believe, contributed to the present out-break of lawlessness, especially in the field of sexual relations. The ethical merit of science is that it is dedicated to discovering and facing the truth. Science challenges all traditional beliefs, conventions, and habits. The tradi-tional conventions about sexual behavior have, in all societies, been restrictive in various degrees. I hold that this is ethically right. However, the more rigid the restriction, the more frequent and flagrant will be the breaches of it, and the more hypocritical will be the prudential concealment of these breaches. Children today are educated—not merely formally but by the Zeitgeist—to have a scientific zeal for the truth and a scientific contempt for shams. Con-sequently, today, the prestige, and therefore the authority, of both parents and governments is being breached by a credibility gap. Present-day children are ready to believe that their parents do not practice what they preach about sexual relations or about anything else.

If this is one cause—and I believe that it is—of the present revolt against traditional conventions about sexual behavior, it is unlikely that the rising generation will be moved to regulate its sexual behavior either by repressive action on the part of the public authorities or even by a voluntary movement for sexual asceticism.

IKEDA: I view the trend toward sexual license in another light. I see its true

19

cause in a weakening of the inner force of life. This weakening has been brought on by the oppressive influences of modern material civilization. The vibrant spirit of love required to establish sex in its proper place in human life cannot be born of enfeebled life force. I am in accord with your belief that, through the operation of love, a way can be found to overcome the present situation, but I think that it is necessary to go one step further and to put faith in the forces of life that generate love itself if we are to expect spiritual efforts to have practical effects. The way to restore humanity to sexual behavior is either to eliminate exterior forces that oppress the spirit or to develop, activate, and strengthen the inner force that is the support and generating origin of life. What can make this possible?

TOYNBEE: The only promising remedy for sexual license will be a positive one. Sexual license is an expression of a loss of faith and hope in mankind's future. The remedy is surely to give the rising generation some objective that is inspiring yet is not utopian. No particular set of rules for sexual conduct is sacrosanct, but human life becomes bestial if human sexual relations are not governed by a set of rules that gives, and that is recognized as giving, human dignity to this most awkward of all the physiological functions that man has in common with his nonhuman fellow animals.

Heredity and Environment

IKEDA: Roughly speaking, there are two schools of genetics: the orthodox school founded by Mendel and Morgan and the Lysenko school founded by the Russian scientist of that name.

The Mendelian school locates the genes, the elements of hereditary transmission, in the living organism itself and holds that the basis of the hereditary phenomenon is the passing of traits from parents to offspring. Genes, which are arranged in precise order within the chromosomes contained in cellular nuclei, follow a fixed mechanism to effect hereditary transmission. Recent research in biochemistry and molecular biology has proved this theory. Further, molecular biology has shown that deoxyribonucleic acid (DNA) is the basic component of the genes, and the work of J. D. Watson and F. H. C. Crick has established the nature of the complex structure of this substance.

Lysenko and other Russian biologists, however, emphasize the role of environment in heredity. According to their theory, heredity consists in the nature of organisms to require certain fixed conditions for the sake of their life and growth and to react to those conditions in certain ways. The Russian scientists insist that heredity must be understood as a part of the metabolic pattern of organisms. I think that the Lysenko approach deserves considerable respect for dealing with heredity phenomena from the standpoint of environmental relationships. But in linking itself with Marxian ideology, in regarding the environment as the only hereditary determinant, and in ignoring the existence of the genes, his theory calls down criticism on Lysenko as a scientist. After the death of Stalin, *Pravda* denounced Lysenko, his school, and its dogma as an obstruction in the path of biological development, thereby revealing the fact that science, when politically distorted by being bound to a specific ideology, cannot progress normally. I think that both the existence of genes and environmental influences are essential elements of genetics.

TOYNBEE: I agree that both genes and environment must be taken into account in any attempt to explain the nature—or, short of that, the mode of operation—of evolution or creation, whichever of these two concepts may appear to come closer to expressing the reality of change.

IKEDA: The efforts and achievements of the Mendel and Lysenko schools warrant just assessment. But for a deeper understanding, heredity must be studied from the viewpoint of interrelationships between living organisms and their surroundings. Such an approach, while of course incorporating research by men like Mendel and Lysenko, will open new vistas in the comprehensive field of heredity.

TOYNBEE: Probably the distinction between heredity and environment is one of those mental analyses of an indivisible reality-in-itself that human minds have to make because of limitations in their capacity for understanding. The establishment of a specific pattern of genes, which is transmitted from one specimen of the species to another by procreation, is tantamount to the establishment of a center for an organism that embraces the entire universe. Of course, this orientation of the universe round one of a virtually infinite number of competing local and temporary centers can be only partial and temporary.

IKEDA: Do you mean that individual members of a species of living things attempt to make themselves the center of the universe?

TOYNBEE: Yes. Each particular specimen of a species dies. Though the mechanism of reproduction through a stable set of genes ensures the perpetuation of a species through a succession of specimens, the species itself may eventually become extinct. Probably the greater number of the species of living beings that have arisen so far since the first appearance of life on this planet are already extinct; the surviving species are probably a small minority. Yet during the brief time span that each particular specimen of a species is alive, this apparently insignificant fraction of the universe is, in a genuine sense, coextensive with the entire universe. The attempt is usually made to organize the entire universe round this particular living being as the universal center, and to an infinitesimal degree, the whole of the universe is truly affected by the individual living being's effort to keep itself alive. Thus the environment of a living being not only includes the whole of the remainder of the universe but also is actually an integral part of the living being itself. The mental distinction between a living being and its environment would, I think, be found to have no counterpart in reality-in-itself, supposing that reality-in-itself were comprehensible to human minds.

IKEDA: Your explanation of the living being and the environment as an indivisible unity corresponds to the Buddhist teaching that is called *Eshō Funi*. The word *Eshō* means the total environment (*e*) and the total greater life force (*shō*). In simple terms, the theory of *Eshō Funi* maintains that, though two separate entities in the phenomenal world, life and environment are essentially one.

TOYNBEE: *Eshō Funi* seems to be a concise explanation of what I suspect the true condition is. A living being's egoistic attempt to organize the universe round itself is the condition for, and the expression of, its vitality. In fact, life and egoism are interchangeable terms. If this is true, it is also true that the price of altruism is death. Altruism, alias love, is an attempt to reverse the natural effort of a living being to organize the universe round itself. Love is a counterattempt, on the living being's part, to devote itself to the universe instead of exploiting the universe. Self-devotion or self-sacrifice means orienting oneself towards some center of the universe that is not oneself.

IKEDA: The major problems of religion and philosophy are attempting to understand the relation of the individual being with the universe and trying to devise ways for the individual self to relate volitionally to the universe.

TOYNBEE: All the great religions and philosophies declare that the proper goal for every living creature is to subdue and extinguish its natural self-centeredness—to die unto itself. They also declare unanimously that this effort is difficult, because it is contrary to nature, but that it is, at the same time, the only true way of self-fulfillment and, therefore, the only true way of attaining self-satisfaction and happiness.

Self-fulfillment through self-subordination and self-sacrifice is a paradox. If this paradox is true and right, the attempt to establish an individual living being as an entity that is separate from the rest of the universe is unnatural from the standpoint of the universe as a whole, though it is natural from the standpoint of the living being trying to assert its separateness and its dominance.

Both self-centeredness (egoism) and love (altruism) testify that reality-in-itself—including obviously the hereditarily determined individual and its environment—is one and indivisible. Self-centeredness is an attempt to reestablish the temporarily and partially disrupted unity of reality by orienting the universe round some particular living being. Love is an attempt to reestablish the unity of reality by abandoning the pursuit of self-centeredness and remerging the particular living being in the indivisible universe. Though love and self-centeredness are antithetical in terms of aims and ethics, they resemble each other in being two impulses whose common field of operation is the universe as a whole. This indicates that the mental distinction between a living being and its environment is nonexistent in reality-in-itself.

IKEDA: According to the principle of *Eshō Funi*, which I explained earlier, universal life and the power and Law inherent in it steadily operate to the end of manifesting themselves. As a result of this process, living bodies are individualized at the same time as the environment is being formed.

It seems to me that the study of hereditary phenomena, if pursued with this idea as a basis of investigation of mutual relations between living bodies and their environments, might lead to new and interesting developments.

Psychosomatic medicine offers an interesting parallel instance of a way in which genetics of the future might develop. Modern Western medical science has developed in the dualistic pattern of physical treatment and psychological treatment. But psychosomatic medicine, by concentrating on the interrelations between mind and body, has evolved a completely new image of human life. It seems possible that a new genetics might do something similar by showing that human life—of course transmitted by means of genetic phenomena—must be understood as maintaining a direct relation with the environment.

23

TOYNBEE: It is well within the limits of credibility that such a new genetics might develop.

Mind and Body

IKEDA: From ancient times, philosophers and theologians have formulated various concepts of the relationship between the mind and the body. The doctrines born of these concepts are numerous and different in kind, but all of them fall into one of two general categories: materialistic and spiritualistic. Followers of both ways of thinking have done much for the sake of cultural development, and I believe that their achievements deserve proper evaluation. For example, by expounding morality and love, spiritualists have contributed greatly to keeping human society truly humane. For their part, the materialists have laid the foundation for the formation and development of modern science.

Still I am unable to embrace either approach without reservation. Although the materialists recognize man's spiritual functions, by considering the physical body the original source of being, they tend to view life itself as material in nature. Furthermore, while agreeing with the spiritualists that reason, intellect, desires, and other mental functions are the bases of a truly humanistic way of life, I cannot subscribe to the philosophy that the physical aspects of human life and physically related human desires are to be despised. Both the materialists and the spiritualists seem to pursue only one aspect of the issue and to fail to grasp the relationship between spirit and body.

TOYNBEE: Yes, I agree that neither materialism nor spiritualism is a satisfying explanation of reality if either is taken as being the exclusive explanation. Matter cannot be comprehended in terms of spirit, nor, conversely, can spirit be comprehended in terms of matter. Each is comprehensible only in terms of a unity that embraces both. We cannot comprehend the indivisibility of the two facets within this psychosomatic unity since we cannot reduce them to a mentally comprehensible unity.

IKEDA: I believe that the relationship between body and spirit is best expressed in the Buddhist concept of *Shikishin Funi.* The word *shiki* represents all phenomena of life that can be understood by means of scientific or physiochemical methods of research. In other words, *shiki* is the material, or phenomenal, aspect of life. *Shin* refers to all of the various noumenal

24

aspects of life and the many kinds of spiritual activities that cannot be grasped in terms of physiochemical methods. Included in *shin* are reason, intellect, and desires that are the object of investigation by spiritualists. In Buddhist teachings these aspects are at the same time separate and united.

Neither *shiki* nor *shin* is more fundamental than the other. They exercise active powers in their individual aspects, and life is only manifest in its truest form when the two become one living entity. The Buddhist doctrine of *Shikishin Funi* (*funi* means indivisible) explains life in terms of a unity of life's two aspects: elements susceptible to explanation in scientific terms and other elements that are a part of the deeper undercurrent on which all life phenomena rest. Materialism concerns itself only with the world of *shiki*, and spiritualism, only with the world of *shin*.

TOYNBEE: Since we can merely analyze a hypothetically real, though mentally incomprehensible, unity into these apparently disparate constituents, I suppose that the concept *Shikishin Funi* is the closest attainable approximation of an understanding of reality-in-itself.

IKEDA: In recent years, psychosomatic medicine and such theories as that of Medald Boss, who deals with the interaction of mental and physical energies in human life, have come close to the Buddhist principle of *Shikishin Funi*. But Buddhism carries the doctrine further by explaining the basic nature of phenomenal life as related to cosmic life. I believe that only when human life is understood as part of the flow of cosmic life will it be possible to go beyond merely recognizing the unity of the spiritual and the physical and to orient the inseparable relationship of body and mind toward the creation of a new kind of life.

TOYNBEE: I believe that the *Shikishin Funi*, which is manifested in every specimen of every species of living creature on this planet, or elsewhere, is part of the flow of cosmic life. As I have said, each single living being is coextensive with, and is therefore identical with, the entire universe. I believe that the Hindu dictum *Tat tvam asi*—meaning that the individual is the universal—expresses the truth about the relation between an individual living being and ultimate reality.

The Subconscious

IKEDA: In the study of the human mind, conscious mental processes—perception, thinking, will—have long been objects of philosophical consideration. In my view, all Western philosophies are built on a study of consciousness. But consciousness is only part of human life.

TOYNBEE: Yes, I agree; consciousness is merely the manifest surface of the psyche. It is like the visible tip of an iceberg, the bulk of which is submerged.

IKEDA: This is why I believe that a total image of the human psyche and of life is impossible unless attention is devoted to the realm of the subconscious lying behind human actions, thoughts, and desires.

TOYNBEE: The subconscious is the source of intuitions that can inspire rational thought but that cannot be reached by the mind so long as the mind is confining its activity to the conscious level. It is recognized that some scientific discoveries that can be, and have eventually been, expressed in logical terms and verified by experiment have been made originally by unverified and nonlogical intuitions that have welled up into the consciousness from the subconscious.

IKEDA: Yes, great scientific discoveries, like the creations of great artists, are often the result of spiritual intuition.

TOYNBEE: The subconscious is undoubtedly the source of poetry and of religious insight. It is the source, too, of all emotions and impulses. The ethical judgments that we make at the level of consciousness distinguish between good and bad emotions and impulses. The deeper into the subconscious that we succeed in carrying our consciousness, the greater becomes the extent of our conscious control over our emotions and impulses. Conscious control enables us to subdue those products of the subconscious that we judge to be bad and to foster those of its products that we judge to be good.

I therefore believe that it is of the utmost importance for human welfare that we should explore the subconscious depths of the human psyche in order to bring as many of these emotions and impulses under as full a conscious control as possible. This is a rewarding spiritual activity, but it is also a difficult one. The subconscious is like the mythical Greek marine god Proteus. It tries to elude control, it resents being controlled when it has been subjected to control, and it has subtle means of taking its revenge on the consciousness

26

for being mastered by it and of breaking loose again when control has been established over it.

IKEDA: The first man to employ natural-science methods to explore the subconscious was the depth-psychologist Sigmund Freud. Naturally, I place very high value on his work and that of others of the latter half of the nineteenth century. But even in ancient times, Buddhist scholars in India had already delved into the depth of the human psyche beneath the level of consciousness.

TOYNBEE: I agree that the discovery and exploration of the subconscious depths of the psyche, which, in the West, started only as recently as Freud's generation, was anticipated in India at least as early as the generation of the Buddha and his Hindu contemporaries, that is to say, at least 2,400 years earlier than Freud. The modern Western attempt to explore and to master the subconscious has not yet progressed beyond a naive and crude early stage. Hindus and Buddhists have been pursuing this quest for a much longer time and have progressed much farther. Westerners have much to learn in this field from Indian and East Asian experience. In books and articles that I have published, I have repeatedly drawn my Western readers' attention to this historical fact, as part of my lifelong attempt to help jolt modern Western man out of his ludicrously mistaken belief that modern Western civilization has made itself superior to all others by outstripping them.

IKEDA: I realize this and I respect your sincere efforts in this line. Two of the leading thinkers in the Indian Vijnanavada school of philosophy, Asanga and Vasubandhu (both fourth century of the Christian era), added new concepts to the then recognized six senses. The traditional six were sight, sound, smell, taste, touch, and a sixth sense that controls and unifies the functions of the other five. The additional concepts added by these great thinkers were a faculty for reason in profound thinking (*manas-vijnana*) and a faculty for deeper insight into the nature of life (*alaya-vijnana*). The seventh sense, the faculty for reason, involves profound speculation; Descartes's *I* of "I think; therefore I am" falls into this category. The Western philosophers followed this far; however, Vasubandhu went further to discover the eighth sense by means of which he was able to look deeper and without illusion into the nature of human life. Chih-i of China (sixth century of the Christian era), by developing the thought of Vasubandhu, evolved a ninth sense (*amala-vijnana*), which arrives at the ultimate spiritual entity activating all other psychological operations. His thought became the seed from which

T'ien-t'ai Buddhism developed. I have briefly touched on these men to show that from ancient times Buddhist thinkers have attempted to understand the deep zones of life beyond the world of consciousness.

TOYNBEE: Of course the efforts of these men produced important results, but I believe that even the conscious surface of the psyche, which is relatively comprehensible, cannot be fully and truly comprehended unless it is seen as being merely a part of an indivisible psychic whole in which the subconscious depths dominate the conscious surface insofar as these subconscious depths are unperceived or are ignored. The value of bringing the subconscious depths, or at least the upper layers of them, into consciousness is that, through becoming conscious of them, we can control them, instead of being controlled by them unawares.

I believe that the Indian Buddhist philosopher Vasubandhu and the Chinese Buddhist philosopher Chih-i did penetrate, with their consciousness, into the lower layers of the subconscious (the spatial word *lower* is inadequate and might be misleading, but a spatial vocabulary, used metaphorically, is the only vocabulary that we have for describing psychic phenomena). I also believe that the ultimate layer of the subconscious abyss of the human psyche is identical with the ultimate reality that underlies the whole universe.

IKEDA: I suspect that your ultimate reality behind the universe corresponds to what Buddhist thought calls the universal life force, which is the source of all phenomena in the universe.

But to move to a somewhat more concrete plane, I should like to ask your opinion of methodologies used in exploring psychic phenomena. Exploration in this particular field of man's mind was stimulated by the introduction and development of Freudian psychoanalysis and depth psychology.

The numerous branches of psychology may be classified roughly into two groups. One is conscious psychology, which deals with the conscious level of the human psyche. The other is depth psychology, which deals with both the conscious and the subconscious levels but which excludes all phenomena incapable of objective verification.

TOYNBEE: The modern Western study of the human psyche is much more recent than the Western study of the inanimate and physical aspect of the phenomenal universe. The Western scientific method that has been worked out for studying the physical aspect of the phenomena has been strikingly successful within its own field. Its prestige had become so great that it was applied unquestioningly to the study of the psychic aspect of the phenomena when the West began, at last, to study this aspect too. As we have said, Buddhists and Hindus began the study of the psyche in India about 2,400 years earlier than Europeans, and in India it was not conducted on the lines of a previously well-established and successful study of the physical aspect of phenomena. The nonphysical Indian approach to the study of psychic phenomena seems to me to be more promising. The modern Western attempt to work out a psychic science on the lines of a preexisting physical science may put Western psychic science in danger of being misled by a false analogy. The study of psychic phenomena is perhaps likely to get nearer to the truth if it is worked out, in the Indian way, on independent lines of its own that suit the nature of this study's psychic subject matter.

IKEDA: That is certainly true. The deep levels of human life are fundamentally different in nature from surface manifestations. They transcend time and space, and for that reason, attempts to measure them by means of ordinary spatial and temporal standards will probably not bring us very close to the true nature of life force itself. Consequently, as you say, it seems that the Indian method of introspection can produce more correct knowledge than attempts to guess about deep-level psychic phenomena on the basis of the methods used to analyze conscious phenomena.

I briefly touched on the two main streams of modern psychological study, but in recent years several new schools of thought have developed and have tried to advance beyond the confines of conventional psychology. One such current is parapsychology, which concentrates on research into supernormal phenomena: telepathy, distance telepathy, clairvoyance, psychokinesis, and precognition. While several experiments in this area have stood tests conducted by conscientious scientists, many so-called successful experiments have been no more than frauds. Some supernormal phenomena can be fully explained by merely delving deeper into the subconscious layers, without attributing them to allegedly extrasensory perceptive functions.

TOYNBEE: Certainly there has been a good deal of fraud in modern Western experiments in the production and observation of psychic phenomena. Probably fraud is easier in psychic than in physical investigations. However, I believe that the majority of performers and observers have acted in good faith, even in cases in which their explanations of the phenomena have been unconvincing. I think this is true not only of the modern Western exploration of the subconscious but also of Indian yoga and Siberian shamanism.

IKEDA: Aside from fraudulent or irrelevant cases, there have occurred phenomena that cannot be explained except by reference to something supernormal. It would be a mistake to discard parapsychology in its entirety. Hypnotism, which was once regarded as a fraud, not a science, has now established itself as a powerful method of psychotherapy. Of course, parapsychological theories must always be subjected to severe verification tests.

Another school of thought, even farther ahead of the mainstreams of psychological research than parapsychology, is spiritualism, which studies the alleged existence of the soul. Completely unrelated to positive science, spiritualism has evolved into what may be called a religious faith. What are your opinions of these approaches to human psychology?

TOYNBEE: I believe that all observable phenomena are normal phenomena. As I see it, the so-called supernormal phenomena that are the subject of so-called parapsychological study are, in truth, normal phenomena of kinds that are either rare or else are common but have been overlooked and neglected in the West till recently. I myself have been a firsthand witness of telepathic communication that was, I know, genuine. I suppose that all living beings have always communicated with each other telepathically and that, even since the invention of human speech, human beings continue to communicate with each other telepathically as well as by word of mouth or by writing.

IKEDA: Conclusions about these supernormal phenomena are important and, consequently, needed. But to praise them excessively as mystical results of some kind of superpower can have grievous consequences. First, it can give rise to mistaken understandings and fraudulent practices. Second, and worse, it can block the way to the discovery of reliable and accurate knowledge about such phenomena. But if thoughts and conclusions on these matters are subjected to excessively severe criticism, all delving into them might be discountenanced. And this might lead to the smothering of heretofore unexplored human abilities and possibilities.

You say that so-called supernormal phenomena are in nature normal. I agree with you to this extent. When the thread of cause and effect among things that are today thought of as supernormal in terms of the results of parapsychological experiments is discovered, those things themselves will probably come to be regarded as normal. The world of animals offers numerous examples of apparently supernormal powers—the homing instincts of some birds and the ability to navigate great distances in migrations—that are now clearly explained by science. If subjected to sincere, careful observation and experimentation, supernormal phenomena too may be similarly explainable.

Much human communication of intentions and ideas is transmitted by words, but there are instances in which words are not used. Oriental peoples place great stress on communications between the spiritual aspects of human beings. This kind of communication (called *ishin-denshin* in Japanese) is unaided by words. I suppose that it corresponds to what you mean by telepathy. It seems to me that mistaken ways of developing this concealed human ability—or perhaps not developing it at all but allowing it to be despised and thus permitting it to atrophy—have prevented it from being manifested as understandably as it might have been.

Something very similar has happened in the case of intuition. Often intuition is less fairly appraised than reason, and as examples of mistaken intuitive guesses become common knowledge, intuition itself is discredited. Since the process by which it operates is unclear, intuition is hastily condemned as unscientific. But the attitude that condemns it invites the danger of forcing man to rely entirely on reason and in this way sacrifice his powers of intuition.

Deep-level consciousness transcends reason and can operate with great acuteness, speed, and accuracy. Though this ability is inherent in life itself, the civilizational development of mankind has weakened it. As a consequence man has come to believe that he can function satisfactorily even if his deep-conscious abilities are inactive. In other words, surface human consciousness, especially reason, has suppressed deeper human consciousness.

TOYNBEE: There is a tendency for an older faculty to atrophy when it is supplemented by a new one. This is unfortunate, because the new faculty seldom performs all the functions of the older one, though it may perform some of the older faculty's functions more effectively and may also perform new functions which the older faculty never did and never could have performed. For instance, among peoples that have become literate, the faculty of memory has been weakened, and perhaps literacy, in its turn, is going to suffer from the use of radio and television as means of communication. In a similar way, the subconscious has, I think, become partially atrophied in human beings through their attainment of consciousness, which has brought with it reason and culture.

We can see the same process at work in the realm of communications technology. Canals have been put out of action by railways, railways by express highways, ships by planes, postal services by telephones. Yet the new instruments do not perform all the functions of the old instruments that they have ruined. In both the material and the spiritual sphere, advances seem to be purchased at the price of losses that we can ill afford.

31

Reason and Intuition

IKEDA: Reason and intuition complement each other in that reason pre-supposes the function of intuition, while intuition is rectified and clarified by reason. The repeated functioning of the faculty of reason can systematize and elucidate wisdom acquired through intuition. Whereas reason generally adopts the analytic approach and resolves complicated subjects into simple constituent elements, intuition grasps a subject as a whole and penetrates directly to its essential nature. Although it might seem that these two oppose each other, I feel that they are closely related aspects of human wisdom and that they have an elevating effect on human nature.

TOYNBEE: The data of sense perception are the raw material for scientific hypotheses. A hypothesis is a tentative explanation of these data. It needs to be followed up by verification. There are two verification tests, both of which must be applied. One test is by reason. Is the particular hypothesis in question consistent with other hypotheses and, in general, with the total body of provisionally accepted knowledge? The second test is by confrontation with the set of phenomena by which the hypothesis has been suggested. Does the hypothesis explain these phenomena satisfactorily? Or are some of them inconsistent with it? Evidently a hypothesis can never be proved correct conclusively and definitively. This is evident because we can never be sure that our inventory of any set of phenomena is complete. At any time in the future, we may become aware of a phenomenon, falling within this set, that has not been observed by us before. The newly observed phenomenon may turn out to be incompatible with the hypothetical explanation of this particular set of phenomena that has been accepted hitherto. A single recalcitrant case is sufficient to discredit the hypothetical explanation of the set of phenomena to which this case belongs.

What is the source of hypotheses? They are not presented to us by the data of sense perception. Hypotheses are not data; they are explanations of data. Nor are hypotheses presented to us by reason. Our reasoning faculty examines and criticizes hypotheses, but it does not originate them. Reason cannot come into action until it already has a hypothesis to work on. Reason and sense perception both operate at the conscious level of the psyche. Our hypotheses are presented to us by intuition, which wells up into the consciousness from the subconscious depths. The consciousness receives intuition from the subconscious. Both reason and sense perception are uncreative. The creative activity of the human psyche is intuitional, and the subconscious is its source.

32

IKEDA: What you have been saying very clearly explains the activities of the great spiritual creators of the world, both the scientists and the religious leaders. Only intuition can provide insight into realms where reason cannot penetrate. But, possibly because of its subjective nature, intuition, if once mistaken, can lead to complacency. The validity of things perceived intuitively must be verified by rational cognizance. A step beyond this process, we see that we require an awareness on a new plane where reason and intuition complement each other. This awareness might be called rational intuition or intuitive reason.

The cases of some of the great thinkers in the field of physics illustrate my point. Einstein's theory of relativity and Newton's discovery of the workings of gravity came about as a result of the intuition of geniuses. But in both cases, immense rational meditation preceded the intuitive moment. It is impossible to treat the great insights of such men on the same level with the fortuitous bright ideas that we all experience from time to time. From the viewpoint of a third party, a truth arrived at through intuition remains a hypothesis that must be proven. But this is obviously not the case for the man who arrived at intuitive truth as a consequence of intensive rational thought. What I mean is this: intuition at work in cases of this kind is not fortuitous intuition but what I have called rational intuition.

TOYNBEE: I understand your point and think it is well taken. But we must remember that both the conscious level and the subconscious level extend on a horizontal plane among human beings and even entire societies. Because sense perception and reason both operate on the conscious level, different human beings are able to compare notes about what they perceive and about how they reason. They can arrive at common accounts of phenomena and common conclusions from their thinking. We call these common accounts and conclusions objective, meaning that these are not private views and thoughts peculiar to a solitary individual and therefore differing from others that are not common to him and to his fellow human beings. But we have no means of knowing whether these common contents of conscious minds are objective in the sense of being genuine and accurate mental reflections of reality-in-itself. They might be merely mass-hallucinations.

Some intuitions are subjective in the sense of being peculiar to a particular individual, and these individual intuitions may be unconvincing for other people. Such intuitions are not self-evident for every mind, yet they may win converts nevertheless. The individual intuitions of scientists, poets, and religious seers are of this kind. Insofar as it has been explored, however, the subconscious appears to consist of a number of distinct psychic layers. There

33

seems to be a layer, below the level of individual intuition, at which the sub-conscious generates myths of the kind that C. G. Jung has labelled "primor-dial images." Like our mental operations at the conscious level, these myths are common to all human beings. Identical primordial images come to the surface in the ritual and the folklore of many different peoples, as well as in the plots of sophisticated plays and novels written by representatives of different civilizations at different times and places. Primordial images carry a high charge of psychic energy and have compelling power. They sometimes overpower the conscious will and carry people into acting in ways that are contrary to their deliberate intentions.

IKEDA: I suspect that Jung's primordial images are what is sometimes called the group mind, which means that in the deep inner parts of the mind of each individual human being is a repository of experience that has been handed down over the ages since mankind first emerged. These experiences are common to all peoples, though they generally remain submerged.

Although it is probably safe to assign religion to the field of intuition, religion supported by nothing but intuition becomes unconvincing. Only when it is illuminated by the light of reason can the intuitive knowledge of religion have realistic life. In this sense, I insist that intuition must be rational intuition. Similarly, because I believe that reason must be supported by intuition, I insist on the need for an intuitive kind of reason.

TOYNBEE: I believe that science and religion derive intuitions from both the individual and the universal layer of the subconscious. In this respect, a scientist's hypotheses are akin to a religious seer's insights, but scientists are more strict than seers in submitting their intuitions to tests in the field of consciousness. Seers are more willing to give dogmatic answers to the funda-mental questions about the nature of the universe and about the significance of human life. These fundamental questions, which most human beings ask at some stage or another in their lives, cannot be given verifiable answers. This is beyond the capacity of human minds. Yet these fundamental questions present themselves to our minds most urgently and demand answers most insistently. The answers given by religious seers are dogmatic in the sense of being unverifiable. (The original meaning of the Greek word *dogma* is an opinion, in contrast to a commonly recognized and acknowledged truth.)

Scientists limit their objectives to observing phenomena, seeking to explain them rationally, and trying to test their conclusions. In contrast to science, religion offers human beings a chart of the mysterious world in which we awoke to consciousness and in which we have to pass our lives. Although

34

this chart is conjectural, we cannot do without it. It is a necessity of life. It is of far greater practical importance for us than most of science's tested and certified surveys of the tiny fraction of the universe that is accessible to us for scientific exploration. Of course science too is a necessity of life, but the science that is indispensable is elementary. Scientific observation and reasoning were required for making the earliest paleolithic tools. This elementary science sufficed to secure the survival of our species. The enormous subsequent advance of science has been superfluous for the purpose of survival, and it may actually end in the self-destruction of mankind.

IKEDA: In the present stage of human history religion and science are, as you say, necessities of life. Because both are required, the two must not oppose each other. In fact, science must be based on religion, and religion must include scientific rationality. I firmly believe that establishing harmony between science and religion would have a revelatory effect on all mankind. In this connection, I think that the words of Albert Einstein—"Science without religion is lame, and religion without science is blind"—are of even greater importance now than when he said them.

TOYNBEE: Science and religion need not and ought not conflict. They are two complementary ways of approaching the universe mentally in order to cope with it. Science is inhibited from trespassing on religion's field. It could not commit this trespass without making unverifiable dogmatic pronouncements and thereby stultifying itself by abandoning its own distinctive procedure of verification. Religion has sometimes trespassed on science's field, but it has had to withdraw when science has claimed possession. Such withdrawals have, however, left religion's own proper field intact.

IKEDA: Religion and the intuitive approach are for the good of mankind. We must awaken all human beings to a realization of their essential value. If we assume this responsibility, we can explore the complementary relations between religion and science in order to find a way to make religion more accessible to all men.

As you pointed out, religious seers are readier to rely solely on intuition and to give dogmatic answers to fundamental questions. By way of contrast, scientists limit themselves to rational explanations and tests of all conclusions arising from those explanations. They rely on human reason for intelligible explanations.

After having recognized the distinctive natures and values of both intuition and reason, we may be able to build a bridge between science and religion and

35

in so doing make the latter easier for modern people to accept. In other words, both science and religion must break free from their established fields and approach each other. By this I do not mean that one may invade the realm of the other; on the contrary, each must respect the other as the two draw closer together. No matter how close together they become, however, the methods of science can never invade the realm of religion.

THE ENVIRONMENT | 2

Oneness of Man and Nature

IKEDA: Only by living in harmony with the natural environment in a give-and-take relation is it possible for man to develop his own life creatively. Based on this approach, Buddhism teaches that the relationship between man and nature is one not of opposition but of mutual dependence. This relationship is described by the term *Eshō Funi*.

Shō stands for *shōhō*, the independent life entity; *e* stands for *ehō*, the environment supporting that life. Since human life influences and depends on its environment, the two—*Eshō*—are inseparable—*Funi*. Should man and his environment be regarded as two separate and opposed entities, it would be impossible to grasp either in true perspective. Instead of remaining fixed and immutable, the environment changes according to the kind of life it supports. Not only are the environments needed for man and, for example, birds different but also the environments of individual humans differ with the characteristics of each person. In this sense, the subjective body and the environment are one indivisible entity. Carrying this concept still further, Buddhist thought finds the ultimate basis of the unity of subject and environment in cosmic life force.

TOYNBEE: A Westerner who has been educated in the Greek and Latin languages and in pre-Christian Greek and Roman literature finds *Eshō Funi* familiar, because this was the Weltanschauung of the pre-Christian Greco-Roman world.

IKEDA: The ancestors of the Japanese people formulated a set of criteria of

37

spiritual judgment based on belief in harmony between man and environment. These criteria had the inherent strength to restrict environmental pollution. Whether these standards emerged from Buddhism or Shinto is beside the point; they did emerge and were effective for a long time, as is proven by the age-old preservation of the beauty of nature in Japan prior to the modern period. But in recent decades, the Japanese have set keeping up with the advanced Western nations as their goal and have abandoned traditional religion, attitudes toward nature, and even ethical relations among human beings. In short, they have launched on a mad course of material greed.

Modern scientific-technological civilization has given virtually free rein to human greed—it is in fact a product of liberated material greed—and unless all of us perceive this fact with maximum clarity and base our judgments on this perception, we will be unable to stop the destruction of our natural environment and the possible annihilation of mankind.

TOYNBEE: Since our ancestors became human, man has been modifying his natural environment in ways that have made it answer more closely to human requirements. In this, mankind has not been singular. Many nonhuman species of living beings have done the same, though, unlike human beings, they have not acted on their environment consciously and deliberately. Till within the last two or three hundred years, however, neither mankind nor any other form of life on this planet has obliterated the natural environment by imposing an artificial environment on it.

It is true that even in the preindustrial age some once fertile regions were turned into unproductive deserts by overgrazing, overcultivation, and deforestation. These violations of *Eshō Funi* were portents of what man has since done to nonhuman nature in the industrial age, yet these earlier human offences against nature were only local and partial. They were kept within limits partly involuntarily, owing to the limitations of human technological power, but man's restriction of his defacement of nonhuman nature was also partly deliberate at this stage. Man was restrained by *Eshō Funi*. This concept and ideal was not confined to Eastern Asia and to the Greco-Roman world; it was, I believe, shared originally by the rest of mankind.

IKEDA: Perhaps, but at the heart of modern scientific civilization flows the conception that man and nature are two opposed entities and that for the sake of human profit it is necessary to conquer nature. The scientific method has been largely instrumental in effecting this conquest.

TOYNBEE: The revolutionary concept of Judaic monotheism opened the way

38

for the deliberate, wholesale violation of *Eshō Funi*. The belief that what I have called the spiritual presence in and behind the universe was concentrated in a single, transcendent, humanlike God involved the further belief that nothing else in the universe is divine. Both man and nonhuman nature were thought to have been created by this hypothetical God, on the analogy of the creation of tools and works of art and institutions by human beings. The Creator was deemed to have the power and the right to dispose of what he had created. According to chapter I, verses 26–30, of the Book of Genesis, God placed the whole of his nonhuman creation at the disposal of his human creatures to exploit in any way that they might choose.

The effect of this revolutionary doctrine was to disrupt the *funi* between *shōhō* and *ehō*. Man was divorced from his natural environment, which was divested of its former aura of divinity. Man was licensed to exploit an environment that was no longer sacrosanct. The salutary respect and awe with which man had originally regarded his environment was thus dispelled by Judaic monotheism in the versions of its Israelite originators and of Christians and Muslims.

IKEDA: In attempting to conquer the natural world, mankind has upset the fixed, basic rhythm of nature. Having suffered and having been brought to the verge of destruction by man's actions, nature is now rebelling against humanity.

I see two reasons for man's having gone so far in the destruction of his natural environment. First, modern man does not regard the natural world as alive in the same sense that man himself is alive; that is, he has thought of nature as something fundamentally different from mankind. Even though the life of the world of nature may be different from that of humanity, man has overlooked the fact that the two kinds of life are mutually related and part of a greater life entity and its fixed rhythm. The second reason springs from the Judaic monotheism that you mentioned. Believing himself to be closest to God of all creatures, man has thought it a matter of course to subjugate all other beings and put them to his service. This idea underlies all aspects of modern thought, and the combination of these two causes has stimulated the growth of the contemporary scientific-technological civilization.

TOYNBEE: The Judaic ideology was first formulated in Palestine as early as the ninth century B.C., yet it was not put into practice unreservedly till the seventeenth century of the Christian era. The practical application of the Judaic ideology has been exceptional among people who have accepted this ideology in theory. The Muslims, for instance, have been more reluctant than any other of the civilized peoples to adopt modern technology and, with it, the ideal and the objective that modern technology serves. Jesus was an orthodox Jew, but according to the reports of his teaching, he taught that economic greed was incompatible with the service of God. He therefore condemned economic planning, the accumulation of capital, technology, and, in general, the glorification of economically remunerative work.

Jesus' sensitiveness to the evil of greed is significant, for Jesus lived in Palestine at a date at which most Palestinian Jews were still peasants, living in harmony with their nonhuman environment in the spirit of *Eshō Funi*. There were few modern-minded financiers and manufacturers in the Palestinian Jewish community in Jesus' time. Conspicuous greed was rare in Jesus' social environment, yet Jesus perceived and denounced the greed that is innate in human nature in all times and places.

The history and teaching and practice of the twelfth-century Western Christian saint Francis of Assisi are still more significant. Francis's father, a wholesale dealer in cloth, was one of the earliest economically successful Western capitalist entrepreneurs. Francis revolted against his father's way of life. Like Siddartha Gautama, the Buddha, who was the son of a minor king, Francis renounced property and deliberately chose to be poor. Like the Buddha again, Francis founded a monastic order to propagate his ideals and his precepts for putting these ideals into practice. Francis was inspired by Jesus, and, though both were brought up in the Judaic tradition, their attitude to *ehō* was the opposite of the attitude implicit in the Judaic ideology. Neither of them approved of the exploitation of nonhuman nature by man. Jesus glorified the uneconomic-mindedness of birds and wildflowers and held this up as an example for his human disciples to follow. Francis recognized the kinship between man and nonhuman nature, both animate and inanimate, and took delight in it. In Buddhist terms, Francis was an enthusiastic believer in, and lover of, *Eshō Funi*. It seems to me that Francis had an intuitive premonition of the future Western cult of greed serviced by scientific technology.

IKEDA: Your suggestion that perhaps Jesus and Saint Francis were in a way admirers of and believers in the ideas represented by the Buddhist term *Eshō Funi* is especially interesting to me because I am convinced that this idea and a large-scale public movement based on it are the way we can put a stop to environmental pollution. Surely it is possible to rechannel and amplify the public energy that has for a long time been part of many other kinds of movements. Doing this, however, requires a revolution in our interpretation of modern civilization.

TOYNBEE: If mankind is not to destroy itself, it must now cleanse the pollution that it has produced and must refrain from producing any more. I believe that this can be done only by cooperation on a worldwide scale. Antipollution measures on a national scale may suffice for restoring the purity of soils, lakes, and rivers, but the greatest threat to the habitability of mankind's environment is the pollution of the air and the sea. Diseases can be spread by aeroplanes pouring poisonous fumes into the stratosphere and by ships dumping poisonous waste products in mid-ocean.

We have now recognized that pollution is a threat to the survival of mankind and that it cannot be cured without restraint of greed. But expediency is not a strong enough incentive. People who have become addicts to greed tend to take a short-term view: "After me, the deluge." They may know that if they fail to restrain their greed, they will be condemning their children to destruction. They may love their children, yet this love may not move them to sacrifice part of their present affluence for the sake of safeguarding their children's future. I believe that nothing short of a religious conversion (using the word *religious* in the broadest sense) will move the present generation in the advanced countries to make immediate sacrifices at their own expense on behalf of *Eshō Funi*. I should like to see *Eshō Funi* adopted all over the world as a religious belief involving a moral obligation. Conversely, I should like to see Francis adopted by Shintoists as a *kami* and by Buddhists as a bodhisattva.

IKEDA: Though I am a Buddhist, I feel that Saint Francis is worthy of great respect. I believe that both Saint Francis and Jesus belong in what we Buddhists call the Bodhisattva world.

TOYNBEE: In order to save mankind from the consequences of technology inspired by greed, I believe that we need worldwide cooperation among the adherents of all religions and philosophies. I hope that Hindus, Buddhists, and Shintoists will take the initiative in this. The adherents of the Judaic religions are handicapped by their paralyzing tradition of exclusiveness and intolerance, which is part of the nemesis of their monotheism. Among the Hindus and the East Asian peoples there has been a tradition of mutual tolerance and respect among adherents of different religions. Between Buddhists and Shintoists in Japan there has been positive cooperation. This is the practice and the spirit that is needed for a concerted worldwide struggle to cure pollution by cutting away its root, which is greed.

Natural and Man-made Disasters

IKEDA: In the past few years, large-scale natural disasters have occurred with alarming frequency in many parts of the world. Some scientists claim that in thousands of years man has rarely experienced so many disasters in so short a time. To cite only a few examples, I might mention the floods in Italy in 1968, the droughts in China and Korea in that same year, the severe worldwide cold waves of 1969, the reported winter and summer three-degree fluctuations in average temperatures in Europe and the United States, and the devastating hot winds, reaching temperatures of 49 degrees Centigrade, that swept through India and Egypt in 1970, leaving many dead in their wake. During 1971, Japan suffered from strange climatic conditions. The Okinawa region experienced a drought, the island of Hokkaido and the northeastern part of Honshu sustained severe damage to rice crops because of unusually cold summer weather, and a typhoon that struck Japan in August behaved in a most erratic fashion.

Meteorologists say that the conditions that plagued America and Europe were caused by unusual atmospheric-pressure distribution of a kind that has not occurred for tens of thousands of years. It is estimated that changes in pressure, by affecting the movements of the atmosphere, have accelerated the earth's rotational speed very slightly, although this speed-up may be only temporary. In the face of these unusual conditions, I cannot help wondering to what extent man's tampering has upset the natural order.

TOYNBEE: Till within living memory, man has been almost as completely at the mercy of nature as the prehuman forms of life. The reversal in the power relation between man and nonhuman nature is still so recent that it is difficult for us to recognize the fact, and it is still more difficult for us to feel and think and act in accordance with this revolutionary new situation.

IKEDA: I suspect that the reversal in the power relation between human beings and nonhuman nature is in some way related to natural disasters. Of course, there are many different ways to explain them. Some people argue that sunspots or alterations in the temperature of seawater are responsible. This may be the case, but even though the direct causes of these unusual occurrences may be natural (like pressure disturbances brought about by sunspots), I feel that mankind's activities are partly at fault.

Scientists who are concerned over the future of mankind feel that there is a possibility that some apparently trivial human action may have triggered alterations in the earth's behavior. I believe that deep within the causes of much of the climatic confusion that spawns so-called natural disasters is always a human element. If my suspicion is justified, such occurrences might be described as man-made disasters in the guise of natural calamities. The human causative element is perfectly apparent in the case of carbon dioxide gas that accumulates in the air of large cities and, by producing the effect of a greenhouse, causes the temperature to rise. It is equally apparent in the case of countless minute floating particles that block out the light of the sun and produce a general chilling effect. Oil dumped into the seas inhibits evaporation of seawater and thus creates climatic alterations.

But dealing with man-made disasters of this kind—that is, disasters about which scientific data are available and fairly well organized—will not enable us to prevent global destruction. In order to ensure the continued existence of the human race and to save our cosmic oasis from catastrophe, mankind must first realize that his behavior influences natural harmony and then strictly regulate any human action that might have adverse effects.

TOYNBEE: We probably underestimate the degree to which man now dominates and modifies his environment. I agree that, beyond the demonstrably man-made environmental disasters, other current environmental disasters, too, are possibly man-made, even though we may not yet be able to trace their human origin.

IKEDA: Of course, disasters occurring before the emergence and worldwide propagation of human civilization were all naturally caused. Humanity, by resisting threats posed by environmental irregularities—natural disasters—gradually overcame those disasters. Engineering projects, disaster-prevention actions, and the science of meteorology developed as a result of human resistance to such threats. The development of hygienics and medical science took place to some extent as a consequence of the urgent need to cope with plagues (a kind of natural disaster) that once ravaged the world. Indeed, most of modern science evolved from the battle with disaster.

But today, man-caused, not natural, disasters threaten to bring the existence of humanity to a halt. Through the intensive use of science, man has developed a power far greater than that of nature for the generation of disaster.

TOYNBEE: It seems unquestionable that man's power over his environment has already reached a degree at which this power will lead to self-destruction if man continues to use it to serve his greed. Human nature is greedy because greed is one of the characteristics of life. Mankind shares this greed with other species of living beings, but unlike nonhuman species, man, thanks to being

43

conscious, can be aware of his greed. He can know that greed, served by power, is destructive and therefore evil, and he can make the difficult moral effort to practice self-restraint.

IKEDA: The only way to put a stop to disasters of the kind we are discussing is to bring about a kind of revolution on the part of each individual human being. Politicians, industrial leaders, and scientists must face the human responsibility in the creation of these disasters.

Some scientists argue that, with further scientific advances, it will one day become possible to end all natural disasters. I do not agree. The belief that further scientific advances will end disasters triggered by environmental pollution and human action is only a way of diverting attention from the essential need for a revolution in human ethics. By blinding man to this need, such confidence in science might lead to greater disasters than any we have yet known. I do not deny the achievements of modern civilization and its use of science in preventing natural disasters to some extent. I do insist, however, that the very acts that have made this prevention possible have often caused man-made disasters or have set off disasters of new kinds.

TOYNBEE: The action required for coping with the evil consequences of power is ethical, not intellectual. But science is an intellectual activity that is ethically neutral. Therefore the effects of the continuing development of science will depend on whether science is applied for good or for bad purposes in the ethical meaning of the words *good* and *bad*. Evils produced by science cannot be cured by science itself.

IKEDA: That is certainly true. Scientific technology must not be used to control and conquer the world of nature, including other living beings. Instead it must be brought into accord with natural rhythm and put to use in such a way as to take maximum advantage of that rhythm. The situation is similar to the case of medicines and surgery, which ought to be used only in order to stimulate and take advantage of the healing powers that are inherent in human life.

Scientists, politicians, and leaders of modern industry, which is based on sophisticated scientific technology, must thoroughly understand the correct uses of scientific technology. Only when they have such an understanding will we be able to prevent the disasters that have arisen from man's rebellion against the natural world.

Developing this attitude requires that all human beings, including scientists, revolutionize their approach to nature from the very innermost part of their living beings. I believe that the profound nature of this revolution demands that religion must take a leading role in scientific-technological civilization. First, religion will bring about a revolution in thought. Then, the human beings who have experienced this revolution will apply scientific technology to the environment. Obviously, scientists and technicians will be the central group making the application. The third stage in the process I envision will be new developments in science and technology. A process of this kind seems to be the only hope for continued scientific development and the cessation of man-made disasters.

TOYNBEE: Science will be used for destructive purposes if we act on the assumption that nature exists for man. This collective egocentric assumption can be overcome only in the field of individual spiritual life. Each human being has to master his own personal egocentricity. Religion is, I agree, the only faculty of human nature that is capable of inspiring human beings to master themselves, either individually or collectively.

Only the religious attitude towards human life and its environment can enable us to recognize once again, as our ancestors recognized, that, in spite of his exceptionally great power, man is a part of nature and must coexist with the rest of nature if nature, and man in his necessary natural environment, are to survive.

Religion seems to me to be a necessity of life for a being that possesses consciousness and that consequently has the power, and hence also the inescapable compulsion, to make choices. The greater man's power, the greater his need for religion. If the application of science is not inspired and directed by religion, science will be applied to the indulgence of greed, and it will serve greed so effectively that it will be destructive.

Urban Problems

Land Prices and High-rise Construction

IKEDA: Today large cities all over the world are faced with problems that are growing more and more complicated and grave. For instance, Japan's major cities are plagued with bad roads, inadequate water supplies, poor sewerage, housing shortages, improper garbage disposal, scanty greenery, traffic congestion, high prices, environmental pollution, dehumanization, and so on.

These problems are, in a sense, a condensation and ensuing eruption of the defects inherent in modern civilization. Obviously, they are problems for governments to solve, and in view of the increasing urbanization of rural areas, drastic measures must be taken immediately.

TOYNBEE: Urbanization is one of the characteristic tendencies of the modern way of life, and the conditions of life in present-day cities are revealing. Like a convex mirror, they show up the blemishes of modern life by exaggerating them. In the world's rapidly growing cities, the present-day evils you have enumerated reach maximum intensity.

The greater part of the world's growing population is silting up in the cities, and the life of the remnant in the shrinking rural areas is being urbanized. Agriculture and animal husbandry are being mechanized as cities themselves spread tentacles, in the shape of express highways, far into the country.

IKEDA: One of the gravest issues accompanying this profoundly disturbing phenomenon is the upward spiral of land prices. Urbanization of population continues to accompany economic growth, and yearly increases in land prices are a concurrent feature of both processes. For many people the idea of owning land and a home has become no more than a dream.

Population growth in Tokyo has reached a peak. In the past few years, a slight decrease in the number of people living in Tokyo has taken place, but city residential conditions have only worsened. This is true because many of the public housing projects built after World War II consisted of wooden structures that have now deteriorated so badly that reconstruction is imperative. Naturally, rents in the new apartment buildings are higher than they were in the old ones. This inevitably works great hardships on the masses of people, who must now pay more for shelter than they did in the past.

TOYNBEE: I realize that these problems are acute in Japan, but the issue is worldwide. Increased land prices are a burning question in Britain today, as the countless articles on housing problems that fill British newspapers indicate. But, because of the enormous population that must be housed in a very limited area, Hong Kong probably has the most serious shelter problem in the world.

The last time we were in Hong Kong, my wife asked to be shown some of the new apartment buildings. The achievement made there in the past decade is astounding, because, in that period, one quarter of the population—that is, one million out of four million people—has been rehoused in high-rise apartment buildings. When a British official took us to see some of the buildings, we greatly admired the orderly way in which the Chinese live under extremely difficult conditions. Because their families are closely united and the children are well disciplined, Chinese people are able to survive under conditions that Europeans would find impossible. Their ability in this line is most impressive.

IKEDA: It may be that many oriental peoples, including the Chinese, are talented at conforming to trying environmental conditions. Still, living in cramped quarters is not easy for anyone, Easterner or Westerner.

Although this too may be a worldwide tendency, it is worth mentioning the huge profits that land brokers are now making in Japan because of the rising prices of real estate. Yearly, lists are published of people in Japan with the largest incomes, and people who have become newly rich on land always occupy high places in the roster. I think that some steps ought to be taken to correct this unwholesome situation.

TOYNBEE: Scandalously large fortunes are being made in Britain too by speculative dealers in land and buildings. These people are prepared to keep their buildings empty for years on end in order to pocket the huge capital gains that they expect to win through the steep increases in the capital value of buildings and sites.

It is wrong for people to make speculative private profit on land, which is one of the necessities of life and which is available in a limited quantity only. Like other necessities—for instance, water and minerals—land ought not to be in the hands of private individuals working for their own selfish gains.

IKEDA: You are correct in saying that land ought not to be in the hands of people, like brokers, who are concerned only with their private financial aggrandizement. Instead it should be made readily available to the ordinary people at prices that everyone can afford. But increasing land prices result directly from great demand. As long as the demand remains large and as long as the system of disposing of real estate is free economic enterprise, it will be impossible to limit rising land prices. The only way that I see out of the situation is the gradual communalization of land.

TOYNBEE: It ought to be controlled, I agree, in the public interest. Land is a scarce commodity, and all other commodities are dependent on access to land. So, too, are all human activities. Therefore, I think that land and buildings ought all to be public property. Dwelling houses now owned by owner-occupiers ought to be expropriated at a generous rate of compensation, and office buildings and factories at a less generous rate. Land and buildings held by speculators ought to be confiscated, and if the speculators are to be given any indemnification at all, it should be considerably lower than the amount that they have invested in their antisocial, speculative activities.

IKEDA: The policy you outline seems the only one open to us, but I suspect that it would take some time to implement. As a more immediate step to relieve the shortage of housing in countries where land is very scarce, the high-rise apartment building is widely employed, but it is not entirely satisfactory. You have mentioned the large numbers of aprtment towers built in Hong Kong. Similar mass apartment settlements are being built in increasing numbers in Japan as well. But the apartments in the new buildings are difficult for ordinary people either to rent or to buy because of the expense involved.

Still another problem has developed from the increase in numbers and sizes of high-rise apartments. Mammoth concrete slabs cut off sunlight and breezes from homes in the immediate neighborhood. This in turn has extremely detrimental physical and psychological effects on the people deprived of these natural benefits.

TOYNBEE: The shutting out of light and breezes from the surroundings is one of the problems accompanying high-rise apartment buildings; there are several others. First, people living in huge apartment blocks are neighbors only in the physical sense. Very little personal contact is established among the dwellers in such buildings, and this is socially very bad. Mothers and children suffer from the very heights and sizes of these buildings. A mother may not have the time to descend from an apartment on the top floor of a building to find a playground for her children and then remain with them while they play. If she cannot herself go down with her children, she may hesitate to let them go alone because she is anxious about what may happen while she is not present to watch over them.

IKEDA: Undoubtedly the blanket reliance on high-rise buildings to solve problems of scarcity of land tends to deepen human estrangement. Such unnatural and antisocial living conditions inevitably bring sorrow. If we are to create living environments in which human beings can lead happy lives, we must plan cities and devise policies for land use that restore harmony with nature. Communalization of land would be one step in the right direction. If high-rise apartment buildings are unavoidable, ample land must be made available for them, and they must be planned to take care of the physical and psychological needs of the dwellers.

TOYNBEE: Assuming that the community has acquired the ownership of all

48

land and buildings, what ought to be the community's policy about high-rise buildings intended for use as dwellings? The speculators have built high-rise apartment houses in order to make maximum private profit. The community would not have this motive for forcing people to live in buildings that are socially and personally unsatisfactory. But the community would still be confronted with the problem of scarcity of land. The Greek geographer Strabo, writing at a date near the beginning of the Christian era, pointed out that the ancient city of Rome would expand from sea to sea if the high-rise buildings there were to be replaced by single-story buildings.

In the present age of population explosion, there is going to be an acute conflict of social interests between two rival claims for the use of land. Which is to have priority? The use for agriculture and pasturage, or the use for housing of a human kind (not high-rise)? I suppose there will have to be a compromise, and perhaps all new dwelling houses will have to be sited on land that is of minimal value for food production. But such sites will be topographically inconvenient and will be expensive to build on, because, for the most part, they will be in rocky, uneven terrain, remote from present concentrations of offices and factories in which the breadwinners will still have to earn their livings. Therefore, we may be forced to decentralize gradually and disperse not only homes but also buildings used for economic production.

Transportation

IKEDA: The automobile is a very inefficient carrier because it takes up too much space for the number of passengers it can transport. In the past, it was especially prized for its speed and for the freedom with which one could use it to travel wherever one wished. But under the conditions of traffic paralysis that prevail now in many parts of the world, the automobile no longer has these two advantages to recommend it. It consumes petroleum, a limited natural resource, and it pollutes the atmosphere with exhaust fumes. The staggering number of people injured and killed in automobile accidents everywhere is shocking and horrifying. In Japan, its too frequent association with death and injury has earned the automobile the grimly facetious appellation "traveling coffin."

In listing the faults of the automobile, I am not advocating the total abolition of automotive transportation. I merely want to stress the danger that if the present trend continues and if the already bad situation grows worse, urban transportation of this kind will come to a standstill.

TOYNBEE: I should like to see the interiors of cities put out of bounds for privately owned cars, with the one exception of doctors' cars. Within this barred zone, I should like to see public transport given a monopoly. This could then be abundant, rapid, and cheap. Privately owned cars approaching a city from the outside should be required, as is already the case in Venice, to park in a car-park on the outskirts. If it is necessary for commercial trucks and vans to visit the interior of the city, they should be allowed to operate there only during the short periods in which the passenger traffic carried by public conveyances is at a minimum. Commercial traffic in the interior should be barred during the rush hours at the beginning and the end of the working day.

IKEDA: Following the example set earlier by New York, Japan has declared vehicular traffic illegal in busy parts of major cities on Sundays and holidays. This leaves broad stretches of cities open to exclusively pedestrian traffic and in that sense is a pleasant thing, but it is scarcely a basic solution to the urban traffic problem.

I feel that the only way to solve the issue is to limit the number of automobiles that can be manufactured and sold to the capacity of the roads and highways. Furthermore, to reduce the number of traffic accidents, each applicant for a driver's license ought to be given personality tests and ought to be subjected to a course in what might be called highway moral education. Of course, as you say, public transportation in cities and suburbs must be developed to the point where restrictions on the number of automobiles will not cause the citizens hardships. Taking these things into consideration, I suspect that the transportation of greatest promise for the city of the future are the subway, the elevated train, the monorail, and other similar means of mass transportation.

TOYNBEE: There should be a limitation of the total number of private cars licensed to travel on roads outside the barred areas, and the conditions for obtaining a driving license should be made more stringent.

In all governmental policy regarding cars, social considerations should be given priority over economic considerations. At present, car manufacturers are encouraged to produce at maximum output, no matter how bad the social effects of their efforts, because maximum output promotes the maximum profits, employment, and exports. This is the policy of a society sacrificing life itself to commercial profit. The evil consequences of this policy are one of the many illustrations of the need to make a radical change in the order of precedence of our values.

50

Returning to Rural Areas

IKEDA: Modern farming makes extensive use of agricultural chemicals and chemical fertilizers, which can be costly. Americans reportedly invest as much in agriculture as in advanced industries. True, such investments have resulted in highly mechanized farming and, therefore, have lightened the labor of the farmers. Artificial fertilizers, however, not only affect the flavor of farm products but also reduce plant resistance to disease-causing bacteria and thus necessitate use of agricultural medicines to counter germs.

According to the report of a Japanese agronomist, when a certain English school fed its pupils lunches made from foods raised with artificial fertilizers, the children were frequently sick. When the school began to give the pupils only farm products grown with natural fertilizer, however, they became healthy and sound. If the report is true, it suggests that crops ought to be raised with natural fertilizer under conditions of natural light and heat.

Agricultural insecticides are no less harmful than artificial fertilizers. They contaminate the natural environment and exterminate many useful insects and small animals as well as pests. Should this situation be left unrectified, such insecticides will eventually threaten man's health and, indeed, his very survival. In view of the evil effects of chemical fertilizers and agricultural insecticides, we are now being forced to initiate a substantial change in our concept of the modernization of farming.

TOYNBEE: I, too, suspect that the recent sensational increase in agricultural productivity through the massive use of fertilizers and insecticides may make the food produced in this new way less nutritious and perhaps even unwholesome. I also suspect that the natural fertility of the soil may eventually be damaged beyond repair by this unnatural treatment.

Nearly ten thousand years of practice have demonstrated that, at a lower level of productivity, agricultural land can be kept permanently fertile by a regime of mixed farming, in which the excrement of domesticated animals is used as manure, and by rotation of crops. Where this is not practicable, fields may be left to lie fallow periodically.

Soil that is good for agriculture is a rare resource: it amounts to only a small percentage of the total land surface of the globe. Therefore soil conservation ought to be given very high priority. Even in the age of traditional farming methods, some areas that were originally fertile were reduced to desert by overcultivation or overgrazing. The risk that, in our greed for an immediate increase in production, we may cause the same kind of devastation on a vaster scale has been greatly exacerbated by recent applications of chemistry to

51

agriculture. Mankind cannot afford to jeopardize the maintenance of its food supply. These considerations certainly suggest that we ought to revert to the traditional methods of agriculture. This will mean reverting to a labor-intensive way of farming.

IKEDA: As you say, reversion to traditional agricultural methods will demand an increased agricultural labor force, which, under current conditions, would be difficult to supply. But as automation increases in urban industries, we may expect the segment of the population employed in such activities to decrease. The needed additional labor could then be provided by superfluous manpower resulting from increasing automatization of industrial processes. It is likely that a reversal in the flow of population, from rural to urban areas, might take place. Industrial work forces may continue to decrease, while farming population continues to increase, with the result that the latter will eventually overtake the former. This seems to be a most desirable course of events, one that will be beneficial to man's physical and mental health, provided that material affluence is guaranteed by automated industries.

It is only to be expected that attempts to use little or no chemical fertilizers or insecticides will encounter fierce resistance from chemical enterprises with immense influence in contemporary industrial society. In order to overcome such opposition, it will be necessary to reform the awareness of the masses of the people and to organize an extensive social movement. The current of human culture must now be rechanneled in a new direction. In modern society, the industrial community has always been the exclusive basis of culture. This basis must now revert to the agricultural community. If that is unfeasible, agriculture and industry must at least advance together on an equal footing.

TOYNBEE: The change you suggest is desirable in the interests not only of agriculture but also of the present urban population. Since the Industrial Revolution, a majority of the population in the technologically and economically advanced countries has been drawn from the rural countryside into the cities. This has been a social disaster, because urban factory work and office work are much less satisfying psychologically than rural agriculture and animal husbandry as a way of life and as a means of earning a livelihood. Urbanization and industrialization have become economic problems, since the progress of automation and computerization is making labor-intensive manual and clerical work superfluous.

The highly urbanized regions are going to have to demobilize their urban population. This will be a painful process, since, within the last two hundred years, town dwellers have become accustomed to urban life, though they have not found ways and means of making it happy. If unemployed ex-industrial workers were evicted from urban slums into rural slums in which they would still be unemployed, their distress and dissatisfaction would increase. It will therefore be a blessing if, just at the time when urban work is becoming redundant, rural work calls for a larger number of laborers.

Even so, the remigration of the majority of the population of the so-called advanced countries from town to country is going to be a difficult, painful, and protracted operation. These countries will probably have to pass through a prolonged crisis before their deindustrializing counterrevolution has been completed. Fortunately, the highly industrialized and urbanized communities are still only a minority of mankind. The majority has not yet departed very far from the rural way of life, based on labor-intensive agriculture and animal husbandry, that has been the economic and social regime of the majority since the beginning of the Neolithic age. For this so-called backward majority, it will be less difficult than it will be for the advanced minority to arrive at the future stable global state that must be attained by mankind as a whole.

This suggests that there may be a dramatic reversal of fortunes. The hitherto advanced countries are likely to have to go through a long period of adversity. The hitherto backward countries are likely to be able to reach the future universal stable state less painfully and more rapidly.

IKEDA: Your forecast that the advanced nations may become in a sense retarded and the backward nations advanced is extremely interesting. It may be that the awakening of interest in young people of the United States and Europe in Japanese Zen and Indian yoga indicates that they consider nonindustrial, noneconomic things to be the most advanced elements of our age. Even if they are correct in this assumption, however, as long as such things as Zen and yoga remain outside the general current of the lives of the people in the advanced countries and are thus no more than exotic cultural objects of interest, they cannot effect a transformation of civilization in general. But the youth of the world might contribute to a massive transformation of civilization if they directed their attention to the traditional production activities and daily living patterns still to be found among some of the peoples of Asia and Africa.

TOYNBEE: If my prognosis is convincing, China may live to congratulate herself retrospectively on her procrastination in industrializing. This cost China a century of weakness and of humiliating ill-treatment, but that may turn out to have been a cheap price to pay for having avoided extreme urbanization and industrialization. On the other hand, the Russians and the Japanese may live to regret that they responded as promptly, vigorously, and effectively as they did to the challenge presented to them by the industrialization of the Western peoples. The Russians and the Japanese responded to this challenge from the West by following suit. They countered by plunging into industrialization up to the neck. On a short view, this seemed to be farsighted. On the longer view that is now beginning to open out, it may prove to have been a shortsightedly precipitate reaction.

Imminent Doom

IKEDA: As many intellectuals are insisting, the future of the human race is anything but bright. When one considers the present state of the world, rapidly recurring worldwide disasters, and scientific data predicting further calamities, one is forced to wonder if humanity will survive into the twenty-first century. Current fears of total cataclysm may in some respects resemble the numerous theories of the End that have appeared from time to time throughout human history.

The prophecies of the End found in Judaism, Christianity, and Islam foresee a final judgment at the hands of God and a subsequent total alteration of universal order. In this sense, they leave room for optimism. Undeniably, however, such optimism could lead to the cessation of reforms in the society of this world. People burdened with actual hardships might well put all their hope in an ideal heaven and, rejecting the actual world, long only for death. The tenacity of Christian belief in a future world and constant forebodings of the collapse of the actual world captured the minds and hearts of many people. This very tenacity is to be seen in the firm belief in the Last Judgment.

But even at the Last Judgment there will be hope for good people. The current theory of the imminent destruction of mankind, on the other hand, leaves no latitude for hope. In the past, even when prophecies of doom gained credence, people continued to believe in the human conscience and the possibility of reform. The currently prevailing theory of the End fails to take into account even the good parts of human life and plunges mankind into despair.

TOYNBEE: At the west end of the Old World, to the west of the regions in which Hinduism and Buddhism have been prevalent, it has been believed that

54

the world, in the form in which we know it, will be brought to an end by the fiat of an almighty god, at a future date this god has fixed in advance but has not revealed. This belief in an End imposed by divine will originated among the Zoroastrians and was adopted from them by the Jews, Christians, and Muslims.

Although ours is not the first age in which mankind has been confronted with the prospect that life in the form in which we have experienced it so far may come to an end, I agree that present circumstances are unprecedented. In the past, mankind has sometimes been threatened with extinction by natural forces beyond human control. But this is the first time that we have known that our future will be decided by what we ourselves do or fail to do.

IKEDA: Noah's flood symbolizes the natural forces that have threatened mankind. Probably peoples of the past regarded natural disasters, like floods, as threats before which human strength is useless. It is scarcely to be wondered that such disasters were linked with ideas about the end of the world. The modern fear of impending doom, however, is a reflection of the bewildering state in which man has used science as a weapon in order to achieve power enough to move the world but has been betrayed by—and is now being driven to destruction by—the very civilization he created.

Upon inquiring into the causes of the current worldwide malaise, we are surprised to find that it is we who have forced ourselves to the brink of death. Had the cause been a natural force, something outside ourselves, we might have lost hope for a while, but we would have risen again to challenge the thing that put our lives in danger. No matter how much science is applied to the problem, it is no easy task to find a way out of the fear that, struggle as hard as we can, all our efforts only speed our progress to catastrophe.

Another interesting difference in past and present interpretations of the nature of impending doom concerns plenty. In the past, famines led people to the contemplation of the End. Ironically, material plenty itself now arouses fear. In other words, abundance of things is creating a new kind of famine. Modern man has brought about conditions, unheard of in the past, in which material things exist in such overabundance that putting them to use involves the danger of shortening life.

TOYNBEE: What you say is true, but we must not be defeatist, passive, or aloof in our reaction to the current evils that threaten mankind's survival. If these evils were caused by forces beyond human control, resignation and submission might be the only course open to us. However, our present evils are man-made and ought to be man-cured as well.

IKEDA: That is the important point. Many basic causes of the threats to man have been suggested, but I feel that the following are the principle ones.

The first cause is weaponry. Nuclear weapons have been created by physics, the branch of modern science that is at present most central in importance. But physics is not the only culpable branch, for biochemistry has unleashed horrors in the form of biochemical weapons.

The second cause is the problem of environmental pollution and destruction, which, by the opening of this decade, achieved alarming proportions. This issue, of course, includes pollution-caused climatic developments and the disrupting of the ecological system. As many ecologists warn, man may find himself gasping his agonizing last in an atmosphere more like muck than like air unless decisive steps are taken quickly.

Were man to apply his wisdom and total energy to the issue, he would be able to transform the nature of a civilization that has generated the threat of global pollution and find a way to solve all political difficulties without resort to nuclear weapons. But as long as mankind remains subordinate to innate greed and egoism and is held firm in the grips of a sense of futility and a fear of impending annihilation, it will be impossible to escape the nagging shadow of imminent global destruction.

TOYNBEE: Our man-made evils have been caused by the greed and aggressiveness that spring from self-centeredness. Therefore, the cure for these evils is to be found in overcoming self-centeredness. Experience tells us that this is a difficult and painful task, but experience also tells us that some human beings have achieved the goal—incompletely, no doubt, yet sufficiently to revolutionize their own conduct and also the conduct of other people who have been inspired by their example. The subjugation of self-centeredness, which some saintly human beings have accomplished to this revolutionary degree, can surely be attained to an extent by all human beings. The saints are only human, and what has been performed by them is not wholly beyond the capacity of the rest of us.

It is shameful that the present threat to man's survival comes from mankind. It would be still more shameful if we were to fail to save ourselves in a situation in which we have the power to save ourselves if we make the spiritual effort to master our self-centeredness. The shamefulness of the situation ought to stimulate us to make the effort, and the knowledge that we have the power to succeed ought to give us hope, courage, and energy for rising to the occasion.

The prospect of destruction by forces or powers beyond human control is paralyzing, because it offers no hope that the destruction can be averted by human action. But, for this reason, passive resignation in the face of this prospect is not demoralizing, because it is not shameful to resign oneself to something that one has no power to prevent. On the other hand, it is shameful, and therefore demoralizing, to allow ourselves to be destroyed by refusing to make an effort that is manifestly within our power and that would manifestly save us if we were willing to make it. Inaction in such circumstances is tantamount to suicide; it is virtually self-destruction.

IKEDA: It is obvious that we must make efforts in order to overcome the situation in which we find ourselves. But I suspect that people today doubt, even despair about, the human ability to exert effective efforts. Some young people display this kind of doubt in spiritless lives dedicated to leisure, violent demonstrations aimed at overthrowing the establishment, or escape in drugs and narcotics. All of these escapist pursuits imply a profound distrust in the human ability to answer deeper questions.

Ending Environmental Pollution

IKEDA: If industrial wastes can be clearly identified and their courses traced, it is relatively easy to put a stop to them. But because everyone living in cities in one way or another contributes to the generation of pollution of many kinds, the solution to this part of the environmental destruction problem is more complicated. In the past, once an urban organization was completed and set in smooth operation, it was capable of dealing with sewage and other pollution generated within its area. Today developments in civilization have increased pollution beyond the scale with which the classic urban structure can cope.

A known number of industrial concerns are responsible for industrially caused environmental pollution, and the majority of the citizens are the victims. Although political regulations, laws, and civic movements can eliminate this kind of pollution, in the case of general urban pollution, the majority of the citizens are at once the guilty parties and the victims.

TOYNBEE: I agree that environmental pollution has two sources: industrial waste and wasteful private consumption by whole populations living under modern urban conditions. I also agree that the first kind of pollution is much less difficult to check than the second.

As you say, industrial waste is produced by a limited number of identifiable business enterprises and probably can be checked effectively by legislation. Private consumption, on the other hand, can be checked only by the voluntary action of innumerable individuals. Sumptuary laws, unlike legislation dealing with industry, have usually proved to be ineffective. Voluntary action for restraining consumption is likely to be ineffective too unless it is inspired by religion.

IKEDA: The problem is difficult but by no means impossible to solve. To effect improvements on the broad scale, each citizen must strive to reform himself by examining his daily life strictly and eliminating from it all acts that are liable to blame as contributory to pollution. For instance, let us examine the trend in the world of motorization. Each year manufacturers urge citizens to buy their newer, sleeker models as if failure to ride in the latest automobile constituted disqualification as a modern man. The advertising campaigns of these manufacturers are very skillful, as are those of the makers of electrical appliances and other articles of daily use, all of whom operate on what is called the principle of built-in obsolescence. But this greed-inspired pandering to innate human selfishness has done much to create the desperate condition in which we now find ourselves. We must become aware that accumulations of the effects of the small acts of daily life could generate a global disaster that might rob our progeny of the right to exist.

TOYNBEE: In the past, when all mankind was poor, our ancestors were constantly threatened with shortages of food, clothing, housing, and other necessities of life. In these circumstances, frugality was held to be a virtue and luxury to be a vice. But, since the Industrial Revolution, frugality has threatened the manufacturers with a lack of markets for their products and has consequently threatened their employees with loss of employment. Therefore, frugality on the consumers' part has become a vice, not a virtue, in the eyes of the manufacturers and their employees. Manufacturers have sought to stimulate consumption artificially by advertising. It is not a coincidence that the advertising business is coeval with the Industrial Revolution.

However, as you have pointed out, the sectional interest of the manufacturers and their employees in stimulating consumption is inimical to the general interest of society. The stimulation of greed by advertising is producing wholesale pollution. This is a threat to the health, and even to the life, of people now alive. Our present greed also threatens to rob future generations by using up irreplaceable resources.

Moreover, greed is an evil in itself. It is a feature of the animality of human nature, but man, besides being an animal, is something more. In indulging our greed, we lose human dignity. Therefore, so far from stimulating our greed, we ought to restrain it—and this on principle, even if greed were not producing the disastrous material effects of pollution for the present generation and of destitution for posterity—if mankind is to survive pollution. Since the Industrial Revolution, manufacturers have been trying, by advertising, to condition the public into giving priority over all other objectives to the maximum satisfaction of greed. We need to reverse the order of our priorities and to make the restraint of greed and the practice of frugality our first objectives. There are at least three grounds for this: the maintenance of human dignity, the protection of our own generation against the danger of pollution, and the conservation for future generations of the limited natural resources of our planet. We need to replace the ideal insinuated by the advertising industry with the ideal exemplified in Buddhist and Christian monasticism.

IKEDA: Precisely. Freedom is of great importance, but deciding which of man's many aspects shall enjoy freedom is still more important. Given unlimited scope of activity, greed oppresses man's loftiest spirit because it inevitably tramples down what is highest in the human mind. When greed has the upper hand, the situation is analogous to what might happen if a wicked criminal were turned loose on an innocent populace. Like the villain, who must be guarded and, if need be, put in bondage for the sake of the good of the people, greed must be restrained for the sake of what is best in man. But this restraint must not be applied socially from the outside; it must arise from the independent self-awareness of the individual.

We must adopt the standpoint that the awareness of the dignity of life must be the basic principle on which all our actions rest. Once we have established this premise, we must go on to take the following concrete actions. First, limit consumption of physical materials to a minimum and devise ways to use waste products in production. This step will both help eliminate environmental pollution and guard against the exhaustion of natural resources. Second, make maximum use of the physical energy of the human body. In addition to reducing pollution and conserving resources, this step will promote and maintain greater human health. Third, be cautious about the unlimited use of medicines, additives to foods, and other chemical products and be aware that harm almost invariably accompanies whatever good these substances do.

Each individual human must put these simple rules into practice in his daily life and must battle with anyone who would endanger the future of mankind by disregarding them. Scientists must make use of their knowledge to enlighten the people, and journalists must apply the power of their words to expose evil occurring in these connections. The housewife can carry on the fight in the home, and the laborer at his place of work. For a movement of this kind to be effective and meaningful, it must have a strong spiritual basis, and I agree with you that the power of religion is required to build this basis.

The kind of religion that is needed must make each individual human being deeply aware of two important things: the truth that the life force of a single person is more important than all the material wealth of the world and the equally important principle that both life and the dignity that is inherent in it can be supported only in harmony with nature.

TOYNBEE: Yes, the present threat to mankind's survival can be removed only by a revolutionary change of heart in individual human beings. This change of heart must be inspired by religion in order to generate the will power needed for putting arduous new ideals into practice.

THE INTELLECT | 3

Education

Goals of Learning

IKEDA: The most important questions in the field of education are the ones devoted to helping man see clearly what he ought to be and how he ought to live. It is true that the pursuit of answers to these questions can produce effects of practical benefit. But such benefits remain side effects. At their best, learning and education are not stimulated solely by the desire for practical benefits, nor do they adopt such benefits as their goals. In modern technological society, however, some people regard learning and science as no more than the servants of utilitarianism. This view in its turn arouses doubt about the value of learning and education.

TOYNBEE: I hold that the goal of education ought to be religious, not mercenary. Education ought to be a search for an understanding of the meaning and the purpose of life and for discovering the right way to live. The right spiritual way is, I believe, fundamentally identical for all human beings. The right practical way too was the same for all mankind in the age before the division of labor was made necessary by the change to complexity from the original simplicity of mankind's social organization and technology.

In the age of technological civilization, education in the right way to live needs to be supplemented by vocational training in special branches of knowledge and kinds of skill. But before entering his profession, everyone who has received professional training ought to take the Hippocratic oath that is prescribed for entrants into the medical profession. Every entrant into any profession ought to pledge himself to use his special knowledge and skill for serving his fellow human beings and not for exploiting them. He should give his obligation of service priority over his incidental need to make a living for himself and for his family. Maximum service, not maximum profit, is the objective to which he should dedicate himself.

IKEDA: You are quite right. By devoting itself to a utilitarianism that over-emphasizes intellectual knowledge and technological skills, education in modern society has had two major bad consequences. First, by making learning a tool of politics and economics, it has robbed learning of its inherent dignity and independence. Second, people engaged in learning and education become the slaves of intellectual knowledge and technological skill, which are the only aspects of learning prized today. As an outcome of this trend, respect for humanity declines. In short, today people are compelled to serve intellectual knowledge and technological skill, which are in turn controlled by politics and economics.

Duration of Learning

IKEDA: School education alone is insufficient to the full development and cultivation of individual abilities. Each person has different talents; each has his own merits and good qualities. The key to meaningful use of talents and characteristics lies in awakening these traits and applying them in daily life and practical situations.

I do not think school performance alone ought to be the sole criterion on which a person's abilities are judged. Not all bright students turn out to be productive and useful citizens, and many people who were not conspicuous for their talents in school become outstanding and able members of society in middle life or even later. In addition, learning today changes so rapidly that often what one learns in school becomes outdated and perhaps useless later on.

TOYNBEE: In the present-day world, in which our knowledge is increasing and our interpretation of it is changing all the time, full-time juvenile education is not enough. This ought to be followed up by lifelong, part-time self-education. What has been learned at the juvenile stage now no longer suffices for the rest of a lifetime. It follows that the degrees that a student has won on leaving his school or university must be regarded not as a lifelong assessment but as merely a provisional judgment. In adult life, each of us ought to continue to be tested and to be reappraised repeatedly. The tests should be a person's practical performance from stage to stage. It is both absurd and unjust to classify a person, once for all, as being first class or third class when he is still only sixteen or only twenty-two years old.

There are slow-growers who blossom late in life. Conversely, there are brilliant starters who fail to fulfill their early promise. Winston Churchill was apparently backward as a child, apparently brilliant as a young man, apparently a failure in middle age, and unquestionably a great man in his sixties. Another man who had a decisive influence on the course of English history was the seventh-century Greek Christian missionary Theodore of Tarsus. When he was sent to reform the Christian church in England, Theodore was about the same age as Churchill was when he was appointed prime minister to save Britain from being conquered. Like Churchill, Theodore accomplished his mission triumphantly. He reformed the church in England in twenty years of strenuous work performed when he was in his sixties and seventies. Illustrations of the converse phenomenon of a disappointing career could of course be cited.

IKEDA: Once a child has grown and has entered society, his ability to do academic study will not be the basis on which his character is judged. In many cases, breadth of character and depth of experience will play the determining part in people's evaluations of him. Although there are differences according to whether the work involved is physical or mental, by and large, in order for a person to manifest and apply his abilities, he must be physically strong and mentally and spiritually sensitive. Academic learning alone cannot develop the body and the mind to the proper degree. To supplement it, we must devise ways of bringing students in contact with society and providing them with varied experiences as often as possible through extracurricular activities and community life. I believe that the kind of education system needed today is one that concentrates on developing the whole human being.

TOYNBEE: I have suggested that one of the advantages of continuing one's education during the adult stage of life is that an adult can bring his personal experience to bear on what he learns academically (that is, at second hand). I will now add that opportunities for gaining practical experience through extracurricular activities and community life ought to be given to juvenile students at the earliest possible stage of their education.

This has been recognized in Britain in the educational system of the so-called public schools. Some of these, which are in truth not public schools but private schools, are open to criticism as preserves of the establishment, yet they do give the older boys opportunities for exercising authority and for acquiring a sense of responsibility. In this respect, British public schools seem to me to have set a valuable example. I was educated in one of these schools. The boy who was the head of this school was admonished in a Greek motto meaning authority is a test of character.

Human abilities are diverse, and all these diverse abilities are socially valuable. Each individual's particular kind of ability ought to be discovered and fostered. This can be done by giving students opportunities for gaining and using practical experience and by continuing, throughout life, the kind of education in which theory and practice are combined so as to supplement and stimulate each other.

Financing Education

IKEDA: Unfortunately, in many countries today, education is conducted under the control of the state and in line with the aims pursued by the government. Learning and research, the fountainheads of education, are especially intimately connected to the needs of states because without governmental financial help, unlimited research in fields involving immense outlays of money would be impossible. In fields related to the national interest, funds are available, and results of research are excellent. Unfair treatment, however, is the fate of fields not directly related to national profit and of scholars whose opinions run counter to those of the state. This mood in the world of learning and research is reflected directly in the world of education, where subjects related to national interest are emphasized while others are slighted.

TOYNBEE: It is undesirable that financing, control, and direction of education should be monopolized by the state, because the state is tempted to subsidize lines of study that seem likely to increase its power. The state is also tempted to give to publicly financed and controlled education an ideological twist in order to condition students into becoming supporters of the ideology of the establishment.

Publicly subsidized education does, of course, have advantages; for example, it gives equal opportunities to all boys and girls. In present-day Britain, some of the leading personalities in all walks of life were children of poor families who had the best education thanks to public subsidization.

IKEDA: Certainly from the viewpoint of equal educational opportunities, subsidies by the government or autonomous public bodies are inevitable because individuals often cannot bear the full burden of school fees. But no tampering with the contents of education must be allowed, and no attempts, even indirect ones, to slant education in one direction or another must be permitted. Our problem is to devise a plan for subsidies that does not run the danger of exerting undue influence on education.

TOYNBEE: In Britain since the end of World War I, we have established semipublic corporations financed from public funds but not controlled by the government. They are administered by autonomous governing bodies. One of these is the University Grants Committee, which now supplies and allocates the greater part of the funds of the British universities. (Only a minor part of these funds is now supplied by students' fees or by private endowments.) The intention is that the government shall abstain from interfering with a semipublic corporation's policy by using the power of the purse. So far, on the whole, this intention has been carried out in practice, but it is still too early to tell whether, in the long run, the autonomy of the University Grants Committee and of other semipublic corporations (e.g., the British Broadcasting Corporation, which is an important educational agency) will continue to be respected by Parliament.

Evidently the device of semipublic corporations is precarious. It is important to make education independent, on a fully secure and permanent basis. For this, I think two conditions are necessary: a permanent financial endowment that is not controlled by the state or by business corporations; a staff of teachers and of educational administrators whose ethical and intellectual standards are so manifestly high that they will be respected and supported by the public.

Such endowments can be provided by irrevocable gifts; that is, gifts made with a legally binding commitment on the donor's part to divest himself and his heirs of all right to interfere in the administration of the endowment. This is the principle of the American private foundations for the advancement of research and education. It is also the principle of the land grants that are one source of revenue of state universities and colleges in the United States. Land is the best form of permanent endowment, because the value of land varies inversely with the value of money, and the value of money tends to depreciate, even at times when inflation is not taking place at its present high rate and rapid pace. The scholarship that I won at Winchester College in 1902 was financed from the income from an endowment of land made by the founder of the college in 1395.

I should like to see all educational institutions in all countries endowed with irrevocable gifts of land on a scale that would make it possible to keep students' fees low and teachers' salaries high. This would ensure freedom from control by the state and by big business. The educational institutions ought to be fully autonomous corporations. The constitutions of these corporations should provide for the representation not only of the educational administrators and the teaching staff but also of the parents (in the case of schools) and of the students (in the case of universities and high schools). The general public ought to be represented, since education is a social activity in which the whole of society is vitally concerned. The determination of the respective powers of these various kinds of participants in the framing and the execution of educational policy would be highly controversial, as is indicated by current controversies over this issue all over the world.

Coeducation

IKEDA: Under the influence of Confucian morality, Japanese education for males and females was conducted separately until the end of World War II. Since then, however, coeducational systems have been established in all public schools from the primary to the university level. I understand that in England too the history of coeducation is comparatively short. What are your views on the good and bad points of the coeducational system?

TOYNBEE: In England, coeducation did not begin until 1870 and then for reasons of economy, not of principle. At that time, the primary and secondary public school systems (i.e., systems paid for out of public resources) were made coeducational, though the private system, including the universities, remained segregated. There were few universities in Britain then—only two in England and four in Scotland—and all of them excluded women from taking degrees. My wife attended Cambridge. She was allowed to take examinations and was awarded first-class honors, but she could not take a degree. In the United States, of course, mixed colleges have long allowed both sexes to attend classes and take degrees together. In Britain today, men and women students mix freely, and there is talk of having mixed colleges of the American kind.

I think that there is much to be said for both the segregated and the mixed systems. At present, coeducation is creating a very serious problem because of sexual promiscuity among students of ages from thirteen to eighteen. This is admittedly an extremely difficult period for the young, a period in which education, mixed or segregated, is likely to encounter many problems. Today there are often cases of young girls' becoming pregnant at fourteen or fifteen. This is not a necessary effect of coeducation, but it is an actual effect and a source of much sorrow and hardship.

When I was fourteen, schools were strictly segregated. There were already separate colleges for women and separate schools for younger girls, but

66

relations between the sexes were closely regulated. We saw each other seldom. This of course eliminated promiscuous sexual relations between boys and girls, but it did not eliminate homosexuality. When I went to boarding school at fourteen, I had never heard of homosexuality. I heard a great deal about it after I got there because it was a frequent subject of conversation. Unfortunately, homosexuality is one of the evils of boarding schools.

Balancing the advantages and disadvantages of the two systems seems very difficult to me. If you attempt to solve the problem of promiscuous heterosexual relations in coeducational institutions by segregating boys from girls, you find yourself with the equally serious problem of homosexual relations.

IKEDA: As you say, there are problems involved in either system. I believe that male and female homosexuality is a relative issue. Some societies accept it, as did ancient Greece; some condemn it. Sexual relations between male and female involve deeper issues since they lead to pregnancy and are therefore closely connected with the dignity of life itself. If I were forced to make a decision, I would say that probably homosexual relations among students are the lesser of the two evils.

In the middle school and high school that I have founded, the sexes are segregated. I took this step in the hope of inspiring the students to devote themselves entirely to their work. Obviously, I should prefer a situation in which sex issues did not occur among students, but since they will occur, I insist that this is a matter for the freedom and conscience of the students.

I believe that an educational institution must teach its students to respect freedom of judgment, help them develop their personalities, and provide them with the knowledge to make their own free judgments. If the pupils of a school persistently make wrong judgments, the school is not adequately fulfilling its duty. For the teacher to attempt to interfere with the students' judgments by exerting undue pressures or by attempting to force them to see things in a particular way reveals the ineptness and perhaps the mental laziness of the teacher. You may think that my approach is too idealistic, but this is the way I look at institutionalized education.

Teaching and Research

IKEDA: It is desirable to separate educators who actually teach from those who are engaged in research or special studies. It is true that education and research belong to entirely different categories, and in more sophisticated academic circles education is often sacrificed in favor of research. But the functional and institutional separation of education and research may deprive

67

the teacher of his role as research scholar and thus rob him of the freshness essential to his work. Even if we separate the teacher and the research scholar, we still must devise ways to promote intercourse between the two and to elevate the quality of the educator.

TOYNBEE: I think that, at the university level of education, teachers ought to be given time and opportunity for research and that this, as well as teaching, ought to be regarded as an essential part of their duties. The function of university education is to teach students how to educate themselves. If the teachers are to do this effectively, I think that they too must continue to educate themselves. For them, the means of self-education is research.

On the other hand, a researcher need not necessarily be a teacher. A vocation for research does not always carry with it a vocation for teaching. I do not think that a researcher is likely to do first-rate work if he spends the whole of his working life on research, to the exclusion of all other activities. If he does this, he will be isolating himself from the general current of human life and will be cutting himself off from the practical experience that cannot be acquired in laboratories and libraries. The most creative researchers have been people who have combined research with some other activity.

In my field, which is historical research, the most eminent historians have not been part-time teachers; they have been part-time politicians, administrators, soldiers, or businessmen. Some of them have carried on their two professions simultaneously; others have retired, voluntarily or compulsorily, from some practical profession partway through their working life and have then taken to writing history. They have succeeded in writing admirable historical works because they have been able to draw on their own firsthand experience. They have taken part themselves in activities of the kind that they have subsequently studied, and this has given them insight and wisdom.

IKEDA: When the research specialist isolates himself from the emotions, the joys, and the sorrows of ordinary human daily-life activities, the results of his research can take odd, even menacing, turns. Your suggestion that people who have spent part of their lives in other fields make the most imaginative researchers offers a hint for a way of dealing with this potential danger.

For the historian and sociologist, the society in which we live is both a valuable source of inspiration and a treasure house of material. Even for the man whose major field of interest involves natural, nonhuman phenomena, society offers important information on the effects the fruits of his research can have on mankind and on the ways human beings will react to them. In this sense, experience with daily social living is essential.

In the light of these connections between research specialists and ordinary citizens, it is evident that the specialist must transmit the topics and outcome of his work to students and the general public in an understandable fashion. Or he must participate in educating the people to the point where they can understand what he has to say. In this way, his research will be examined by disinterested human beings. Their outlook may give him a fresh viewpoint for further research. It may also correct the course of development of—or halt altogether—research that threatens to lead to danger.

Literature's Influence

IKEDA: Thinking about the role of literature reminds me of Jean-Paul Sartre's famous question: what can literature do for the starved? There has been a great deal of controversy over the role of literature in the modern age. Some writers and critics, believing that literature can play an effective role, are struggling to create a new socially effective literary art, whereas others have become nihilists.

TOYNBEE: What can literature do for the starved? The answer becomes clear if we also ask: what can scientific research do for the starved? Scientific research can do little or nothing for the starved if it makes the feeding of the starved its deliberate objective and if it limits its activity to trying to achieve this desirable, practical aim. Science, operating with these blinkers, will fail, because by confining itself to this limited purpose, it will have handicapped itself for making important new scientific discoveries, either useless ones or useful ones. Scientific research leads to discoveries only when it is pursued for its own sake—that is to say, for the satisfaction of intellectual curiosity without any utilitarian *arrière-pensée*. Some of the discoveries made by research undertaken without social or other ulterior motive turn out—unintentionally, unexpectedly, and surprisingly—to have socially useful applications. The truth of this apparent paradox has been demonstrated so often and so con-vincingly that many private business corporations existing to make financial profits have found that it pays to endow scientific researchers and to give them a free hand to follow up any line of research into which their curiosity may lead them, instead of directing their research towards particular objectives with obvious value for the corporation's line of business. This paradoxical truth about science holds good for literature.

The literary works of the great nineteenth-century Russian novelist Tolstoy have had a worldwide effect in awaking the conscience of the rich and powerful minority to try, even at the expense of their own privileges, to reform society in many ways, including the feeding of the starved.

Tolstoy's attitude to life went through two stages, distinguished by a sharp break at his conversion. In each of these stages his attitude at the time was reflected in the character of his published works. During his preconversion stage, Tolstoy wrote spontaneously, simply to satisfy his impulse to produce creative literature. After his conversion, he held that the pursuit of art for art's sake was self-indulgent and socially irresponsible and that an artist ought deliberately to devote his genius to the promotion of human welfare. Tolstoy's postconversion publications were directed towards this limited utilitarian objective. His preconversion publications, however, not only were superior, judged by the criterion of purely literary merit, but also have been more influential socially than his postconversion publications, which were deliberately aimed at producing social results. His preconversion books move readers by their literary merit and therefore inspire them to try to reform society on lines that are implicit in the novels but were not Tolstoy's conscious aim in writing.

The communist regime in the Soviet Union has adopted Tolstoy's postconversion view of the function of literature. The Soviet government holds that literary work ought to be harnessed for the production of social welfare. (Their interpretation of social welfare is much narrower and more controversial than Tolstoy's; for the Russian communists, social welfare means the promotion of the communist ideology and of the Soviet government's power, but this difference does not invalidate the comparison.) The consequence has been a marked decline in both the literary merit and the social influence of Russian literature. Under the communist regime, Russian writers who have followed the party line have been sterile, while those who have written spontaneously, as their creative spirit has moved them to write, have been discouraged and hampered, even when they have not been subjected to actual persecution.

IKEDA: Although I cannot speak in detail on the subject since I possess only limited information about current conditions in the Soviet Union, I suspect that what you say is correct and that the troubles faced by Solzhenitsyn derive from governmental pressure applied to literary artists.

TOYNBEE: The pre-1917 Russian imperial regime, too, disliked and feared literary freedom, but, being less doctrinaire than the present communist regime, the tsar's government perceived that the effect of trying to dragoon

Russian writers would be counterproductive from the government's point of view. They saw that this would increase the writers' influence instead of diminishing it.

The lesson of modern Russian history seems to me to be that literature is likely to have a practical effect in proportion to its spontaneity in giving expression to the writer's creative impulse. This is a paradox only in appearance, for being creative means drawing inspiration from the wellsprings of human spiritual life.

IKEDA: Without doubt, the literary artist, like the scientist, must be spiritually free if he is to produce great works. Literature that is tied to social objectives is not worthy of the name. If literature is to do anything at all for the starving, it must not be limited to fixed purposes but must spring from a free creative spirit.

To continue along these lines, we might expand our examination of literature and the political regime. Is a Marxist literature possible, or can literature grow within the so-called spiritual kingdom of Christianity? Historical examples show that literatures bound by ideologies have been unable to evoke universal response. For example, fifty years after the Russian Revolution, the Russians have produced no literary works superior to those of Dostoevski.

TOYNBEE: Generally, there are two different motives for refusing to allow freedom of expression. One motive is concern for maintaining ideological orthodoxy (Christian, Muslim, Marxist, capitalist, or what not); the other is concern for maintaining ethical standards.

Censorship on theological grounds does have a blighting effect on literature, and in my opinion, it is never justified in any circumstances. Ideological censorship, however, is easy to administer. The decision as to whether the expression of some thought or feeling is admissible or inadmissible is made by the fiat of all-powerful autocratic political or ecclesiastical authorities. Censorship on moral grounds presents more difficult problems. Few people would content that incitement—in private, on the radio, or on television—to indulge in sexual promiscuity or perversion, drug-taking or alcoholism, and physical violence ought to be entirely free in all circumstances. The exposure of the young to possibly corrupting influences would be considered inadmissible by most adults. But there is no consensus on the questions of what is corrupting and of where the line should be drawn between permission and restriction. Moreover, it is arguable that any restriction is likely to be counterproductive— that its effect will probably be to stimulate curiosity and to arouse opposition.

71

THE INTELLECT

IKEDA: Since literature is the spirit of an age and a mirror reflecting the trends occurring in the society producing it, many literary currents arise in an age of multiple values like the present one. Pornography may be only a reflection of one aspect of the changing attitudes of our times. I cannot believe, however, that the current rage for such literature will persist, because both greed for and the satisfaction resulting from pornography are fleeting. The time will come when the masses of the people will no longer pay attention to pornography. We must not, of course, overlook the fact that pornography can corrupt the young and bring disorder to society. At present some people are voicing the opinion that stronger control is needed on pornography from the ethical and moral standpoints. Still I am fundamentally opposed to all restrictions on the freedom of expression. Past experience shows all too vividly how censorship, once admitted in any form, can soon extend to matters of thought, faith, and religion.

TOYNBEE: The establishment has no moral right to use its power for suppressing all religions and philosophies and ideologies except its own. Religion, or art, that is heterodox in the eyes of the establishment cannot flourish in a totalitarian climate. In such a climate, orthodox literature, and art too, may wilt if the regime is so oppressive and inquisitorial that even an orthodox writer's or artist's first concern must be to avoid the risk of falling foul of the censors. This anxiety will kill the spontaneity that is the enabling condition for creativeness.

At the same time, it is a historical fact that some great works of literature and art have been produced under totalitarian regimes: the regime of Christian countries from the fourth to the seventeenth century of the Christian era and the regime of Muslim countries down to a still more recent date.

A poet or an artist may be so completely in tune with the prevalent ideology and so rapturously inspired by it that he will be unconscious of being manacled by the totalitarian regime under which he is living and working. As long as he is unconscious of restraint, he will be spiritually free.

Dante was aware, no doubt, that in Western Christendom in his time there were heretics who were being convicted and being put to death. Perhaps Dante took it for granted that this way of dealing with heretics was right, and it may never have occurred to him that he himself might have been a heretic. This state of mind that I have attributed to Dante was probably shared by the artists who made the pictures, statues, and icons for Christian churches and by the composers of the words and music of the Christian liturgy. If it had been put to Dante that he was living under a totalitarian regime and that he was not a free man, he would, I believe, have denied this in good faith.

72

Totalitarian regimes differ, of course, in the degree of their oppressiveness. Medieval Christendom would have seemed to a Hindu or an East Asian observer to be totalitarian, and his diagnosis would have been correct. Yet Dante was, I believe, no less free spiritually than he would have been if he had been a poet in pre-Christian Italy or in the India or Eastern Asia of his own time, where there was a plurality of religions and where persecution on religious grounds was rare and relatively mild.

The nineteenth-century Russian novelists, on the other hand, were aware of, and affected by, the oppressiveness of the Russian imperial regime. Under the present Soviet regime, it would be difficult to imagine a Russian communist counterpart of the medieval Western Christian poet Dante who would be so devout a believer in the established communist faith that he could express the doctrine and mythology of Marxism-Leninism in sublime poetry with complete spontaneity and with no uneasy awareness of the dark cloud of totalitarian intolerance lowering over his head.

Under the Marxist-Leninist regime, the price of spiritual independence is certainly persecution, and this may come to be its price outside the frontiers of the present communist countries if a worldwide totalitarian regime is going to be—as I suspect it may—a necessary agency for the stabilization of mankind's chaotic affairs.

The Greek poet Aeschylus has said, in two lapidary words, that suffering is the only way of learning. The experience of suffering was certainly one source of Dante's poetry. Dante suffered nothing at the hands of the totalitarian ecclesiastical regime under which he breathed and felt and thought with perfect freedom, but he was crossed in love and he was exiled from his native city-state. If he had not suffered these two severe afflictions, his *Vita Nuova* and his *Divina Commedia* might never have come to birth.

IKEDA: The profound faith that made Dante free within the framework of medieval Christianity may have arisen from his sense of his own sinfulness as a human being. He employed strong faith as a source of power in the forming of his own unshakable self.

In a case like Dante's, there is no question of calculated action to achieve practical social aims. In the instance of the nineteenth-century Russian writers, however, such action was an important goal. Some writers, sensing the futility of their social tasks, become nihilists. Today, too, upon seeing how powerless literature is to feed the poor, some artists have become nihilists. Perhaps the modern fondness for intensely introspective art has contributed to the nihilistic despair of writers.

TOYNBEE: Nihilism means, I suppose, a despair and rejection of human life and of the universe without any vision of an alternative. If this negative reaction is powerful and widespread, it is likely to express itself in literature as well as in other forms. A potent literary expression of a state of mind may fortify this state of mind. For this reason I feel that nihilistic literature is deplorable.

Introspection has two possible alternative objectives. It may be a retreat into one's self from contact with other people and with the universe, or it may be a search, in the subconscious depths of the psyche, for contact with the ultimate spiritual reality. Introspection with the first of these objectives is isolationist; introspection with the second objective is unitive. The first is negative; the second is positive. Introspective literature may be negative, according to the nature of the introspection by which it is inspired. I deplore introspective literature that is negative, but I welcome it if it is positive.

I do not think that it is the function of literature to propagate any particular Weltanschauung, good or bad. Literature with a conscious social or metaphysical aim is likely to defeat its own purpose. The proper function of literature is to describe, and to comment on, the facts and the problems of human life. I think literature ought to be candid but courageous.

IKEDA: Whereas the goal of literature ought not to be rigidly fixed, literature must have a sense of mission that can serve as a motivating factor. Somewhere in the freedom afforded the writer there must be a sincere concern with human suffering—even a subconscious awareness—if the writer is to produce works that will appeal to all people. The struggle to nurture it may be hard, but I am convinced that we must evolve a literature that can do something to save the starved.

TOYNBEE: True art for art's sake is art for life's sake too. Of course, art does sterilize itself if the artist turns himself into a professional specialist who writes primarily or exclusively for his fellow specialists, instead of writing for all his fellow men. As I see it, this is not art for art's sake; it is art for the practitioner's sake. This is a false view even of the practitioner's interests. I therefore hold that it is unfortunate and that it is a symptom of social sickness when either literature or science or scholarship becomes esoteric.

IKEDA: My hope is for a literature that can give the people of our age courage. I cannot condone literature that finds beauty in a vision of humanity falling head on into hell. Instead I prefer to seek the dignity of life in the image of humanity living in sincerity and good will.

74

TOYNBEE: Literature ought to face the evils and difficulties of life without despairing of human nature's ability to respond victoriously to life's challenges. We must strive to win the battle of life, though we have no guarantee that we will.

Intellectuals and the Masses

IKEDA: Many civilizations have preserved the distinction between intellectuals and the masses, but I think that modern society ought to discard it. We must adopt the premise that human beings are human beings before they are members of either the intellectual group or the masses. From this standpoint, it becomes clear that no demarcation line can be drawn between the two. People of the highest intellectual power lead roughly the same kind of daily life as all other human beings, and among the so-called masses there are people of the highest intellectual powers. A brilliant physicist may be no match for an ordinary housewife in balancing a domestic budget. Indeed, it may be only rarity that gives the physicist his great social esteem.

TOYNBEE: The most important aspect of human beings is their common humanity. A human being has to be human before he can be any particular kind of human being: black or white, Buddhist or Confucian, Jew or gentile, intellectual or lowbrow. The most important human experiences are universal and inescapable. Every human being has been born and is going to die. The difficulty of being a conscious living being and the mysteriousness of the universe in which we find ourselves are the same for intellectuals and nonintellectuals. Human beings of both classes are confronted by the same inexorable facts of life and death.

It is a symptom of social ill health when a society is divided into an intelligentsia and the masses and when each of these two sections of the society feels that the other section is alien. Russia suffered from this social malady after her sudden, rapid, forcible, and superficial Westernization by Peter the Great. The intelligentsia (a Russian word) was a new class brought into existence by Peter the Great's policy of inducting Russia into Western society. The Russian intelligentsia consisted of Westernized Russians whose function was to enable the nation to participate in the life of Western society. They were an unhappy class because their conversion to the Western way of life cut them off from their fellow Russians without making them fully at home in the West. In the nineteenth century, many of them lived as expatriates in

75

Western countries, partly voluntarily and partly as political refugees, for their Western education alienated the intelligentsia from the autocratic native Russian regime that had called them into existence.

The magnificent nineteenth-century Russian novels are products of the Russian genius inspired by the Russian intelligentsia's malaise. In Tolstoy's novel *Anna Karenina* there is an illuminating scene in which Levin, a landowner who has been converted to Western liberalism, calls a meeting of his serfs with the intention of giving them shares in his land. The peasants are bewildered and suspicious; they cannot understand their master's motives, and they do not believe in his sincerity. The landowner is baffled and exasperated. The encounter produces no positive results.

The Russian Revolution of 1917 was made by members of the Russian intelligentsia, most of whom had spent many years in exile in the West. Their program was to reform the Russian way of life on so-called advanced Western lines. When those people came into power, scenes like the one I described from Tolstoy's novel were enacted on the grand scale in real life. The revolutionary Westernized Russian intellectuals and the native Russian masses misunderstood each other. Since the revolutionary intellectuals had seized power, they imposed their alien Western ideology on the Russian people by force, in the manner of the native Russian autocratic regime, which they had overthrown as missionaries of modern enlightenment.

IKEDA: In some respects there are similarities between the Russian experience and that of the Japanese since the Meiji Restoration in 1868. Seeing that long centuries of isolation from the rest of the world had left the nation backward in some areas, the leaders of the Meiji government frenetically learned everything they could from the West. The fever to learn from the West affects Japanese society even today, when intellectuals are not judged on the basis of their own wisdom but on the basis of how much they know about the ideas and philosophies of Western scholars.

This of course widens the gap between the intellectuals and the ordinary people. Though intellectuals ought to use their intellects and knowledge to make contributions to the lives of the common people, with whom they ought to maintain a strong sense of relationship, in fact, they tend to divide themselves into small cliques with highly specialized interests. (The tendency to do this may be related to the analytical and discriminatory operations of the intellect.) They adopt the self-satisfied stand that they themselves are creatures very different from the common run of man. Unfortunately, however, in divorcing themselves from the common people, intellectuals rob themselves of a base of support and in this way invite their own downfall.

76

It is not surprising that the masses should refuse to recognize the value of an intellectual class that alienates itself in this way and that, from the standpoint of ordinary men, is capable of doing nothing but talking. Although something can be said in defense of the attitude of the masses, mutual alienation is a great tragedy for society.

TOYNBEE: In general, when the intellectuals are alienated from the masses, they tend to lose touch with the universal realities of human life, while the masses tend to be deprived of the intellectual culture that ought to be made accessible to every human being to the full extent of his capacity for it. In the present-day Western world there is an unhealthy tendency for the intellectuals to form closed circles of professional specialists who live and work exclusively for each other. These intellectuals despise the general public for being nonprofessional and ignorant; the public ignores the intellectuals, because it finds them unintelligible and unpractical. This mutual alienation is bad for both parties and bad for society.

IKEDA: You have brought up a very important point. I think that the closed circles of professional specialists you mention have developed at least partly because of the nature of modern learning, which has become overspecialized as scientific technology has advanced at a rapid pace. Because of their inability to grasp the meaning of such learning, the masses either blindly adulate or harbor animosity against the intellectuals. For their part, the intellectuals tend to look down on the masses, who, they feel, could not possibly understand them or their activities.

Today, as learning reaches higher levels, it tends to become so departmentalized that the uninitiated find it incomprehensible. To solve the difficulty, it is now essential for learning to follow the reverse course; that is, it must become generalized instead of specialized and inclusive instead of divided. The world of learning must deemphasize the ivory-tower attitude and emphasize closeness with the people whom it must serve.

TOYNBEE: I agree emphatically in deploring excessive specialization. This alienates the specialist and the public—including the intelligent but nonspecialized members of the public—from each other. The specialist is tempted to despise nonspecialists as laymen. Nonspecialists are tempted to write off the specialist as useless to anyone who is outside the specialist's own narrow coterie. I myself think that the nonspecialists are right. The specialist gets a distorted view, even in his own special field, if he studies it in isolation from its setting. Specialization seems to me to be a bad approach for trying to understand and to deal with the modern world, because all peoples, all sides of life, and all activities are becoming increasingly interdependent. We are living in a world in which we need a global outlook.

IKEDA: That is true, but perhaps the nature of education today plays a part in sponsoring the development of isolated groups of intellectuals. First of all, in order to obtain the kind of education required for serious intellectual pursuits, one must have time and money. The student, who is totally dependent on his family for support throughout his formal education, must concentrate on study and can do little to help himself financially. In other words, a completely external condition—financial position—can determine whether a young person has a chance to develop his intellectual abilities and prepare himself for a career of an intellectual kind or must go out into the world and do manual labor as quickly as possible in order to contribute to his family's well-being.

In some instances, the state or a foundation of some kind either pays or advances expenses for education of extraordinarily talented but poor students. But the number of such lucky young people is extremely limited. Perhaps the majority, discriminated against for reasons completely beyond their control, come to resent the fortunate few whose road to education is easy.

TOYNBEE: I agree with you to an extent, but the picture is somewhat more complicated. To become an intellectual a person needs three things: intellectual ability—a gift of nature that is very unequally distributed; the will to work hard and to behave well—virtues that are within the individual's power to practice; and a prolonged education—this requires money, which has to be provided either by the student's parents or by some public source, because it involves the postponement of the date at which the intellectual will earn his own living.

An intellectual and his community thus have mutual moral obligations. The intellectual owes it to society to perform a useful social service in return for the social resources that have been invested in his education. Conversely, society owes it to the intellectual to remunerate him sufficiently to enable him to do his work efficiently, assuming that this work is socially valuable.

In Britain, in my generation, scholarships were few, and the competition for them was, I think, too severe. Of course, even under the most adverse conditions, extremely high ability has always won and always will. But, if conditions are very hard, all but the highest ability may be deprived of its chance of realizing its potentiality for serving the community.

IKEDA: For people who are not fortunate enough to have the time or money to obtain a formal education in their youth, provisions ought to be made for study courses that working people can take. By setting up something like a lifetime educational system, we might be able to go a long way toward bridging the gap between the intellectuals and the masses.

TOYNBEE: I agree that ample time and money ought to be provided for part-time adult education and that a person's working hours and pay ought to be adjusted so as to make it possible for anyone who has the ability and the will to combine a continuous part-time education with the earning of his living throughout his working life. I see the following good reasons for this: lifelong part-time education is the surest way of raising the intellectual and moral level of the masses; conditions of life are now changing so greatly, within the span of a single lifetime, that we need to continue adapting ourselves to these changes; the experience of responsible grown-up life is a valuable aid to education in all circumstances; and, for this reason, education can be more fruitful during the adult stage of life than during adolescence, even if adult education cannot be a full-time occupation.

IKEDA: Certainly the only way to solve the problem is to make efforts of the kind we have been discussing. For both intellectuals and nonintellectuals, the important thing today is to set as a goal the reform of the injustices and inequalities we see around us. But as long as the intellectuals and the masses continue to distrust each other, they will never come together to make meaningful contributions to such reform. We must take our common humanity as our great premise and realize that it is mankind as a whole, not any one class or group, that has been the true moving power in history. If all classes come together in a concerted effort to improve society, a lasting bond between intellectuals and nonintellectuals will inevitably develop. And this could provide a key to other problems extending to civilization as a whole and to mankind's continued existence.

TOYNBEE: Without doubt, today we need to recognize our common humanity and live together as members of a single family. I believe that religion is the field in which the intellectuals and the masses have the best chance of once again finding common ground.

Intellectual and Artistic Involvement

IKEDA: Some people disapprove of intellectuals, writers, and artists who show active interest in current sociopolitical issues. There is some truth in the idea that intellectuals and artists run the danger of losing their purity and integrity when they become implicated in political problems. Since man cannot live apart from society, however, we are all inevitably connected in one way or another with politics. It is the fate of modern man to be unable to live as a recluse. Intellectuals and artists dwelling in ivory towers or isolated ateliers cannot do truly valid and vital work.

TOYNBEE: It is impossible to be an intellectual or an artist without first being a human being, and a human being is a social animal. He is implicated in the problems of human life, both those that are universal and perennial and those that are peculiar to his own time and place. An intellectual or artist who ignored the universal and perennial problems would be stultifying himself. If the reason for his ignoring them were indifference or blindness, he would be uninspired and therefore uninspiring. There have been some supremely great thinkers and artists who have concentrated their energies on the universal and perennial problems but have been unresponsive to the problems of their own time and place. Plato did not feel spiritually at home in his native Athens; Goethe did not participate politically or even emotionally in the encounter between Germany and Napoleon, though Goethe cannot have been unaware that this encounter was a turning point in his country's history. At the opposite extreme, Marx and Lenin were so passionately concerned with the problems of their own time and place that Marx turned his philosophy into a program for political action, and Lenin carried out Marx's program in Russia by capturing control of the Russian state and using his power to make the Russian Revolution.

IKEDA: Such brilliant philosophers and writers as Socrates, Plato, Rousseau, Goethe, Marx, Lenin, and Dostoevski changed the course of human history through their ideas and works because they were actively involved. They criticized the prevailing thoughts of their times and put forward ideas that transcended them. When scholars write theses and give lectures before students and when writers or artists publish or exhibit their works, they offer their thoughts and intentions to their fellow men and in this way influence society and politics. The greater the artistic or scholarly work, the greater its influence on the times and the stronger the likelihood that the work may pave the way for great political change.

It is not wrong for intellectuals and artists to be interested in politics or to be actively engaged in reforming the conditions of their time. On the other hand, it is of paramount importance that they avoid becoming so deeply involved in politics that they lose their souls to the evil of power and thus destroy themselves and others.

TOYNBEE: I agree that an intellectual's or artists's right relation with the problems of his own time and place is a middle way. He ought to be neither wholly aloof from these topical problems nor wholly engaged in them. As examples of men of letters who have found this middle way I would single out the nineteenth-century Russian novelists Turgenev, Dostoevski, and Tolstoy. As examples of philosophers who have found the middle way I would single out Zeno, the founder of the Stoic school, and Epicurus. These two Greek philosophers lived in a generation in which city-states ceased to provide a satisfying social and ethical framework for Greek life. The Greeks found themselves spiritually disoriented. Zeno and Epicurus worked out for their Greek contemporaries new attitudes that made it possible for Greek life to go on after the Greeks' traditional master-institution, the city-state, had collapsed.

IKEDA: The middle way is excellent, but in actual practice it is very difficult to follow. Artists and intellectuals who have been unable to follow the middle way have often fallen prey to power and have consequently stifled the germination of their own creative work. It may indeed be the large number of such cases that has given rise to concern over the relationship between politics and power. In the light of these difficulties, what steps do you recommend to intellectuals and artists who participate in politics?

TOYNBEE: It seems to me that the French maxim *noblesse oblige* is a valid rule of conduct for intellectuals and artists if we interpret the word *noblesse* as meaning not aristocratic ancestry but humanity; that is, a human being's built-in moral obligations. Socrates, the plebeian, like his aristocratic pupil Plato, was concerned primarily with the universal and perennial problems, but, unlike Plato, Socrates participated in the political life of his native city-state of Athens. Although Socrates did not go out of his way to intervene in controversial politics, if he thought it necessary to take an unpopular political line, he did not hesitate when he considered such action part of his civic duty. At least once he voted publicly in the Athenian assembly against a motion that was very popular but was morally very wrong. He allowed himself to be condemned to death rather than declare, against his own conviction and contrary to the truth, that his teaching had been morally corrupting. After having been condemned, he refused to take an opportunity of escaping to a place of refuge abroad. Socrates's practice of neither seeking nor shirking political involvement seems to me to be the right practice for an intellectual or artist.

IKEDA: If I compare the middle way as chosen by Socrates to the way chosen by Siddartha Gautama, the Buddha, I find that as a way of living, Socrates' approach fails to convince me. Gautama, who was born a prince into a royal household, might have established a political regime of great mercy because he was a young man of intense sensitivity. But since he had been enlightened to the fact that politics or economics cannot save mankind from suffering, he decided to follow the way of ascetic discipline.

It was not that Gautama was uninterested in politics. Even after his enlightenment, he continued to teach both his own royal relatives and rich men— the people who held controlling power in the city-states of ancient India— in the hope of making Buddhist teachings the ideological foundation of political action. The ideal of the Buddha was the establishment of a path that surpasses politics and leads humanity to true happiness. During the lifetime of the Buddha and throughout the history of Buddhism, political leaders have leveled persecutions against Buddhists. Characteristically, however, Buddhists have not attempted to deal with political powers on their own level but have always approached them from a more elevated plane.

In contrast, Socrates, in order to defend his ideas, confronted the city-state authorities head on and chose death rather than submission. The nature of his death may have increased the influence of Socrates' teachings on later centuries. But even without putting himself in a position where he was forced to face a tragic death, the Buddha has had an influence as great as that of Socrates or of Christ. I cannot condone the deliberate choice of a tragic death because such an act stimulates people to hate the politics and the people that were instrumental in bringing the death about. The point of my comparison between Socrates and Buddha is this. Socrates ultimately chose to meet his political persecuters on their own ground. The Buddhist approach, which seems to me the better one, is to attempt to elevate one's persecuters to a higher level where direct and possibly tragic encounters are no longer necessary.

Limits of the Scientific Intellect

IKEDA: As far as the rational light of science can penetrate, it clarifies the things it adopts as objects of research. I like to think of this kind of scientific thinking as the eye of science. You and I agree that, because of its limitations, science must not become so important that man tends to regard it as omnipotent. We further agree that, in dealing with the issues that science cannot successfully explain, religion offers mankind faith and important spiritual support. But to make the importance of both religion and science clearer, I think we might try to find out wherein religious thought differs from what I have called the eye of science.

By the *eye of science* I mean a power to understand. By turning on objects of inquiry a trained and refined eye of rational thought, we can illuminate those objects and find in them constant and universal laws. In discovering such laws by means of the power of reason, it is inevitable that we apply the analytical method and that we then make generalizations and abstractions. Furthermore, the analytical method invariably requires a quantitative treatment of its objects.

TOYNBEE: In making an arbitrary abstraction from the total content of the data of sense perception, science succeeds in taking an objective view of its selective field of observation, if we define the word *objective* as meaning a phenomenon or a thought that is necessarily identical for all human minds if they compare notes about it. On the other hand, if we define *objective* as meaning a genuine and accurate reflection of reality-in-itself, I think we have to conclude that science's abstraction from the phenomena is likely to be still more remote from reality-in-itself, by at least one further remove, than the phenomena are before they have been processed and pruned by science. Science claims that it is clarifying the phenomena, but it could no less convincingly be accused of disfiguring them.

IKEDA: The picture emerging from the process of abstraction and quantification by the eye of science is not quite identical with the true nature of the object. It appears to me that herein lie the essential limitations beyond which the eye of science cannot see.

TOYNBEE: Science deliberately ignores those properties of phenomena that are not common to all the specimens of a species and that therefore cannot be expressed in quantitative terms. The price of quantification is the ignoring of uniqueness. This is a high price, because, in truth, uniqueness, as well as uniformity, is an intrinsic and essential property of phenomena. Each of the specimens of the so-called inanimate species of phenomena is unique to some extent. The element of uniqueness is relatively still more significant in living beings, and in conscious living beings its significance reaches the maximum. It is therefore no mere accident that the selective mental procedure of science has been most successful when applied to inanimate phenomena (in physics and in inorganic chemistry); it has been less successful in its application to living organisms (in organic chemistry and in biology); it has been still less successful in its application to the conscious layer of the psyche (in epistemology and in logic).

It has only recently ventured to begin the exploration of the subconscious layers of the psyche, which Indian philosophy was exploring about two and a half millennia earlier. It is still too early to foresee whether science is going to succeed or to fail in this most recent and most difficult of its enterprises, but it is clear that this is a crucial case for testing science's ability to enable us to know and understand phenomena. Of all the phenomena that are accessible to human minds, psychic events at the subconscious level are probably both the most important for us and the most elusive for science.

IKEDA: When the scientific method works, as it always does, from analysis to generalization, some peculiarities and individual traits of the phenomena being observed are lost. For example, things that cannot be treated in quantitative terms or that cannot be universalized are discarded. When the object of study is humanity, the individual workings of the mind and spirit and the subtle characteristics of emotion and consciousness are rejected.

TOYNBEE: Science has been successful in the degree to which it has ignored those features of phenomena that are of the greatest importance to human beings for all purposes except those of technology. For nontechnological purposes, the translation of qualitative impressions into quantitative notations is an intellectual and aesthetic impoverishment. The sounds that we hear and the colors that we see are more significant and more satisfying for us than the quantities to which they are reduced by the sciences of acoustics and optics.

IKEDA: Because of its limits, science views everything from a strictly material viewpoint. When the object of research is a living thing, the individuality innate in its unique life is abstracted and buried in the general concept of life. In other words, scientific thinking inevitably includes a process of turning life into a mere compound of matter.

84

TOYNBEE: When we say that a human being is a cipher, we disparage him. We mean that he is deficient in the distinctive, significant, and valuable qualities of human nature. Yet science literally reduces a human being to a cipher when it renders in numerical notations its account of his spirit and of the psychosomatic organism with which his spirit is associated. It reduces him to a cipher in another way when it substitutes for his personal name a number on an identity card or on a card to be fed into a computer.

IKEDA: The scientific way of thinking regards life lightly and causes us to lose sight of the true nature of living human beings. These undesirable aspects of scientific thinking come to the forefront because modern man forgets that the aspects of science that tend to reduce men to ciphers and to abandon individuality are no more than means to the attainment of partial ends. The trouble arises when people begin regarding these means as absolute ends in themselves.

As long as the operations are only part of a process to uncover some kind of truth, it might be permissible to treat human beings as ciphers, formulas, or means. But such methods must never be permitted in the management of society or other large organizations or in any case when human beings are the actual objects of the activity in question.

TOYNBEE: A human being can be manipulated insofar as he can be dehumanized. Probably this was first discovered in the practice of war. It was found that a human being must be hypnotized by drill to convince him to risk his own life in trying to kill other human beings with whom he has no quarrel. Bureaucratization and computerization are alternative ways of making human beings amenable to the wills of other people. Manipulation is technology, whether it is performed on human beings, nonhuman living beings, or inanimate things. Technology is facilitated by quantification, and though quantification intellectually misrepresents and aesthetically defaces the object to which it is applied, its serviceableness for technology makes it a generator of power, over both nonhuman nature and people. Thus science is of importance for one practical purpose, namely, technological manipulation.

Is the augmentation of the potency of technology by science through quantification good or bad? It is neither good nor bad intrinsically. The question has to be answered ad hoc. The answer depends on whether or not the moral standard of the human wielder of the power conferred by science is high enough to ensure that he will exercise his enhanced power for good, not for evil.

85

IKEDA: That is true. The power of science is intrinsically neutral. It is nonetheless important to decide whether human beings ought to regard science as absolute or limited. This decision becomes an essential basis for independent human judgments.

In order to complement the limited capabilities of the eye of science and thus to permit science to prove its true worth, we need another eye that can probe more profoundly and extensively into the true aspects of things and bring to light the properties unique to each of them.

Buddhism uses the figure of speech of five kinds of eyes to represent ways of looking at things: the eye of man, the eye of heaven, the eye of wisdom, the eye of the Law, and the eye of the Buddha. The eye of man is normal physical visual observation and the perceptions gained through it. The eye of heaven indicates a leader's sharp insight into delicate changes in the human mind. The eye of science is incorporated within the eye of wisdom, for the latter represents the cognitive faculty of throwing the light of reason on objects, abstracting them, and discovering universal laws in them.

The eye of the Law and the eye of the Buddha are the power to penetrate the truth of life more profoundly and from a more humanistic approach than is possible with the eye of wisdom. The eye of the Law means the ability to see all things as they truly are. This eye is developed by polishing one's life— in Buddhism, the word *polish* used in this kind of context denotes bringing forth from the depths of life a feeling of compassion—and employing this polished life as a mirror in which to view all things. The eye of the Buddha means the penetrating insight that discerns the pulsating energy of life and all aspects of the universe; to embody them in oneself; and, using this reactivated vital force, to perceive the realities of life, society, and the universe.

The Buddhist concept of the five eyes shows the way to awaken and to enhance the faculty of the wisdom behind reason and sense—the wisdom contained in the innermost part of life. Only by first cultivating and activating the eye of the Law and the eye of the Buddha is it possible to transcend the essential limitations of scientific thinking as a function of the eye of wisdom and to cause science to emit an even more brilliant light of reason.

TOYNBEE: The eye of the Law and the eye of the Buddha supplement and correct the eye of man (sense perception), the eye of heaven (psychological insight), and the eye of wisdom (the faculty of reason, including the scientific way of using this faculty). Like the eye of wisdom, the eye of the Law and the eye of the Buddha are not merely ways of seeing: they are also ways of acting. The compassion that is evoked by the eye of the Law seems to me to be the antidote for the dehumanizing effect of science.

HEALTH
AND WELFARE

4

Practitioners of the Healing Art

IKEDA: Because the object of medical study and practice is the health of the human mind and body, the question of ethics in medical science deserves close attention. Western medical science has made astounding progress. Especially in the latter half of this century, advances in biology and biochemistry and development in surgery and anesthetics have made it possible for the surgeon to insert his scalpel into the heart and the brain, regions that until recently have been held sacred and inviolable. Transplantations of internal organs and replacement of organs with artificial counterparts are about to become generally practicable. It may soon be feasible even to go to the extreme of replacing one's personality with that of another by brain transplantation. Progress in pharmacology has reached the stage where it is no longer mere dreaming to conceive of freely controlling memory, thought, and desires by means of drugs.

As the power of medical science to control life increases, the way the physician uses his skills becomes a question of great concern. Today, if put to good use, medicine can make immeasurable contributions to human happiness. Put to ill use, it destroys life.

Unfortunately, some physicians today seem to have lost respect for human life and to have lowered their ethical standards. Even before the twentieth century, there were undoubtedly unethical physicians, but their numbers were small. Since medicine at that time did not wield the great power it has today, the lowered ethics of a few doctors did not constitute a serious problem. In the past in Japan, medicine was known as *jinjutsu,* or the benevolent healing art; doctors were respected and trusted as practitioners of this art.

TOYNBEE: Certainly medicine ought to be a healing art. The dignity of the physician, or the surgeon, requires him to make the service of his fellow human beings his first concern and to give priority to this over the earning of a livelihood for himself and for his family. Of course, the economic by-product of a liberal profession is not only legitimate, it is also necessary.

IKEDA: People no longer trust and respect doctors as practitioners of the healing art. Medical treatment based on personal communication between the physician and the patient is disappearing.

Some causes of the ethical deterioration among doctors may, of course, be found in the doctors themselves, but, in addition, the general tendency in our civilization to regard life lightly causes many physicians to misuse the powers of medicine.

TOYNBEE: Your assumption seems correct. In recent years in the United States the practitioners of the medical profession have been criticized by the public on the ground that they pursue their profession primarily as a money-making enterprise for themselves, and no longer as a service. The medical or surgical specialist whose first concern is to sell his skill at the highest price the market will bear may be an expert technician, but he can hardly be his patient's humane and compassionate friend.

Is it possible for a physician to be his patient's friend—a relation that carries with it an emotional involvement—and at the same time to be a cool-headed scientific technician—a task that requires emotional detachment? The medical profession is beneficent, and the military profession is maleficent, yet the two professions have one feature in common. The physician and the soldier both have to do their work in constant contact with physical and mental suffering, with the fear of death, with death itself, and with grief at bereavement. Unless they can detach themselves emotionally, they will not be able to do their professional work efficiently. Yet unless the physician can be compassionate besides being detached, he will not be a fully adequate practitioner of his profession.

IKEDA: What you say has especially deep meaning because in recent years doctors who are fully adequate in this sense are in great demand. We must attempt to examine individual attitudes of doctors in connection with the lowered ethics of the profession and from the standpoint of the one-sided development of medical science.

Medical science has been able to make great forward strides because general science provided it with effective methods of examining diseases. Science, however, contains within its very nature a marked proclivity for viewing all things objectively, holding them at arm's length, and dissecting them with the scalpel of reason. When treated scientifically, the natural world becomes something isolated from itself. It has then no more than an objective existence. In like fashion, when submitted to scientific study, human life becomes an object stripped of spiritual communication with the physician.

Under such circumstances, the physician naturally regards human life as something purely material. Doctors become nothing more than expert technicians. The nature of the psychological influence this attitude has on a doctor was vividly related to me by a physician of my acquaintance. He told me that often, after a number of years of working as a surgeon, the doctor finds that the patient lying in the bed before him ceases to seem to be a living human being and becomes only a material body.

The more deeply imbued in the scientific way of thinking the doctor becomes, the more his mind is exposed to the danger of regarding humans as mere physical entities. The inescapable dilemma of modern medical science is this: science itself alters the personalities of the doctors who must employ its knowledge and skills and, at the same time, robs those doctors of respect for life.

Although medicine requires a cool, rational basis of science, it must also manifest warm human sentiment; there must be the desire to regard the life of another human as something subjective and a mental posture that venerates spiritual communication among people.

TOYNBEE: To this end, the doctor must be both the cool-headed technician and the compassionate, concerned friend. Is it possible to be simultaneously loving and aloof? Adherents of the theistic religions would answer that the physician ought to do his work for the love of God and that this will enable him to combine two emotional states that might otherwise be incompatible. Medieval Christian hospitals were dedicated to saints, and Roman Catholic Christian nuns did, and do, serve God by nursing the sick. The present-day secular nursing profession in the West, in Protestant as well as in Catholic Christian countries, originated in the nursing work of some of the Catholic religious orders. A present-day secular nurse's uniform and the title *sister* used in Britain for nurses are reminders of the profession's historical origin. The pre-Christian Greek medical profession was dedicated to the Greek god of healing, Asclepius.

IKEDA: It is vitally important that members of the medical profession should have religous faith. In fact, the only way out of the dilemma facing modern medicine is a humanism firmly based on faith and a clear insight into the essence of life and human nature. I am convinced that the only way to remedy the situation facing modern medicine is to be found in the kind of philosophy of life I see in Buddhism.

TOYNBEE: You have suggested that in the West Christianity is now in decline and that an alternative inspiration for the medical profession might be found in Buddhism. I agree that it seems hardly possible for anyone to be a spiritually and ethically adequate physician unless he has some religious or philosophical view of, and attitude towards, human life and towards the universe in which mankind finds itself.

Organ Transplantation

IKEDA: Heart transplantation is the most spectacular and the most controversial of the organ transplant operations. Since Dr. Christian Barnard performed the first heart transplant in December, 1967, worldwide public debate has raged around the topic from the moral, philosophical, and religious viewpoints. In Japan, the heart transplant operation performed by Dr. Juro Wada at the Sapporo Medical School in August, 1968, remains a focal point of controversy, particularly in regard to the question of whether his decision to undertake that operation was morally justifiable. Divergent views of the issue were expressed by a number of doctors at the national convention of the Japan Medical Association in 1971.

Unlike kidney transplants, heart transplantation inevitably involves the death of the donor. This awakens apprehension that since it is necessary to maintain the integrity of heart tissue, expediency may lead to the use of a heart before all doubt about the death of the donor has been removed. Dr. Wada contends that, in reaching his decision to perform the heart transplant, he chose to save the life of one man rather than be forced to see the death of two.

My opinion on organ transplanting in general is that, in cases like those of the kidneys or the cornea, the operations are permissible if they are backed up by adequate medical reasons. Present-day medical technology may not be able to ensure adequate success in all cases of kidney transplants, but once the condition of the recipient has been taken into consideration, it is permissible to allow the doctor to decide whether such an operation is warranted. In these instances and in cases of cornea transplants, judgment of death is not an issue.

Deciding whether the donor is dead, however, is crucial to the transplantation of the heart, liver, and brain, if research ever reaches the point where this last operation is feasible. Including opinions of medical scholars in my consideration, I believe that, as a principle, the transplantation of these organs must not be performed as long as medical and surgical techniques remain at their present level. Brain transplantation especially must be forbidden because it entails replacing the essential part of the recipient's thinking self with that of another. In the cases of heart and liver transplantation, I believe doctors must refrain from such operations until scientifically unquestionable grounds for determining death have been established.

TOYNBEE: Your comments embrace three separate issues, which I should like to distinguish from each other. First, is the transplantation of organs, or of some particular organ, desirable or undesirable in principle? Second, if we judge that it is desirable in principle, is it desirable in practice at the present stage of medical knowledge and technical skill? Third, is it desirable in practice at the present level of ethical standards and conduct?

The criterion for deciding the question of principle is, as I see it, a conviction that the paramount consideration should be the preservation of human rights, the most important of which is, to my mind, the maintenance of human dignity. A human being has a right not to be deprived of life against his will, and it would be a violation of human dignity if a human being were to be used, against his will, as a means—even a means for preserving another human life.

But suppose that a human being is already dead but that his heart is still alive in the sense that, if successfully transplanted, it would provide an effective living heart for a living person whose life would then be saved. Suppose, again, that a living person volunteers to sacrifice his own life to save another person's, as, in the Greek myth, Alcestis is said to have voluntarily descended to Hades in lieu of her husband, or as, in everyday life, people sometimes lose their lives by drowning or by fire in trying to rescue others. Suppose, finally, that a dead person's brain is available for transplantation and that a living person, whose own brain is damaged, asks to have the dead person's brain transferred to him, in spite of his knowing that this may involve for him a change of personality.

In all these three hypothetical cases, it seems to me that transplantation would be consistent with human dignity or would actually be required by it.

91

If I myself recognized that I was becoming senile or was going out of my mind, I believe I should wish to exchange my damaged brain for an intact brain if I thought that, with this, I could be an asset, instead of a liability, to myself and to my fellow human beings.

The answer to the second question is comparatively simple. It would be better not to attempt, for the present, a particular transplantation if medical science is still unable to establish a satisfactory criterion for determining the moment of death in the light of the current state of medical and surgical knowledge and skill, if medical science is not yet able to predict what the effect of the transplantation is likely to be, or if surgical skill is not yet sufficiently advanced in this field to be able to offer more than a slight hope of success.

The third question is perhaps the most difficult of the three. In the light of past experience, medical knowledge and surgical skill seem likely to improve; this likelihood makes it reasonable to hope that if a particular transplantation is held to be unwarrantable professionally at the present stage, it may become warrantable professionally in the course of time. But experience offers no corresponding expectation that ethical standards and conduct will rise. There is no evidence that they have risen since our ancestors became human.

IKEDA: It is sometimes impossible to preserve the life of one person without a heart transplant. When it is clear that the patient will not survive without recourse to heart transplantation and when there is an appropriate donor, the operation may be permissible. But the decision to perform transplant surgery in such a case must be made not only by the transplant team of doctors but also through consultation with immunologists, brain surgeons, other specialists, philosophers, and jurists. Even when a heart transplant is undertaken after such consultation, as a matter of course, the doctors responsible for removing the donor's heart must be distinct from the doctors responsible for planting it in the recipient. Furthermore, it is necessary to obligate the team to announce publicly details of operative and postoperative progress as well as of surgical procedures.

TOYNBEE: If a particular transplantation is held to be legitimate in principle and also to be technically feasible, the decision whether or not it is to be attempted in a particular case ought to be taken by a team. Different members of this team may have different ethical standards and may live up to their standards in different degrees. They will also have different personal relations to the case. The recipient and the donor (if still alive) will be intimately concerned, and so will their respective relatives and friends. The surgeons who would be removing the organ and grafting it will also be concerned very closely; expert consultants and representatives of the law and of the public authorities will be relatively detached. The degree of each party's involvement may affect his ethical conduct in dealing with the case.

IKEDA: I maintain that we must abide by the basic principle that organ transplants involving the inevitable death of the donor ought not be performed at the present state of knowledge. I object to organ transplantation in general at the present time because, in the first place, the definition of death has yet to be clarified and, in the second, because there is yet no established medical method for overcoming the rejection reactions that offset the effectiveness of organ transplantation. In the future, even should the problems of rejection be solved, I feel that medical science must strive to develop the field of artificial organs instead of relying to a great extent on organ transplants.

TOYNBEE: This is a particular instance of a general problem. An increase in scientific knowledge and in technical skill brings with it an increase in power. An increase in power confronts people with the responsibility of making choices that were not open to them previously. This widening of the range of choice may create ethical problems that have no precedents.

Medical Treatment: Scientific and Total

IKEDA: As scholars of psychosomatic medicine point out, Western medical science, because of its analytic approach and specialized attitudes towards life, misconceives the true nature of human illness. It considers illness a separate entity and, though it possesses great knowledge about pathological conditions, disregards the human beings who actually suffer from illness.

TOYNBEE: Unfortunately, in the West within the last three centuries, medical science has gone the same way as science in general. It has taken an analytic, selective, and specializing turn. The medical specialist limits himself to dealing with some single organ or with some single physical malady. The specialist does not deal with all of the person whose organ or malady he is treating, and the general practitioner, who does do this, is looked down upon by the specialist as a jack-of-all-trades who is master of none.

In the United States, modern Western medical specialization has been carried to extremes. There the general practitioner is almost extinct. Specialists have their offices in a row under the same roof, and the patient is passed from one to another. The patient's problem is how to discover which of the specialists he ought to consult first. The patient has no general practitioner to make a diagnosis for him. Once my wife had a bad sore throat when we arrived on the campus of an American college. The wife of the president of the college had to guess which specialist would probably be the right one for my wife to visit.

IKEDA: If your wife's illness had been a matter of life or death, finding just the right specialist might have been a very urgent matter. Medical specialists have their value, but an ill person suffers with his whole being, not with just the pathologically affected part. The cause of illness is likely to be pathological alteration in an organ or tissue, but many other factors, including psychological ones, inevitably enter the picture. Furthermore, the pathological alteration as such does not comprise the whole of the living being.

The most distressing thing about Western medical science is the outcome that excess concern with pathologically altered parts of the body has for the individual patient. For instance, doctors sometimes become so engrossed in pathological manifestations and ignore the total life of the individual to such an extent that the patient's condition worsens as a consequence of treatment. In extreme instances, when surgical or pharmaceutical treatment has been called successful, the patient has died.

TOYNBEE: It is because such things can happen that I place great emphasis on the importance of the general practitioner. The term *family doctor* often used for the general practitioner hits the mark. The general practitioner is not a mere technician and not even a mere scientific technician. He is the friend and confidant of all the members of the family whom he attends, and he applies his technical skill effectively because he applies it with a human understanding of his patients and a human relation with them of mutual regard and trust.

The general practitioner does not run the specialist's occupational risk of being handicapped by conceit. He recognizes the limits of his own general knowledge and skill, and when he judges that he has reached these limits, he calls in the appropriate specialist. Of course, the general practitioner must know who the appropriate doctor is when a specialist's aid is required. In medicine, diagnosis is all important. The first diagnosis is made by the general practitioner; it may be incomplete or even erroneous, but it is the indispensable first step. The general practitioner's services continue to be needed from first to last, because, unlike the specialist, he has a personal knowledge of the patient and of his environment. Unless the specialist acts in the light of the knowledge that only the family doctor can supply, he will be using his skill blindly and therefore perhaps more harmfully than beneficially.

IKEDA: I think it is greatly to be lamented that the family doctor is becoming rare. But all hope of a general view incorporating the patient and his environment has not been lost. In spite of specialization and departmentalization, which have been the salient characteristics of modern Western medicine, some people have recognized the danger and have tried to do something about it. For instance, Hans Selye, noted for his stress theory, and people interested in psychosomatic medicine have tried to grasp human life as a whole. I think that these new trends deserve praise as the fruits of the efforts of doctors who are trying to arrive at a humane medical science. At the same time, I think it would be helpful to the growth of such a science to reexamine the value of the medical system evolved over the ages by the wisdom and experience of the peoples of the Orient.

In China, doctors who have studied Western medicine and others who are proficient in oriental medicine are cooperating with each other in the treatment of patients. In Japan, too, the idea of oriental medicine has gradually been reevaluated and is now popular among the people. Although it is not yet a general tendency, a number of medical students are trying to acquire knowledge and skill in oriental medicine. This turn in events has two causes. First, defects in Western medicine have become increasingly apparent. Second, oriental medicine is attractive to patients because it attempts to understand the sick person as a whole, without considering him and his illness separately.

While examining a patient's sickness thoroughly, practitioners of oriental medicine try to restore the whole human to a normal, healthy condition. In contrast to Western medicine, which tracks down the physical causes of illness and uses surgical treatment and medicines to cure them, oriental medicine is primarily concerned with the patient, not the illness. It insists on examining the sick person's condition thoroughly and tries to detect the differences between the patient's healthy and sick states. It first examines all of the patient's symptoms, then analyzes them from the standpoint of the total living organism before initiating treatment.

The whole life of the person is regarded as the patient's condition. Oriental medicine fits these conditions into a total picture including the environment and the rhythm of the universe (weather, climate, and other natural features).

On the basis of this approach, treatment is carried out in accordance with the theory of dual cosmic forces (Yin and Yang) and the five traditional natural elements (air, fire, water, metal, earth). This theory, which is a basic oriental view of life, represents the attempt to understand the relationships between the universe and mankind in terms of macrocosm and microcosm. Although in general it is correct, it is in need of revision. The flaws in this theory have been reflected in oriental medical science.

The unfortunate deflection of this philosophy from its true path is not the only defect in oriental medicine. It lacks the kind of modern scientific thinking that is characteristic of Western medicine. To make oriental medicine all that it should be, it is essential to introduce into it pathological analyses and physical definitions based on the light of reason.

TOYNBEE: The method of oriental medicine seems to be the same as the method of Greek medicine in the fifth century B.C., as expounded in the writings of Hippocrates and his colleagues and pupils. Greek medicine studied and treated the patient as a psychosomatic and spiritual unity in his social and physical environment. Modern Western medicine is derived historically from Greek medicine, and the original Greek method is still followed by the modern Western general practitioner.

The distinction between the roles of the specialist and the general practitioner in Western countries where the general practitioner still survives seems to me to coincide with the difference between oriental and modern Western medicine. Surely these two approaches are complementary, not mutually exclusive. The patient needs both, but, if I were forced to choose, I would stay in a country in which there were still general practitioners, and I would do without specialists. The specialist is valuable; the general practitioner is indispensable.

IKEDA: It seems to me that the best thing we could do now would be to foster the unification of the two systems in a new system that would take advantage of the good points of both. That is, we could then have a medicine that makes full use of the scientific method of Western medicine while not losing sight of the oriental medical approach toward an understanding of the entire being of the patient.

Assisting the Age d

IKEDA: In advanced countries of the West, as the average life span lengthens and the birthrate decreases, elderly people account for a very large part of the total population. Accompanying this phenomenon is increased concern over the question of caring for the aged. Growing numbers of homes for the elderly and more complete pension systems indicate this concern. This question is of pressing urgency in Japan. Is it equally important in Britain, where a sound welfare system has already been established?

TOYNBEE: Yes, it is certainly equally important in Britain, as it is in other welfare systems. Old people, including myself, every week draw a national pension, and there are old people's homes. But such a place is not a psychological or spiritual substitute for the three-generation family in which grandparents, parents, and children all live together and share truly human relations. One of my school-fellows is one year older than I. When his wife died some years ago, his daughter-in-law invited him to live with her and her husband. While his grandchildren were small, he used to drive them to school. In this practical way, he took part in the family life until his grandchildren grew up. His son is a farmer, who employs workers. Now my friend drives the workers' children to school. He still takes part in the family life. It is important that his son is a farmer. He lives in the country and, therefore, has room in his house for his father as well as his wife and children. In towns, most people have to live in very small houses or small apartments where there is no room for more than parents and children.

IKEDA: I agree that institutions can never replace family relations. At least as much, and probably more, attention as is devoted to the planning of welfare facilities must be given to the spiritual assets of old people. It is not necessarily true that homes for the aged and social security "to the grave" are the greatest gifts we can give our elders. There are numerous reports of suicides among old people living in nations with highly advanced social security systems. As the smaller, more tightly nuclearized family gains predominance, the tendency is to take increased advantage of the institutions for the elderly. But sending old people away to such places may bring them nothing but despair.

I believe that the most important point is giving elderly people a reason to go on living; this is more urgent than building institutionalized homes. Giving them this reason to live must not be attempted in isolation from the actualities of society, because a consciousness of participating in social activities strength-

97

ens one's will to go on. Making elderly people realize that they are not being discarded, that they can still play important social roles, and that they can remain active members of the social group by creating things of value on their own is the most important reason for living we can offer.

TOYNBEE: The problem of how to save human beings from the psychological distress of feeling themselves to be socially superfluous is the same for those who are pushed out of employment by old age as for those who are thrown out of it by the automation of industry. The evil effects of urbanization break up the traditional three-generation family, which included grandparents, and make physical neighbors social strangers.

I agree emphatically that social security in the economic sense does not compensate for the psychological insecurity of being socially superfluous. An institutional home for the aged, however well equipped with medical care and with material comforts and amenities, is psychologically a camouflaged internment camp.

IKEDA: Unfortunately, that is true. And it has a detrimental effect on old people. Once removed from social responsibility and allowed to slacken his pace, a person begins to age rapidly. That same person can stay young and vigorous, however, if he plays an active part in the world. Instead of coddling older people, overlooking their importance to society, and attempting to deprive them of meaningful occupation, we ought to help them to realize that they are indispensable to society.

In a number of respects, people of advanced age have much to offer. First, they are more persevering and responsible in relation to a given task. Second, though old people may be physically weaker than the young, in many cases spiritually and mentally there is little age-related difference between the two groups. Many elderly people have been able to put their rich experience of life to good use and have made brilliant contributions to society. Providing the elderly with occupations that take advantage of their special abilities and letting them know that the contribution they have to make is greatly needed are the steps we must take.

TOYNBEE: The increase in the average length of effective working life is helpful both to the individual and to society, but it merely postpones the problem of old age in an urbanized and automated civilization. This problem, however, does not arise for an old person who has a socially useful occupation that requires mental, but not physical, activity and who retains his mental capacity and vigor till his death. I have known at least three mental workers who have lived to beyond the age of ninety without losing their mental powers. But I have also known other people who have died mentally before their physical death. This is a dreadful hazard, and it is on the increase. Modern medicine has been sensationally successful in prolonging physical life but has had no corresponding success in prolonging mental life. Today it is a gravely important matter to decide whether the medical profession should keep a senile person physically alive by the means now at its disposal or let nature release the patient from his humiliating living death.

To retain one's mental faculties to the end of life is a piece of good fortune for anyone—of course above all for a mental worker. Most people, however, are still physical workers; I have known farmers who have had to retire from work, owing to physical incapacitation, with the bleak prospect of many years of purposeless and meaningless life.

IKEDA: Dealing with the elderly in the vast group of people whose work is strictly physical is a much more difficult issue. Perhaps providing them with institutionalized homes and offering them chances to do light physical work that gives a sense of importance, and maybe even of friendly rivalry, would be one answer.

Though there may be many cases in which senility makes it impossible for old people to continue working in one field of endeavor, those same people probably have abilities in other fields that might make them useful participants in social life. Organizations devoted to discovering these abilities and guiding the elderly in applying them are needed. Facilities for the care of the elderly must be deeply connected with the rest of society, they must encourage activity, and they must afford opportunities to do meaningful work.

TOYNBEE: At my present age, I am singularly fortunate. My wife is alive; I still have the most precious form of human companionship. My mind is unimpaired, though my physical strength has been reduced by a coronary thrombosis. However, I can still answer questions, both orally and in writing, and I can still write articles and books. What is more, other people are willing to publish my books and articles, and they wish to interview me on television or by means of tape-recordings or written questions. The longer I live under these happy conditions, the more sadly I grieve for the fate of those of my contemporaries who were killed in World War I when they were between the ages of twenty and thirty. I grieve still more for a lifelong friend, three months younger than myself, who, happily, is now dead but who, before dying, gradually became senile, though never so senile as to cease to be distressed by what was happening to him.

99

IKEDA: Your friend's predicament certainly evokes great sympathy. Buddhist teaching lists aging among the four great afflictions of human life: birth, aging, illness, and death. It seems to me that the way a person chooses to live when he has reached an advanced age depends on his inner strength and on his view of life. This problem is an excellent one for the field of religion. On the practical plane, society owes its older members the chance to make a way for themselves.

GNP or Gross National Welfare

IKEDA: Both socialism and capitalism have serious flaws. Capitalism has sacrificed the happiness and welfare of individual human beings to the pursuit of profit. Socialism has suppressed human liberty for the sake of standardized equality. Failure to take into consideration the dignity of human life is behind the faults of both systems. The same thing is true of nations now striving to establish welfare societies because, though they revise their systems and proclaim their search for general well-being and happiness, the good they attempt is entirely material in its orientation. At present there is no nation that can guarantee its people spiritual welfare rooted in respect for the dignity of life.

TOYNBEE: In the field of human affairs, the maintenance of human dignity ought to be our objective and the criterion of judgment for the rightness or wrongness of the means we use to attain that objective. Human dignity demands both freedom and equality. These two necessities are not mutually exclusive. Capitalists and socialists, however, have made the mistake of considering them mutually exclusive because the visions of these two ideologies are limited to the economic level. Human life and activity operate on a number of different levels, each having its own requirements.

   At the economic level there ought to be equality and restraint on greed. At this level, we need regimentation; for the sake of human dignity, we ought to acquiesce in socialistic management of mankind's economic affairs. This is a fair price to pay for social justice and for survival. On the other hand, at the spiritual level, freedom is as indispensable for human dignity as regimentation is at the economic level.

   To draw a parallel with the workings of the human body, I might say that economic regimentation liberates the human being and allows him to act freely on the spiritual level as, in psychosomatic life, the automatic func-

100

tioning of the heart and lungs liberates the brain to serve as the physical locus of consciousness and will.

IKEDA: In saying that capitalism and socialism operate only on the economic level, you have touched on a point of great significance. The current trend is to regard production and economy as the total of human society and not merely as a subsystem, which is in fact all that they are. This great modern illusion has wrongly put all other aspects of human activity—culture, religion, technology, and politics—in a position where they are subject to and must serve the needs of the economy.

The belief that economic expansion and growth are the sum total of human society has already swept over the whole globe. As long as we permit the economy to run its own independent course, we are headed along a path that will lead to the loss of the right to exist on earth.

The time has come for us to revise our way of thinking about the precedence currently being given to economic matters. We must put the economy in a place subordinate to culture and education, and we must devote all our energy to the creation of a richly humane society in which the economy will promote human spiritual development and will serve as a means of enabling human beings to manifest their creative abilities.

I recommend that the already existing economic theories and systems be examined from the standpoint of this basic idea, because such an appraisal will make obvious the indispensability of economic controls, administration, and planning to human society. In addition, it will make clear the significance of incorporating socialist methods in capitalist societies.

Of course, economic controls, administration, and planning must be carried out for the sake of humanity. If they are allowed to become ends in themselves, they will increase the danger of the establishment of totalitarian or dictatorial governments. But controls based on human ideals must be applied on a global scale to halt the exhaustion of the world's resources and the destruction and pollution of the environment. Religion and philosophy must be the ultimate basis of our actions if we are to succeed in a program of this vast scale.

TOYNBEE: I agree with you. My hope for the twenty-first century is that it will see the establishment of a global human society that is socialistic at the economic level and free-minded at the spiritual level. Economic freedom for one person or community often spells servitude for others, but spiritual freedom has no such drawbacks. Everyone can be spiritually free without encroaching on the liberty of anyone else. Indeed widespread spiritual freedom means mutual enrichment, not impoverishment.

IKEDA: Economic equality and spiritual freedom are certainly desirable but may be difficult to achieve. In order to establish control over economics, a highly concentrated and powerful authority is needed. People who are concerned with the maintenance of such authority often hesitate to recognize even the spiritual freedom of others. Nevertheless, your approach provides many suggestions that will be useful in thinking about the society of the future.

But let us turn for a moment to contemporary efforts to establish welfare states in some of the advanced nations of the world like Britain, West Germany, Norway, Sweden, Denmark, and New Zealand. There are many unresolved problems in these attempts, one of which concerns the economy of the nation, and I think this problem applies especially to Britain.

As the distribution of wealth becomes more equal and as the lives of the people become more stable, economic growth tends to slow down or even to stagnate. In other words, the very achievement of the ideal of the welfare state inevitably acts as a brake on the economic growth of the country.

A second problem has to do with the attitudes of the people themselves. As social security becomes a reality, the citizens lose independence and grow to rely more and more on services provided by the state. This can have a great influence on the formative years of young people and can even play a part in growing crime rates in this age group.

The third, and in my opinion the most important, problem in the welfare state is a weakened understanding of the meaning of life, a loss of the competitive spirit, and the growing difficulty people find in manifesting their creative talents. In welfare states a number of complicated difficulties in addition to these three are likely to arise in connection with urban structures, the environment, natural resources, population growth, and so on.

In presenting this list of weak points I am by no means categorically rejecting the welfare system. On the contrary, I am one of the people who earnestly hope for the establishment of such a system in Japan. I consider it a social goal that we must strive to achieve because, if based on harmony with human spiritual and material welfare, it can be a step in the direction of the ideal human society.

TOYNBEE: I have lived to see the partial establishment of a welfare state in Britain. This social revolution, fortunately a bloodless one, has been accepted with good temper by the former privileged minority, whose privileges have been reduced through the achievement of a greater degree of social justice. But in Britain the welfare state is incomplete, for the economy is still mainly conducted on the basis of competitive private enterprise for profit. Unionized industrial workers have now joined the capitalists in running this economic rat race. Moreover, there still exists a minority that has been left below the poverty line and a perhaps larger section of the nation that is now being squeezed economically between the capitalists and the trades unionists.

The so-called developed countries are all moving toward the introduction of the welfare-state system, and in all of them—indeed in most of the so-called developing countries too with some exceptions like Burma—there is a demand for economic growth with the objective of raising the individual's material standard of living. I believe that a global rise in the material standard of living is impracticable. So far, the countries and the classes within these countries that have succeeded in raising their own material standard of living have accomplished this by exploiting their economically weaker fellow human beings. Even the prosperous minority will not be able to increase its prosperity ad infinitum. The irreplaceable material resources of this planet are limited. The prosperous minority has been consuming these resources at an accelerating pace. Meanwhile, the increase in the planet's population is also accelerating, especially in the poorest countries and classes. It seems likely that, in the near future, worldwide economic stabilization will be the only alternative to worldwide catastrophe.

Present-day society sees success and happiness in terms of ever-increasing economic affluence. This objective is not only economically unattainable but also spiritually unsatisfying. It does, however, provide an incentive for exertion and a zest for work. Conversely, the fear of impoverishment acts as a spur in a society in which economic activity is competitive.

I agree that, insofar as the welfare state gives economic security, it weakens the incentive to work. If the state guarantees some of the necessities of life— education for children, pensions for the old, and free medical care for all— adults will tend to regard wages as a child regards its pocket money: as windfalls that can be spent on the gratification of immediate, childish desires. People then cease to regard wages as something primarily to be spent on school and medical fees, or as something to be saved for the stage of life when earnings stop. A welfare state does encourage its citizens to feel that their basic needs are provided for, even if they themselves do their work lazily and inefficiently and even if, in consequence of extorting higher wages for less and worse work, they eventually put themselves out of employment.

Economic security of this kind makes for a decline in economic productivity and for unhappiness. When it is possible to get something for nothing, it is tempting to take advantage of the opportunity. At first, this is pleasant; ultimately it is depressing, for life becomes dull and meaningless when exertion is deadened by eliminating incentives.

IKEDA: I see a possibility for solving these problems only on the spiritual plane. Unfortunately, however, until now, attempts at welfare societies have been almost entirely material in their orientation. The generally accepted interpretation of this kind of society is one in which the social security system works well; in which there is total employment; and in which food, clothing, and housing are guaranteed by means of a taxation program. But all of these things are material. Adequate consideration of the spiritual aspects of welfare are left unnoticed. Still I am aware that a level of material security is essential to the elevation of the spiritual life. In Japanese we have a proverb that puts the issue succinctly: one only learns social graces when one has enough to wear and to eat.

It is necessary now to effect a fundamental turnabout in the popular way of thinking about the relations between the spiritual and the material. Elevation of the level of spiritual welfare must become our first concern, and raising of the physical level of welfare must be given second priority. In other words, precedence ought to go to raising the cultural, religious, educational, scholarly, and artistic levels of society. Social security programs, total employment, and other material aspects of welfare must be developed for the sake of the construction of a high-level spiritual society. If spiritual and cultural matters are placed first in the welfare programs of states, the problems of decreasing desire to work and loss of a reason to live will be solved, and human creative talents will have an opportunity to manifest themselves to the full.

For example, it is important to give elderly people adequate housing and annuities, but it is probably even more important to give them the chance to experience the beauty of a picture, to enjoy the pleasure of creating things themselves, to enjoy meeting and discussing matters with their children and grandchildren, and to share in a wide range of social intercourse. Active participation in religious activities and practices of faith too are of importance. In other words, it is imperative to give people the opportunity to develop and maintain their own objectives for living. Of course, together with this, it is desirable that the wealth of a nation be equitably distributed, that the citizens enjoy material stability, and that the national economy pursue a course of gradual growth.

On an international scale, the advanced nations that strive to achieve a welfare state must not turn their eyes only to their own domestic issues but must give thought to the affairs of the so-called developing nations as well. Nations that are ready to modify their own tempos of growth for the sake of devoting attention to the welfare of their own peoples must not attempt to hamper the economic growth of the developing nations. On the contrary, they must make positive efforts to assist the less advanced countries and to bridge the gap between themselves and the poorer members in the international community. This is related to what you mean by world international economic stability.

TOYNBEE: If the world's economy were to become stabilized and automated, a majority of the population would probably become economically unemployed. There will be a ceiling on everyone's material standard of living, and, in a welfare state, the differentials between the material standards of different classes and professions will be relatively small, whereas everyone will enjoy economic security in the sense that the necessities of life will be guaranteed. Under such a regime, people have no economic incentive; they are therefore unhappy as long as they continue to see happiness primarily in terms of material success and satisfaction. They will be unable to regain happiness unless they reorient their ambitions. They will have to renounce economic ambitions and cultivate spiritual ambitions. In order to carry out this spiritual revolution, they will need to work out their own clear analyses of the meaning and nature of life.

IKEDA: Emphatically a spiritual revolution is indispensable to human welfare. Man cannot hope to find happiness in revolutions in systems and technology alone. For many years I have been insisting on the vital importance of what I call a human revolution because I am convinced that changes arising from the deepest strata of life are the only way to a solution to mankind's dilemma. Furthermore, long-term thinking in connection with the deepest levels of life will make human beings painfully aware of the folly they have committed in connection with economics. One outstanding example of this folly is the Japanese attitude toward the gross national product, or GNP.

As is well known, following World War II Japan set out to catch up with America and the nations of Europe and if possible to surpass them in the field of economic production. In a spirit of greed for profit, Japan launched a vigorous program of high-level economic growth. But what have been the results? The Japanese people have been forced to labor hard and long under inhuman circumstances. There has been no sign of improvement of conditions. Industrial and other kinds of pollution have spread over the nation. Japanese products, it is true, have reached the markets of most parts of the world. But whereas at first these products were greeted with surprise, they are now met with antagonism. At last the Japanese government has started advertising itself as being in favor of a welfare state, but how serious it is and how effective its efforts will be are questions that remain in grave doubt.

The GNP is probably a valid indication of the economic power of a state, but I think it is time to give precedence to what I call GNW, or gross national welfare. Instead of knowing how much a country produces in a year, it is far more important to know how well that product serves the needs of the citizens. In the GNW, of course, primary consideration ought to be given to cultural and spiritual welfare.

TOYNBEE: Gross national product is not an index of even the economic prosperity of the human beings who compose a nation. Statisticians divide the figure for the GNP by the figure for the national population and call the resulting dividend average per capita income. This notion is meaningless, and the quantification of it is culpably misleading. A figure for average per capita material damage would be more meaningful, for although, in such areas as housing, the damage from the increase of the GNP in an economically competitive society is unevenly distributed, pollution of the air, soil, water, and other constituents of the natural environment adversely affects all the inhabitants of a country. Pollution may poison a rich mother's child as well as a poor mother's child.

In a nation in which the first national priority is the increase of the GNP, economic competition between individuals and classes is likely to be intense; therefore, the inequality of the distribution of the GNP is likely to be aggravated. For instance, in present-day Britain, which is partly a welfare state, housing conditions are shockingly bad for the minority below the poverty line. In other words, Britain fails to guarantee the necessities of life to all her citizens.

I agree that we ought to aim not at gross national product but at gross national welfare. My tests of welfare would be these: the degree of harmony and mutual kindness among the participants in the society; the average per capita spiritual welfare, which determines the degree of harmony and mutual kindness; the average standard of self-mastery, which is the key to spiritual welfare; the degree to which the society forgoes profit for the sake of avoiding pollution, both material and spiritual. The last test gauges the extent to which the society has succeeded in giving spiritual welfare priority over material wealth.

The Profession of Motherhood

IKEDA: The problem of guiding a child along the paths that lead to adulthood is one of the greatest responsibilities and greatest privileges of the human mother. The task requires great effort and subtle psychological understanding, but it cannot be accomplished without boundless love. Because the possibilities of development in infancy are limitless, the nature of early impressions on the very young mind is of paramount importance. It is a grave mistake to think that using nurseries and similar institutions to relieve mothers of the burden of caring for their children is the way to true women's liberation.

TOYNBEE: I agree emphatically that the mother in the home environment is irreplaceable as the educator of her children in the early years of life during which a child's character and temperament are formed. Part of a child's personality is, I suppose, determined by the genes transmitted to it physically by its parents through the sexual union by which the child has been pro-created. But character is formed by an interaction between a person's heredity and his response to his environment, and it seems to be agreed that, though character can be modified at all stages of life, the decisive developments occur during the first five years and that, at this formative stage, the major environmental agency is the mother's educational influence, if the child is brought up by its mother in the family's home.

In Britain during World War II, many children were removed from their mothers' care and placed in impersonal institutions to mobilize women for war-work. Psychologists who have studied the histories of some of these children as they grew to adulthood now agree that the lasting aftereffects of the upheaval in early life were bad.

IKEDA: The future of human society depends on education, and the first educational imprints made on the infant's mind ought to be warm and human, not official and institutionalized.

In material production and related activities, the male assumes the lead, but in the matter of caring for and cultivating the highly sensitive and receptive infant life and in guiding that life to adulthood, women are more skillful than men. I think this is true because women are more alert to subtle psychological changes and because it is their nature to be able to give self-sacrificing love.

A child absorbs with great sensitivity the mother's teachings and training, her actions, her emotions, and the whole image of a human being. And in this process, the child imperceptibly amasses personality traits and thus inherits fundamental human culture. An old proverb says that the child is the mirror of the mother. Institutions may conduct courses of education and may impart great knowledge to their charges, but it is beyond their power to give all that a mother and a family can give.

TOYNBEE: To enable women to impart knowledge and love to the young while developing and taking advantage of their other talents, we ought to try to create a society that will be neither a men's society nor a women's society but will suit the convenience of human beings of both sexes. For a human being, liberty is the freedom to fulfill potentialities, including those potentialities that are not common to both sexes but are peculiar to each sex as a consequence of its distinctive physiological and psychological characteristics.

IKEDA: I too think it is desirable to create a society that provides both sexes with opportunities to manifest and develop their potentials and that grants equal rewards for equal work no matter who does it. The women's liberation movement, however, is wrong in demanding that women be freed from their tasks as housewives and mothers. The advocates of this movement are right in insisting that modern society has not advanced to the point where women can develop and display their talents as easily as men and that women are treated unfairly in the matter of salaries. These things need correcting. But to liberate women from the jobs of bearing children, a task which is theirs biologically, and of raising them and caring for the home is to invite disaster for humanity. Furthermore, in abandoning these tasks, women would be throwing away their most important strong point. It seems to me that women would find it more to their advantage, and more convincing to men, to hold firmly to these all important tasks and, in addition, to demand equal opportunities for development and equal remuneration for labor. Many problems arise, however, when women try to combine employment in other fields with the responsibilities of home and family.

TOYNBEE: The first solution for this problem is to rearrange the division of labor so that part-time jobs of other kinds will be available for mothers during the period in their life when they are bearing and rearing children. Time can be saved for mothers by the mechanization of household chores. The psychological problem is more difficult. Even if time can be provided for a woman to do both a mother's work and some part-time work of another kind, it may be difficult for her to divide her attention and her concern satisfactorily. Her children on the one side and her professional colleagues on the other side may feel, with some resentment, that she is not giving them their due share of her attention and concern.

108

Another solution has been opened up by the recent increase in the average length of the effective period of working life as a result of the advance of medical science. A woman can now obtain a complete higher education; can then qualify for practicing a profession; can then marry, bear children, and bring them up, while continuing to practice her profession to a sufficient extent to keep her hand in and to keep abreast of current developments; and then eventually, when all her children are grown up, can practice her profession full-time. She will probably then still be in the prime of life—at least in a society in which the number of children in a family is limited voluntarily by family planning. Motherhood is such an important and rewarding potentiality that it is normal for a woman to want to be a mother.

Human beings are stimulated to do good work if they are given emoluments and the status that the work deserves. Under an economic regime of free enterprise, the chief status symbol is (perhaps unfortunately) pay. I therefore suggest that mothers, like other educators, ought to be paid a salary; that this salary ought to be high; and that it ought to be paid directly to the mothers themselves, so that they will have an earned income of their own, independent of their husbands' income. The bill for mothers' salaries would make a large demand on the community's general wages fund, and, to find the money for this, the amount distributed in wages to men would have to be reduced considerably. In our present-day society, such a redistribution of the community's income between men and women in women's favor would carry with it a rise in women's social status.

IKEDA: Your proposal is excellent and reasonable. It would relieve women from the feeling of being victimized as a result of their tasks in bearing and raising children. At the same time, it would make clear to all of society the immense difficulties of a mother's work. Until now, society, especially male society, has regarded raising children as no more than woman's natural task. As a consequence, women have come to look on motherhood as an irksome job imposed on them by their sex. Some of them now ask to be relieved of this burden.

Before a woman is a mother or a wife she is a human being. I consider the women's liberation movement mistaken in claiming that women do not wish to be tied to their homes and their families because they are human beings. But I must hasten to add that I realize that there are large numbers of women who are content to find lifetime employment in some profession—not only in the field of religion. Naturally the rights of these women too must be protected.

109

TOYNBEE: In my opinion, the liberation to which women have a right will not be complete unless and until women who prefer to forgo marriage, in order to spend the whole of their working life in some full-time profession other than motherhood, are given a full opportunity to lead a professional life on equal terms with men. However, even if a woman's renunciation of motherhood has been deliberate, she may suffer psychologically from the nonfulfillment of such an important female potentiality, just as, conversely, a woman may be partially frustrated by the fulfillment of her potentiality for motherhood if she has a very compulsive vocation to pursue some other profession.

On the whole, I have the impression that this second form of frustration is less psychologically damaging for a woman than the frustration that she may suffer through forgoing motherhood. I think the happiest solution will be to rearrange the world's work to make it possible for a woman to combine being a mother with spending part of her working life on following some other profession as well. In any case, insofar as, and for so long as, she serves society as a mother, I feel sure that a woman ought to be given the high status and big salary that the key profession of motherhood deserves. Her status ought to be at least as high as, say, a professor's or a magistrate's or a pilot's, and her salary ought to be of a corresponding size.

For a child, a mother's love and care are psychologically indispensable. Now that women have a number of alternatives to motherhood, society can no longer leave it to nature to ensure that good mothers are forthcoming in sufficient numbers. Society ought therefore to cater for a supply of good mothers by making this profession, which men are physiologically incapable of taking up, sufficiently attractive for women. Motherhood ought to be both highly honored and generously remunerated.

Breeding to the Limit

IKEDA: It is generally accepted that birth control in the developing countries, which are largely responsible for the modern population explosion, is an important step in resolving the difficulty. However, there are obstacles in the path of its realization. For instance, there is the moral issue. Many people, especially those who regard children as so-called gifts of God, feel that it is immoral to destroy prenatal human life artificially. As a religious man, I am deeply conscious of the paramount, irreplaceable value of human life; I deeply believe that all human actions must be based on an awareness of the

110

greatness of life. On the other hand, birth control—the lessening to some extent of the possibility of giving birth—is by no means trampling on the dignity of life. On the contrary, if such measures can alleviate the chronic starvation of the developing nations, they are a practical way to demonstrate even greater respect for life. As long as it effectively promotes the continued survival and expansion of mankind, birth control deserves our support.

TOYNBEE: Recently the advance of science has affected the problem of human sexual relations in two ways. Science has reduced the rate of premature deaths—especially deaths in infancy and women's deaths in childbirth—and has increased the average length of life. This has been happening not only in the developed countries but in the developing countries too. In addition, science has discovered means that are effective and apparently physically harmless for women to have sexual intercourse without incurring the natural liability of becoming pregnant.

The first of the two effects of science has been to cause a population explosion. The death rate can be reduced quickly and easily by public-health measures, but reduction in the birthrate requires voluntary action by individuals. This, in turn, requires not only a knowledge of, and access to, new scientific means of avoiding pregnancy but also a break with mankind's traditional habit of breeding to the limit. Consequently, the adoption of birth control to offset the already achieved reduction in the death rate is slowest in the developing countries. The peoples of these countries are both the largest and the poorest part of mankind.

The impulse to breed to the limit has, no doubt, been implanted by nature in man, as in all the nonhuman species of living beings, as a device (this purposive language is, of course, not to be taken literally) for ensuring the survival of the species. In man, this natural impulse has been rationalized by being translated into religious sanctions. It has been believed that a man must make sure of leaving behind him male descendants to perform rites that are held to be necessary for the welfare of the dead man's spirit; or, as in the doctrine of the Judaic religions, man has been commanded by God to "be fruitful and multiply and replenish the Earth and subdue it." (Chapter 1, verse 28, of the Book of Genesis in the Jewish Torah, which Christians call The Old Testament.)

IKEDA: The attitude that man must breed to the limit must be changed, for if it is allowed to go unaltered it will further aggravate the population crisis and will effectively destroy respect for life. The simple-minded idea that having children proves the virility of the male and the fecundity of the female persists in some places. The only way to dispel this misconception is to strive to enlighten the people on the importance of birth control. Religious rules on the subject are perhaps harder to deal with.

TOYNBEE: Supposed religious injunctions for breeding to the limit are, in my opinion, superstitions that are neither factually true not morally binding. Nevertheless, they increase the psychological difficulty of breaking with an ancient habit in the conduct of one of the most intimate affairs of life. I deplore the pronouncement of Pope Paul VI reaffirming the traditional Christian veto on the use of any artificial method of restricting the number of births, with the exception of the avoidance of sexual intercourse during those phases in the sexual cycle of a woman's life in which intercourse is most likely to result in pregnancy. This permitted exception is illogical, for a calculated periodical abstention is just as much a deliberate human interference with the course of nature as is the use of contraceptives.

I hold that the criterion ought to be not supposed religious commands or vetoes but the maintenance of human dignity. Until human science discovered how to reduce the death rate and to limit the birthrate, man was in the same humiliating position as defenseless species of nonhuman living beings, like the rabbit. Human communities, like rabbit communities, were decimated by predators (in man's case, since the dawn of civilization, man himself has been the most destructive predator on human life, apart from bacteria and viruses). Therefore human communities, like rabbit communities, have produced a maximum number of offspring in order to offset a maximum number of casualties. It is unseemly for human beings to behave like rabbits. Rabbits have nothing to lose, whereas human beings can and do lose spiritual dignity. This loss is self-inflicted when the progress of science has made it unnecessary as well as undesirable.

IKEDA: It is likely that, when they are first promulgated, religious regulations —like the Catholic veto on birth control—are designed with an eye to protecting the dignity of life. But when they cease to be able to change with the times, such rules must be revised or abandoned. It is by no means certain that methods good in one historical age will be appropriate in another. The true spirit of religion is to adopt only those measures that protect the dignity of life.

TOYNBEE: Human dignity requires the procreation not of the maximum number of children but of the optimum number. The optimum number can be defined as the number that, under the technological and social conditions of a particular time and place, will give each child brought into the world and the whole society as well the optimum standard of living—reckoning the standard in spiritual terms and regarding the material standard as a means to a spiritual end instead of as an end in itself.

We ought not to be deterred by religious vetoes from using, for human spiritual welfare, the new power that the progress of science has placed in our hands. The power to prevent sexual intercourse from resulting in pregnancy can be misused for indulging the sexual appetite without dignity or love. But, alternatively, it can be used beneficently for the welfare of children, of their mothers, and of society. We ought not to deprive ourselves of the use of this new power for welfare, though of course we ought to do our utmost to induce the younger generation to refrain from misusing the same power.

IKEDA: National governments ought to be the leaders in spreading required knowledge about birth control, especially since its good effects will have great influence on national economies.

Of course, in the process of promoting birth control, we will encounter many problems. For example, as technical knowledge about birth control becomes more widely available, sex might well move in the mistaken direction of pure hedonism, as you have suggested. Reduction in the size of the family unit will have repercussions on the housing problem. As the members of the younger generation decrease in number, the available labor population will fall off, and the older generation will be called upon to play a bigger part. Because it will greatly influence industry, alteration in the population structure will necessitate the study of such methods as labor reduction. As this brief outline suggests, many aspects of birth control require thought.

TOYNBEE: You have pointed out that a sudden reduction of the number of births is bound to produce an imbalance in the respective sizes of the age groups within a community. This imbalance, however, will be only temporary. Meanwhile, the temporary increase in the relative number of old people will be offset by the increase in the average length of effective working life that will have been brought about by improvements in nutrition and medical care, both public and personal.

IKEDA: It is sometimes said that married couples should be required to limit themselves to two children. Some scholars go so far as to insist that in the future couples producing more than three children ought to be penalized. Such legal restraint may be right or wrong, but I agree that some restrictive measure is needed. What method do you think would be effective?

113

TOYNBEE: Reduction of the number of children ought to be voluntary as far as possible, but an exclusively voluntary change of the ancient and deeply ingrained habit of breeding to the limit is unlikely to bring about the necessary amount of reduction. I expect that society, represented by the public authorities, will have to impose a compulsory limit on the number of children that are brought into the world. In the past, this has been taken, as a matter of course, to be solely the concern of parents. There have been cases in which the procreation of large families has been rewarded by the public authorities either positively or at least negatively. But, hitherto, even the most totalitarian governments have refrained from taking direct action either to enlarge or to reduce the size of families. However, I expect that it is going to be recognized —and this in the practical form of drastic political action—that the number of children brought into the world is not just a private concern of parents but a public concern in which the public authorities have a right and duty not only to intervene but also to take effective steps to ensure that they, and not the parents, shall have the last word.

IKEDA: I too suspect that some form of public governmental restriction will be inevitable. Although it is to be hoped that the people would take suitable steps voluntarily and would accustom themselves to small families, I am afraid that by the time this desirable state had been reached, disaster from overpopulation would already be upon us. The implementation of population controls, however, will give rise to a variety of problems. Mankind has always believed that increasing the human population is the natural course to follow. Social structures and ideas about daily living have been built on this principle; changing them will be extremely difficult.

One problem generated by reductions in the numbers of births will involve education. Limits on the number of children may prove to be a serious handicap to character formation. A child with few or no brothers or sisters tends to depend excessively on the parents, who for their part become overprotective. Lacking a spirit of independence, children spoiled by such parents often become selfish. In prewar Japan, the average family consisted of more than five children. Since World War II, few married couples have produced more than three children. The decrease in the number of births has undeniably had adverse effects on the character formation of postwar children.

TOYNBEE: In the relatively large families that have been normal in the past, children were educated not only by their parents but also by each other. Learning to get on with each other and to look after each other was one of the most important parts of the rising generation's education in sociality. This is the heart of human education, since man is a social animal who cannot survive if his sociality is not properly developed. A family of half a dozen children is a miniature society and, as such, has an informal, but potent, educative social effect. The same effect cannot be produced by a family that is limited to a maximum of two or three children.

IKEDA: Relations among children are more than a mere means of transmitting knowledge; they are vital to character formation. Although adults always treat children as immature and inexperienced, children living and playing together regard each other as individual and equal personalities. Situations arising from such equality teach children to control their selfishness and train them to know how to deal with other children who are weaker than they. Character training of this kind takes place among brothers and sisters in a single family and in neighborhood groups that generally form when families in a region have many children. But when families are small, opportunities for social intercourse with contemporaries diminish, and the ties between parents and children become stronger.

TOYNBEE: How are we to ensure families in which the number of children will not fall below the minimum figure that is requisite to the children's own interest? We have to look for some way of reconciling the children's interest in growing up in a miniature society of their own with the general interest of mankind in reducing the birthrate.

These two interests conflict with each other in a family of the structure that, unfortunately, has become normal in the urbanized section of present-day society. The typical urban family is now restricted to a single married couple with their nonadult children. But this limited family is a recent phenomenon. It is a product of the industrialization and urbanization of an increasingly large minority of mankind within the last two hundred years. The traditional family, in all human societies, has been a three-generation family consisting of grandparents, their sons and daughters together with their respective wives and husbands, and all the middle generation's children. In a three-generation family of the traditional structure, first cousins are brought up under the same roof as, or, short of that, next door to, their first cousins. Relations among cousins are as close as those among brothers and sisters. In a three-generation family, there would be enough children to form a miniature society, even if the maximum number for each married couple were—voluntarily or compulsorily—restricted to a maximum of two or three.

Can the traditional three-generation family be preserved even in those present-day societies where it still survives? And can it be reestablished in

115

societies in which it has recently been replaced by the two-generation family? The solution of this problem is going to be difficult for the already urbanized minority of mankind. A partial solution may be found in the decentralization of our present gigantic urban populations. However, this decentralization can be carried out only gradually, and a certain number of large urban agglomerations seem likely to remain a permanent feature of human social life. We must therefore work out some method of making the three-generation family feasible under urban conditions.

MAN AS THE SOCIAL ANIMAL | 5

The Labor Movement

IKEDA: The labor movement seems to have arrived at an important turning point. Since the living conditions of the working classes have improved in recent years, economic demands, which were once the main driving force of the movement, have receded somewhat into the background. Demands for working conditions permitting individuals to display their abilities are gaining strength. In addition, the working classes are becoming more aware of their role in society. For instance, they sometimes raise protests when they learn that the factories where they work are sources of environmental pollution or are manufacturing military weapons. In terms of political power, the unions often become support organizations for particular parties. Men with political ambitions regard the holding of union offices as good training for later political candidacy. Unfortunately, political ambition frequently creates a gap between union leaders and ordinary members.

Although a consciousness among laboring people of the existence of something called the working class is highly developed in the West, it is less pronounced in Japan. This is because, from as early as the feudal period of Japanese history, industry has been organized around the family in a family-like system. Even in vast modern enterprises, workers generally do not rise up against management; they tend instead to feel the need to combine their strength with that of all other parts of the organization for the general good of the firm.

Although some sociologists describe the family-style approach to business as a purely Japanese phenomenon, it seems to me that, as business everywhere tends to internationalize, closer family relations between management and labor will become increasingly important. For instance, as competition between two large automotive companies—let us say Ford and Benz—grows stiffer, it would seem that the workers in each factory would come to feel greater solidarity with the management of their own company than with the workers in the competing company, even though the concept of a working class is supposed to cut across nationalities.

TOYNBEE: So far Japan has enjoyed happier relations between capital and labor than Britain, where the paternalistic tradition died out before the outbreak of the Industrial Revolution. In the first stage of industrialization, employers were merciless in exploiting the new industrial working class. The workers comforted themselves by looking forward to the eventual replacement of private enterprise by socialism. They hoped that the state would take control of the country's economic life and would then impose social justice by regimentation. The British workers tried to protect themselves against exploitation, until a socialist state could come into being, by forming trades unions. Britain has not yet become a socialist country. On the other hand, the trades unions have become so powerful that they have gone over from a defensive to an offensive posture.

The increase in the workers' strength has been due partly to their own action in unionizing each trade more comprehensively and partly to the increased vulnerability of British society to dislocation caused by strikes. As the progress of technology has made the whole community more dependent on such public utilities as gas, electricity, water supply, and postal services, unionized workers in these key industries can now extort pay increases by damaging the nation's economy or even paralyzing its life. In consequence, the trades unions have become, in practice, beneficiaries of the economic regime of unrestricted competitive private enterprise of which they were once the victims. Unionized workers are now even more strongly opposed to socialism—that is, to the limitation of prices and incomes by legislation— than their capitalist employers are.

IKEDA: Yes, this is a very important thing to keep in mind when attempting to analyze the labor movement of the new age.

TOYNBEE: It will be an important consideration in the future, but it is very important even now. In present-day Britain, unhappily, class war has broken out again, but the dividing line between the classes involved is a new one. Now that the equipment of industry has become extremely costly, production stoppages caused by strikes are ruinous for the employers of industrial labor. Employers are therefore inclined to concede the workers' demands for wage increases and to try to recoup their losses by raising the consumer prices of their products. The class war in Britain today is between two groups: people who have the power to increase their incomes either by obtaining higher wages for indispensable work or by raising consumer prices for necessities of life, and people who do not have the power to take either of these steps. The first class includes both the employers of industrial labor and their employees.

Of course, increases in wages and prices are partly illusory in terms of money, because money itself depreciates as increases in money-wages and money-prices lag behind increases in production. Nevertheless, industrialists and unionized workers can offset inflation for themselves by constantly increasing the amounts of their money-wages and money-prices, whereas the rest of the community cannot do this and must manage on fixed incomes, even though the money itself has lost value. Thus, in effect, people who can obtain higher wages and those who can demand higher prices for their products are robbing people who cannot.

I should be surprised if there were no comparable developments in Japan, where employers and workers cooperate with each other much more effectively than they do in Britain. In other words, I should be surprised if Japanese management and labor were not cooperating at the expense of the consumer.

IKEDA: Unfortunately an identical tendency has grown extremely pronounced in Japan in the past decade. To take only one example, I might mention the problem of the railroads, which are an absolutely indispensable means of transportation for the millions of Japanese people who must commute. Almost every year, labor organizations within the railway systems make demands for increased wages. The strikes they hold to force management to meet their requirements paralyze large segments of the population. In order to keep the railways operating, management must grant the workers their wage increases, but to make up for the financial loss caused by increased wages, they must raise railway fares. In short, labor strikes for more money, and it is the ordinary people who must bear the financial burden of higher wages for railway workers.

TOYNBEE: That is unfair, but ironically enough demands for wage increases sometimes work to the detriment of the people who make them. Frequent increases in wages and prices make it impossible for an industry to hold its own in competition with its rivals. For example, in Britain today, rises in wages and prices are swelling the ranks of the unemployed and increasing the

119

number of bankruptcies. So far, however, this shrinkage of available employment has not deterred workers in vital industries from taking utmost advantage of the continuing strength of their bargaining position.

IKEDA: In the past, guaranteeing workers' rights and the improvement of working and living conditions were aims of paramount importance. Now, however, new aims must be added to the older ones. The right to a full and happy life for all classes—not just for the laborers—must be guaranteed. We must establish as one of our major aims the development of a resistance to social abuses that threaten the very survival of humanity. In basic terms, the labor movement must cease being one that gives precedence to the satisfaction of greed and become one that strives to ensure fundamental protection for all mankind. Obviously, the new labor movement must never lose sight of its fundamental aims and must never allow itself to become isolated from reality.

TOYNBEE: A new movement is very much to be desired because, if things continue as they are, I am afraid the outlook cannot be bright. My conclusion is that private competitive economic enterprise is condemning itself to death because all parties fail to restrain their greed. The ethical—or, perhaps, unethical—postulate of the ideology of competitive economic enterprise is that greed is a virtue, not a vice. But this postulate is contrary to truth, and falsehood brings nemesis. Unrestrained greed is self-destructive because it takes suicidally short views. I believe that, in all industrial countries in which maximum private profit is the motive for production, the competitive economic system will become unworkable. When this happens, socialism will eventually be imposed by a dictatorial regime. This will be resisted as bitterly by the workers as by their employers because, temporarily, workers, too, have benefited from a system that exploited them in the first stages of its history.

It might appear that I am Marxian in forecasting the advent of socialism, but I am not Marxian in my ethical judgments. Marx denigrated the employers of labor and idealized the workers. Lenin, however, became disillusioned with the workers and, after a time, dragooned them. In my view, the strictures Marx made on the employers of his time apply to the workers of my time. Human nature is the same in both employers and workers.

IKEDA: I agree with you. The starting point of any reform must be an accurate evaluation of human nature. All past revolutions have devoted insufficient study to the basics of human nature and have attempted to rebuild society by means of reconstruction of no more than systems and institutions. It is true that these revolutions have succeeded in some fields, but it is their very lack of attention to human nature that has caused them to fail in bringing about a total renovation of man's society.

TOYNBEE: Human nature is greedy, and greed leads to disaster if it is not restrained. In economics, as in all other human activities, self-mastery is, I believe, the only way to self-salvation.

Earlier you said that it is essential that we make a shift from a search for the satisfaction of human greed to a pursuit of fundamental protection for mankind. I agree with you, but I fear that this shift will not be voluntary. I am afraid that it will be imposed by a dictatorial regime. All parties to the process of industrial production will resign themselves to this regime, which they will reluctantly recognize as a lesser evil than the complete economic disaster toward which the present system of private enterprise seems to be leading. I hope that if the dictatorial regime I foresee succeeds in carrying out its revolutionary mandate, it will then be replaced by a milder regime that is more democratically representative of the subjects of the world state, which, I believe, must be founded on some kind of world dictatorship.

IKEDA: You have stated a belief that, in economics as in all other human activities, self-mastery is the only way to self-salvation. I agree with you on these points. But you fear that a shift in the labor movement from a desire to satisfy greed to a desire to protect human rights cannot be made voluntarily, but must be imposed by a dictatorial regime. I regard this statement with considerable apprehension and feel that it must be the objective view of a historian analyzing the possibilities of the future. Surely it is not an expression of the way future trends ought to go.

TOYNBEE: Indeed not. I do not hope for the establishment of a dictatorship. I fear it. In itself, dictatorship is an absolute evil. Still, in the past, the dictatorial system has often been part of the unavoidable price of great social change. No matter how unwillingly, peoples have tolerated dictatorships because they seemed less evil than any alternative they could provide or imagine. In short, it has been much easier to establish a dictatorship than to rid society of another kind of system that has proved unworkable.

Tokugawa Ieyasu in Japan, Han Liu Pang in China, and Augustus in the Roman Empire were dictators; all three succeeded in establishing dictatorial regimes that lasted when similar regimes created by their predecessors, Toyotomi Hideyoshi, Shih Huang-ti, and Julius Caesar, had failed. Why? They were succeessful because they kept their dictatorships within the limits that public opinion considered compatible with avoiding the greater evil.

Dictatorship, then, was the lesser evil elected to forestall the greater evil of social and political anarchy.

People are not fated to bring dictatorship upon themselves. But when dictatorship occurs, it is the nemesis of unrestrained selfishness and antisocial behavior. I fear that stabilization of the present world, at least in material terms, may not be possible without a degree of dictatorship.

IKEDA: I see your point, but if I recapitulate briefly, I think I will be able to show that there is a way to avoid dictatorship. Undeniably the growing power of the labor movement and unlimited greed on the part of economic powers adversely affect the lives of the ordinary people and tend to bring society to the brink of great disorder. As long as leaders of trades unions and industrialists continue to regard fellow human beings as sacrifices necessary to their relentless pursuit of material wealth, dictatorship may be the way the people must choose to restore social order. But there is a way to halt this apparently inevitable development.

For example, I mentioned labor unions that rose in protest against their employers because the factories where they worked were either aggravating environmental pollution or producing military weapons. Before these union members took these brave stands, they probably engaged in some kind of introspective analysis that might be termed self-revolution and that was probably based on ideas not unlike religious belief. Their actions were altruistic; they were for the good and protection of all society, not for the aggrandizement of the workers or the unions. They spoke out against their employers for polluting the environment with industrial wastes or for producing armaments that pose the threat of disaster for all mankind.

If the leadership and membership of the labor movement can equip themselves with the kind of religious ideas, broad knowledge, and courage shown by the people in my example, it will be possible to avert both uncontrollable social disorder and dictatorship. The condition on which self-revolution is based is the development of a personality that is capable of feeling innate human suffering deep within the substance of life's being. The kind of personality that can harmonize with all of society is the personality imbued with the spirit of compassion.

The road to self-revolution is not easy; it demands intense and strict religious discipline and practice. But as long as he is guided by a philosophy of life and a religion that clarifies the truths of existence, man is capable of self-revolution.

Leisure and Its Uses

IKEDA: Under ordinary working conditions, each worker's daily activities are predetermined by his place of duty. The individual laborer must do no more than perform his assignment precisely and efficiently; he does not need to worry about what to do next. When he is confronted with leisure time, however, he must plot his own course of action. This entails mental work, which to some people is almost torture.

TOYNBEE: Leisure enlarges our scope for making choices, and since having to choose may be an agonizing responsibility, human nature shies away from leisure. It shies away from democracy for a similar reason.

A human being can be relieved of the responsibility of decision making by being dehumanized, as he is when he is turned into the equivalent of a cog in a machine. The traditional recipes for dehumanization are political dictatorship and military discipline and drill. But since the time of the Industrial Revolution, these older dehumanizing anesthetics have been supplemented by the monotony of minutely organized work in mechanized factories. The political police and the drill sergeant have been reinforced by the impersonal tyranny of the conveyor belt. Today technology is making the further advance from scientifically managed machine tending to automation. This is promising—or threatening—to provide for everybody the leisure that hitherto had been the privilege of a minority.

IKEDA: In some future, if slightly farfetched, age, all production activities may become the work of machines, electronic computers, and robots. Human work will still be necessary for making basic production plans and for instructing computers, but a special elite will perform these tasks. The majority of people, freed from labor, will have to think seriously of how to spend their days. In other words, leisure will become a problem. Given circumstances of this kind, artists, writers, and others who find joy in using their creative abilities will not be bored by extra free time: they will know how to use it meaningfully. People whose creative talents are less developed, however, may be forced to resort to meaningless amusements to consume the extra free time afforded them by reduced work. I believe that man is fundamentally a creative animal, indeed a being that cannot live without experiencing the joy of the creative act. I see the solution to the leisure problem in finding ways to cultivate and develop creative talents.

TOYNBEE: It will be necessary to develop both those talents and an awareness

123

of the importance of using them, because people who have enjoyed leisure in the past have not always employed it to good advantage. For instance, the privileged minority have sometimes found their leisure so irksome a burden that they have rid themselves of it by inventing artificial work either in the frivolous form of sport or in the sinister form of war. Aside from artificial time-consumers of this kind, these drones have had only one task: the maintenance, by force, of privileges that they enjoy without having earned them by performing social services.

In contrast to this group, a creative minority within the privileged minority have found leisure a blessing instead of a burden. These have been the people who, even in a whole life of leisure devoted to work, have had so many things to do that they could not carry out their full agenda. In the past, the problem of leisure has been peculiar to the idle, privileged minority, but in the automation age, the majority will be confronted with it.

If leisure is as truly undesirable as the passion to escape it and its responsibilities suggests, then in the automation age, a privileged minority will still exist, but it will be a minority for whom work, not leisure, can be provided. This minority will be the handful of workers employed in building, tending, and programing the computers that will have deprived other human beings of obligatory employment.

During the preautomation age, the majority of people have been compelled to work to earn their living, but their attitude toward their tasks has been ambivalent. When forced to work, they have resented labor as a burden from which only the privileged minority have unfairly been spared. But when these same people have been out of work, they have resented their unemployment even though the work they lost was monotonous, fatiguing, and disagreeable.

IKEDA: Resentment at being out of work is understandable. In fact, even should labor become unnecessary as a means of making a livelihood, it will continue to be essential for a truly human way of life. Work gives human beings the joy of creativity. This is true for both the blacksmith and the farmer, who can see the direct results of their work, and for the employee of a gigantic enterprise who cannot see the results of his efforts.

Our civilization has developed in the belief that reduction of working hours and increase of leisure time are related to greater human happiness. To a certain extent, this is true, but there is a limit. I cannot say whether we have already reached that limit. Nonetheless, this phenomenon, like all others, has its positive and its negative aspects. When the limit of tolerance is reached, the negative aspects inevitably evoke a reaction on the part of the people.

124

TOYNBEE: Unemployment has many disadvantages of course. The most obvious, but not the most serious, of the sufferings caused by being out of work is economic impoverishment. But the psychological misery caused by unemployment is even more distressing. An ex-worker with nothing to do feels that he has become socially superfluous. This is humiliating because man is a social animal and social redundancy seems to reduce him to personal nullity. Worse still, to be out of work is to be at leisure. Unless the unemployed worker is one of those rare creative persons who have more ready-made employment than they can find time or strength for in a lifetime of complete leisure, he must confront the ultimate question of human destiny. This problem immediately besets a human being when he ceases to be employed in earning a living or stops engaging in uneconomical self-employment, no matter whether that self-employment is frivolous, mischievous, or creative.

The question of human destiny lies in wait for every human being, however obtuse or insensitive he may be, for it is impossible to be conscious without being exposed to the possibility of becoming aware that being human is an awkward plight and a terrifying mystery. Few people live out their lives without facing this plight and this mystery occasionally at times of personal crisis. Chronic unemployment can do what momentary crises do: it can confront a person inescapably with the problem of human destiny.

Is it a blessing or a curse to be compelled to look this problem in the face? Most human beings behave as if it were a curse. If they are not anesthetized by compulsory work, they invent unnecessary work to anesthetize themselves. If they drop out of society and thus lose their access to social anesthetics, they anesthetize themselves physically with intoxicants or drugs.

IKEDA: I think the core of the matter is this. No matter how much leisure one has or how much one works, the important thing is for human beings to establish their independence and live in a creative fashion.

In spite of the modern trend to consider reduction of labor hours as entirely good, it must be remembered that work has two major aspects. It may cause suffering at times, but it also provides humanity with the joy of being creative. Consequently, it is an error to look at only one side of the picture and to argue that merely increasing leisure time will in some sense liberate mankind and turn sorrow into gladness.

I believe that we must create a general social system in which each individual can work as much as he wants, not under compulsion but on his own initiative and according to his talents and aptitudes. This system must also provide for the effective use of leisure time.

125

TOYNBEE: What you say is true, but let me return briefly to the point of using leisure to grapple with the problem of human destiny. There are people who regard leisure used in this way as a blessing. Facing the problem of human destiny is another name for religion and philosophy. Among the creative minority within the privileged minority, whose privilege was once leisure itself, there have always been persons who have devoted their creative faculties to religion and philosophy instead of to art, science, or technology.

If it is possible for some human beings to find self-fulfillment in a lifetime of leisure devoted to the study of man's ultimate spiritual problems, is not this a potential form of self-fulfillment for all human beings? It must be, if it is true, as it surely is, that the question of human destiny lies in wait for every human being who awakens to consciousness.

Since man is a social animal, religion has a social as well as a personal facet. Anchorites—Hindu, Buddhist, and Christian—have felt that, in responding to the demands of their own spiritual life, they have been performing a social function. Their service to society has been recognized and acknowledged by their fellow human beings.

Religion seems to be the most promising field in which to look for a solution to the problems created by automation. Religion is a personal and a social activity. However hard we may try to elude it, religion will confront us at some time or other in the course of our lives. Even if it were possible to elude religion altogether, the price of the escape would be nothing less than the forfeiture of our humanity.

Sense of Value in Social Organization

IKEDA: One of the things of which we are most basically aware in discussions of modern culture is the problem of organizations. Together with technology and communications, organization is a major pillar of our civilization. As such, it has been a source of blessing for mankind. At the same time, it undeniably poses a grave threat. Society, itself an organizational form created by man, reflects human intentions. But social mechanisms occasionally function in totally undesirable ways. It is one of the tragedies of our times that the autonomous action of organized society sometimes suppresses and even rejects humanity.

TOYNBEE: Yes, organizations sometimes produce results that are contrary to the ideas of their founders. This makes it seem as if they acquire wills of their

126

own and as if they establish their own objectives, which differ from the objectives of their participants. The truth is, I suppose, that organizations do not become autonomous personalities but that the persons governing them make it their first concern to guarantee the continued existence of the organizations for which they are responsible. These same people make it their second concern to achieve the immediate, narrow purpose for which their organization was founded without taking into consideration wider effects and ultimate consequences.

IKEDA: An extreme manifestation of the harm that can result from ignoring wider effects and ultimate consequences is the environmental pollution caused by highly industrialized society. There are a number of causes of environmental pollution, but the basic one is failure to realize the relationship between man and nature. This failure resulted in the development of value principles based on the idea that man ought to conquer nature instead of recognizing his place as part of the universe.

At certain points in historical time, ideas and actions that have now caused great harm were highly esteemed. Historically speaking, these ideas and actions were not originally motivated by inhumane impulses. On the contrary, in the majority of cases, they grew from the best of personal human intentions. But as they accumulated and became part of the social mechanism, basically good human intentions grew into organizations and social evils that distorted and sometimes utterly defeated the original aims. For example, a certain medicine may bring great benefit to man. Mass industrial production of that same medicine, however, can result in pollutant waste products that become the source of immense harm. But when matters reach this stage, it is not easy to halt production of the medicine, because it will have become the very life of the organization manufacturing it. Halting production, then, would wreck that organization.

TOYNBEE: Sometimes basically good organizations create impasses for themselves and their individual members. For instance, the executive head of a trades union may be so successful in obtaining wage increases for his union members that eventually the industry employing them goes bankrupt, thus putting all of the union men permanently out of work. The higher wages won by the trades union cease to be paid, and the members are reduced to living on doles from the state. This result is contrary to the wishes of the trades union executive, the members of the union, and the government. It is the consequence of shortsighted operation of an organization.

127

IKEDA: That is true. People many years ago warned of this danger, but their warnings went unheeded. From the middle of the nineteenth century, when the problem of organization was not as apparent as it is now, some philosophers and thinkers with admirable foresight expressed their opinions on the issue, without effecting solutions. Ironically even Marxism and socialism, which attempted to save the laboring classes—victims of the capitalist society—inevitably became tainted when their ideals were converted into social systems.

The tendency for organizations, societies, and systems to fail to achieve ideal goals led many people to believe that the problems inherent in them are unsolvable. But rejection of organization as such leads to the rejection of all group control or, in other words, to nihilism and anarchism.

TOYNBEE: Nihilism and anarchism are, I think, the first reactions to the miscarriage of organization. For instance, the angry young men and the hippies of today demonstrate against the failures of the economic system of competitive private enterprise oriented toward maximum profit. Irate reactions against a system hasten the collapse of the organization against which they are gestures of protest. The next reaction is likely to be a drastic dictatorial regime.

IKEDA: I am very much afraid that a drastic dictatorial regime might arise. Still I hope that it will be possible to avoid such a regime by rebuilding modern society. Many different people have tried various ways to deal with the contradictions in social organization. Some attempt to resolve them within the frameworks of the same organizations on which man has relied in the past. Other people regard this approach as nonsense and attempt to form broad movements based on individual independence. In my opinion, true solutions cannot result from the reformation of the system or structure of a given society. It is essential to begin with a reexamination of the values that form the basis of individual human action. First we must try to define the way of life that has most universal value for contemporary man. Then we can take a fresh view of individual attitudes and practical action. In brief, after first having established a universal criterion of value, we must attempt to discover optimum organizations and systems that will contribute to the realization of that value. My idea of the way in which to rebuild modern civilization is to define a philosophy for our times—in philosophy I include religion—and to bring about a revolution in human awareness based on that philosophy. This amounts to a revolution in human beings themselves. Having accomplished this, we can proceed to renovate organizations and society.

128

TOYNBEE: I agree that the sickness of modern society can be cured only by a spiritual revolution in the hearts and minds of human beings. Social maladies cannot be remedied by organizational changes; all attempts at such remedies are superficial. They either reject all organization, or they merely replace one kind of organization with another. The only effective cures are spiritual. Every social organization or institution is based on a philosophy or a religion, and the organization is only as good or as bad as the spiritual basis on which it is founded.

I agree that mankind needs a new spiritual basis. If and when a basis is found to heal our present social sickness, a new and more satisfactory form of society can be built on this new and better spiritual foundation. Short of this, I see no possibility of a cure.

IKEDA: A new spiritual basis is needed, one that is deeply related to the kinds of values held by the people. Human values must never be narrow; they must never be oriented toward satisfying only the aims of individuals, groups, races, nations, or ideologies. Human values must be universal. In the past, narrow values have led to tragedy. As the twentieth century draws to a close, our values must be broad and deep.

The question of the kind of life human beings ought to lead cannot be solved within the framework of accepted social commonplaces and mere common sense. This is true because man himself is not limited to a single society in a single country but is part of a chain connecting humanity, the natural phenomena of the whole earth, and the cosmos. That is to say, man is part, but only a part, of the universe.

Generally speaking, until now a great deal of attention has been paid to man's social aspects; that is, to one facet of his being. But the existence of the cosmic life force that is the original source of all mankind has often been treated lightly. The lack of attention to this issue is all the more regrettable because the question of life force has an important bearing on the basic equality of all living things.

When man is recognized as part of the life force underlying all things, it becomes immediately clear that discrimination directed toward neighbors, other races, other biological beings, nature, or anything in the whole universe is wrong because, in terms of cosmic life force, all existing things are equal and united. The nature of man as part of the life force is a universal issue transcending societies, nations, and races. Man as a mere social being, on the other hand, changes with the historical period, country, and race. In order for human beings to lead lives worthy of their humanity, they must return to a cognizance of their nature as part of the universal life force and must regard this as the basis of all their actions. Once they have adopted this attitude, they will be able to create the sense of value that is urgently needed today. This sense of value will give paramount place to life itself, and it will devote major concern to solving the questions involved with life, for these are the ones that determine the answers to all other questions.

Allegiance to Organizations

IKEDA: Practically everyone belongs to a number of organizations: enterprises, political groups, national groups, or other organized bodies. Enterprises themselves are members of national or international federations, and nations participate in far-reaching defense organizations or other international groups like the United Nations. Within these organizations the individual human being inevitably has rights or duties that in one way or another restrain him. This is a very important issue in connection with the freedom of modern man.

TOYNBEE: The widespread plurality of allegiances to institutions, which characterizes our era, was initiated by a spiritual and political revolution that took place in Western countries in the latter part of the seventeenth century. One of its distinctive features is the so-called annihilation of distance resulting from advances in technology. This in turn means that some of the most important and attractive of the organizations among which mankind's allegiances are distributed are no longer such geographically compact and localized organizations as nations and states.

IKEDA: Yes, today the organizations that are important from both the individual and the general social standpoints are formed in accordance with function rather than on the basis of geographical proximity. These organizations are growing increasingly complicated. Often sophisticated scientific technology is used as a means of controlling the membership of organizations. Under such circumstances, protecting the independence, freedom, and dignity of the individual becomes both more difficult and more pressing. Mankind has often faced problems involving relations with the natural elements, but today, one of the most serious of our problems is relations among human beings. This is the problem of organization.

In the past, in many instances, organizations were monolithic in the sense that political organizations fulfilled economic and religious functions as well.

130

This meant that the person at the top exercised control over all these fields of human experience. Although this state of affairs is undesirable from the standpoint of modern man, in times when humanity had to battle with nature for survival, such organizations may have been inevitable.

TOYNBEE: I think that the most oppressive and therefore the most undesirable institutions have been those of the monolithic type that demand exclusive allegiance from their human participants. Classical examples are states in which governments use political power either to impose on their subjects adherence to an officially established religion or, short of that, to penalize those of their subjects who adhere to other religions. This kind of institutional tyranny has been less common in Eastern Asia and India than it has been at the western end of the Old World since the rise there of religions of the Judaic family. In Christian states, from the fourth to the seventeenth century, and in Muslim states until a more recent time, the established religion was given a monopoly or, at least, a privileged position. Communism in present-day communist states enjoys a similarly privileged position. This is not surprising, since communism emanated from Christianity and is, in truth, a nontheistic Christian heresy.

In contrast to the monistic regimes that formerly prevailed in Christian and Muslim countries, the whole of the noncommunist world today is multi-institutional. Multiinstitutionalism has always prevailed in India and Eastern Asia.

IKEDA: Perhaps this has something to do with the nature of the gods worshipped by different peoples. Religions in the Judaic tradition believe in an absolute god who is omniscient and omnipotent. Under the authority of this one god, all activities are combined into one culture. In contrast, Asian peoples have always thought in terms of polytheistic pantheons of deities, each god in which is responsible for a certain aspect of human acitivity. For instance, farmers have an agricultural god and fisherman a deity devoted to fishing.

TOYNBEE: Certainly India and other Asian countries have always had a plurality of religions and philosophies. The case of China, though somewhat different, nonetheless illustrates your point. It is true that the established philosophy of the Chinese Empire from 136 B.C., during the reign of Han Wu-ti, until 1905, was Confucianism. But this did not prevent either the survival of Taoism or the introduction of Buddhism. Furthermore, the ninth-century Confucian persecutions of Buddhism were briefer and milder than persecutions of alien religions by Christians and Muslims or by the communist states.

IKEDA: In connection with the topic of man's relation to organizations, I might mention a kind of family organization that was probably common among peoples in both the East and the West in the past but that has altered greatly in recent decades, especially in Japan.

In the past, the head of a family exercised virtual life-and-death control over all family members. The feudal lord, who was both head of his own family and, by extension, head of a wider-reaching clan, held his people in such total subjection that he could deprive them of freedom for no more than going against his will or incurring his displeasure. Although such a lord might be compared to a modern autonomous chief, the system that gives to one man powers as great as this now seems grossly unfair. Modern man, especially in the free, advanced nations, enjoys greater freedom from direct force than ever before in history. His basic human rights are guaranteed. The only organization capable of supressing or invalidating these rights is the state. Even in this case, action must be taken in accordance with laws that are established, even if in an indirect way, by the will of the people. The attainment of such freedom is one of mankind's greatest advances.

TOYNBEE: The family and most other organizations today are very different from what they were long ago for an important reason. Today's major organizations are diasporas whose representatives do not account for a majority in any one locality because they are scattered all over the globe.

Before the invention of modern means of communication, diasporas were unusual. First, geographical distances made it difficult to maintain contact among members of a group unless they were concentrated in one place. As a consequence, localized organizations were considered normal in the pre-mechanization age, especially at the western end of the Old World after its conversion to Christianity and Islam. The geographical limitations imposed on organizations bred great intolerance among their participants. Intolerance of the Christian and Muslim kind has now spread to those non-Western countries whose governments have adopted communism.

IKEDA: Do you think it can be said that the state represents a continuation into modern times of localized organizations of the kind prevalent in the pre-mechanization age and of the patriarchal system?

TOYNBEE: Perhaps, but in many respects the diaspora today is more important. I said that in the age before the invention of modern means of communications diasporas were unusual, but they were by no means nonexistent. The classic example of a premechanization-age diaspora is the Jewish one. The Jewish diaspora still exists side by side with other later diasporas that, like the Jewish one, are held together by religious bonds. The Parsees are a case in point. But in modern times a number of worldwide nonreligious diasporas have come into being. Examples of this kind of diaspora include the physicists, physicians, and students of the whole world. For many people today, participation in a diaspora is a more important social fact of life than participation in a local organization. For instance, being a doctor can be considered, from a doctor's standpoint, more significant than being a citizen of a particular state.

The present-day possibility of participating simultaneously in a number of different organizations promotes individual liberty. Allegiances to worldwide diasporas, which cut across allegiances to local organizations, are both safeguards for individual liberty and milestones on the road towards the social unification of mankind on a global scale.

IKEDA: It would seem that the possibility of participating in worldwide diasporas instead of remaining anchored to geographically limited organizations would expand the freedom of the individual human being. But in fact is the individual's liberty enlarged or expanded in modern organizations of the kind you describe?

As a result of belonging simultaneously to a number of different organizations, the human being can be forced into a peculiar situation. For example, a man who belongs to many organizations is forced to abide by the regulations and demands of each. In doing his utmost to live up to the code of one group, he can inadvertently act contrary to the code or purposes of another organization of which he is a member. Of course, at the hands of any organization short of a national state, retaliation incurred by the transgressor as a result of such a mistake would take the form of indirect, psychological coercion. Direct physical coercion is less frequently encountered today than it was under older totalitarian systems. Still, though a third party might not understand his reaction, the person submitted to it will find psychological and indirect pressure as difficult to bear as direct, physical coercion. Indeed, stresses building up from this kind of pressure often lead to psychological disorders. Certainly this is one of the negative aspects of simultaneous participation in many organizations.

TOYNBEE: Yes, without doubt simultaneous allegiances to a number of organizations liberate the individual but at the price of sometimes involving him in conflicts of loyalties. The individual may find himself compelled to decide which of two or more incompatible loyalties is to receive paramount allegiance. The necessity to choose may have damaging psychological effects even when it does not entail penalty or persecution. But the power to choose among a wide range of alternatives is more consonant with human dignity and more conducive to human happiness than constraint to give allegiance to a single organization. Condemnation to exclusive allegiance is bad enough if it is forcibly imposed against the individual's will. It is still worse if the individual voluntarily gives exclusive allegiance to an institution because he is unaware of the existence of alternatives.

IKEDA: I suspect that the heart of the trouble with organizations and conflicting loyalties is to be found in the reactionary nature of groups that refuse to break with their old ways. Organizations come into being as the result of the need to satisfy various needs of the individual. They start and end with the individual, for whose protection they are created. When the individual has the independent ability to judge his own actions in relation to the decisions and administrative policies of an organization, he becomes aware of this point of origin of all organizations. Consequently, each human being must nurture within himself a strong awareness of his own independence.

People who manage organizations must adopt the following attitude. First, instead of viewing the organization as a mechanism, they must think of it as a sophisticated life body made up of human beings, each of whom is a part, no matter how small, of the whole. Each of these parts deserves the same degree of respect as the entire organization. In short, the individual exists within the organization, and the organization within the individual. Managers of institutions must adopt this attitude, and each individual must regard the idea expressed in it as the definition of his relation to the particular organization.

TOYNBEE: I agree emphatically that the raison d'être of organizations of all kinds is the welfare of the individuals who are its participants. To subordinate or sacrifice the welfare of people to the maintenance or aggrandizement of an institution is a reversal of the proper relation between institutions and human beings. This is an evil against which we must be perpetually on guard, because the authorities responsible for the administration of institutions are always likely to be tempted to give first priority to their incidental and contingent duty of maintaining the institution, whereas their proper paramount duty is to ensure that the institution ministers to human welfare. This is the test of any institution's value. If an institution fails to pass this test, it ought to be reformed or abolished. To seek to maintain it unaltered under these circumstances is an antisocial act.

IKEDA: Organizations exist for human beings and not human beings for organizations. Each member of an organization must have the wisdom to judge whether the organization's actions and circumstances agree with its aims. In addition, he must have the power of judgment and application to reform that organization if it ever runs counter to its own purposes.

I believe that the question of human beings and organizations is going to become increasingly important to human happiness. Someone once said that humanity has never been successful in political matters. But if man persists in making failures, human misery may never fade from the earth.

The Establishment and the Generation Gap

IKEDA: I believe that the differing attitudes of the two groups toward the establishment to some extent explain the existence of the gap between the younger and the older generations. Probably all generations agree on the importance of freedom, equality, respect for the individual, and respect for life itself. Although older people value the individual, they tend to favor the establishment. Believing that the establishment protects them and their interests, they are willing to do anything to guard it, even if doing so entails laying down their own lives in sacrifice. For people who feel this way, respect for life and freedom are only ideas, whereas the protection of the establishment is an actual and basic premise of all action.

The diametrically opposed attitude of the younger generations is that the establishment, which ought to protect them, is in fact the greatest threat to their lives and freedom. This viewpoint evolves from the knowledge that the older generations have lost life and liberty for the establishment because they believed it promised security. Youth considers such sacrifices extremely foolish.

The desire of the older generation to protect the establishment arises from the interweaving of its security with their own rights and interests. When the people who are now the older generation were young, they suffered bitter experiences because of their predecessors' authority over them. Now they have power in their own hands, but ironically the younger people who must follow them someday refuse to recognize the validity of the establishment on which the authority of the older generation rests. Young people today are painfully aware of the urgent need to protect humanity. They therefore mock the pride of the establishment and go so far as to try to destroy it entirely. If we are to understand the actions of the young people, we must try to understand the emotions that prompt them.

Their basic objection is to the consciousness of special privileges entertained by many participants in the establishment. Each age has had its own establishment, and each establishment has changed with the passing of time. No matter what the nature of the establishment of the moment, however, those who could not become part of it have been estranged from it. The young today are banded together in resistance against this apparently inevitable estrangement and against the ideas that support it.

One of the manifestations of opposition to the establishment today is the violent wave of so-called student power that has swept most countries. Related to the student movement are the hippies, who attempt to flout the establishment by abandoning some of its traditional symbols: moderate dress, neatness in such things as hair style, and so on. By adopting their own unusual costumes and allowing their hair to grow long, the hippies are trying to set up a counterculture. This so-called subculture is spreading widely.

We cannot know at present how extensive the effects of the youth resistance will be. It seems, however, that ordinary people will continue to find their actions unintelligible. Still, as the emotions supporting the actions of the younger generations become generally assimilated and reach wider realms, the generations dedicated to the support of the establishment are beginning to feel insecure. They even tend to lose confidence in their own acts on behalf of the protection of the establishment.

With the passing of time, the present older generation must give way. It is only a matter of time before the young of today become the wielders of leadership powers.

TOYNBEE: As you point out, there is today a worldwide revolt against the establishment. This is nothing new in itself. In Pharaonic Egypt the establishment that built the Pyramids in the age of the Old Kingdom was overthrown at the fall of the Sixth Dynasty; in the Greco-Roman world the establishment was overthrown in the third century of the Christian era; in France it was overthrown in the French Revolution; in China it was overthrown at the fall of the Ch'ing Dynasty, after having kept its seat in the saddle—or having recovered its seat whenever it temporarily lost it—for a longer period of time than any other establishment of which we have a record, except the Pharaonic Egyptian.

The distinctive feature of the present worldwide reaction against the establishment is that the revolt has mainly taken the form of a war between the rising generation and the middle-aged generation within the establishment itself. It is true that many of the previous revolts against establishments have been led by young members of the establishment itself; it is also true that, in the present worldwide revolt, the people below the poverty line, both in the rich countries and in the poor countries, constitute the majority of the insurgents. But the revolt, en masse, of the rising generation within the establishment is the peculiar feature of the present general disorder.

IKEDA: Of course, there have been struggles between the establishment and the antiestablishment in all ages. But in the past it was usual for the established elements to have the upper hand and for the antiestablishment to be suppressed. When the former became too rotten and inconsistent to be tolerated, it was overthrown by the antiestablishment, and a social transformation was brought about.

As you say, the difference between all past struggles of this kind and the present one is to be found in the nature of the antiestablishment element. The Hebrew and the Germanic peoples who overthrew the Greco-Roman establishment entered that establishment and worked a revolution from within. The Germanic mercenaries who toppled the West Roman Empire had been a major support of the establishment, but they were fundamentally outside it. In the case of the French Revolution, too, the bourgeoisie were part of the *ancien régime*, but they were not part of the privileged establishment made up of the aristocrats and the clergy.

In contrast to these cases, the students who are the major force in the present antiestablishment movement are at the same time the children of the people at the heart of the current establishment. They are what might be called the reserve forces who according to tradition ought to become establishment leaders in the future.

TOYNBEE: I can see several different causes of the present revolt of the rising generation within the establishment itself. First, the middle-aged generation now in power is manifestly failing to manage the world's affairs satisfactorily. Second, owing to the acceleration in the advance of technology, things are changing so fast and are taking such a menacing turn that the rising generation now fears that, before it will have had time to take over, the middle-aged generation may have let mankind be overpowered by some perhaps irremediable catastrophe. Third, the rising generation is alienated from its elders because, in the so-called advanced countries, the establishment's activities and ways of life have lost attractiveness and prestige. There used to be some

137

glamor in the life of Brahmans, samurai, elder statesmen of the Meiji era, Roman senators, and Wall Street tycoons. But there is no glamor in the life of a present-day corporation man, civil servant, or trades union official. The dullness as well as the ineffectiveness of the present-day establishment has provoked its children to revolt against it.

This war between different generations within the establishment is aggravating the dangerousness of a situation that is fearfully dangerous in itself. Therefore we must try both to mend this situation and to end the generation-war that it has provoked.

IKEDA: In order to solve this double danger, we must strive to find a road along which the now sundered generations can walk together.

TOYNBEE: The tension between the generations might be mitigated if the young could be made to see that no generation ever has, or has had, a free hand and that each generation, when it comes into power in its turn, finds that its freedom of action is limited by karma. The rising generation despises and detests the middle-aged generation even more for its apparent insincerity and hypocrisy than for its obvious ineffectiveness and dullness. No doubt the middle-aged generation in the establishment is insincere and hypocritical to some extent, but it is almost certainly less so than it seems to be. While it may genuinely wish to carry out some of the radical reforms that the rising generation is demanding, it may also be finding—without succeeding in explaining this articulately—that it is being handicapped by its karma heritage and that it is unable to modify this heritage by its own efforts sufficiently to make changes in the state of the world that it is wanting and trying to make bona fide.

IKEDA: Your example points up the weakness and fragility of humanity in the face of karma and destiny. The young people of the antiestablishment faction, too, must think about these things. But they seem convinced that they can manage anything by means of reasoning powers and high ideals. Such an attitude may be one of the virtues of youth; for people in positions of authority and responsibility, the problem of irrevocable fate always arises. The most idealistic of young people find that actuality cannot be dealt with successfully by means of ideals and reason alone. In the life of each individual lurk karma and greed. In the lives of all persons engaged in creating any society are unfathomable destinies, all of which overlap and interweave to form reality. Once a person has stepped into this complicated set of circumstances, it is difficult to advance without losing sight of the light of ideals. The impor-

tant premise for bridging the generation gap is for all concerned to understand themselves and others as human beings burdened with the same kinds
of karma-created faults and weaknesses.

TOYNBEE: The cleavage between the establishment and the rest of mankind
is part of our karma heritage. Will we be able to modify our karma to the
extent of closing this social gap that opened at the dawn of civilization, at
least five thousand years ago? Will we succeed in abolishing the establishment
by merging it in the mass of mankind? I agree that this must be our objective,
because I agree that the privileges of the establishment are irreconcilable with
the dignity of man and that, in the conflict of interests between the establishment and humanity, we ought to give humanity precedence. This is right in
itself, and it is also the necessary condition for making peace between the
warring generations. However, history shows that this is a difficult enterprise.
The Pharaonic Egyptian establishment, like its Chinese counterpart, was
repeatedly reinstated after having been repeatedly deposed. The French and
Russian revolutions deposed old establishments only to open the way for the
installation of new ones.

IKEDA: The important thing in this connection, of course, is knowing how to
abolish the karmic, or destined, evil that exists within man. Why do the people
in power within an establishment monopolize authority and trample on
human dignity? Why does an establishment that came into being for the
sake of preserving human happiness and peace end up by bringing humanity
nothing but misery and by threatening peace? I am convinced that the reason
why all overthrowals of old establishments in history have inevitably resulted
in the creation of new establishments is that people have been unable to eradi-
cate the basic evil karma within themselves. But is karma unalterable as has
sometimes been argued?

The teachings of Nichiren Daishōnin hold that by coming directly to terms
with karma and with human nature, it becomes possible to change both. The
dignity of human life lies in the possibility of developing and changing
karma.

If the older and the younger generations adopt as a starting point the recognition of the dignity of humanity in this sense, I am confident a way would
open for reunion. This in turn would lead to reconstruction of the establishment and the educational system, and the creation of a whole new order.
To this end, all notions of sacrificing people for the good of the establishment
must be abandoned. In more concrete terms, all nations must give up the right
of belligerence and do away with military conscription. It goes without saying

that no other social organization can be permitted to have authority that infringes on or threatens respect for humanity or safety of life.

Although, given present world conditions, carrying out this kind of program is by no means easy, if the dignity of life is to be recognized ethically, what I have outlined is a natural course to follow. It all depends on whether human beings revolutionize their awareness. Whether they do this depends in turn on the possession of religious ideals to guide their actions and energy to carry out their projects.

TOYNBEE: I think that, basically at any rate, we are in agreement. We shall not truly succeed in solving the establishment question if we achieve no more than the redistribution of mankind's surplus product on an equitable differential scale. I share your opinion that recognition of the dignity of man is essential. But the dignity of man requires that all professions shall become liberal professions. We have to abolish both conveyor-belt man and organization man. It ought to be made possible for everyone to earn his living by doing work that is of intrinsic value and that is felt to be such by the worker himself. At present, most people do their work in order to earn the maximum remuneration and not for the sake of the value of the work itself. The profit motive ought no longer to be given top priority. But this most desirable change of motivation can be brought about only by a change of heart, and this most desirable change of heart can be brought about only by an inward spiritual change. This change has to be made at the religious level, not at the economic level, and it has to be made by every human being individually.

Neutrality of the Mass Media

IKEDA: Mass communications influence many fields of contemporary society and to an extent characterize our age. Radio waves instantaneously transmit news of happenings in one country to most of the world, and television makes this news more vivid by bringing visual images of occurrences into private homes.

TOYNBEE: Modern technology has enormously extended the scale on which the public can be reached instantaneously by direct visual and auditory means of communication. In the past, a public speaker was not equipped with loudspeakers, nor could he broadcast his voice and image by radio and by television. Therefore the human body's natural capacity limited his audience to the number of people who could assemble close enough to him to be able to hear and see him simultaneously. The Greek philosopher Aristotle estimated this number to be not more than five thousand, and accordingly he held that the maximum size of the enfranchised citizen body ought to be no more than five thousand in a state in which the form of government is direct democracy.

By contrast, radio and television broadcasts can be picked up instantaneously by anyone throughout the world. Newspapers and books take longer to distribute, even if they are dispatched by air. Even then, they are accessible only to the literate portion of mankind, and, although in some countries—Japan, New Zealand, Germany—nearly 100 percent of the population is literate, a majority of the population of the whole world is still illiterate. Inevitably the printed word has less influence than the spoken word and the visible images that are accessible to the illiterate majority and that can be conveyed instantaneously. This is unfortunate. What is heard through the radio, and what is heard and seen on the television screen, is ephemeral. It vanishes as swiftly as it is transmitted; the listener's and viewer's only record of it is in his memory, a natural faculty that is notoriously unreliable.

IKEDA: Since the influence of mass communications is vast, they are constantly accompanied by the danger that they may become tools for manipulating the people. Furthermore, even if such manipulation is unconscious, mass communications nonetheless contribute to the formation of world views and to the slanting of those views in one direction or another.

TOYNBEE: The influence of mass-communications media is certainly vast, and the people who control these media can use them for manipulating their public. This power of manipulation is not a monopoly of the conscious level of the psyche of the listener or viewer himself. The operators of the media can make their message penetrate through the conscious surface of the psyche to subconscious depths. They can manipulate their public's subconscious for their own purposes. In the United States, some years ago, private business concerns that had bought radio and television time for advertizing their goods or services used the media for addressing not the conscious surface but the subconscious levels of the psyche as a strategy for making the public purchase their wares involuntarily. This manoeuver rightly evoked vigorous protests. In France under President de Gaulle's regime, the opposition was likewise right in complaining of the government's monopoly of the use of the media of instantaneous mass communication. The opposition maintained that this was an illegitimate exercise of governmental power.

IKEDA: The importance of neutrality in these media is apparent, but the problem of establishing such neutrality is by no means easy. Take for example a newspaper picture of victims in the Vietnam War. In fact, the people shown in the objective photograph may be neither Vietnamese from the South nor members of the Northern Viet Cong. It all depends on what the captions say; they can slant the picture and the mind of the reader in either way.

Or if the television camera, trained on a clash between radical students and the police, shows the violent attack of a wild-eyed student virtually leaping from the camera into the living room, the viewer is likely to look critically on these young people. If, however, the camera shows the police using weapons to quell the students, sympathy will probably flow in the other direction. Since it is impossible to flash two pictures at once into the viewer's living room, in such cases neutrality in the strictest sense is impossible. Still I believe that neutrality is a vital condition that we ought to require of mass communications.

But in what does maintaining neutrality consist? It is very difficult to obtain true neutrality by adding the right half to the left half of an issue and cutting the resultant sum down the middle. Politics frequently involve questions of neutrality, but in these instances there is a great difference between the strengths of government power holders and of the people, for as long as the government maintains a firm grip on power, it has an overwhelming edge. Consequently, if the mass media assume a position halfway between the people and the government, though this seems neutral, in effect it is not. We must keep this point in mind when thinking about true neutrality, which is at best a vague concept, usually varying with the case of the moment.

TOYNBEE: I agree emphatically that this enormous new power to influence people, which has been created by modern technology, ought to be employed neutrally. But we need to clarify the meaning of neutrality and to find a governing body that will be both willing and free to employ the media in the neutral way that is desired.

Neutrality is fairly easy to define when, for instance, it is a question of apportioning the use of the media for political propaganda at election time in a democratically governed country. Time should be apportioned between the competing political parties in proportion to their numerical strength. The financial charge for the allotted time should be proportionate to the respective sizes of the several parties' campaign funds (the figures should be disclosed and be verified). These apportionments should be made not by the government of the day and not by any political organization but by the authority that has been empowered to administer the media.

142

However, the distinction between good and bad and between right and wrong is made individually by every human being and collectively by every human community. There is extreme disagreement about what particular things are good and bad, and what particular actions are right and wrong. But there is unanimous agreement in drawing the intellectual distinction between the two categories and in holding that it is our moral duty to take sides with what we deem to be right and good, against what we deem to be wrong and bad. These facts raise the question whether it is right, and indeed whether it is possible, to be neutral between right and wrong or between good and bad.

For instance, in the moral codes of most societies, political tyranny, personal dishonesty, the use of violence by private persons in a country's domestic life, and pornography are stigmatized as bad and wrong, though the precise definition of these evils will vary. There are also practices and institutions whose moral status is controversial, even among the members of one and the same society. Examples are war, capital punishment, suicide, homosexuality. Is neutrality right or possible between what is good and bad and between what is right and wrong in the judgment of an individual or of a community?

I myself believe that, in this situation, neutrality is not possible and that, if it were possible, it would not be right. To try to be neutral between what one deems to be right and what one deems to be wrong is tantamount to taking sides with what one deems to be wrong, since this would be a breach of one's moral duty to take sides with what one deems to be right.

IKEDA: In moral matters, as you say, neutrality is impossible between issues of right and wrong, but practically speaking, I am forced to insist that the neutrality of the mass media is essential. As a guideline for defining this kind of practical neutrality, I might offer this suggestion. The mass communications media must consistently protect the rights of the people and deliver their news from the viewpoint of respect for life.

TOYNBEE: Subject to the important and substantial proviso that neutrality is impossible between right and wrong, I agree that the mass media ought to be used neutrally. Indeed, I would go so far as to suggest that the authority that administers the media ought to give to people whom this authority deems to be morally in the wrong an opportunity for stating their case, though this without concealing the fact that the authority's own judgment on these people is adverse.

But how are we to recruit the members of an authority that is to be neutral? And how are we to ensure that a neutral-minded authority will be free to

administer the media neutrally in practice? I do not think that either appoint-
ment by the government or election by the electorate is likely to produce a
neutral-minded governing body for the mass media. I suggest that this body's
members should be selected on the basis of the merit of individuals. But what
means can we find of financing the administration of the mass media without
exposing the governing body to financial pressure? On this criterion, we must
reject, as sources for this body's revenue, both tax money allocated by the
political public authorities and fees for advertizing paid by private business
concerns. An alternative is to charge a fee for listening licenses and viewing
licenses. This would limit the use of the media to people who can afford to
pay the fee. However, in any case the mass media can be used only by people
who can afford to buy or hire the receiving apparatus. Compared to the cost
of this indispensable apparatus, the cost of a licensing fee on a sufficient scale
to pay for the service would be small.

Restrictions on Freedom of the Press

IKEDA: In modern constitutional states, freedom of expression, including
freedom of speech and freedom of the press, is recognized, but issues concerning the effects of verbal and printed statements on the public inevitably give
rise to problems of limitations. Generally accepted restrictions on freedom of
expression concern the following fields: public morals, state secrets, individual
personalities. The current trend in advanced Western countries to liberalize
controls on pornography is well under way. Some people are of the opinion
that this tendency is undesirable from the standpoint of juvenile education,
but in my view their apprehension cannot be justified. I can by no means condone the use of political pressures in attempts to control matters of this kind.
By nature, man tends to become more curious about things kept in strict
secret. Instead of hiding sex, we ought to help young people obtain a correct
view of it.

TOYNBEE: Concealment may do no harm in some cases, but it cannot do
any good. For instance, I was brought up in a time when, in English middle-
class families, sex was regarded as so embarrassing that children were told
nothing about it. When I was ten or twelve years old, my father made an
attempt at explaining the sex act to me, but his embarrassment was so great
that his explanation was very difficult for me to understand. Later one of my
school masters tried to clarify things for me, but he had no more success than

144

my father because he was just as shy about the subject. Before I got married, I went to a doctor in England and asked him to help me; oddly enough, even this professional man found frank talk on the matter too much and, instead of giving me an explanation, lent me a textbook with diagrams. This was my premarital sexual education, and it was absurd. I did not develop a taste for pornography as a consequence of these early experiences, but I can see how secretiveness might lead people to do so. I agree, fully, that if sex is talked about openly it will lose some of its titillating appeal and will take its natural place in human life.

IKEDA: True freedom means freedom to reject pornography as well as freedom to accept it. In other words, I do not adopt a stand of completely unrestricted license for pornography, but I do insist that restrictions must be limited to conformity with the basic principle of freedom of choice.

Now let us turn for a moment to the issue of restrictions on freedom of expression in connection with what are generally called state secrets. It is undesirable, even dangerous, for states to engage in confidential enterprises that must be kept secret from the people and from other nations. The state ought to be a public utility; therefore, I think that it must not have secrets under any circumstances. In fact, the people must explode national secrets and courageously and watchfully see to it that governments do not lead them along dangerous paths.

TOYNBEE: State secrets are an index of the barbarousness of politics, particularly international politics. In the course of the two world wars, I spent about a decade as a temporary government servant, working at times with secret documents. I intensely disliked the secrecy of this work. The motive for secrecy in state matters is the intention to injure the governments and peoples of other states and the fear of being injured by them. When I was working temporarily in the Foreign Office, each official was given a bunch of keys for locking and unlocking the boxes in which secret documents were carried from place to place. Because I did not want to spend the rest of my life working with papers that had to remain hidden, I refused each time when, at the end of the war, I was invited to remain permanently in government service.

Openness is one of the reasons why modern science has been able to make great progress. Until the discovery of a way to split the atom and of a way to harness nuclear energy, scientific research and discoveries were completely open. Everything new was published, and everyone exchanged information with everyone else. Scientists knew no political barriers. Scientific journals were naturally published in many languages; any scientific library had all journals, and all were available to everyone. Since the invention of atomic weapons, however, nuclear science, at any rate, has become subject to the wills of governments and to the rules of secrecy of government services. I fear that this may happen in other branches of science as well. We must resist this danger and we must fight to recover the freedom of science. In this realm and in others there ought to be no state secrets.

Of course, a man who has sworn to keep state secrets and then accepts bribes to betray them has committed an act that is morally wrong from the personal standpoint. But it seems to me that in Britain punishments for such acts are disproportionate to their gravity. We have done away with the death penalty in Britain. Murder is punishable by life imprisonment, though sometimes the term of the sentence is shortened. A man who sells state secrets is liable to the same punishment, and it may even turn out that he is more severely punished than a murderer who is given time off for good behavior.

IKEDA: That kind of disproportionate punishment is wrong, especially in the light of my belief that state secrets ought not to exist in the first place.

The one field of the three in which I do insist on restrictions on freedom of expression—press, and other—is that of infringement on the privacy of the individual. There is no way to restrict gossip, but the individual must have the right to protest against, and legally to suspend publication of, printed matter containing unconfirmed rumors involving him.

TOYNBEE: Yes, private life ought to be protected from improper publicity. In 1939, my eldest son committed suicide. Immediately after the news was published, we were surrounded by reporters who pestered us without stopping. My wife and I begged them to go away, but they insisted that if they did not get the story they would lose their jobs. When we decided to talk to them, they were embarrassed and we were distressed. This is one of the bad effects of the relentless pursuit of sensational news.

Not long ago, there was a running fight between a famous woman and a photographer who was apparently persecuting her. The photographer argued that he had a right to earn a living by following the woman and her children and tormenting them by taking pictures. She claimed, and quite rightly, that her private life is her own. I agreed with her and thought that she ought to have been protected. No photographer should have the right to harass other people in order to make money for himself. In cases like this, the freedom of the press ought to be subjected to restrictions.

Abolition of the Death Penalty

IKEDA: Unfortunately the death penalty is still in effect in Japan and in most other countries. I should be very interested to hear how the British abolished it.

TOYNBEE: I am very glad that the death penalty has been abolished in Britain. But the abolition is not surprising. Long before this step was taken, there had been a tacit understanding in Britain between police and criminals that both parties should refrain not merely from using arms but even from carrying them. Criminals were not persuaded to give up committing crimes, such as robbery, but they were willing to commit their crimes without using physical violence, so long as the police were willing to refrain from using violence against the criminals. The common purpose was to keep violence to a minimum. Logically, the abolition of the death penalty ought to have been a big further step along this humane road; the response on the criminals' part ought to have been the abolition of murder.

Unhappily, in Britain, the abolition of the death penalty has been followed by the murdering of policemen who have been trying to arrest criminals, as is their duty. Now that the death penalty has been abolished, a criminal may calculate that, if the police capture him, he is going to be imprisoned for a long term if the crime that he has committed is a serious one. Supposing that he now murders a policeman and is then captured, the worst that can happen to him is that he will be imprisoned for a still longer term. On the other hand, if he murders a policeman who is on the point of capturing him, he may escape capture entirely. The criminal is therefore tempted to murder the police. In this new situation, the task of the police has become more dangerous; therefore, the police have been suggesting that the death penalty ought to be reimposed as the punishment for murder in cases in which the victim is a policeman performing his duty.

IKEDA: Of course, I can sympathize with the British police, but, as events in other countries prove, the reinstitution of the death penalty will not put a stop to the murdering of policemen. My reason for insisting that the death penalty ought to be abolished everywhere is based on Buddhist respect for the dignity of life. People advocating the abolition of the death penalty usually advance one of two ideas as substantiation of the validity of their position: one man has no right to judge and execute another; abolition of the death penalty will not increase the number of crimes committed. Those in favor of the extreme punishment are adamant that the death penalty reduces the number of crimes perpetrated. Whether it has this effect or not, the concept

147

of the death penalty involves the taking of life as a warning to other people or as a retaliation for crime. But one retaliation, by inevitably leading to another, sets in motion a course of wicked acts. I feel that life, as an absolute entity worthy of the profoundest respect, must never be treated as a means of achieving anything other than life itself. The dignity of life is an end in itself; therefore, when social restraint is necessary, it is certainly better to devise a method that does not tamper with life. The use of the death penalty as a warning manifests a regrettable tendency that has long plagued human society and that seems to be on the increase today. That tendency is the habit of undervaluing life.

War is one of the major causes of the undervaluing of life. In almost all cases, wars are waged by states acting in their own interests. Human life is regarded as no more than a means to the end of victory and, as such, is thought to be expendable. No crime committed by man is as heinous as this. As long as this monster crime is permitted to go unchecked, other human crimes will continue on a widening and deepening scale.

TOYNBEE: I hope the death penalty will be abolished in all countries for the following two cogent reasons. No human being has a moral right to deprive another human being of his life. As you insist, the abolition of the death penalty requires the simultaneous abolition of war. It is illogical to hold that we have no right to put to death, by the least inhumane means possible, a single human being who has committed some grave crime, like murder, against individual fellow human beings and against human society, yet at the same time to consider that, in war, it is legitimate to kill and wound countless human beings by the most cruel and barbarous means. Soldiers have committed no offense against their fellow human beings until they have been compelled, at the risk of losing their own lives, to try to kill so-called enemy soldiers, against whom they have no personal grievance. War not only murders people, it compels people to become murderers, and it causes these two crimes not just individually but en masse.

The second cogent reason for abolishing the death penalty and war is that killing is irrevocable. So long as a human being is alive, he has the possibility of reforming himself morally, even if he has been a criminal whose crimes have been serious and frequent.

IKEDA: I agree that abolishing the death penalty ought to be accompanied by the simultaneous abolition of war. If this should prove temporarily impossible, at least nuclear warfare must be forbidden. If I were willing, even hypothetically, to entertain the enforcement of the death penalty—and I am not—no one would be as justly repaid with such punishment as those who might bring about a nuclear war. I am certainly not condoning the death penalty; I am merely saying that all mankind must take a firm attitude toward the annihilation of the greatest crime—that of murder by means of nuclear weapons—by cutting it off at the very roots.

I greet the current worldwide groping for ways to abolish the death penalty with happiness, but I should like to see mankind go one step further and create a society in which the penalty would be unnecessary because no serious crimes would be committed. For the sake of society, we must give thought to halting the trend to undervalue life. At the same time, we must determine practical attitudes to take toward crime. As one measure, I advocate patiently attempting to awaken the conscience of people who commit crimes. In that way it would be possible to convince them of the wrong they have done. Under no circumstances, however, ought states to be allowed to impose the death penalty, for in executing this punishment, the state itself becomes a murderer. As I have mentioned earlier, when social punishment of some kind is absolutely necessary, a recourse other than the death penalty must be found.

TOYNBEE: In a country in which the death penalty has been abolished, the alternative cannot be to give a convicted criminal the amount of personal freedom to which fellow citizens who have no criminal record are legally, as well as morally, entitled. If we hold that a murderer has a right to remain alive, we must also hold that his noncriminal neighbors have a right to be protected against the risk of being murdered by him. A convicted murderer must therefore be kept imprisoned unless and until it is guessed—and this can be only a guess, never a certainty—that, if set free, he will no longer be a danger to other people. The purpose of imprisonment ought not to be vindictive; it ought to be strictly precautionary and, beyond this negative aim, positively educative and ameliorative. A prison ought, as far as possible, to be a school in which a criminal is taught how to reform himself. But how far is this possible? Education is effective in proportion to the degree of its voluntariness. In education, as in other relations between people, compulsion tends to arouse resistance. A school that is a prison is a school in which compulsion and the resentment aroused by compulsion are at a maximum both objectively and in the consciousness of the prisoner himself.

IKEDA: Only educators with extraordinary enthusiasm and devotion to their task and their charges will be able to overcome these admittedly great obstacles in the path of effective prison education. I am in agreement with your interpretation of corrective penal systems and with your hope that the death penalty be abolished in all countries, but I am certain that a spirit of religious mercy will have to spread over the entire world before this can happen. Only then will mankind become aware of the true meaning of the gravity of life; only then will he be awakened to the dignity of life.

Suicide and Euthanasia

IKEDA: Do you agree that to take one's own life is contrary to the basic dignity of life?

TOYNBEE: I think that to deprive another of life is the greatest evil. The decision whether or not to terminate one's own life must, in my view, be left to the well-considered judgment of the individual. Similarly, whether or not to approve of suicide must depend on the particular circumstances of the case at hand.

If a person is not *compos mentis,* I think that he should be prevented from committing suicide, if prevention is possible. Even if he is *compos mentis,* I think he should be prevented, if possible, if he appears to be acting on impulse in reaction to some difficulty that makes life seem unbearable at the moment but that, in other people's judgment, could be solved if the man is prevented from putting an end to his life. The irrevocability of death tells in favor of trying to prevent the commission of suicide, as it tells in favor of refraining from imposing the death penalty and in favor of abolishing war. The deliberate cutting short of one's life, either by oneself or by one's fellow men, is undesirable in all cases in which it is true that "while there is life there is hope."

There are, however, cases in which there is no longer any hope, though there is still life. In such instances, when the person is *compos mentis,* I hold that a well-considered wish to die ought not to be thwarted. If a person in this situation asks for euthanasia, I hold that his request ought to be granted. If he prefers to commit suicide, I hold, most decidedly, that no attempt ought to be made to prevent him.

IKEDA: I consider pleasure and pain complementary in the logical sense and on a par in the ethical sense. I believe that people must be admonished against sacrificing life for the sake of pleasure (as sometimes occurs in cases of indulgence in narcotics) and against sacrificing life for the sake of escape from pain.

TOYNBEE: I define euthanasia as the killing of a human being not in order to punish him and not in order to protect other people against him but as an act of mercy for him. A person who is *compos mentis* may wish to die and may ask to be put to death because he is finding it unbearable to remain alive; bereavement or incapacitation may have made life intolerable, or he may feel that it is incompatible with his own human dignity to be a burden on other people and perhaps to be taking for himself skilled medical attention and nursing that, in his opinion, might be better used for the benefit of other patients. Ought this person's request to be put to death be rejected? I believe that it ought not to be. I believe that to refuse his request in these circumstances is a violation of the human dignity to which he has a sacred right.

The question is more difficult in the case of a person who is suffering unbearably, physically or mentally or both, but is not *compos mentis*. In this case, the decision has to be taken for the patient by other people: the medical profession, the government, the patient's friends and relatives. In this situation, we would not hesitate to put a nonhuman animal out of its misery. Does not a human being have the same right? If we hesitate to say that he has, it is because we regard the killing of a human being as a more serious act than the killing of a nonhuman animal. But is not this hesitation cowardly and blameworthy if the human patient is suffering unbearably and if there is no prospect of a cure, or even of alleviation?

If, in these circumstances, we hesitate to kill, need we also hesitate to refrain from keeping the patient alive? Recently, medical science has discovered previously unknown ways of keeping mortally sick people alive physically. Is it not a misuse of this new-found medical skill to employ it for prolonging lives whose prolongation seems not merciful but unmerciful? In these circumstances, it is surely reasonable to let the patient die. Yet, if we let someone die when we have the power to keep him alive, is this ethically tantamount to putting him to death?

The question whether euthanasia is justified in the case of persons who are not *compos mentis* and who are therefore not capable of either asking for it or declining it is so difficult that I believe that the least objectionable solution is for the decision to be taken ad hoc, in each individual case, by a panel of responsible persons. The composition of such panels would have to be prescribed by law, but the law ought not to lay down in advance the decisions that a panel appointed in accordance with the law shall take.

IKEDA: If we grant that euthanasia ought to be approved under certain conditions, your suggestion for a way to deal with it is convincing. Nevertheless, I cannot condone the shortening of life by physical, chemical, or any other external means. I do agree, however, that it is unnecessary to waste efforts on keeping alive hopelessly ill people—the so-called human vegetables whose brains no longer function or whose bodies cannot take in nourishment unaided—even though modern science has the ability to prolong such lives even when there is no longer a possibility of effective treatment. I agree with you on this point because I feel that a human being who has reached such a condition is no longer functioning as a human being and in a sense is dead already.

In criticizing euthanasia, I am not thinking of truly hopeless people but of persons who, though in virtually unbearable suffering at the time, do have a period of life left to them, a period in which they can possibly achieve something worthwhile or maybe even brilliant. The person who is suffering may not see this possibility, and it is the duty of those around him to point it out to him as convincingly as possible. While recognizing that freedom to assist another to escape unbearable pain by taking his life or to seek death for oneself is a logical conclusion of humanistic thought, I am afraid that, should this idea be regarded with less than maximum caution, it could degenerate into the kind of undervaluing of life that I have often condemned.

For example, if people come to regard euthanasia as totally acceptable, is it not possible that the elderly who, as a result of illness, are bedridden and dependent on the care of others for whom they can no longer do anything in return might feel guilty about simply remaining alive? In cases of this kind, recognizing euthanasia as born of a spirit of mercy might deprive all society of compassion.

I believe that whatever means are available ought to be applied in attempts to lessen suffering. Maximum efforts must be made to this end. But human agencies must not be allowed to affect the inherent right of life itself to survive.

Pleasure and pain have no intrinsic dignity, whereas life has a dignity for which there is no equivalent. Consequently, no pleasure and no pain can weigh as much in the scales of judgment as the dignity of life.

TOYNBEE: But if, as you suggest, controls must be imposed on the human desire to end life under apparently impossible conditions, ought those controls to be official? In Britain at present, even in these circumstances, it is possible to commit suicide only surreptitiously, by stealth. This seems to me to be inhumane and also to be a violation of human dignity. Supposing that I myself had taken a well-considered decision to commit suicide, I should certainly feel it outrageous that I should be able to do this only by deliberately deceiving other people.

I had two friends who did commit suicide by a well-considered decision that seemed to them, and seems to me, to have been ethically right. One of these friends was an artist who had had a stroke. She knew that she would never be able to practice her art again and that, for as long as she went on living, she would have to be nursed. Before her stroke, she was giving something of positive value to the world in the works of art that she was creating. After her stroke, she was involuntarily taking much and giving nothing in return. Feeling this to be incompatible with her dignity as a human being, she put an end to a life that, in her opinion, had changed from a plus value to a minus value for herself and for other people. My other friend was a writer who was being overtaken by incurable blindness.

Both these friends had to make sure that they would be able to contrive to commit suicide without being detected and prevented. Both were successful, but the need to avoid being hindered was an aggravation of a tragic situation. I feel that this aggravation of their plight was an unjustifiable additional affliction for them. In cases such as these two, I hold that suicide is legitimate and that to put obstacles in the way of it is very wrong.

IKEDA: The cases of your friends arouse sympathy, but I still insist that one must regard one's own life with the same maximum respect that one must give the life of another person. Talents and the ability to reason are only a part, not all, of the total entity of life. To argue that once a person's abilities have failed, he can no longer live in a meaningful way is to put too narrow an interpretation on life itself. Should this attitude become widely accepted, talentless people might come to be considered unworthy of living. As you say, on ethical grounds, it may not be praiseworthy to cling to life when one is a burden on others. Nevertheless, I doubt that even people who have fallen into this extremely unhappy situation should choose death at once.

Undeniably some people attempt to end suffering and to find freedom by the willful decision to end life. But is whatever they attain in this way true freedom? When life runs contrary to the will of the individual and becomes bondage, the freedom to overcome tribulation seems to vanish. All that is left is the so-called freedom of deciding whether, as Hamlet says, "to be or not to be." Under these circumstances, choosing death is flying from the "slings and arrows of outrageous fortune" or, as it appears to me, allowing oneself to be washed away by fate.

Whether to accept or reject suicide and euthanasia depends ultimately on the individual's broad view of religion—or of life and death. For example, in the Japan of the past, when the honor of one's name was held in paramount esteem, samurai felt justified—sometimes impelled—to commit hara-kiri to cleanse their names of disgrace. In contrast, in England and other

Christian countries, religious teachings forbade suicide (while, ironically, establishing no serious restrictions against killing in duels for the sake of clearing an individual's honor). Earlier you said that, in contemporary Britain, suicide must be committed by stealth. I suspect that there is a religious element in the social conditions necessitating secrecy in taking one's life.

TOYNBEE: There is, in Britain, a historical reason why suicide is discountenanced and is made humiliatingly and cruelly difficult. According to Christian doctrine, a human being who commits suicide is committing an offense against God. He is trespassing on God's prerogative. God alone has the right to decree the moment at which a human being is to die.

I do not believe in the existence of a humanlike God. If I did believe that he existed, I should have no means of knowing what prerogatives in the realm of human affairs he chooses to keep in his own hands. I should, however, assume that God's hypothetical regulations are consistent with each other. I should therefore assume that if God forbids a human being to kill himself, he forbids him, *a fortiori*, to kill other people whether by murder or in war or by imposing the death penalty for crimes. Conversely, I should assume that God also forbids medical aid and nursing. The prolongation of life by human action, as well as the cutting short of life by human action, would be an offense against God if it were true that God alone has the right to decree the length of time for which a human being is to live.

IKEDA: The Buddhist point of view is quite different. To our way of thinking, it is the greater life force that deserves reverence and not an anthropomorphic deity. Consequently, in keeping with the dignity of life, it is wrong for a person to kill, but it is good to prolong life for whatever period is possible as long as this action does not involve sacrifice on the part of other human beings. Am I correct in assuming that Christians, to an extent at any rate, agree that it is wrong to take life—no matter whose—but not wrong to prolong life?

TOYNBEE: Yes, but in general, Christian practice has been inconsistent with Christian theory. A person who has committed suicide is not allowed to be buried in the consecrated ground adjoining a Christian church. On the other hand, a soldier who has been killed in the act of trying to kill enemy soldiers is buried with Christian rites and will perhaps have a monument erected in his honor. Christians honor the medical profession. (Christian Scientists are unique among Christians in forbidding their adherents to receive medical aid.)

I myself was brought up as a Christian, but I was educated in pre-Christian

154

Greek and Roman literature and history, and my non-Christian education has had more influence on me than my ancestral Christian religion. The pre-Christian Greeks and Romans had no taboo against committing suicide. They held that freedom to commit suicide was one of the basic human rights. They also held that there were situations in which suicide was the only course that was consistent with the preservation of a person's human dignity, and people who committed suicide in these circumstances were highly honored. For instance, the Greek philosopher Democritus was honored not only for his intellectual achievements—he was the father of the atomic theory of the structure of matter—but also for his refusal to go on living when he had become aware that his mental powers were failing. Democritus is said to have committed suicide by deliberately starving himself to death. No one attempted to keep him alive by feeding him forcibly. Cato, one of Julius Caesar's political opponents, committed suicide rather than fall under Caesar's unconstitutional and dictatorial rule, imposed by military force. Cato had been an unpractical and unsuccessful politician, but, thanks to the glory that he won by committing suicide for the sake of his human dignity, he became posthumously, for the next century and a half, the most formidable opponent of the Caesarean autocratic Roman imperial regime.

Many modern Westerners, including me, have supposed that the pre-Christian Greeks' and Romans' approbation of suicide for the sake of maintaining human dignity has also been the attitude towards suicide in India and Eastern Asia in all ages. I have seen it stated that under the imperial regime in China, an official censor who felt duty-bound to criticize the reigning emperor would also feel an obligation to follow this by committing suicide. I thought that the Forty-seven Ronin were admired in Japan and that the Southern Buddhist monks who have burnt themselves to death in South Vietnam during the American occupation have had the same kind of posthumous influence as Cato. Is my impression mistaken because of ignorance?

IKEDA: As you say, from ancient times in China and Japan suicide has been relatively common and has exerted a considerable influence on the attitudes of the peoples. Especially in Japan when the code of the samurai held sway, suicide was praised as part of an elevated morality. Today, the Japanese legal code prescribes penalties for assisting in suicide but none for suicide or suicide attempts. Many examples of euthanasia, too, could probably be cited. In the Meiji period, a leading novelist named Ogai Mori, who was also a doctor, wrote a novel about a man considered a criminal for having assisted in euthanasia.

I think that we might find an ideological reason—apart from political considerations—in the self-immolation of the Vietnamese monks. I suspect that the Southern Buddhist doctrine that the flesh is fundamentally unclean may have influenced these men to some extent.

Nevertheless, Northern Buddhism asserts that all life is a precious vessel containing the Buddha nature or the Buddha world. In other words, life itself is of value without equivalent, and above this value it is doubly precious because the Buddha nature is latent in it. The Buddha world may be briefly outlined in the following ways. It is the wisdom that has determined the ultimate nature of the universe and of life force. It is the entity containing the boundless life force, which is one with individualized life. It is the wellspring of all true happiness. Though Buddhist literature contains nothing specifically prohibiting suicide and euthanasia, on the basis of Buddhist belief in the dignity of life it cannot be considered to condone it. In order to discuss whether these acts are justified, we are forced to approach the question by reasoning from Buddhist teachings.

Buddhism presupposes that life exists throughout past, present, and future, as does karma. Suffering does not end with death but, incorporated in karma, continues to exist even after death. Karma will never alter unless the individual changes it by his own efforts. This Buddhist concept evidently removes all grounds for justification of euthanasia since the suffering that inspires a longing for death does not end with death. I disapprove of suicide on the grounds that, according to the Buddhist principle, all life is a vessel embracing the most valuable of treasures.

It is of course impossible to provide objective proof of the uninterrupted continuity of life. Consequently, attitudes toward euthanasia and suicide from this objectively unverifiable premise must be a matter of faith. But as long as human life is considered invaluable and irreplaceable, deliberate action to cut it short must not be pardoned.

TOYNBEE: The Greeks and Romans, like the Chinese and Japanese, sanctioned suicide and euthanasia; the two are combined in hara-kiri, in which sadistic self-disembowelment is followed immediately by merciful decapitation. You maintain that the East Asian and pre-Christian West Eurasian attitude is incompatible with the principles of Buddhism, as it is with the principles of Christianity.

My Hellenic education has prevailed over my Christian education. Consequently, I feel that suicide and euthanasia are fundamental and indispensable human rights. I feel that a human being's human dignity is violated by other people when he is kept alive by them against his will, in accordance with principles in which these other people believe but in which the person primarily concerned perhaps does not believe. I also hold that a human being is violating his own dignity if he fails to commit suicide in certain circumstances.

We agree that human dignity is the supreme human value, but we do not agree about the relation between human dignity and suicide or euthanasia.

IKEDA: I do not deny your assertion that human beings have the right to kill themselves, but I insist that the decision of when to end life ought to be left to the life force itself. Intellect, reasoning, and emotion are superficial attributes of the life force, but they are not the life force. They must protect the life force and work to the end that the life force can manifest itself in loftier ways. Consequently, intellect, reason, and emotions do not have the right to destroy total life or to decide when it shall terminate. Only life itself has this right. Life may terminate itself as the result of karma from the past or perhaps as a consequence of some malfunction of the physical mechanism that supports its continuation. No matter which is the cause, the termination of life is determined at a level beyond human consciousness and is unrelated to intellect and emotion.

Naturally, if intellect, reasoning, and emotion are to contribute to the loftier manifestation of life force, they must strive for justice, courage, and benevolence. Even if in the pursuit of these ideals there are things that threaten total life force, the quest must be approved. Distorting justice, falling prey to cowardice, and sacrificing others for the sake of self-protection amounts to damaging the dignity of the life force. Consequently, even Buddhism teaches that to protect the justice of the Law, a person must not begrudge his life if it is to be given for altruistic reasons. The ideas you illustrate by means of reference to the ancient Greeks and Romans and particularly Cato are imbued with courage, justice, and high human dignity. In this sense, Cato is to be praised and the idea he represents deserves approval. Still, suicide is an error. Cato may have given Caesar a psychological shock by killing himself, but he did not save Rome from a dictatorial government. Had Cato chosen to live and fight, he might have been defeated. But he would have served as a powerful example for people in later generations who loved freedom.

II

POLITICAL

AND

INTERNATIONAL LIFE

THE SECOND HALF OF THIS CENTURY | 6

The United States

The Frontier Spirit

IKEDA: There are people who suggest that the American defeat in Vietnam was not merely political and military but moral as well. If this is true, one wonders what significance it will have for the future of the United States. A large number of European nations and peoples have to try to live together harmoniously in a confined area. In America this is not the case. The very spaciousness of the American continent has given rise to what is called the frontier spirit, but this spirit, which was originally a challenge to the natural rigors of an uncultivated terrain, seems to overlook the existence of other peoples. When the Americans are forced to deal with other nations and peoples, the frontier spirit asserts itself in the form of attempts to bring to bear the immense power of the United States. The defeat in Vietnam suggests that perhaps the frontier spirit has reached an impasse.

TOYNBEE: The Americans have long tended to overlook human beings in their attitudes toward other lands. Thinking of the North American continent as an unpeopled zone of nothing but wild animals, forests, and deserts, they took no account of the native human inhabitants, whom they treated as no more than part of the flora and fauna. This spirit—the frontier spirit—is the attitude that the Americans translated into policy and that they employed in dealing with Vietnam. The discovery that the Vietnamese are not flora and fauna but human beings just like the citizens of the United States has given

161

the Americans a shock. The defeat in Vietnam was indeed a moral one. More important, it was a lesson that I hope the Americans will take to heart.

But we Europeans must not be smug on this issue. We have not always been so very harmonious in our relations with one another. Not all European countries can boast of the successful harmonizing of peoples speaking different languages and following different religions that is characteristic of Switzerland. In Belgium, for example, very serious problems arise out of the rivalry between the French and Flemish language groups. Europeans have no right to be conceited about their harmony with each other, though we do not have anything comparable to the American frontier spirit.

IKEDA: There are probably very few cases in which different races have lived in complete harmony in a single country for long periods. In some instances, all goes badly for a while, then conditions improve. In other instances, everything is harmonious between the peoples for a time, and then something happens to spoil the situation. The case of the Koreans living in Japan belongs in the second category. In ancient times and in the middle ages, the Koreans were welcomed and honored in Japan as representatives of an advanced culture. It was not until much later times that the Japanese came to treat the Koreans with condescension or worse. Though the situation has improved since the end of World War II, the problem is not yet completely solved.

The lack of racial harmony in the United States, however, takes on enlarged importance because it is reflected strongly in American international politics. It then becomes even more important because of the immense influence of American politics on the politics of all other nations.

TOYNBEE: It is true that the frontier spirit and the prejudices underlying it have led the United States to magnify her mistakes by projecting them into the field of international politics. I think that she will be forced to give up the frontier spirit in Southeast Asia. It proved disastrous in Vietnam, and it created a quarrel between the president and the Congress over Cambodia.

The case with Israel is different for a number of reasons. From the cynical standpoint, one must admit the importance and the unfortunate nature of the effect of the American Jewish vote on the actions of American politicians. Second is the fantastic—to a rationalist like me—but undeniable belief in some American religious circles that Israel is the promised land in fact as it is in the Old Testament and consequently belongs by right to the Jews. The groups that hold this opinion are the old-fashioned, so-called Bible Christians, who are numerous in the United States. Finally, the Americans apply the frontier spirit to their approach to the Israel question by considering the

162

Arabs, as they considered the American Indians, to be a people with no rights in the face of the superior Israelis. As long as she has American support, Israel will be able to resist a just, give-and-take peace with the Arabs. But by a strange piece of good luck the Arabs have found bargaining power. They happen to be the owners of by far the largest reserves of petroleum in the world. Petroleum elsewhere is growing scarce, and the question remains whether the Americans are willing to sacrifice automobiles and heating for the sake of Israel.

Both the United States and the Soviet Union are eager to improve their relations and to end the cold war, but as long as danger exists in the Middle East, war might flare up between the two powerful nations against the wishes of both. It is to everyone's interest to settle the Middle East question; to do this, the Americans must change their present, emotional, and, in my view, irrational attitude toward Israel and the Arabs. This change obviously entails an alteration in at least the application of the frontier spirit.

Uneasy Activists Abroad

IKEDA: There is no doubt that the United States has been an important focal point in world history in this century. The role she played in bringing democracy and liberty to a Europe ravaged by fascism during World War II is especially praiseworthy. On the other hand, it is impossible to overlook the mistakes made by the United States in involving the world in the cold war with the Soviet Union and in the Korean and Vietnamese wars. Even within the United States, antiwar movements played a part in bringing the war in Vietnam—the "dirty war"—to an end. We can only wonder what future path the United States will follow in relation to international politics. Will she return to the positions set forth in the Monroe Doctrine, or will she attempt to maintain her rights as a leader in a world in which she is a superpower?

TOYNBEE: In the Neutrality Act, passed by the Congress at the beginning of World War II, the United States announced her determination to stay out of war. Had it not been for Pearl Harbor, she might never have entered the war. Surprisingly, however, after the war and until this day, the United States has pursued an activist international policy entirely contrary to all of her previous policies, beginning with the famous warning by the founding fathers against foreign entanglements.

It is worthwhile to note that most of America's activist policies have been directed against the communists, and especially against the Soviet Union. Even though she has fought two world wars with Germany and one with

163

Japan, the United States, apart from the actual fighting, has shown very little antagonism against these two nations, whereas, since 1917, she has reacted violently against the Soviet Union. Why should this be?

It seems to me that the Americans are so inward-oriented that they do not think of communism as something to be dealt with in the field of international politics. Instead, they regard it as a domestic threat to the pockets of rich American citizens. Japan and Germany threatened American political security, but they did not threaten to communalize or otherwise expropriate American wealth, as the very basic idea of communism does.

IKEDA: My interpretation of the current flowing throughout American history is the desire to create an ideal country. Since the times of colonization and early development, the people of America have embraced the hope of breaking with the Old World and creating an ideal society in the New World. The Monroe Doctrine was a means toward devoting themselves to the unhampered development of their own country.

In the twentieth century, however, American isolationism no longer works. I suspect that the Americans entered both of the world wars most grudgingly. After World War II, when they opened their eyes to the immense world-swaying powers they wield, they probably decided to expand their dream of an ideal nation to a worldwide scale. This, I believe, gave rise to their activist policies.

Unfortunately, their attempts to achieve their ends have been based on force. I do not deny the important effects American idealism has had on the world, but I cannot condone reliance on force of arms. To pursue the ideal course they have in mind, the Americans ought to rely on culture instead of on weaponry.

TOYNBEE: Yes, that is true. Fortunately the quarrel between China and the Soviet Union has relieved the Americans of some of their fear that communism may upset their domestic situation. I hope that the resultant relaxation of tensions will lead the United States to take a less militant and belligerent policy toward China and the Soviet Union, since it is of great importance for the whole world that these three powers should work together for the benefit of the human race.

Racial Unrest at Home

IKEDA: The most pressing problem facing the United States on the home front is that of racial discrimination. The Anglo-Saxon whites have long controlled leadership in America. The other white peoples—for instance, the citizens of Latin descent—the blacks, and the American Indians, the original inhabitants of the land, have been forced into a miserable position.

TOYNBEE: The Americans certainly have this problem. The Anglo-Saxon whites occupy a special position of superiority, but they share it with whites of German, Scandinavian, and Dutch origin.

Racial discrimination, however, is by no means an exclusively American phenomenon. In Britain, the number of blacks is very small compared with the number in the United States, yet the British manifest the same hateful emotions toward them. All of us must be humble in criticizing the Americans on this point. We British long ago drove the previous inhabitants of Britain into the mountains of Wales, but the Welsh have not forgotten the experience. The Japanese, too, pushed the Ainu farther and farther north, till they are now confined almost entirely to Hokkaido. Of course there are very few Ainu left to remember what happened to their ancestors, but at some time in their history they must have recalled that they once owned much of the land, and they must have regretted the loss of it and resented the people who took it from them. So you see, many other peoples have racial prejudices and have done very much the same thing that the Americans did in taking land away from the American Indians.

IKEDA: Prejudices of any kind are thorny problems, and prejudices based on emotion, like those entertained by some Americans, are especially difficult. The American people and government are, I feel sure, trying to do what they can to improve the racial situation, but their task is a hard one.

Some Americans have gone so far as to suggest the creation of independent states for the blacks and American Indians. As the case of Israel suggests, this might be an answer. But as long as the opposing parties continue to hate each other, the creation of independent states would not stop the fighting. In the final analysis, the only way to bring peace is to strive to eliminate hatred and prejudice.

TOYNBEE: I am afraid that both blacks and whites who put their hope in independent states show excessive optimism. Some American Indians demand independent states within the United States, but the history of the reservations on which these Indians live is sad. They have been given the worst possible lands, and these have been badly administered. The white South Africans are trying to push their blacks into very poor substitutes for independent states. These settlements are called Bantustans, but they do not have much hope of success. I think that black America and white America are going to have to live together and that they are going to have to do so on terms of equality and of mutual regard and friendship.

IKEDA: Clearly the racial problems arising within a single nation are difficult to solve. Do you have any good examples of cases in which harmony among peoples living together has been achieved?

TOYNBEE: Hawaii is an unusual case, of course, but European-Americans, Japanese-Americans, and Chinese-Americans all live together there and inter-marry with apparent harmony. If this can be done in Hawaii, it can be done in other places as well.

The Space Exploration Race

IKEDA: I admit the significance of programs of space exploration for their achievements thus far, but I cannot readily assent to their unrestricted con-tinuance, because they demand increasing financial outlays. The most urgent need of our time is to relieve the miseries afflicting the earth. Even the greatest space success will be meaningless if it is achieved at the sacrifice of the welfare of the inhabitants of our own planet. Nations are free to stake their prestige on vehement competition, but if this puts so heavy a strain on their national budgets that sufficient appropriations for solving more important problems, such as poverty and industrial hazards to life, are not forthcoming, all their effort becomes useless and, worse, harmful.

Nations ought to establish the promotion of happiness on earth as the premise of their space projects and, acting on this premise, ought to coor-dinate progress in this field with developments in other branches of science and technology. Allotments for space efforts must always be in reasonable proportion to the size of the national budget.

TOYNBEE: I am not opposed to space exploration in principle. There is virtue in the courage, skill, and coordinated action that this enterprise de-mands, and there is value in the additions that it makes to our knowledge of the physical cosmos. I am, however, opposed to present space exploration for two reasons, which you mention. First, the dominant, present incentive is not scientific curiosity; it is the competition between the United States and the Soviet Union for ascendancy on this planet—a competition in which the

166

prestige conferred by successful feats of space exploration counts, like the possession of nuclear weapons, as one of the weights in the rival scales. Second, the expenditure on space exploration, which is immense, ought not to have been given priority over meeting the needs of the poverty-stricken majority of the human race, who are still short of food, clothing, and shelter. Mankind's resources are limited; therefore, the question of priorities for their use is important.

IKEDA: Geophysical observations at the South Pole are smoothly carried out with the close cooperation of all involved countries. Similarly, well-coordinated space projects jointly sponsored by participating nations would undoubtedly produce exceedingly good results in terms of scientific and technological development and in terms of the money saved. I admit that military considerations might prevent such plans from working as easily as is the case with the Antarctic expeditions.

TOYNBEE: If and when the material standard of living of the poverty-stricken three quarters of mankind has been raised to the present level of the affluent minority, then I should be in favor of considering whether space exploration is, or is not, the first priority for the expenditure of mankind's surplus. If and when we do decide that we are justified, socially and ethically, in going ahead with space exploration, I agree that this ought to be conducted as a global cooperative effort, and not as a politically motivated competition between the Soviet Union and the United States.

In present circumstances, space exploration seems to be an extravagance that is unjustifiable, because it is being indulged in at the expense of the poor. I expect that future generations will condemn it retrospectively as having been a rich minority's antisocial folly like the building of the Pyramids, Angkor, and Louis XIV's palace at Versailles.

Japan and Britain

Democracy

IKEDA: Britain and Japan have several things in common in terms of history. As far as political structure is concerned, both nations now adopt the constitutional-monarchy system. The thrones of the British king and the Japanese emperor are perhaps the most stable in the world. In some points, however, Britain and Japan contrast very sharply. For example, democracy and the ideas of liberty and freedom have a long history in Britain. Though subjected to severe trials in the past, these institutions are now deeply rooted in the British way of life. By contrast, in Japan, democracy, liberty, and freedom have a history of a mere quarter of a century. They were not won by the people as a result of long, hard struggles but were transplanted by the Americans after World War II. Although Japanese democracy may be compared to a horticultural graft, it was neither born in a native climate nor planted in well-cultivated soil. There is, therefore, a large gap between Japanese democracy and traditional Japanese ways of thinking about society and human consciousness, both of which are of crucial importance in the functioning of democratic institutions.

TOYNBEE: The British-American type of constitutional government is, of course, a peculiar, and partly fortuitous, product of a long, local, historical development. It is therefore not surprising that, in countries in which it is exotic, it has not been found easy to copy and to operate. Even France, which had so much in common with Britain in its medieval institutions, has found our kind of constitutional government difficult to manage.

IKEDA: For the sake of argument, let us assume that it is desirable to establish a democracy of the best possible kind in Japan. What can we Japanese learn from Britain? To what causes do you attribute the success of the British system? I feel the most fundamentally important condition is for each person to be subjectively individual and independent. To a British citizen, my statement is probably only too obvious, but in Japan, this kind of essential independence is sometimes a forgotten issue. I am convinced that without individuality and independence attempting to establish democracy is building on shifting sand.

TOYNBEE: As I see it, the relative success of parliamentary constitutional government in Britain is due to the following factors: (1) Deliberate political moderation dating from the reaction against political violence in the seventeenth century. (2) The organization of the conduct of parliamentary business through the two-party system. (The high price of this is the regimentation of the individual member of Parliament; the electorate now votes by secret ballot; the member of Parliament must vote publicly and is disciplined by his party if he does not vote in accordance with the party line, just as the industrial worker is disciplined by his union if he does not join in a strike.) (3) A tacit understanding between the two parties that, on fundamental questions, they will give priority to the national interest instead of manoeuvering for selfish advantage. (4) A recognition that political opposition is compatible with personal goodwill and friendship.

Since World War II, the British tradition regarding points (3) and (4) has shown some disquieting signs of breaking down—for example, over legislation about industrial relations and over the issue of joining the European Economic Community.

At a more fundamental level than the operation of the British political constitution, I think the British people's success in preserving individual liberty during the last three centuries is due to the tradition that the individual citizen has a moral obligation to incur personal risks, and, if necessary, to make personal sacrifices, in taking a stand on questions of principle.

In an Anglo-German discussion meeting after World War II, I found that the Germans were surprised to learn that I had once had to resign from a professorial chair over the issue of academic freedom. I happened to mention this incident casually, in illustrating some point about British public life. I took my resignation as a matter of course, but the Germans said that they found it illuminating. They had supposed, they said, that British individual liberty was just a gift of the gods. They had not inquired into its basis and had not realized that it is maintained only by the constant efforts of individuals. I think this point is quite important.

Diplomacy

IKEDA: Britain and Japan are both island countries located off the shores of continental nations. Each of them faces the United States across a large body of water.

TOYNBEE: The geographical locations of Japan and Britain make it necessary for these two insular countries, which are offshore islands of the Old World, to have close relations with both the adjacent parts of the continental Old World and with the New World—especially, of course, with the United States. I believe that for both countries relations with their neighboring continents are going to prove more important than their relations with America. Therefore, I expect, and hope, that each of them will become associated with a regional group of adjacent countries—Eastern Asia in Japan's case, and Europe in Britain's. I also hope that these regional associations will be stepping stones, not obstacles, to an eventual union of all mankind on a worldwide scale.

IKEDA: Diplomacy is an area of contrast between Britain and Japan. Britain led the free nations in the recognition of China. As a member of the European community, she takes an active part in dealing with European problems. In other words, Britain attempts to maintain a neutral stand. Japan, on the contrary, is far from being neutral in her diplomacy. I must admit that Japan's policy toward the United States is servile in still allowing Japanese territory to be used for American military bases. Japanese opinion in general is that, though it should not damage friendly relations with America, the government must establish an independent foreign policy.

In terms of history and tradition, relations between Britian and the United States and between Japan and the United States differ sharply. For a long time, Britain and the United States have enjoyed almost familylike relations. Both were among the victors in World War II, whereas Japan was on the losing side. Perhaps this historical background accounts for the very different attitudes toward the United States taken by the two countries. Not once in the thirty years since the end of World War II has Japan taken a firm stand against the United States. Our relations with the United States are comparatively new. The almost miraculous economic recovery of Japan in the postwar period took place under American protection. But it is now time that we abandoned our servile posture and adopted an attitude of neutrality. I feel that in the long run this would be to the advantage of the United States and would help to maintain friendly relations between our two nations over a longer period.

TOYNBEE: I should say that there has been some subservience in Britain's, as well as in Japan's, attitude to the United States. The British, till lately, have had a snobbish wish to rank as one of the overseas peoples, and not as Europeans. This snobbery has blinded them to the harsh truth that Britain's much-prized "special relation" with the United States is one of a satellite that the Americans have no intention of taking into economic partnership. The notion that the "special relation" could solve Britain's economic problems seems as illusory as the notion that British problems could be solved by participation in the Commonwealth. In my view, Britain's economic future lies in membership in the European Economic Community, in which it will be one among a number of equal partners.

For Japan, economic partnership with China is not yet actually within reach, but eventually Japan's economic future will probably lead to such a relationship. In an association with China and the other East Asian countries, Japan would be fully independent of the United States.

IKEDA: To speak frankly, Japan has not been fulfilling her responsibilities to the other Asian countries. While extending economic aid to nations promising conditions advantageous to Japan, she is less generous to countries where it is feared that invested funds might be slow in producing returns. On the other hand, the Japanese make economic inroads into all the Asian countries so eagerly that they have been dubbed "Yellow Yankees." At present, Japan devotes great energy to an economic diplomacy unfortunately oriented toward increasing Japanese wealth.

A better economic diplomacy would be to use wealth to help poor nations. In the future it will be important for Japan to devote attention to developing a cultural diplomacy, especially with other Asian nations, in order to deal with questions of education and health and to sponsor exchanges of technology and knowledge.

TOYNBEE: Though today far outstripped by Japan in economic development, Britain, too, is part of the world's rich minority. I agree that the rich countries have a moral obligation to help the poor countries and to refrain from exploiting them. The economic aid given to the poor countries by the continental members of the European Economic Community is, I believe, greater, in proportion to the gross national product of E.E.C. countries—as well as in absolute figures—than the aid given by Britain. As the third richest country in the world in terms of gross national product, Japan has a proportionate obligation.

I agree that aid should not be merely economic. The best form of economic aid is the acceptance, by the economically stronger of two trading partners, of equitable terms of trade. This is preferable to doles that we offset by unfair terms of trade and by the export of profits from investments in underdeveloped countries. These countries ought to be helped to help themselves, and, for this purpose, aid in the fields of education, art, health, science, and technology can be very efficacious.

No Candidate for King

IKEDA: In considering the factors contributing to the success of British parliamentary democracy, it is interesting to examine the role of the institution of the crown. Japan, like Britain, has maintained a modified monarchical system while adopting a democratic method of government. At first glance, monarchy and democracy seem contradictory, but they have lived side by side in Britain for a long time. Perhaps it is British traditionalism that has made it possible for the two to coexist.

TOYNBEE: Even before the modern revival of the worship of the collective power of local sovereign states, political power always attracted some degree of emotional attachment—a feeling of reverence, if not of affection—on the part of the subjects of a government. Usually the emotion is directed toward the holders of power.

Under the Japanese and the British monarchical regimes, the exercise of power and the attraction of sentiment are divided between different persons. The sentiment is concentrated on a sovereign, who does not exercise the power, and the holders of the power do not attract the sentiment. In the histories of both countries, this separation between power and prestige has not been deliberately contrived. It has been the result of undesigned historical developments. The result of the split is sometimes—I think correctly—interpreted as a fortunate accident.

IKEDA: No matter whether it was accidental or deliberate, the separation of the king, or emperor, as an object of reverence from the executive wielders of power was fortunate, because people in power, far from being regarded with reverence, are often feared or even hated. In order to bring together and guide the strengths of a people, something that awakens a feeling of veneration is essential. The British division between these two aspects of leadership greatly facilitated the early political stabilization of the country—earlier than that of any other European nation—and the manifestation of the abilities and talents of the British people. Similarly, I believe that the same division helped Japan to create her own independent culture in spite of numerous instances of internal strife, changes of leadership, and rivalry with foreign powers. At any rate, since the time when the local national state became a prevalent phenomenon throughout the world until the present, the division between the object of reverential respect and the holders of political power has had salutary effects.

TOYNBEE: Under absolute monarchy (as in imperial China and in Pharaonic Egypt) the ruler comes into office either by hereditary succession or by adoption or by revolution. Besides being the focus of loyalty, he wields the whole collective power of the state, insofar as he is personally capable of wielding it. If an officially absolute monarch is politically inefficient, the power that is nominally his is actually exercised by members of his household who have no constitutional mandate for exercising it. Thus, under an absolute

172

monarchy in all circumstances, power is exercised arbitrarily. This system is surely inferior to the Japanese and British systems.

However, the Japanese and British systems have not solved all the problems of government. The de facto holders of power, who exercise this power in the official sovereign's name, are inevitably tempted to try to draw on the crown's prestige for winning public support for their policies. Conversely, the crown is obliged to endorse, and to assume official responsibility for policies carried out in the crown's name in which the crown has had no say. A constitutional monarch's role is psychologically unrewarding.

IKEDA: Monarchy is on the decline all over the world. As I mentioned earlier, since monarchy differs in character according to the nation in which it came into being, generalities about it are difficult to make. But what do you think the future is—or ought to be—of constitutional monarchy as a system?

TOYNBEE: Probably the present constitutional monarchies—Japanese, British, Dutch, Belgian, Danish, Norwegian, Swedish—are likely to survive longer than any others. If they too eventually disappear, this will not be through their being overthrown; it will probably be because no member of the royal or imperial family will be willing to take over such an unattractive job. In the language of industrial relations, constitutional monarchies are likely to be ended by strikes.

In the course of the present century the number of monarchies has already dwindled. Monarchy was abolished in Austria-Hungary, Germany, and Turkey as a result of defeats in World War I. In the Arab world since the end of World War II, monarchy has already been abolished in Egypt, Iraq, the Yemen, and Libya, and it is obviously now precarious in those Arab countries that are still under monarchical rule.

Monarchy of all kinds, both absolute and honorary, has been the focus of the emotional attachment of the subjects of a state. This emotional attachment has been a form of religious worship. States have, in fact, been felt to be gods. It looks as if the progressive disappearance of monarchies is an indication that states are ceasing to be felt to be gods and are coming to be seen as public utilities. I hold that this change in attitude to states is highly desirable.

173

Demise of the Local State

IKEDA: The tendency for the prestige of the state to decrease, especially since the end of World War II, has been most remarkable in the so-called advanced nations, where state structure has reached a high level and its greatest fulfillment. But the idea of the state is not indispensable to human life, nor is it something worthy of the highest respect. Quite the contrary, excessive devotion to the state invites many serious threats to the future of humanity.

TOYNBEE: Nationalism—the worship of the collective power of a local national state—has been a principal post-Christian Western religion, embraced by more people more intensely than any other modern religion. It has become worldwide. Today there are about 140 officially sovereign local states, each of which has been treated as a god with a divine right to commit all kinds of atrocities. A sovereign local state has not been subject to any law, either in theory or in practice. I agree, however, that the worship of local national states has been decreasing since World War II.

IKEDA: One of the reasons for the decrease may be the intensification of international exchange in cultural, economic, and other fields of endeavor. As international activities gain precedence, they leave little room for the intrusion of the authority of the local state. Today, as an outcome of increased international contacts among peoples, it is widely thought that state authority inhibits freedom of action.

　　Another reason contributing to the loss of respect for the state is the foreseeable possibility of nuclear warfare, which one state alone cannot successfully prevent. In the field of international relations, the so-called superstates monopolize the right to make significant pronouncements. But no one monopolizes all power, and none can risk warfare without the massive assistance of allies. Still, the large nations maintain a firm grip on leadership rights in group defense systems. This means that while small and moderate-sized nations belonging to these systems may make bold statements in international affairs, what they have to say is likely to be ignored. In other words, national states of all sizes and degrees of power are shackled by the inability to go to war independently because of the destructiveness of nuclear arms. Going to war independently has been one of the traditional rights of the national state.

TOYNBEE: I think your first and second points, taken together, are the chief causes of the collapse of the authority of the deified local states. One effect of the recent advance in technology has been a great increase in the scale of human activities of all kinds, military and civil. We are approaching the point at which the only effective scale for operations of any importance will be the global scale. This means that local national states, which were once the most convenient units for human activities, have now become highly inconvenient and indeed positively obstructive insofar as they still have power. Moreover, while the scale of operations has been increasing, the size of the local states has been diminishing. Today, the habitable part of the land-surface of the globe is divided into about twice as many local states as there were within the same area before World War II.

IKEDA: Still a third cause of the loss of prestige of the state is the trend for big business and labor unions with independent aims to organize their own social groups cutting across national allegiances. In some instances, the individual's sense of being a member of such a group is stronger than his awareness of citizenship in a given state.

TOYNBEE: This too is important. Some private organizations for economic purposes—business corporations and trades unions—have become more powerful than governments and therefore more important to their members than political citizenship. Governments cannot hold their own against business corporations that grow to multinational dimensions. Governments cannot even hold their own against some trades unions that are still confined within the frontiers of a single state. In England, the state made itself irresistibly superior in power to all private individuals or organizations in about the year 1500. This imposition of the supremacy of the state, which was achieved in England by King Henry VII, was achieved in Japan by Toyotomi Hideyoshi and Tokugawa Ieyasu about a century later. But, in Britain today, the trades unions are able to defy the state, as the barons were able to defy it in England before Henry VII broke their power.

IKEDA: Still another cause is the current tendency for the individual to oppose the establishment. In many cases, when the state comes to represent the establishment, the people strongly resist its displays of authority or power.

TOYNBEE: But this is nothing new. I believe that all states of all kinds have always been controlled by the establishment and have been manipulated by the establishment to serve the establishment's interest. Therefore, insofar as the masses have become alienated from the establishment, they have also become hostile to the state whose subjects they are.

175

IKEDA: Because of the traditional relationships between state and citizens, the state frequently employs high-sounding causes to drag its people into warfare. Even this deception did less harm in the past, when military men usually came from certain classes of society and entered military service voluntarily. With conscription, however, an immensely greater part of the national population must risk death in case of war. World War I, by showing how horrible war is, became a contributory factor in the destruction of the absolutism of the state.

TOYNBEE: It is true that states have been discredited by the great changes for the worse that have taken place in the character of warfare since 1914. Twentieth-century wars everywhere have been accompanied by atrocities of the kind committed in seventeenth-century Western wars, which were more violent and bloodier than the wars of the eighteenth and nineteenth centuries.

Apart from the atrocities that have again become accompaniments of war since 1914, the effect even of so-called legitimate acts of war has become prohibitively destructive. Military casualties have become huge, as have civilian casualties, since improvement in weapons (the invention of airborne nuclear bombs) has obliterated the former distinction between noncombatants and combatants. In Vietnam, defoliation has rapidly devastated the countryside in the way in which it is being devastated more gradually elsewhere by the excessive use of insecticides in agriculture.

IKEDA: As we have outlined them, then, the numerous factors contributing to discrediting the state in modern times are interwoven in a very complicated way, but I think the Tokyo tribunal that tried Japanese war criminals after World War II is a major symbol of these factors.

The trials were held to enable the victors to try the vanquished for offenses against peace and humanity. Of course, inhuman criminal acts were perpetrated by soldiers on the winning side as well. But in spite of this, the winners unilaterally tried those on the losing side whom they considered responsible. In not a few instances, the verdicts were insufficiently substantiated, and the conduct of the trials themselves was not strictly impartial.

Apart from these problematical points, in areas that went largely unnoticed at the time, the trials were commendable. First, they recognized the value of humanity and peace and insisted that they ought to be inviolable. I believe that their insistence that violators of peace and human rights, even when acting under military or governmental orders, must be held culpable for their acts will be of historic importance.

In contrast, neither Kaiser Wilhelm II nor his generals were held accountable for criminal acts after World War I. In those days, the acts of the state, no matter how tragic their consequences, were immune from being stigmatized as criminal. The case was entirely different after World War II, because the idea that the will of the state is absolute and that the state is worthy of all respect had collapsed. For this reason, I think the military tribunals illustrate a rejection of the authority of the state and symbolize an important historical development.

TOYNBEE: The Nuremberg and Tokyo trials of war criminals symbolized and advertised a historic change in mankind's attitude to war. These trials signified that war had come to be seen as the crime that it is, and no longer as the legitimate prerogative of sovereign governments deemed divine and therefore not amenable to human laws. But these trials were unjust in the sense that they were conducted by the victors against the vanquished and that the victors did not put on trial any of their own politicians and military authorities, though some of these ought, in equity, to have been indicted on the same charges.

IKEDA: All of this makes us stop to reconsider the definition of war criminals. Ought trials like those held in Nuremburg and Tokyo to be conducted? If so, who must be put on trial? In what form ought the trials to be held, and what ought to be the standards on which they are to be based?

TOYNBEE: Every participant in an institution has some degree of personal responsibility for the acts committed in his name by the persons who are in control of that institution. If the electorate in the United States were to set up a war tribunal for trying American war criminals in the Vietnam War, I think the prosecution should not be limited to presidents, commanders in chief, and civilian and military subordinates. The American electorate ought to indict the whole of itself, since the electorate bears the ultimate responsibility in a state that has a democratic constitution.

IKEDA: In other words, the people are responsible for the actions of the state. This ought to mean that the state exists to express the will of the people and that it is therefore a utility and not an object of worshipful reverence. For this reason, I am in accord with the thought that, ideally, the world ought to be unified under one global government and that the state as we understand it today ought to vanish. Still, desirable as this may be, we must alter our way of thinking about the state until we can reach the stage in social and political development where national states cease to exist. My feeling is

177

that it is sufficient to regard the state as a regional unit reflecting social or cultural characteristics of groups of people or as, at most, a convenient administrative unit.

TOYNBEE: I hold that the local states ought to be deprived of their sovereignty and subordinated to the sovereignty of a global world government. Even then, local states would still have a useful, and indeed indispensable, municipal role to play as units for local administration—the role played in a federal state by its constituent states. As the scale of all operations continues to increase, I expect to see more of the former administrative powers of local states pass into the hands of the world government, but there will probably be an irreducible residue of functions for which it will be convenient to retain administrative decentralization. The cumulative weight of these considerations makes me agree that the world's present 140 local states ought not to, and cannot, remain political units with the sovereign right to make war and at the same time have the last word in human affairs of nonmilitary kinds.

IKEDA: What is your evaluation of the state as a contemporary institution in relation to the individual human being? And what expectation do you have for the state of the future?

TOYNBEE: As I have said previously, I regard the state of which I am a citizen as a public utility, like the organizations that supply me with water, gas, and electricity. I feel that it is my civic duty to pay my taxes as well as my other bills, and that it is my moral duty to make an honest declaration of my income to the income tax authorities. But I do not feel that I and my fellow citizens have a religious duty to sacrifice our lives in war on behalf of our own state, and, *a fortiori*, I do not feel that we have an obligation or a right to kill and maim citizens of other states or to devastate their land. My own paramount loyalty is to mankind, not to my local state and not to the establishment by which this state is controlled.

However, my attitude is merely one individual's attitude. Mankind in the mass will have to be induced to give up its traditional religious devotion to local states if the local states are to be confined to what seems to me to be their proper and legitimate function. I should like to see states deconsecrated and nonhuman nature reconsecrated.

Countries Susceptible to Communism

IKEDA: Although China, India, and the Western Asian nations built great civilizations that left brilliant marks on the history of mankind, in recent centuries, after having been subjected to the colonial imperialism of the Western European nations, they have declined. Now that they have regained their independence and sovereignty, these countries are walking the agonizing road of reconstruction. India and the Western Asian countries are still far behind the West because of political instability and insufficient social capital. By contrast, China has successfully embarked on a course of reconstruction under firmly established communist rule that has stabilized her political situation and given her a socialist, planned economy and a resultant accumulation of social capital. If India and the West Asian nations are to follow China's lead, might they not do better under communist rule?

Of course, communism alone does not explain China's success. She was fortunate enough to have in Mao Tse-tung a leader of high caliber, a great man of the kind whose presence is of immense importance to a nation. Mao has been able to create a new China by assimilating Marxism-Leninism in the historic and spiritual tradition of his nation. Without doubt, it is owing to Mao's great leadership that the Chinese communist revolution succeeded.

TOYNBEE: I diagnose communism as a religion and specifically as a new representative of the Judaic species, in which the Judaic mythology has been preserved under the disguise of a nontheistic vocabulary. One common characteristic of all the Judaic religions is tight organization and strong discipline. This is the positive side of their exclusiveness and intolerance.

People need discipline and submit to it in a crisis, and all the non-Western civilized societies have been in crisis since the time Western civilization started to make its impact on them. This challenge has compelled them to try to make a forced march in order to catch up in those fields—above all, in the field of technology—in which the modern West has been temporarily more powerful than the rest of the world. A forced march requires discipline of a military kind. Communism provides discipline of just this kind. Therefore, communism is a helpful religion for a society that has to try to achieve the tour de force of assimilating an alien civilization, especially when that society is threatened with total collapse if its self-transformation is not sufficiently rapid and drastic.

IKEDA: I agree that communism is a religion, but one aspect that sets it apart from other religions is the fact that it is concerned solely with the questions of

179

living in this life and does not attempt to deal with life beyond death. I suspect that one of the things that makes it easy for China to accept a practical, this-world religion like communism is the traditional Chinese lack of interest in absolute, supernatural beings and a generally rationalistic approach to life. Though Taoism is colored with mysticism, Confucianism is a completely rational political and life philosophy. The religious psychology that Confucianism exemplifies is part of the rational tradition that assisted the Chinese in accepting the teachings of Marxism-Leninism.

Allah of the religions of the Islamic countries of Western Asia is not only an absolute deity but also the arbiter of things of this life. Although it is impossible to say that the Islamic countries will never accept communism, I do not think they have the background that will allow them to assimilate it with the ease the Chinese have shown.

TOYNBEE: Communism—in one of its aspects, a left-handed form of the modern Western religion of scientific rationalism—is relatively easy to adopt in a country, such as China, where the predominant indigenous tradition, like Confucianism, is rationalistic and authoritarian. So far, the Muslims have proved to be allergic to communism. This is certainly surprising, for Islam is a more rational form of Judaic religion than Christianity, and it is also at least equally authoritarian. The word *Islam* means self-surrender. The Turks, who are as proud an ex-imperial people as the Chinese, have paid for their slowness in assimilating Western civilization by suffering humiliations like those once inflicted on the Chinese. Yet the Turks, unlike the Chinese, eventually made their forced march without resorting to communism. The Arabs have been far more severely humiliated than the Turks, yet they, too, have been allergic to communism, notwithstanding their having compromised themselves with communism externally by accepting Russian aid against Israel and against the United States. The imperviousness of Islam to communism puzzles me.

IKEDA: I consider the imperviousness to communism of the Islamic nations to be the result of the exclusiveness of Allah, an absolute god ruling over everything both in this world and the world beyond. Allah leaves no room for the introduction of communism and its claim to control human activities in actual life.

TOYNBEE: It is true in principle that the Muslims accept only the authority of Allah as interpreted by recognized experts in the Mohammedan law. But in practice, since an early date in Islamic history, they have accepted auto-

180

cratic, political, secular rule. Of course, the secular rulers are supposed to obey the Islamic religious law, the last word in which lies with the recognized experts; actually most Islamic governments have been very despotic.

Today modern nationalism has infected the Islamic world. Two countries are outstanding examples of its effects: one is Turkey after World War I and the other is Pakistan following the British abdication from power there.

The first thing the Turks did after World War I was to abolish the Ottoman dynasty. This is not contrary to Islamic law, which does not decree that the Muslims must be governed by autocrats. But some of the Turkish reformers' steps did violate Islamic law and therefore greatly shocked other Muslims. The Turks secularized the state by abolishing the caliphate, which was the succession to the political, as distinct from the religious, functions of the prophet Mohammed. In addition, they translated the Koran into Turkish, whereas according to the law of Islam it must be only in Arabic. In other words, in Turkey nationalism proved stronger than the law of Islam.

Pakistan, a somewhat different case, became a state owing to the desire of Indian Muslims to unite. Previously they had lived all over India and had, like Hindu Indians, belonged to many different races, but they decided to band together to form a state of their own. Assuming that Islam would transcend racial and language differences, they concentrated all Indian Muslims in what is now West Pakistan and in what is now Bangladesh. They never dreamed that Islam could not be a permanently effective bond between the two regions. But trouble was not long erupting. The people of Bangladesh refused to accept Urdu, the official language of West Pakistan, as their own official language. They also refused to use the Arabic alphabet and clung instead to the Bengali script common to Hindu and Muslim Bengalis. In other words, in Bangladesh, as earlier in Turkey, nationalism prevailed over Islam. Now, of course, Bangladesh has seceded from Pakistan on nationalistic grounds.

All of this has been a terrible blow to Islamic unity, but Islam, after all, is no more immune to nationalism than Christianity. In the case of both of these faiths, fanaticism has been transferred from the religion to the nation.

IKEDA: In other words, the strong binding power that Islam once had is now a force leading Muslims in the direction of nationalism.

But the change to nationalism can be seen in the communization of China as well. China by no means followed a direct course to communism; it traveled by means of a nationalistic detour. The effect of that experience is still pronounced in the Chinese national character.

This Chinese duality is extremely interesting, especially since communism has consistently presented itself as the ideology that will abolish ideas of race and nation. Of course, under the banners of antiimperialism and anticolonialism, communists have aided nations and peoples in all parts of the world; nevertheless, they have always insisted that the abolition of nations and the unity of all peoples is their ideal. The ideal, however, does not agree entirely with current conditions in China. In thinking about the now latent factors that will someday determine the path China takes, I think we may have to alter our terminology; that is, I think the national character of China and the Chinese cannot be adequately described in terms like *pure communist* or *pure nationalist*.

The important question for us to answer now is what is the background of the complexity of the Chinese, and to find an answer, we must once again examine the spirit of Confucianism, which has been a ruling force throughout Chinese history.

Confucianism teaches that the individual human being must abide by the greater order and therefore must recognize the authority of people placed above him. The object of respect changes with the situation and may be parents, seniors, kings, or leaders. The ideal human being is typified as what is usually translated as the Confucian gentleman who is aware of the way of Heaven. These ideals were coordinated into a set of moral political rulings advocating moral behavior, worship, government, and peace. I believe that the same code of behavior exists for the people of China today. For this reason, it was only natural for them to become faithful followers of the leadership—no matter that it teaches the principles of Marx, Lenin, and Mao.

The situation involved in the communization of Soviet Russia was something quite different. The Russian Orthodox Christian Church, which held sway over the Russian people for centuries, was mystical and irrational. With the revolution, Lenin completely altered the course of Russian life by channeling it into materialism and rationalism. The suddenness and violence of this immense social upheaval took a heavy toll in destruction and human sacrifice. Although the methods employed by the Soviet leaders were unyielding, their application in Russia suggests that a communist revolution is possible in other countries where the prevailing religion is antimaterialistic and irrational. When the Russian Revolution occurred, no other nation in the world had ever been converted completely to communism. Since the revolution, however, a number of nations have followed a similar course, though they have moved through periods of trial-and-error experimentation. Looking at the present conditions of those nations, we can say that communism does not invariably result in an ideal society.

TOYNBEE: Like communism, Eastern Orthodox Christianity is authoritarian. Perhaps this partly explains why it has been possible for communism (and also for its predecessor in Russia, the Western, "enlightened," absolute monarchy introduced by Peter the Great) to capture Russia, in spite of the discord between Western communist and precommunist rationalism and the nonrationalism of Christianity. I suspect that this discord is not really as great as it appears, because communism has retained a large measure of its ancestral Judaic irrationality beneath its rationalistic mask. For example, the idea of the dictatorship of the proletariate has much in common with the Judaic idea of the chosen people. Neither of these attitudes is either rational or wholesome.

IKEDA: What do you think of communism's chances of being adopted in other societies? For example, in India the irrational Hindu tradition is an integral and deeply rooted part of daily life and social customs. Hinduism has created the strong Indian caste system. Do you think that communism with its class struggle and ideal of a classless society can work a revolution in a nation like India?

TOYNBEE: Communism has an unpromising opening in a profoundly non-rationalistic society, like the Hindu, or in a society that does not need to make a forced march in order to catch up with the West.

World-embracing Patriotism

IKEDA: Essentially the wish to love and to promote the development of the country and society in which one lives is a special manifestation of the basic human trait to love one's own life and to stimulate one's own growth. In itself, this is a very important issue for mankind. Without the wish and the vitality underlying it, human society would not have developed to its present state. But once the natural love of the society in which one lives is brought into and used in confrontations between nations, it begins to take on a suspicious coloration, for in such cases, nationalism, which is entirely different from pure patriotism, distorts the basic human expression of love for home.

Too often pure patriotism has been distorted, misused, and trampled on in the name of belligerent nationalism. When this happens, love of country is transformed into hatred of or the belittling of other lands; a sense of common existence with one's own society becomes self-sacrifice for the sake of the state.

183

TOYNBEE: The kind of patriotism that led so many of the world's young people to tragedy and destruction in both the world wars and in most of the other wars that have been waged since the American and French revolutions is, as I see it, an ancient religion into which the Western peoples relapsed when they found themselves in the religious vacuum produced by the modern loss of belief in their ancestral religion, Christianity. This resuscitated pre-Christian religion is the worship of the collective power of a local community. This was the religion of the citizens of each of the Sumerian and the Greek city-states.

In Greco-Roman history, this worship of local collective power was eventually replaced by the worship of the collective power of the Roman Empire. Roman imperial power was worldwide in the sense that the Roman Empire was all that is under heaven as far as the inhabitants of the Roman Empire knew. However, it was contemporaneous for centuries with the longer lived Chinese empire, which was likewise all that is under heaven as far as its inhabitants knew. The Christian martyrs held that the worship of Roman imperial power was an unsatisfying and unsatisfactory religion, and they sacrificed their lives rather than perform the rites that signified acceptance of this religion.

In my opinion, the Christian martyrs were right. The worship of the god Caesar and the goddess Rome was a less maleficent form of the worship of collective human power than the worship of Athena, the goddess who had stood for the local collective power of the city-state of Athens. The worship of worldwide collective human power gave mankind political unity and therefore peace. But collective human power, whether local or worldwide, is surely not a fit object for worship.

IKEDA: I agree that collective human power, whether local or worldwide, is the basis on which rests the awareness of nation and of antagonism between nation and nation. I further agree that this power and the concept of the national state are not suitable objects of worship. As civilization has advanced, the life basis of modern man has expanded to worldwide limits; that is to say, the land in which one lives today is the entire world. Consequently, the feeling that the earth is one's homeland and a love of all mankind must take the place of the narrow patriotism of the past. When world-embracing patriotism gains precedence, national patriotism will sink to the level of loyalty to a locality.

TOYNBEE: Now that the whole of mankind's habitat has been unified at the technological level, we need to unify it at the emotional level. The political

184

devotion that, hitherto, has been given to local patches of our habitat and to local peoples and governments of these patches must now be transferred to the whole human race and to the entire world—indeed, to the universe. The Stoic school of Greek philosophy held that man is a citizen of the universe. The Neo-Confucian Chinese philosopher Ch'eng Hao held that man (or *jen*) regards heaven and earth and all things as one body. To him there is nothing that is not himself. He regards the world as one family.

I believe that the right object of worship for man is the ultimate spiritual reality within and beyond and behind the universe. As I see it, this ultimate reality is love. I agree with the Neo-Confucian philosopher Wang Yang-ming (1472–1529), who says that the highest goal is the ultimate principle of manifesting character and loving people. I hold that man ought to follow love, even if it leads him to self-sacrifice. Love is the spiritual impulse to give instead of to take. It is the impulse to bring the self back into harmony with the rest of the universe, from which the self has been estranged by its innate, but not unconquerable, self-centeredness.

ARMS AND WAR | 7

Economic Growth and War

IKEDA: The nature of war has been described as an armed version of politics and diplomacy, but while politics today remains a partial cause, economic factors seem to play a larger role in warfare and military preparations. The problem of abolishing warfare requires study from many angles; there are many causative elements behind the necessity for nations to expend vast parts of their budgets on war. But under current conditions, the most important problem is devising a way to secure economic prosperity while avoiding confrontations that might lead to warfare.

TOYNBEE: This statement by Clausewitz—a philosophizing, Prussian, military staff officer—that war is diplomacy carried on by other means is intentionally provocative in that it ignores the ethical difference between discussion for the sake of agreement and a physical trial of strength in which a conflict of interests or a difference of views is settled by brute force. It might be nearer the truth to say that war is the nemesis of the failure of diplomacy. It is true that sometimes war has settled disputes that diplomacy has failed to solve, but the price of settlement by means of war has been widespread death and devastation leading to the creation of new problems that are often dealt with by more wars leading in turn to still more wars. History shows that the settlement of a dispute by war is seldom satisfactory and is therefore seldom permanent.

IKEDA: War is undeniably an evil and a danger to the dignity of life. Equally undeniable, however, is the stimulation war has given to economic and technological development. In the modern world, war and preparation for it seem to be deeply related to economic needs. At any rate, war is a way of disposing of surpluses in the immense industrial productive power of our society. In a state of emergency, all resources of a country are mobilized; war takes precedence over everything. Activities of society are controlled and systematized for the purposes of war and reorganized in their most rational and effective forms for the final goal of victory. At such times, a strength unimaginable under ordinary conditions is added to the general effort.

Under the impetus of the two world wars, aircraft, rockets, and atomic power were rapidly researched and developed. After the wars ended, peaceful uses of these brought blessings to mankind. By increasing demand and the need for labor, war and war preparations play an important role in stabilizing economic development, but a kind of repetitive cycle is established in which vast economies bring about wars and wars stimulate further economic growth.

TOYNBEE: The fifth-century B.C. Greek philosopher Heraclitus said that war is the father of all things. War has been a stimulus for technological and economic development. The sinews of war are economic resources, and the weapons of war are products of technology. Belligerents develop their technological inventiveness and their economic resources to the utmost because the energies are keyed up to the highest pitch when they are fighting for their lives. Here, however, we come to the nemesis of war. Since one war tends to breed more wars, the accompanying progress of technology and the increase in a community's surplus product that can be expended on war tend to make each successive war more devastating than its predecessors, until finally warfare becomes so chronic and so destructive that it must be abolished by doing away with the sovereignty of the warring local states.

IKEDA: War now threatens our civilization and our continued existence on this globe. We must do something to alter the basic nature of economics so that it no longer stimulates warfare. There are a number of factors aside from war that can promote economic growth. For instance, expanding and improving our social security and educational systems, providing better housing for our people, and giving massive foreign aid to underdeveloped countries would demand sums sufficiently vast to support the economies of most nations.

TOYNBEE: War is only the most costly of a number of alternative possible economic stimuli; being the most costly, it is surely the least desirable.

There will be no lack of nonmilitary stimuli for us in the immediate future.

187

In the fast approaching next stage of history, mankind will have to exert itself to the utmost in order simply to secure its survival. We shall have to stabilize the world's economy, stop the population explosion, and revive religion as the major human concern that it has been in the past and that it ought always to be. We shall have more than enough work on our hands to call out all our best energies. We will not need war, nor will we be able to afford it.

Peaceful Utilization of Atomic Power

IKEDA: As a future source of energy, atomic power is an important subject for consideration. The First International Conference on the Peaceful Use of Atomic Power, held in Geneva in 1955, paved the way for developments in this direction. Since then, advanced countries have been competing to promote the peaceful application of this promising source of power.

Coal, the major power source from the nineteenth till the early twentieth century, has already given way to petroleum. Even petroleum, which still plays a leading role in modern industry, will be exhausted in the not-too-remote future. Rapidly expanding industry is squandering the energy resources that nature has untiringly built up from time immemorial. Even atomic energy is not inexhaustible. Since it is produced from mineral resources, the time will come when it too will no longer be available. Nevertheless, as a power source it has a great future since its per-unit quantum of energy can successfully replace petroleum and coal.

Atomic power, however, is a very dangerous, two-edged sword. While it may contribute tremendously to the welfare of mankind, its misuse may blot out the human race. Disposal of fuels, general handling, and a number of similar problems are much more serious in the case of atomic energy than in the case of petroleum or coal. Although there is no objection to peaceful uses of atomic power, great effort and research are needed to overcome the difficulties involved and to prevent possible damage.

Of all the problems connected with atomic power, the most difficult is how to prevent the results of studies primarily aimed at peaceful use from being abused for warlike purposes.

TOYNBEE: For the reasons you give, the development of atomic power for peaceful purposes is desirable and is indeed indispensable. I agree that this is the most dangerous of all the inanimate sources of power that have been harnessed, so far, by man.

IKEDA: I should like to propose an international body, perhaps established by the United Nations, to conduct periodic inspections of the achievements of all nations in the atomic field. Naturally, the body must be invested with the authority necessary to execute its duties. No nations, including those that apparently do not have atomic weapons, should be allowed to refuse the inspections. As a matter of course, atomic disarmament must precede full-scale peaceful use of atomic power. If total abolition at one stroke proves to be difficult, step-by-step measures must be taken. In this, as in all technological fields, innovations must be made public for the common good of the human race.

My proposal must naturally be applied to the internal zones of all countries. In Japan, though we are pursuing research for the peaceful use of atomic energy, in the spirit of our constitution we will not allow its conversion to military purposes. In order to prevent the military use of this energy in all countries, we must establish an inspection body aligned with no political interest and composed of private citizens as well as scholars. This body must be able to conduct its investigations at any time without intervention from governments.

A still more fundamental problem than peaceful utilization of atomic power is solving issues that lead to conflicts between nations that possess nuclear weapons, because this situation is bound up with the peace and welfare of humanity.

TOYNBEE: Unless and until the people of the world agree to renounce the use of atomic power for war and unless and until we have established a world authority with effective power to ensure that this renunciation is scrupulously honored in practice, it will not be safe for us to go ahead with the use of atomic power for peaceful purposes.

An effective world authority for controlling the use of atomic energy pre-supposes the establishment of an effective world government—by this I mean a government that will be able to enforce its will throughout the world as effectively as Ch'in Shih Huang-ti was able to enforce his will throughout China after the year 221 B.C. and as effectively as Hideyoshi and Ieyasu were able to enforce their wills throughout Japan.

Proxy Wars and Asia

IKEDA: Tension and opposition between the huge powers like the Soviet Union, China, and the United States threaten the medium and small nations of Asia and other parts of the world. Do you believe that the world is likely to suffer other tragedies like the Vietnam War? If such a proxy war, in which great powers fight without declaring themselves openly as belligerents, happens again, what steps can medium and small nations take to avoid becoming involved?

TOYNBEE: Unhappily, no matter how cautious small and medium nations may be, they are likely to become involved in wars of this kind against their wishes. For instance, Cambodia, a small unmilitary nation of very peaceful people, fell victim to American policy in Southeast Asia. The United States determined that North and South Vietnam should not be united. North Vietnam challenged the American decision and decided to take military action. But the only way to do this was to operate along the Ho Chi Minh trail through Cambodia. The Cambodians were powerless. If they had tried to stop the course of events, the North Vietnamese would have overrun their country. Prince Sihanouk had no choice but to allow the North Vietnamese to have their way. Then President Nixon very wrongly extended the war into Cambodia with the result that civil war raged through and destroyed this once peaceful nation. The most tragic aspect has been the powerlessness and blamelessness of the Cambodians.

Other Southeast Asian countries, too, have been sucked into the Vietnamese conflict. Thailand, like Japan an independent nation that has never known colonial rule, could scarcely refuse when the United States pressed for permission to build air bases on her soil. Thus Thailand unwillingly became implicated in the war. Australia and New Zealand, small nations that saw from the fall of Singapore that Britain could no longer protect them, turned to the United States because these two nations had a very real, if unfounded, fear of East Asia. The United States then compelled them to take part in the Vietnam War against their inclinations.

IKEDA: It does seem likely that in a world controlled almost entirely by force it will be difficult for small and medium nations, no matter how cautious, to avoid becoming embroiled in wars in one way or another. Still I think that Cambodia, Australia, and New Zealand had another choice open to them. They could have adamantly proclaimed their complete neutrality. Cambodia could have refused passage across her land to North and South Vietnamese alike. Thailand could have said no when the United States asked for permission to build bases on her land. And New Zealand and Australia could have rejected the proposal that they send troops to fight in Vietnam.

Obviously this would have put a damper on relations between Cambodia and China and the Soviet Union, and between Thailand, Australia, and New Zealand and the United States. But this brings us to the more basic issue of the validity of the mutual-defense and group-security ethics that dominate relations among nations in this age of preoccupation with military power.

This is a large and troublesome issue, but it seems imperative to me to devise new ethics in a world where the fires of war spread quickly from one country to another. Of course, mutual defense and collective security have performed important services. When Nazi Germany and militarist Japan were overrunning and suppressing small and medium nations, collective security helped give the victim countries some protection. On the other side of the coin, this same idea played a causative role in the generation of two world wars. Since the days of those wars, the very nature of warfare has been changed by the development of nuclear weapons. Today there can be no war for the sake of the protection of justice since war itself destroys justice.

As you said, Cambodia, Thailand, Australia, and New Zealand were drawn into the Vietnam War completely against their will. In the light of the fact that situations of this kind can emerge, it is imperative to make changes in the fundamental basis of international ethics. Since it would be very difficult to leave each nation entirely on its own, all nations should come together to deliberate in order to decide the posture they ought to take. Under circumstances of this kind, large, powerful nations would be unable to drag smaller nations into their conflicts. Moreover, such group deliberation might contribute to the ending of warfare itself.

TOYNBEE: Of course, it is not always merely alignments of the kind you describe in terms of collective security agreements that involve nations in the conflicts of other nations. Take for example the tragic case of Lebanon, whose population composition and geographical location almost inevitably involve her in the belligerency of her next-door neighbor, Israel. Though a small nation, Lebanon is by far the most modernized and advanced of the Arab countries. Once entirely a Christian country, Lebanon inherited a large Muslim population when, after World War I, France took over former Turkish territory in Lebanon and Syria and doubled the size of the Lebanese Republic by adding big stretches of Muslim territory to it. Today the Christian and Muslim elements of the Lebanese population are about equal in size, though the Christians are richer and more efficient. Naturally the Muslims, who do

191

not like being under Christian domination, sympathize with Arab guerrillas. This means that the issue between Israel and Lebanon becomes a domestic Lebanese issue between the Muslims and Christians. This situation has brought Lebanon to the verge of civil war. Although she has been very careful, Lebanon has been unable to stop Arab guerrillas who operate from Lebanon or the Israelis who make raids on Lebanon in retaliation against the guerrillas. This is Lebanon's tragedy, but it is not Lebanon's fault.

IKEDA: The Lebanese problem is of the very touchy kind in which a difficult domestic split, by becoming associated with an international dispute, threatens to drag an entire nation into war. I think that to resolve such an issue, the disagreeing domestic powers must create a situation in which complete fair play is possible; that is, the situation must allow them to use their own forces boldly and effectively to solve their own problems. If they are prevented from doing this and despair sets in, they are likely to seek outside assistance; this will inevitably threaten their own national security.

TOYNBEE: You have touched on two very important points that need further amplification: fair play, or social justice, and despair. It is very wicked to drive a people to despair by depriving them of social justice. This has been the case with the Palestinian guerrillas. Ever since the Balfour Declaration of 1917, the world has treated the native Palestinians as ciphers who are expendable and who do not count. The Palestinians, however, are human beings, who, like the Vietnamese, resent this treatment and give vent to their resentment by means of senseless acts of guerrilla warfare and terrorism. It is only a minority of the people who resort to these methods, but even the minority illustrates the point that despair leads to eruptions of violence.

Similar situations can be seen in other parts of the world where one people has oppressed or wrongly treated a suppressed people: the American Indians at Wounded Knee, the black guerrillas in Rhodesia. The answer to the problem is simple; do justice to the American Indians, the Palestinians, the Rhodesian blacks, and the world will not be forced to suffer the horrors of Wounded Knee and guerrilla crimes—or Israeli retaliation, which is in itself criminal.

IKEDA: You are absolutely correct. The first requirement of the people in authority in any nation is that they treat all the people under their authority with fairness and that they provide all their people—not just a select group—with equality of rights and opportunities. This attitude is a fundamental condition of politics and is essential both to the happiness of individual peoples and to the peace of the world.

192

Before leaving this topic, I should like to return to what we have called proxy wars and ask why, in your opinion, so many of the conflicts of this kind that have occurred since World War II have taken place in the East.

TOYNBEE: The reason why there have been wars in the Middle East and in Korea and Southeast Asia is that in those parts of the world, the United States could go to war without risking the serious danger of Russian or Chinese intervention. The black African nations are too weak yet to wage war, and the South American nations are too divided among themselves and too greatly dominated by the United States. As for Europe, as long as the United States and the Soviet Union fail to establish firm good relations, Europe is too dangerous a place to risk warfare.

Self-defense and the Japanese Constitution

IKEDA: Since the beginning of history, most nations have maintained military power for the sake of self-defense. Far from being an exception to this rule, our own age has expanded the range of military might beyond anything conceivable in the past. The amounts of money required to support modern military establishments have become proportionately vast. Nations possessing nuclear weapons claim that self-defense is their basic purpose. But the size of their nuclear arsenals far exceeds what would be needed to defend them from invasion. Their weapons are so huge in scale and so horrendous in nature that, were they ever to be used, the enemy nation, the nation launching the weapon, and perhaps the whole world would be put in the gravest jeopardy. All of this leads me to think that modern military power must be regarded as very different from the self-defense forces with which man has been familiar throughout the ages. I see no grounds for justifying military power in the world today.

TOYNBEE: The most effective means of national self-defense under the present international dispensation is to renounce the possession of physical armaments and the maintenance of armed forces with the exception of a national police force for the preservation of domestic law and order with a minimal use of weapons. The renunciation of armaments and armed forces designed for defense against attack by some foreign local sovereign power must, of course, be accompanied by the renunciation of any national actions or policies that are genuinely injurious to foreign countries and that give foreign governments legitimate grounds for complaint.

Most governments and most private individuals now agree that aggression by one local sovereign state against another is a crime. It is significant that the national ministries and national budgets that are designed for making war are nowadays usually labelled not "war ministries" and "war budgets," and never "aggression ministries" and "aggression budgets," but "defense ministries" and "defense budgets."

IKEDA: Worse than these euphemisms is the downright trickery of calling on young people to sacrifice their lives for the fiction of self-defense masking belligerence. Too often, political powers employ the excuse of national defense to conduct invasions that plunge the invaded and the invaders into the depths of misery. I am convinced that examples of warfare conducted for the sake of verifiable self-defense are rare.

TOYNBEE: Yet, in truth, to organize, to arm, and to recruit for defense cannot be distinguished in advance from making the same preparations with intention to attack. Therefore, preparations that are ostensibly for defense excite the suspicion that they may really be intended for attack. This moves a state that feels itself threatened to make counter-preparations, and, once an armaments race has begun, either of the competitors may be tempted to try to win the race by launching a surprise attack and seeking to justify this act of aggression by calling it a preventive war.

After the defeat of Germany in World War I, Denmark refused to reannex from Germany the part of Slesvik in which a majority of the population is German, in spite of the fact that the whole of Slesvik had been taken from Denmark by Prussia and Austria in the war of 1864. Then, between the two world wars, Denmark virtually disarmed herself. In World War II, Germany occupied Denmark militarily without provocation, but the frontier between Denmark and Germany, which had been drawn after World War I, was one of the few (in the territories temporarily occupied by his armies) that Hitler refrained from revising to Germany's advantage. Thus Denmark's policy of self-disarmament, combined with her previous refusal to commit a territorial injustice, would have been justified, even if Germany had won World War II.

The thesis that the best defense is the renunciation of the means of physical self-defense has not been accepted by most of the world's smaller sovereign states. For instance, Switzerland and Sweden, two sovereign states committed to a policy of neutrality, maintain formidable armaments as deterrents against aggression. Switzerland's armaments did preserve her neutrality in both world wars. Sweden, too, succeeded in escaping belligerency in both world wars, but in World War II she escaped it only because Germany did not see any strategic

194

advantage in attacking Sweden. Moreover, as the price for leaving Sweden's neutrality inviolate, Germany exacted from Sweden certain transit facilities in wartime that were perhaps not strictly compatible with the neutrality that Sweden professed.

IKEDA: Article 9 of the Japanese constitution renounces all types of war potential. There is much controversy as to whether this clause forbids even the maintenance of armed forces for purposes of self-defense. The discussion is focused not so much on technical interpretation as on how to preserve the security of Japan in the present international climate.

Those in favor of rearmament point out that all the countries of the world except Japan possess military forces. According to them, it is only natural that an independent nation should be armed to protect itself. They further insist that, should all forms of war potential be renounced and should the right of belligerence be entirely denied, then and only then will the right of self-defense, even though theoretically recognized, lose its practical meaning. Others, opposed to this reasoning, argue that the exercise of the right of self-defense does not necessarily require military might and that the policy of absolute nonarmament is, in itself, a powerful weapon in current international relations.

The right of self-defense is the right of a state to protect its own existence against imminent and unjust aggression by other countries. Raised to a social level, man's supreme natural right to protect his own life becomes the state's right of self-defense. It is axiomatic, then, that no nation should use this right to endanger the lives of the people of another country. This is the essential nature of the right of self-defense.

As things stand now, however, the right of self-defense presupposes aggression by other nations; consequently, the international community is charged with a war potential that gravely threatens the survival of mankind. In order to defend itself against this vast war machine, a country must possess prodigious war capabilities of its own; therefore, self-defense by means of arms has reached its limits. Solving this problem will be impossible as long as we continue to regard the right of self-defense as no more than the right of one state to safeguard itself against another and as long as we consider war potential the sole means of exercising this right. We have entered an age in which it is time to return to first principles, to start afresh with a broader view. Our new point of departure must be the right of survival of the people of the whole world, not of one nation alone.

From this standpoint, I take pride in the spirit of the Japanese constitution which renounces all forms of war potential and declares its determination to preserve our security and existence, trusting in the justice and faith of the peace-loving peoples of the world. This spirit must be preserved.

TOYNBEE: It would be a disastrous mistake on Japan's part to abrogate—or, even worse, to infringe without abrogating—Article 9 of the present Japanese constitution. Whatever may be the general future course of international relations, I think it is going to be of vital importance for Japan to establish good relations with China. In Chinese eyes, Japan's policy concerning Article 9 of her constitution is going to be the test of Japan's intentions towards China. Japanese rearmament, even if this were bona fide for self-defense and not for aggression, would arouse suspicion and hostility in China. In Chinese minds, it would awake memories of 1894 and of 1931–45. It might even tempt China, when her atomic armament becomes sufficiently advanced, to wage a so-called preventive war against Japan.

On the other hand, so long as Japan abides by Article 9, she will be in no danger of being attacked by China, even if China makes herself a first-class atomic power. China's territorial ambitions are probably limited to recovering the frontiers that she had attained in 1796. Beyond those frontiers, I suppose China's aims are negative. No doubt she wishes to obtain the withdrawal of the armed forces of the United States from Eastern Asia and from adjacent waters, but there is no indication that China wishes to occupy any of the Asian territories in which the United States now has troops and bases.

Therefore, adherence to Article 9 is, in my opinion, advantageous to Japan even in the present anarchic state of international relations. Of course, if the peoples of the world were to succeed in bringing this anarchy to an end by establishing a global government, this would prove, in a striking way, the Japanese people's wisdom and prescience in anticipating the course of history by writing Article 9 into their constitution.

IKEDA: Although Japanese economic power is expanding into the international field, it is awakening animosity in many parts of the world. As I observe this state of affairs, I cannot help recalling the position in which our nation found itself before the outbreak of World War II. Do you think Japan will again be put in a position of international isolation in the future? If so, how do you feel this can be prevented?

TOYNBEE: No, Japan has played too important a part in the economic life of the world as a whole for the rest of the nations ever to leave her out again, even if only for material reasons. Clearly, China and the Soviet Union are competing for Japanese assistance in developing their economies.

The problem as I see it is the extreme degree of Japanese economic success in recent years. The balance of trade has been too much in Japan's favor. On the long-term view, if nations are to trade successfully with each other, the balance between them must be equal, though it may swing to the advantage of one side or the other for brief periods. I hope that Japan will realize that in her trade with other nations—with the United States for instance—she must import to a value roughly equivalent to that of her exports.

I suspect that this is realized in Japan. Japan must be neither stronger nor weaker, neither defeated nor victorious, but equal with the other nations of the world. Being human, all of us will probably always bargain very hard with each other and try to get the advantage for our own side. Nevertheless, I hope that we shall all arrive at the point where we entertain a wholesome sense of justice for our fellow peoples. No, I do not think that Japan will ever be isolated again, but I do think that all nations will have to exercise consideration for all others.

Future Police Forces

IKEDA: As a Buddhist, I advocate absolute pacifism and the abolition of all military preparedness. But for the sake of discussion, let us assume that we ought to recognize the existence of domestic police forces for the preservation of law and order within a country. If mankind ever achieves world government, such police forces must be placed directly under the administration of that government. In other words, we must strive to establish a politically united world, and then we must submit all arms to the resulting global administration.

TOYNBEE: In planning what to do with armaments, our objective ought to be to reduce to a minimum their quantity, their deadliness, and their utilization.

Let us assume that mankind has succeeded in establishing a world government that has made it impossible for its component local states ever to go to war again. Let us also assume that these local states have been prohibited from retaining any national armaments of any kind and that this veto has been effectively enforced. I think the world state will still need an armed police force. It has not been found possible to do without police altogether in any local state—not even in one that is well governed and in which most of the citizens are law abiding. There is always a residual antisocial minority that

197

must be restrained. What is true today of a well-governed local state will, I believe, be true of a well-governed world state, if we succeed in establishing one.

IKEDA: I too think that some force for the preservation of law and order is always essential. Without it, good people would be made to suffer and would be left without protectors. Never in any society have evil and injustice been completely eradicated. Unfortunately, in the world today they seem to be more powerful than good and justice.

TOYNBEE: If we agree, then, that a police force will be needed, we are faced with two questions. How should the world-state police force be recruited? How should it be armed?

I hold that the world-state police force, like the present civilian staff of the United Nations, ought to be directly recruited by the world government itself and that its individual members ought to pay allegiance to the world government. The world police force ought not to be composed of contingents supplied by the constituent local states, for each of these would pay allegiance to its own local government and would subordinate to this its loyalty to the world government, a loyalty that ought to be paramount. The local states would need to be allowed to maintain local police forces for local purposes, but the size and the armament of a local police force would have to be kept within limits making it incapable of being misused for the unconstitutional and antisocial purpose of defying the world government's authority.

The world government will have to command sufficient force to be able to impose peace, on the most equitable terms practicable, in areas in which injustice, conflict, and violence amount to serious breaches of world peace and serious violations of individual and collective human rights. For instance, it would have to put an end to the oppression of blacks by whites in South Africa, of Arabs by Israelis in the Middle East, and of Roman Catholic Christians by Protestant Christians in Northern Ireland. The world government would have to depose the present oppressive local establishments under arrangements that would protect these ex-tyrants from being victimized, in their turn, by their own former victims.

Even if effective guarantees for the deposed local establishments were worked out, these guarantees would need to be enforced; and even if the local establishments were assured in advance of being effectively protected by the world government after their own deposition, they might try to resist by force of arms the world government's action for deposing them. In view of this possibility, it seems to me to be clear that the world government would need

198

to have a police force of its own, that this force would need to be armed, and that its armaments would need to be sufficiently potent to enable it to be sure of overcoming the utmost possible local resistance that it might encounter in carrying out its duty to establish worldwide peace, which could be done only by imposing order and enforcing justice. Considering the innate selfishness of human nature and the particularly truculent present temper of those oppressive local establishments that will have to be deposed, I fear that, in some cases at any rate, these will take up arms in order to resist being deposed and will therefore be deposed only at the cost of bloodshed.

IKEDA: I am painfully aware that the world today is very far from the ideal in which a moderate police force would suffice. I agree that a world police force is needed now and probably will be needed in the future. Even so, armaments themselves must be rigidly controlled. As a practical step, all nations ought to renounce at least nuclear weapons.

Nuclear arms have developed so rapidly in the years following World War II that they are now much deadlier than the atomic bombs dropped on Hiroshima and Nagasaki. Means of delivering them, too, have developed: intercontinental ballistic missiles, many kinds of aircraft with nuclear armaments, and submarines capable of firing undersea ballistic missiles. Our planet is constantly threatened with the terror of total destruction at the push of a button.

All of us living in this age must make up our minds firmly that to produce, possess, or use nuclear arms is wrong. If we do not, either the human race will be destroyed, or our successors in coming generations will fall heir to this horrible threat. No matter to what high levels our civilization and culture advance, as long as nuclear arms continue to exist, mankind can take no pride in its achievements.

Hiroshima and Nagasaki proved how horrible nuclear destruction is; they showed how diseases caused by radioactivity gnaw at human lives long after the damage to cities has been repaired. All the people of the world must recognize these terrifying facts.

TOYNBEE: Without waiting for the creation of world government, the still sovereign local governments ought to be compelled by their subjects to destroy all the nuclear weapons that at least five local governments already possess and to undertake never to acquire nuclear armaments in the future. I insist that a future world government ought to deny itself the possession of nuclear armaments and that this self-imposed veto ought to be one of the fundamental articles of the world government's constitution.

199

The very nature of nuclear weapons and of the means of employing them makes it impossible to use them in war except for the insane purpose of the mutual annihilation of the belligerents. The built-in indiscriminateness of nuclear weapons makes them, *a fortiori*, unusable for police work. The South African whites, the Northern Ireland Protestants, and the Israeli army of occupation in Arab territory could not be coerced with nuclear weapons. They could, of course, be annihilated with nuclear weapons, but this would involve in most cases the simultaneous annihilation of far larger numbers of their victims. Since the purpose of the exercise would be to liberate these victims, any attempt to accomplish this purpose by the use of nuclear weapons would be fantastically self-defeating.

Insofar as police forces for local establishments need to be armed, the armaments ought to be limited to conventional weapons, and these should be weapons of types that can subdue, with the minimum amount of wounding and killing, rioters who are using lethal weapons to resist the enforcement of the law. The law-enforcing police ought to use nonlethal weapons as far as possible: rubber bullets that inflict bruises but not wounds, gas that incapacitates temporarily without producing permanent harmful effects, and splashes of temporarily indelible colored paint on clothes and skin that will make a rioter identifiable and thus make it harder for him to escape being arrested and convicted.

Hitherto, scientific technology has been applied to devising and using weapons for the purpose of making the conduct of hostilities more lethal and more devastating. Although we ought to continue to apply scientific technology to the use of organized physical force, our objective ought to be reversed. We should devise weapons that will enable both the world government's police force and local police forces loyally supporting the world government to impose the orders of the legally constituted public authorities with the minimum infliction of damage to violent resisters and, above all, to innocent passers-by and to livestock, crops, and valuable inanimate property.

IKEDA: The idea of developing weapons that temporarily incapacitate without causing serious damage to people or to anything around them is excellent. There is no reason why scientific skill cannot produce such weapons. Scientists, of course, but more important, politicians, would do very well to turn their thinking into these channels.

The Nature and Future of War

IKEDA: Biologists tell us that *Homo sapiens* is the only species known to kill its fellows with systematic violence and cruelty. Do you believe that war is something humanity is destined to suffer? How do you think we can avoid a global nuclear war and achieve lasting peace?

TOYNBEE: Our present knowledge about human feelings, thoughts, value judgments, and actions extends backwards in time no farther than the most recent period of human history; that is, no farther than the period for which there are surviving contemporary records in writing. This period is only the latest five thousand years, and our ancestors may have become human one million years ago. The dating depends on the stage in our ancestors' evolution at which we guess, from the evidence of bones and tools, that they had become self-conscious, that is, fully human. Even if we were to count none of the now extinct species of hominids as being fully human and were to confine the term *human* to the sole surviving species, the so-called *Homo sapiens*, the human race would already have been at least two or three hundred thousand years old. Even this is a long span of time compared to the latest five thousand years.

It is certainly true that, during the last five thousand years, war has been one of the major institutions of mankind. We have spent on war by far the greatest part of our surplus product; that is, the greatest part of what we have produced in excess of the product spent on bare subsistence—spent, that is to say, on keeping ourselves alive and on saving our species from becoming extinct. But surely war is impossible without the production of a surplus, because war requires the uneconomic use of working time, food rations, materials, and industry for the conversion of these materials into weapons and other military equipment. As far as we know, no human community possessed the surplus needed for going to war before the draining and irrigation of the lower basins of the Tigris-Euphrates and the Nile, and this was not completed very long before about 3000 B.C. The earliest surviving depictions of war in Sumerian and Egyptian visual art and the earliest written records of wars are of about the same date. I conclude that war is no older than civilization and that, since the two are coeval, war is one of the congenital diseases of civilization.

War is not identical with violence and cruelty. It is a particular manifestation of human violence and cruelty. I believe that these evil impulses are innate in human nature and are intrinsic to life itself. Every individual living organism is potentially violent and cruel. War is an organized and institutionalized com-

201

mission of cruel violence. In war, human beings fight and kill each other under orders from public authorities—governments of states or improvised government in civil wars. Soldiers fight without personal animosity. Most of them are not acquainted with each other personally.

IKEDA: You have said that man has spent much of his surplus product on war, but I think he has in fact spent much more than surplus in terms of destroyed homes, ravaged agricultural lands, and the common necessities of life that are taken from ordinary people in wartime. An interesting example of the amount of a people's production that must be spent on military matters is the samurai of medieval Japan. Considered the highest of all Japanese social classes, they exploited the agricultural and commercial classes. Even in modern Japan a not completely dissimilar situation exists. As the self-defense forces grow larger, improvements in the living conditions of ordinary people must be sacrificed to support them. Even minimal welfare systems cannot be established. Homes for urban laborers remain inadequate because the money that ought to go into such projects is channeled into the defense budget. I suspect, however, that all countries in the world that have some kind of military preparedness face a similar dilemma.

TOYNBEE: Without doubt they do, but let me return to your earlier question. Is war part of the fate of human nature? For the historical reason that I have mentioned, I think that it is not. I do think that violence and cruelty are innate in human nature. As you point out, biologists tell us that man is the only known species of living being on this planet that fights fellow members of his own species to the death. When male animals of other species fight each other for winning the females, one combatant eventually surrenders and the victor then spares his life. Crimes of violence, not stopping short of murder, have, we may suppose, been committed by our ancestors ever since they became human. But, even within the last five thousand years, human violence and cruelty have not manifested themselves in the form of war at all times and places.

Japan, for instance, seems to have been free from domestic warfare, though not from aggressive border warfare against the Ainu, for more than five hundred years, ending in the twelfth century of the Christian era. After that, Japan tormented herself with incessant civil wars for more than four hundred years. Under the Tokugawa regime from the early seventeenth until the middle of the nineteenth century too, she was at peace, both at home and abroad. Since 1945 Japan has renounced war.

The Norwegians were not at war at any date between 1814 and 1940, but

202

in the Viking age they were one of the most warlike peoples in the world, and they fought vigorously in World War II after they had been attacked and invaded.

During the periods of Japanese and Norwegian history that were free from war, there were still private murders and public executions in both nations. This shows that we must distinguish war from our nonmilitary killing and violence.

IKEDA: You are absolutely correct in insisting on this distinction. Execution for crime is perhaps different, but murder is always an act of the individual. Even when committed by a gang or criminal organization, the basic situation is unchanged, since the decision to become a member of an organization that commits such crimes is based on individual motivation. Murder occurs in all lands, and all nations forbid it strictly and punish it severely. The same nations that punish murder, an individual act, however, have no systems of punishment against warfare, a criminal act committed by nations. The barbaric law that has obtained throughout the ages is that he who wins is just. But the contradiction inherent in this idea is so blatant that no one can find such a definition of justice tenable. Nonetheless, man has given tacit assent to this irrational law for thousands of years.

Tacit approval seems to suggest that people regard warfare, or conditions based on warfare, as the normal circumstance among nations. It is apparently thought essential to be prepared for war at all times and to be at sword point with all neighboring nations. Peace, then, becomes no more than the interval between wars. I do not believe that this is the way things ought to be.

In my view, all people must come to think of peace—the time when no human beings fear any others, when all trust and love each other—as the natural and ordinary way of life. Only when this belief is our guiding principle can a truly human society be created. I regard the propagation of such belief and the consequent building of a human society as the prime duty of political leaders, philosophers, and intellectuals.

TOYNBEE: War can be abolished, even if it were to prove impossible to cure all human beings of committing nonmilitary crimes of violence. I think the invention of nuclear weapons makes it probable that we shall succeed in abolishing war, in spite of the difficulty of giving up a habit that is five thousand years old. The assumption underlying the institution of war was that one of the belligerents would win, that the other would lose, and that the advantage of victory for the winner would be greater than the cost. This calculation often proved wrong. Wars were often disastrous for the victors too.

But it is clear that, in a war fought with nuclear weapons, there can be no such thing as even a costly victory. This prospect deprives states of a rational incentive for going to war.

However, human nature is only partially rational. It is conceivable that we might irrationally commit mass suicide. The institution of war cannot be abolished without replacing it by a new institution: world government. War, even in the nuclear age, will remain a possibility so long as the present 140 local states have not subordinated themselves to a single worldwide authority equipped with effective power to compel even the most powerful local states to keep the peace.

CHOOSING
A POLITICAL SYSTEM | 8

Qualities of a Good Leader

IKEDA: One by one the heroes and leaders of the age of World War II have died or become inactive. Today, with the exception of Mao Tse-tung, there seem to be no towering figures capable of global influence. It is difficult to know whether the absence of heroes is fortunate or unfortunate. It is a sign of progress when conditions no longer require the concentration in one human being of sufficient power to make him a charismatic leader whose judgments influence the whole world. It is good that the democratic mechanism of society operates so satisfactorily that there is no need to rely on leaders whose powers extend over a vast scale. The question is quite different, however, if one interprets the lack of outstanding figures as an indication that contemporary democratic society is unable to produce leaders of great ability and appeal.

TOYNBEE: I fear that we may not have seen the last of the charismatic dictatorial leaders. Of course, constitutional government with the maximum participation of as many citizens as possible is the political objective at which we ought to aim, but the present-day world needs such drastic political and social changes, and needs them so urgently, that I doubt whether it will be possible to achieve them constitutionally.

I think that personal leadership is needed for every collective enterprise of any kind, even for enterprises that are organized on the most democratic lines possible. Leadership of a democratic enterprise, organization, or institution is a more delicate and difficult task than charismatic, dictatorial leadership. A leader of the latter kind obtains the obedience of his subjects partly by force and partly by arousing irrational emotions. Under a democratic regime, the leader ought to obtain his fellow citizens' cooperation by convincing them rationally that the policy he is proposing is right, and he ought to conduct this rational dialogue with them at a low emotional temperature.

IKEDA: The difference between the two kinds of leadership is of the greatest importance. As you say, democratic leadership is both more difficult and more delicate. Democratic leaders must always deal with prescribing the nature of systems and structures for the management of society. These systems and structures must be created in accordance with the rules of democracy, the theories of which must be the background for all management. The human heart, however, invariably harbors the greedy desire to stabilize and expand the rights and privileges of the individual, even at the expense of others. When the man in authority allows this desire to hold sway over his thoughts and actions, the system or structure that he is supposed to guide for the good of the majority can become an absolute in itself, and the ideals on which it is based can be overlooked.

Because the present global situation is neither peaceful nor stable, for the sake of solutions to the many problems facing mankind, a leadership based on wisdom and high ideals is essential. In a democracy, the leader must always be judged unemotionally on the basis of his leadership principles and the extent to which he is able to put those principles into practice. If applied sensibly and unfailingly, this kind of judgment can be an important help in preventing the emergence of charismatic leaders.

TOYNBEE: If a democratic regime is to work satisfactorily, it needs a leader who is neither a trickster nor a demagogue but a person of such manifest ethical and intellectual worth that his fellow citizens will follow his lead without having to be either coerced or emotionally excited. Such a leader is hard to find and, if found, may be reluctant to undertake the difficult and thankless task of guiding his fellow citizens. The leader's role is obviously of the greatest social importance; to undertake it for altruistic reasons requires a very high degree of public spirit and unselfishness.

The democratic leaders in our time who have come the closest to playing their difficult role satisfactorily are, in my judgment, Franklin D. Roosevelt, Winston Churchill, and Jawaharlal Nehru. Yet Roosevelt—and even Nehru—was not completely candid in his relations with his constituents. Moreover, each of the three had the advantage of being called to office in a crisis, when even democracies are amenable to being induced to endure hardships and to make sacrifices.

IKEDA: Yes, in time of trouble, people are likely to be easier to lead. It is possible to say that Roosevelt and Churchill were fortunate to come into power at a time of national crisis, which gave them the opportunity to exercise their talents to the full. But the situation would have gone from crisis to disaster if these men had lacked great talent.

I feel that the power entrusted to leaders in a democracy must always be temporally limited. When a man's term in power is over, the people ought to judge his actions in office and decide whether to retain him in his position of leadership or oust him in favor of someone else. In other words, the characteristic of the democratic leader, in contrast to the dictator, ought to be the awareness that the power he exercises while in office, no matter how great it is, originates with the people and is subject to their judgment. I realize that this system has a serious flaw. Because he is constantly aware of the surveillance of the people, a man in office who wants to remain there might adopt policies merely because they are popular and because in following them he ensures his continuation in power.

TOYNBEE: A democratic leader must steer a middle course between two undesirable alternatives, and his room for manoeuver between them is narrow. On the one hand, he may be tempted to pander to the wishes of his constituents, even when he judges their wishes to be misguided. If he does this, he will be virtually abdicating from his role of leadership and will be betraying his trust. The opposite undesirable alternative is for him to trick his constituents into voting for a policy that he judges to be right but that they would have rejected if it had been put to them candidly. This, too, is a betrayal of the leader's trust. Moreover, his fraud is likely to be detected sooner or later, and then he will be discredited.

IKEDA: I agree that the leader must not deceive himself for the sake of ingratiating himself with the people and that he must not deceive the people for the sake of putting through his own ideas. In all things, he must base his thinking and his actions on truth and faithfulness, for the moment that he attempts to fool either himself or the people, he forfeits his qualifications as a leader. There is nothing more disturbing in a society than a politician who is devoted solely to securing his own authority at all costs.

In this respect I greatly admire the attitude that Winston Churchill took. He served heroically to save Britain during the nightmare of World War II, but when the fighting was over and he was told that the people did not consider him suited to the reconstruction task, in a manly fashion he gave over his political authority to Clement Atlee's Labor Party.

207

I require that the politician be true and faithful to himself and to the people and that he be entirely just in his actions. The qualifications of a good leader— courage, justice, courtesy, practical wisdom, dignity, and generosity—can only be manifested if the man who would be a leader is prepared to enter into dialogues with the people, do battle for their sake, and die with them if need be. Furthermore, the true value of the leader depends on how well he prepares those who will follow in his footsteps. He must train his followers not with the idea of personal advantage or the fulfillment of personal greed but with the welfare and future of all humanity in mind.

But as you say, leaders of this caliber are rare today. Moreover, many of the historical personages who have caused immense stir and in some cases accomplished great things have been people whose personalities fail to elicit respect.

TOYNBEE: In a nondemocratic state, in which the leader rules by exercising force and by arousing emotion, the high-minded unself-seeking fanatic—like Robespierre or Lenin—is sometimes more disastrous and less effective than a cold-blooded and cynical but cunning and tactful careerist. The Chinese Emperor Han Liu Pang, the Roman Emperor Augustus, and the Arab Caliph Muawiyah are three examples of the calculating, careerist leader. Each of the three took over an imperial government that had come to grief as a result of a previous leader's tactlessness; each of the three succeeded, thanks to his own savoir faire, in reestablishing a broken-down imperial regime and putting it on a durable basis. The savoir faire of these men was not admirable ethically, but, in the circumstances, it was politically expedient.

I do not think that any regime of any kind can be operated successfully by a leader whose personality is mediocre. In the history of the United States, there have been some mediocre presidents who have been more harmful to the country than demagogues and tricksters. In the history of the Soviet Union, while Leonid Brezhnev is, no doubt, preferable to the monster Joseph Stalin, he seems to be a poor exchange for his temperamental and dynamic predecessor Nikita Khrushchev.

Safeguards against Fascism

IKEDA: Recently, in countries like the United States where administrative controls extend into an increasing number of social areas, there has been some concern about the danger of a turn toward fascism. Though fascism and democracy are fundamentally opposite, fascism does sometimes wear a mask of democracy. Indeed, democracy can be the soil in which the seed of fascism grows. I think that at this point we could advantageously turn to this question to try to find out two things: the issues on which most caution must be exercised if we are to prevent the rise of a new fascism; the areas in democracy that might most easily lead to the rise of fascism. Because of the danger that democracy can degenerate into mob rule, we must be constantly watchful.

TOYNBEE: Democracy has certainly sometimes degenerated into mob rule. A notorious instance is Athenian democracy in the fifth century B.C. The poor majority of the citizens voted the taxes that the rich had to pay, and when Athenian democracy was discredited by a defeat in a great war, the rich seized the opportunity to set up a violent fascist regime. This regime was quickly overthrown, and democracy was reestablished at Athens, but the abuses associated with democracy were not corrected.

IKEDA: As long as the number of people who are desperately disappointed in democracy remains small, there is little worry about the political system, but should profound dissatisfaction become the prevailing attitude, fascism might find a footing.

Modern history proves that the true nature of fascism is never apparent at the outset. Historically it has often arisen without announcing itself and has at first assumed a perfectly legal platform within a democratic society. Therefore, it is essential to spy out its traits before any of them has a chance to develop into full-scale fascism. In the beginning, Nazism was only a small right-wing reactionary party in the basically democratic Weimar Republic. How did this group, ironically employing democratic elections, grow from no more than one among several small parties into the leading party and then into a firmly established dictatorship? Hitler's evil genius as a manipulator of the masses without doubt played a part, but closer analysis shows that this was not all of the story. In the early days, the people of all classes supported the Nazi line of thought, without, I dare say, having an inkling of the horrifying situation they were inviting. Especially after the worldwide panic of 1929, small businessmen, white-collar workers, farmers, and the overwhelming majority of students, discouraged by Germany's defeat in World War I and frightened by economic conditions, followed the lead of the Nazi party because they regarded it as the one political organ that would fulfill their needs.

TOYNBEE: A poverty-stricken minority is politically powerless. On the other hand, a lower middle class that is being squeezed between the capitalist and the trades unionist wings of the establishment is capable of organizing itself and taking the offensive against both these privileged classes. The insurgent lower middle class was the explosive social force that carried Hitler into power in Germany in the 1930s. Since no one else was willing to help them, they helped themselves by organizing themselves into the National Socialist Party and by capturing control of the government. I agree that Hitler's demagogic genius would not, by itself, have enabled him to become the dictator of Germany if there had not been a discontented class in Germany to which Hitler could offer redress in return for their acceptance of him as their leader.

IKEDA: The Germans of the time entrusted themselves too readily to the Nazi party in the hope of finding solutions to their admittedly pressing difficulties. They failed, however, to be able to see that the methods the Nazis followed would inflict infinitely greater grief on other peoples. Made impatient by their hardships and unable to see the harm the Nazis could do, the Germans naturally could not foretell that the peoples on whom they were inflicting injury would one day rise up against them with immense strength. This blindness led to the frustration of Germany's national hopes and to her own self-destruction.

Sorrowfully we must admit that it is a very human characteristic to be extremely sensitive to one's own pain and singularly insensitive to the suffering of others. Nevertheless, for the sake of the preservation of freedom, each individual human being must possess the mental ability to assess the effects of the political acts of his system on the lives and well-being of other people. I feel that the only way to ensure that all human beings have this kind of ability is to provide them with a sound philosophy based on love and respect for all humanity. Such a philosophy will help develop individual wisdom, and wisdom alone can prevent the rise of fascism. I am certain that, for the sake of the defense of democracy, each individual must have the intelligence to examine closely the fundamental nature of everything that happens around him. Individual good sense is the best way to guard democracy against the rise of fascism.

TOYNBEE: In my opinion, the best safeguard against fascism is to establish social justice to the maximum possible extent. Complete social justice is difficult to attain, because the establishment—whatever its social composition happens to be—usually insists on a differential distribution of the community's wealth. For instance, in present-day Britain differentials are insisted upon by trades unionists as well as by capitalists. Consequently, there are usually some classes in a community that are left out in the cold. If the injustice with which they are treated by their more powerful fellow citizens is gross, these penalized classes will seize any opportunity to overthrow the regime that has failed to give them a fair deal, as happened in Germany in 1933. The closer a regime approximates being socially just, the greater its stability. But social justice is an elusive objective because there is no agreed criterion for deciding what is the just allocation of the community's wealth among the different social classes of which the community is composed.

The Nature, Means, and Ends of Power

IKEDA: The idea that the end justifies the means has been the driving force of many organizations and is prevalent today in many fields of endeavor. People engaged in political power struggles have argued that application of this principle is unavoidable. The fascists are an extreme example of such a group. Since we must prevent the appearance of other groups like the fascists, we must clearly understand the proper relationship between ends and means. My interpretation of the problem is that an end depends to a large extent on the means used to achieve it. In other words, the process by which a goal is reached must prove the justness of the goal itself.

TOYNBEE: An end does not justify a means. Means and ends must be ethically consistent. This principle is borne out by experience. It is psychologically impossible to do right at stage two by deliberately doing wrong at stage one. If one is wrong at the outset, it is impossible to reach a righteous goal.

IKEDA: One thing that makes it especially important to examine the means of modern organizations is the nature of the goals they announce. The case is somewhat different with organizations frankly professing prejudiced views; but in many cases goals expressed by groups have a breadth of applicability that makes them attractive to many people. Such goals arouse sympathy because they seem to meet human needs. Since these goals frequently involve vague, abstract ideas, however, it is difficult to ascertain their good and bad points and hard to grasp the nature of the groups or movements professing them. In such cases, it is inevitable that we examine the means employed by those organizations and groups. I agree with you that ends and means must be ethically consistent, for if the means contradict the ends, the ends themselves degenerate into meaningless slogans.

211

TOYNBEE: The fallacy of the idea of attaining good ends by following bad means is the theme of Dostoevski's novel *The Possessed*, with its satanic hero. It is also the lesson that can be derived from the careers of two high-minded revolutionaries, Robespierre and Lenin. They were both unself-seeking men who had dedicated themselves sincerely and wholeheartedly to working for the welfare of mankind. But they made the mistake (an ethical mistake as well as an intellectual one) of thinking that their aims were so good and the attainment of those aims was so important that violence was a justifiable means. Consequently, instead of creating earthly paradises, Robespierre produced the Terror and Lenin, a totalitarian regime.

IKEDA: Your examples illustrate the need for the lofty ideals of a goal to be reflected in the means used to achieve that goal. It seems to me that the worldwide peace movements would do well both to clarify the processes by which they intend to realize the high programs they set and to conform those processes to their ideals. But even when a high goal is achieved by ideal means, inevitably the problem of power and its abuse arises. This issue is one that demands constant wary attention.

Society requires order. To maintain order, authority is essential. Authority manifests itself in terms of power that constrains and sometimes oppresses the actions of human beings. Power in its turn often becomes an evil restricting human freedom and infringing on human rights. In other words, though by nature power ought to be wielded for the protection of humanity and for the fulfillment of beneficial aims, because of the psychological motives and the aims of the person controlling authority, it frequently becomes an evil.

The words *abuse of authority* carry two shades of meaning. First, they can suggest the essential degeneration of the power-holder as a result of an intensification of his own selfishness and lust for glory. Second, they can represent the invasions of human rights and the danger of threat to life itself that such invasions imply. Still, power can be used correctly as long as the person in authority has a pure spirit that inspires him to protect human happiness and justice and to prevent his own authority from causing harm. Obviously human beings expect and hope for this kind of exercise of power.

But, unfortunately, man is not by nature always good, and circumstances often rob him of spiritual purity. This situation brings about uses of power that sacrifice many human beings for the sake of the happiness and power of a small group of power-holders. Although abuse of power might seem to be a problem related primarily to people in authority, the role of the masses subjected to power is highly important in the creation of a climate in which misuse of authority can grow.

TOYNBEE: Power held and exercised over others by one or more persons is an inescapable factor in human life because man is a social animal and power is automatically generated by social relations. Of course, it is possible for power to be used for good instead of for evil, but since every living being is by nature self-centered and greedy, a human being who acquires power is strongly tempted to misuse it for his own selfish advantage at the expense of the interests of the people who are in his power.

Since man is a social animal, the first priority on the agenda of a society is always to save society from disintegrating into an anarchy that would make it impossible for the participants in the society to survive. Consequently, there are situations in which even an unjust exercise of power is the lesser evil, and this is why the victims of a power-holder sometimes acquiesce in the unjust use of his authority over them. In other words, they hope that, at the price of allowing the man in power to do as he likes, they can save society from disintegration. Of course, they often miscalculate. In 1933, the German people submitted to Hitler in the hope that he would prove to be their savior. Instead, he deliberately involved them in World War II and thus brought on Germany a disaster far greater than those that she incurred in the worldwide financial crisis of 1929 or even in her defeat in World War I.

IKEDA: The desire to preserve a prevailing system can become a support for the abuse of power. But I might bring up another psychological aspect that gives impetus to the development of tyranny. There are many people who gladly debase themselves before the mighty in the hope of being admitted into the powerful group and of sharing in whatever profits are being made. In this way, great evil attracts petty evil. The great evil grips its smaller adherents firmly and, sapping their strength, grows ever stronger. The self-propagating characteristic of misused power is an evil of the most awesome kind.

TOYNBEE: Yes, and that self-propagating ability can find great range for development in large societies. For instance, today all peoples are coalescing into a worldwide society. But that society is in the danger of disintegrating for several reasons. First, the existence of 140 sovereign states, largely in discord among themselves, threatens total political anarchy. Second, the population explosion presents immense problems. Third, sensational recent progress in technology has conferred new power on a minority of mankind, who have appropriated that power to themselves. This powerful group may be called the rich minority of the world's peoples. It is using its power to indulge its own greed by consuming a grossly unfair share of the world's resources, many of which are unrenewable and irreplaceable.

213

IKEDA: By just such actions as you mention, man is becoming the greatest single threat to his own existence. Unless we learn how to govern ourselves more successfully, we run the risk of plummeting into a whirlpool of destruction. The problem of power and authority is an intensely concentrated case of the need for human beings to learn self-control.

TOYNBEE: You mentioned the danger of our falling into a whirlpool of destruction. To amplify somewhat on that point, I might say that it seems as if mankind may suddenly wake up to a realization of the truth that the greed of the rich, working together with the increasing numbers of the poor and with anarchy in international relations, threatens the whole world with imminent disaster. I suspect that a worldwide totalitarian movement of the communist-fascist kind may overthrow existing institutions—such as local sovereignty, political democracy, economic private free enterprise—and that at the eleventh hour, some such totalitarian movement will stabilize human affairs by taking drastic actions in which indispensable fundamental reforms will be intertwined with atrocious acts of injustice. This worldwide revolutionary movement may take the form of a global politico-religious organization that will produce a new ideology of its own. The chief plank of the global party platform will probably be stabilization in all departments of life at any price.

 When this revolutionary work has been accomplished under the leadership of a ruthless world dictator, I suspect that a reaction will take place and that the necessary stabilization will be remodeled into a milder and therefore more durable form. This will be accomplished by a second world dictator who will be more tactful in his actions because he will have learned by experience that his predecessor's ruthlessness turned out to be counterproductive.

IKEDA: Your forecast is both bold and disturbing. I constantly pray that a totalitarian government that tramples on the freedom of the individual may never rise again. Please explain in more detail the basis on which you make this estimation of the future.

TOYNBEE: Although I could give many more illustrations of my point, in fact I have in mind three cases taken from Japanese, Chinese, and Roman history. Tokugawa Ieyasu, who followed Toyotomi Hideyoshi, established the long-lived Tokugawa regime. Ch'in Shih Huang-ti founded the Imperial Ch'in, which lasted a brief fourteen years (221–207 B.C.). His successor, Han Liu Pang, however, created a Chinese imperial regime that lasted, on and off, for more than twenty-one centuries. Similarly, Augustus, who followed Julius

Caesar, established a Roman imperial system that lasted from 31 B.C. until A.D. 284 in its original form and in a more autocratic form at Constantinople till A.D. 1204.

In all three of these cases, even the more moderate imperial regimes that followed the drastic initial ones sometimes, and to some extent, exercised their powers unjustly and oppressively, though, on an average, they were lesser evils than any possible alternative in the particular circumstances of their times and places.

IKEDA: I can believe that the collapse of human society could lead to the establishment of a worldwide dictatorship. Though obviously social questions are important, the true cause of abuse of power lies in the evil that—like good —is a basic element in human life. Consequently, throughout our search for peace and happiness, the problem of abuse of power may persist, even if all others are solved.

TOYNBEE: I agree that the essential evil of power is an innate tendency in human nature and that we must search for means of mitigating this evil. I believe that the only effective means is the subordination of egotism or greed to altruism or love in the conduct of individuals. In other words, self-mastery is the only way to happiness for the individual and for all humanity.

IKEDA: Realizing and putting into practice the means you describe are the major issues facing mankind today. The first essential is basic self-awareness and self-mastery on the part of the individual human being. But we must strive to channel our thoughts about all of society in the same direction. A human revolution is needed to produce both individuals and a society in which altruism is the prevailing spirit. To prevent that revolution from resulting in a totalitarianism that would infringe on the dignity of the individual, we must ensure that it is based on a philosophy and a religion that have the power to convince all people. In addition, we must make certain that this philosophy is born of the spontaneous awaking of each person.

Democracy or Dictatorship

IKEDA: Several outstanding writers and scholars have attempted to analyze the increasing importance of the masses of humanity. Perhaps the classic in the field is *Revolt of the Masses* by the Spanish writer Jose Ortega y Gasset.

Other noteworthy writers in the field include Erich Fromm, who described the tendency of the masses to attempt to flee from freedom toward dictatorial systems, and David Riesman, who made a study of what he calls the lonely crowd. These and other outstanding works in a similar vein have repeatedly analyzed the relationship between the dictator and the masses, especially as this relation was manifested in the case of Nazi Germany. But none of the research dealing with the relation between the masses and the governing system has discussed ways of preventing the people from falling under the control of a dictator.

Unfortunately, the modern trend is for human beings in the aggregate to be led into foolishness, ignorance of their rights, and the irresponsible pursuit of pleasure. Though superficially the masses sing the praises of human rights and freedom, in fact they are losing their faith in democracy. Under these conditions, mankind may well be on a dangerous road where one mistake leads to either overwhelmingly powerful dictatorship or to totalitarianism.

TOYNBEE: Human beings acquiesce in, or even welcome or demand, dictatorships for two reasons that are distinct and different in kind. One reason is psychological and perennial; the other is environmental and occasional. The perennial psychological reason for accepting dictatorship is that it relieves all individuals, except, of course, the dictator himself, of the agony of having to make crucial choices. The occasional environmental reason is the onset of some physical or social emergency.

A danger is easier to surmount if the people who are exposed to it put themselves under a single individual's command, instead of each trying to cope with the common danger uncoordinatedly. Traveling by plane or ship or by camel caravan would be prohibitively dangerous if the travelers did not submit to the dictatorship of a captain for the duration of their journey. Similarly, in a social emergency, people find that submission to a dictatorship is a lesser evil than the continuance of anarchy.

The wish to survive an emergency is a less formidable cause of dictatorship than the wish to escape the agonizing responsibility of making choices. *Dictator* is, in origin, a technical term in the initial republican Roman constitution. In an emergency, the constitutionally elected public officers voluntarily suspended their exercise of power and appointed, on their own initiative, a dictator with autocratic powers to replace them for the duration of the emergency. This system worked successfully till 133 B.C., when Rome's emergency was made chronic by intractable economic and social maladies. A century later, dictatorship became a permanent institution at Rome. The reason for its permanence was that the body of citizens had become perma-

216

nently apathetic. They had lost the belief that they could manage their own affairs without running into disaster.

The present-day world is intolerably anarchic. Mankind's survival now depends on a technology with a worldwide range of operation, but even this is being paralyzed by the continuing partition of the globe among 140 discordant, sovereign, local states. It therefore seems likely that, sooner or later, the modern world will be unified politically by the dictatorial method by which Ch'in Shih Huang-ti unified China in the third century B.C., when the Chinese people had become sick and tired of the turbulent conditions of the period of the Warring States.

IKEDA: It is true that human beings acquiesce in almost any governmental system that promises improved conditions. But I feel that the true nature of the system itself, no matter whether it is called monarchy, dictatorship, or rule by an intellectual elite, depends on the attitude of the people in power. Since democracy provides the most effective checks on power abuse, it is the most generally acceptable governmental system available to us at present. Of course, it has its drawbacks, but it is bad to dwell too long on them, for this can inspire the sentimental desire for a return to the monarchies of the past or the wish to achieve security by establishing new dictatorships.

As long as the masses preserve their apparently innate desire for dictatorships in time of crisis, it is essential to devise ways of averting the danger of the emergence of dictators. I believe that the only way to do this is to elevate the educational and moral levels of the masses. The solution to the problem lies in shaking the people out of their lethargy and evolving systems in which maximum participation by a maximum number of people prevents power itself from getting out of control.

What I will say now is related to what you earlier described as the environmental and temporary reason for the emergence of a dictatorship. Let us suppose that a social body is engaged in violent conflict with another social body. Under such circumstances, it may be advantageous to concentrate the controlling power in the hands of an individual or of a group. At such times, quick judgments and the ability to conform to changing circumstances are important, since lack of speed in making decisions could give the enemy a vital advantage that might lead to defeat and possibly the destruction of all members of the losing social group. In cases of this kind, the actions of all members must be based on the decisions of the leader: obedience must be obligatory and insubordination forbidden.

In times of peace, on the other hand, the situation is entirely different. In a peaceful society, where the existence of groups and the lives of its individual

217

members do not hang on the issue of defeat or victory, the quality of the contents of judgments and decisions is more important than the speed with which they are made.

In the case of a nation, there are many different needs and desires to be satisfied. Multitudes of individual human beings form themselves into multifarious groups, each with its own ideals and aims. In these circumstances, the main task of authority is to try to ensure harmony and the equitable satisfaction of the needs and demands of many groups, each of which may be energetically asserting its own claims in competition with some or all of the others. Exercise of authority, then, is not directed against an external enemy but is brought to bear on individual and group elements within the society.

Ideally power ought to be put to use so as to reflect the wills of all members of society equally. In the light of these considerations, while realizing that it has its flaws and that it can easily fall into a number of traps, I am forced to the conclusion that democracy is the most desirable governmental system.

TOYNBEE: Even a permanent dictatorship is a lesser evil than incurable anarchy, yet dictatorship is a calamity nevertheless. The alternative is an effective constitutional regime in which as many members of the citizen-body as possible participate as actively as possible in the management of public affairs. In the present-day world, this is vitally important. But the citizens will not make the effort to participate actively unless they feel it credible that their participation will be effective in fact.

IKEDA: Seizing upon this danger, some people argue against democracy on the basis of the opinion that the citizens are fools incapable of thinking for themselves and therefore not to be entrusted with the right of selecting their leaders. In many instances, the leading advocates of this theory are people with aristocratic leanings or members of an intellectual elite.

One of the most glaring flaws in democracy stems from the very fact that the people select the man they find most attractive for a number of reasons, some good, some bad. For instance, it is not unusual for a man to rise to political position as a result of popular election merely because he is a skillful manipulator of public opinion. On the other hand, the populace sometimes ignores diligent and earnest leaders who are poor at advertising themselves. In extreme cases, the public may employ the democratic system to elect and put into virtually complete power a man whose aim is to destroy democracy and set himself up as a dictator. The reason that some critics object to a democracy in which all of the people participate is this weakness, which is undeniably part of the system. But it is an error to brand an entire citizen-body as fools because of the possibility of mistakes of this kind. Instead, it is the duty of the intellectual elite to strive to lift the masses from ignorance. The mass is no more foolish than its individual components, and all of us have our share of foolishness. By means of education that raises the intellectual level of the populace, much can be done to mitigate this fault. At the same time, power must be dispersed over as wide a base as possible so that a maximum number of the members of society can exercise their rights by direct participation in government.

TOYNBEE: You have pointed out the criticisms of democracy voiced by people that you say are usually either aristocratic in sympathy or members of an intellectual elite. I suspect that lack of confidence is more widespread than you suggest. By nature, democracy requires the complete trust of its citizens, but there are two major threats to that indispensable confidence. One of these threats is perennial, the other peculiar to the present-day world.

The perennial threat is the difficulty of electing worthy public officers. Constitutional government breeds politicians; that is, people who make politics their career and who become professionals in the art of persuading the electorate to put them in power and to keep them there. The practice of this professional art enables politicians to win elections, but it does not enable them to win the electorate's respect. The electorate elects them yet despises them, and the discrediting of the politicians discredits the constitutional political regime, which enables the politicians—through the electorate's fault—to be elected to offices of which they are unworthy. Recently the credibility gap between politicians' pretences and their performance has become wide. The public has seen through the politicians' insincerity and inadequacy, but it has not seen how to elect more respectable rulers. The present wide-spread disillusionment with politicians, together with the failure to translate disillusionment into reform, is putting democracy in jeopardy.

The threat to democracy that is peculiar to the present-day world is the portentous increase in quantities and magnitudes. This is an effect of two causes: the population explosion and the increase in the scale of operations and in the volume of production of technology. Man now feels himself dwarfed by his environment, both his social environment and the artificial material environment that has been imposed on the natural environment by technology's triumphant success. Present-day man's social environment has become depressingly impersonal; his material environment has become crushingly massive. This experience of life saps man's ability to believe that he can be an effectively responsible participant in society, and this skepticism lowers his self-respect and, with it, his ethical standards.

Therefore, it is now supremely important to enable the individual to continue to be socially effective; in order to make this possible, the individual must be convinced that he is being given a chance of effectiveness by present-day institutions; and, in order to convince him, we have to make our institutions genuinely and manifestly participational. Because of the adverse circumstances I have already described, creating participational institutions will be difficult, but we must not give way to despair and to the resignation and passivity that would follow.

Even if the world's present emergency were to make a temporary world dictatorship the only alternative to the self-imposed extinction of mankind, we can draw inspiration from the Romans in the republican age, who did succeed repeatedly in reverting to constitutional government from temporary dictatorships as soon as the emergencies that had required the dictatorships were over. Our attitude ought to be that of travelers who submit to a captain's dictation while they are *en voyage*, but, as a matter of course, resume their personal freedom of action as soon as their perilous journey is over.

IKEDA: In the past, people have often attempted to combat the evil of one system by means of the challenge of a new system. But at the instant when the evil of the old way was overcome by the good of a different system, new evil inevitably resulted. The Meiji Restoration in nineteenth-century Japan and the Russian and French revolutions illustrate my meaning.

Of course each system has its own faults and merits. In the future, the extent to which it contributes to the happiness of humanity must be the major criterion for judging a system. In other words, we cannot afford to forget that the majority must assume basic initiative in all systems. If the people do not take this initiative, no matter how ideal the system may appear to be, it will degenerate into a regime of evil and oppression.

Democracy or Meritocracy

IKEDA: Each nation should attempt to adopt the political system that best suits its own national personality, educational level, international position, and level of economic development. Consequently, the communist system appeals to peoples whose majority own nothing and who are oppressed by a minority of the wealthy. On the other hand, the same system finds small welcome in nations where the majority are owners and where the general economic level is high. Though it is impossible to make blanket judgments as to which systems are good and which are bad, the elevation of the people's intellectual and educational levels and the creation of general affluence always meet unconditional approval.

What is the ideal political system for a nation that enjoys both high intellectual and educational levels and economic plenty? The consensus of current opinion seems to be that democracy is the ideal, but I sense the need to examine this system in the light of moral principles that cannot be measured in terms of either educational level or economic plenty.

TOYNBEE: Man has been amazingly resourceful and inventive in his technology and no less amazingly unfertile and uncreative in his politics. The number of alternative possible political systems so far discovered is small, and most of these systems, when applied, have proved, on trial, to be unsatisfactory. In my view, the case for democracy can be put most judiciously in negative terms: democracy is the least bad of the political systems that man has yet hit upon.

But democracy too has it defects. One of the gravest is the tendency of people living under a parliamentary democracy to give ultimate loyalty to the small, less important group instead of to the large, important group. By this I mean that people too often put the interests of a political party above those of the nation and those of the nation above the interests of mankind as a whole.

The second serious flaw in democracy is insincerity. Considerable pressure is sometimes exerted on politicians to make them follow the party line, even when that line goes against their own consciences. Indeed, some politicians are very ready to sacrifice their consciences to personal ambition. On a somewhat wider scale, for the sake of political tactics, people often pretend to support policies in which they do not really believe. The attitude of the British Labor Party about joining the European Economic Community is a case in point, as was the official attitude of the West German Christian Democratic Union about concluding treaties with Poland and the Soviet Union that recognize the de facto postwar frontiers.

IKEDA: It seems to me that the absence of a firmly established sense of morality in the masses is the source of the major flaw in modern democracy. But even when it was at the peak of its glory, Athenian democracy, too, contained the seed of the failing that later brought it to the level of mass rule. It is sometimes pointed out that today the United States and the nations of Western Europe face a similar crisis.

221

TOYNBEE: The golden age of Athenian democracy was the first century after its inauguration. In that age, power was already in the hands of the masses according to the Athenian constitution, but in practice the masses still allowed themselves to be guided by aristocrats, as, in the first chapter of the history of the United States, the Americans allowed themselves to be guided by the aristocratic Founding Fathers.

However, even in the initial golden age of Athenian democracy, the masses yielded to two temptations. They turned the tables on the well-to-do minority of their fellow countrymen by taxing them crushingly and by exacting from them public services that were only nominally voluntary. In the second place, the masses misused Athenian naval power. The navy depended on the masses to provide oarsmen for warships. Seizing upon the power that this dependence gave them, the masses used the navy to reduce to the level of subjects other Greek states that were officially allies of Athens. Athens then bullied and fleeced these states by coercing them with her superior force. Athenian democracy was denounced as a bad system of government by contemporary Athenian intellectuals—for instance, by the historian Thucydides and by the philosopher Plato. But their judgment must not be accepted without reserve. They were not unprejudiced, for they were members of the well-to-do minority. Yet their strictures on the domestic and foreign policies of democratic Athens were based on firsthand experience and are borne out to a large extent by undisputed historical facts.

It is significant that, at Athens, democracy was short-lived. It lasted for less than two centuries and was then succeeded by a moderate oligarchical regime that lasted for about three times as long—in fact, for as long as the Athenian city-state itself. The system survived under Roman suzerainty till at least the third century of the Christian era. This oligarchic regime was moderate by comparison with the intemperateness of the preceding democratic regime, yet postdemocratic Athenian oligarchy, too, was socially unjust. Under this regime, Athens was governed by, and in the interest of, a minority consisting of rentiers (specifically, rural landlords who lived parasitically on rents extracted from the cultivators of the soil). The scholar-gentry who governed the Chinese Empire for more than two millennia were counterparts of the postdemocratic Athenian governing class.

IKEDA: There are people who maintain that modern democracy, like that of ancient Athens, is likely to be short-lived and that it will be succeeded by an oligarchy of the intellectual elite.

TOYNBEE: As I see it, neither a selfish minority nor a selfish majority is likely to provide good government. I should prefer a constitution that gave the majority the negative power to control the government by the exercise of a veto on issues in which the majority's vital interests are at stake, without giving the majority the positive power to conduct the government. I think the best governing body would be a meritocracy, but even the most impartially and efficiently selected meritocracy ought not to be exempted from popular control, since the ablest and most public-spirited human beings are still subject to human failings and since in itself power corrupts.

The governing meritocracy that I have in mind ought not to be recruited by popular election. One of the worst features of democracy, both direct and representative, is that democratic politicians are tempted to make their own election or reelection their first priority and to act with an eye to this rather than to what they believe to be the true public interest. This weakness is illustrated by the history of the American presidency since Jackson's era and by the history of the Athenian board of generals (*strategoi*) in the post-Periclean age of Athenian democracy. I would be in favor of retaining an elective, representative, democratic constitution for the recruitment of the organ for popular control of the government, but I would rule out election as a method for recruiting the governing meritocracy. I should like to see this governing body recruited partly by co-optation and partly by nomination, the nominees being appointed by socially and culturally important nonpolitical and noneconomic institutions.

IKEDA: In modern democracy, the tendency is for the majority to participate in a negative instead of in a positive fashion and for the intellectual elite to exercise increasing control. In this sense, the present situation seems to be close to your idea of a meritocracy. I am afraid, however, that if your meritocracy were realized, the split between the masses and the elite would become more pronounced and deeper.

Aside from this difficulty, I entertain a number of other doubts about meritocracy. You say that part of the leadership will be co-opted and part nominated. Who will have the right to nominate the leaders and what will determine their qualifications? You further say that the general population would have the right to control the meritocracy but not the right to select it. What method of control could the people use under such circumstances?

The majority of the population will have a veto concerning issues of vital importance to them, but I feel that the people will find it difficult to understand to what extent a particular policy will affect their vital interests. For instance, a number of policies taken individually might seem perfectly innocent, whereas in accumulation they could pose a grave threat. Granted that the meritocracy someday replaces modern democracy, I feel that a number of difficulties connected with it must be solved before it can become a satisfactory governing system.

The high level of morality, breadth of intellectural vision, and accuracy of judgment required of the people by meritocracy and democracy are the same. Unless the masses possess these qualities, neither system can exist.

I respect equality among all people. I prefer to support a system in which all kinds of people can participate on an equal footing. I believe that the most important thing is to elevate the morality and intellectual capacity of the masses to a level that will enable them to shoulder the burden of the democratic system.

TOYNBEE: I agree that the most important thing is to elevate the morality and intellectual capacity of the masses. Undoubtedly this is the only sure way to bring about the improvement in politics that is so urgently needed. But the time factor may be prohibitive. Accelerated technological change has speeded up social and political change proportionately. The masses may be overtaken by catastrophe long before they have time to reach the moral and intellectual level at which they would be able to raise politics above the danger point.

The meritocracy that I advocate is a way of buying time by installing a caretaker regime, or a body of administrators like those in the British civil service in India and the Chinese imperial civil service. These men were recruited by competitive examination.

I admit, however, that the histories of these civil services, though honorable and successful on the whole, reveal the following weaknesses of the meritocracy. "All power corrupts, and absolute power corrupts absolutely," as Lord Acton said. A meritocracy may honestly do what it believes to be in the best interests of the masses, but it may actually be blinded to those interests by isolation from the masses or by a subconscious wish to remain indispensable. The British civil service in India, generally considered largely successful, illustrates my point.

I see the weakness of government by meritocracy as well as I understand the dangers of parliamentary democracy with an intellectually and morally uneducated electorate. Unfortunately, I fear that mankind's appallingly bad past record in politics may be surpassed by the badness of his future performance.

ONE WORLD | 9

International Currency

IKEDA: Although the purpose of the present currency system is said to be to prevent the repetition of the monetary chaos of the 1930s, in fact it may be regarded as the product of the postwar monetary policies of the United States. At the conclusion of World War II, the United States was—and for that matter remains—economically the most powerful country in the world. But as long as the currencies of the world are supported and therefore tremendously influenced by the dollar, any weakness in American currency obviously puts the world monetary system in turmoil. It is by no means desirable for the currency of one nation to control the economic actions of all other nations. As long as there is fluctuation in the value of currency itself, it is impossible to hope for stabilized economic activities. The problem is not a temporary one. It is something with which most nations of the world are now trying to deal. But even if a provisional solution is found, the problem will inevitably arise again. Consequently, I am convinced that the only way to solve the dollar crisis is to totally revise the international currency system.

TOYNBEE: The peoples of the world are now knit together so closely on the economic plane that they cannot do without active and massive international trade and investment on a worldwide scale. Some countries—Japan, Britain, West Germany—depend on foreign trade for their livelihoods. But there cannot be worldwide trade and investment without a worldwide common standard of value in terms of which the citizens of different countries can conclude business contracts with each other and can then make or receive the payments

225

due for the execution of these contracts. Moreover, this worldwide standard must be stable in terms of purchasing power, for people doing business must be able to see ahead. They must have assurance that contracts based on calculations made in terms of the present value of the common standard will not be made ruinous by unpredictable changes in its value before the transactions have been completed.

So far, there has been no world currency. The world is still divided politically into a number of sovereign states, and one of the prerogatives of local sovereignty is to have a national currency that can be increased or decreased in value by the action of the government and of the citizens of the state in question.

If national currencies had been the sole medium of exchange, international business transactions would have been impossible. For these, some equivalent of a world currency is necessary. The traditional common measure for relating the values of national currencies to each other has been gold. But the use of gold for this purpose has at least two serious weaknesses. (1) The intrinsic economic value of gold, as a metal for use in technology, is small. Gold has been prized not for its utility but for its rarity. The high valuation of gold is superstitious, not rational. (2) Owing to the rarity of gold, the supply of it bears no relation to the demand for it in its role as the equivalent of an international currency. In the nineteenth century, the increase in the gold supply, through the discovery of new sources in California and Australia, happened to keep pace, more or less, with the contemporary increase in the volume of international trade and investment. But this was only accidental.

After the Industrial Revolution, gold alone would no longer have provided an adequate medium of exchange if it had not been supplemented—and largely replaced in practice—by the use, for international transactions, of some particular national currency with a value that was not only truly stable in terms of gold but was also believed to be stable. In the nineteenth century, the British pound sterling played this role. Today, the pound has been almost entirely replaced by the United States dollar. But now the dollar, as well as the pound, has proved too weak to perform this function for the world. At the present moment, there is no worldwide common measure of value. A number of important currencies are now floating in terms of their relation to the dollar, and this loss of a common measure of value is having a paralyzing effect on international business transactions.

A world currency will not be stable and will not inspire the confidence in its stability that is the necessary condition for concluding contracts in terms of any currency if it is not based on something that, unlike gold, has an intrinsic, practical value that is both stable and high.

There are a number of material commodities that have a higher practical value than gold. But no material commodity has any value at all unless and until it is utilized by human action. Petroleum, for instance, had no value until human beings discovered how to tap it, how to refine it, and how to construct engines in which the refined product of petroleum could be made to serve as a material driving force. The ultimate source of value is human productivity, and in this there are three indispensable factors: skill, work, and cooperation. The most important of the three is cooperation, for any economic enterprise of any importance has to be the joint enterprise of a number of participants. If the participants fall out with each other (as in disputes over the division of the rewards for their joint production), work will be paralyzed, and skill will be deprived of opportunities. This point is illustrated by the current sabotaging of production by industrial disputes in the so-called developed countries.

Mankind's economic productivity is, it seems to me, the only source of economic value. If this is the truth, a worldwide medium of economic exchange ought to be based on mankind's economic productivity. But how are these two things to be related to each other? The essential requirement for a worldwide medium of exchange is that its value shall be stable and shall be believed to be stable. But productivity, though it is the true source of value, suffers from the same weakness as gold, the dollar, and the pound. Like these former common measures of value, productivity is unstable.

Productivity varies in degree from country to country and from age to age; it is also at the mercy of human caprice. The skill that is now applied to technology and to business management might run short if the world's skillful minority were to turn its attention away from economics to philosophy or art. Work might run short if the workers were to choose to work less hard and to give less time to work and more time to leisure, instead of giving priority to earning the maximum amount of pay. And productivity might be hamstrung if the participants in production were to become less cooperative and more combative in their relations with each other.

If, for some or all of these reasons, mankind's productivity were to decrease, the quantity of a world currency based on productivity would have to be reduced proportionately. Is it possible to give to a world medium of economic exchange the stability that is a sine qua non while at the same time basing this world currency on mankind's productivity (which is, I believe, the only real source of value but is evidently also highly unstable)? This seems to me to be the problem that the world's experts have to solve. I can state the problem as I see it, but I cannot offer any suggestions for a solution, for I do not have even the rudiments of the necessary expertise.

227

IKEDA: The problem is serious and difficult. It is desirable to strive to alter the world economic system from one based on independent national units to one made up of compound or federated national units, for only in this way will it be possible to stabilize currency while expanding the scope of economic activities. For the sake of achieving this kind of system, I might cite what I consider to be an ideal approach.

First is the development of an economic community in Europe. This is now being achieved. The creation of a unified economic sphere is the European Economic Community's short-term step toward a long-term aim of political unity for its members. Should this long-term goal be reached, the establishment of a European Economic Community currency system or of a central European bank would become entirely possible. This, in turn, would lighten the present reliance on the American dollar and might lead to the kind of world bank proposed by John Maynard Keynes.

Then we would need to set up a communal body like the European Economic Community in other economic spheres. In the case of Asia, the development of such a body faces a number of obstacles. First, of course, are differences among political systems: some Asian nations are capitalist, some are communist, and some are neither. The considerable differences among Asian national economic structures are a roadblock in the path to unity. At present I cannot think that a communal economic body will be easy to establish in Asia. Consequently, worldwide economics will probably rely on the American dollar as a basic currency for some time yet. In saying this, however, I do not imply that differences in political system and ideology make the birth of an Asian economic community impossible. On the contrary, since economic needs themselves are common to all men, regional economic unity must be one of our goals, for efforts in that direction are tantamount to contributions to world unity.

East Asia's Role

IKEDA: In spite of apparent improvements in relations between China and the United States, it seems likely that their future stands may be much like the ones held by the United States and the Soviet Union; that is, they may attempt to maintain a balance of power by means of vast arsenals of nuclear weapons. Should matters turn out this way, the other Asian nations will remain anxious and insecure.

TOYNBEE: So far, the detente between the United States and the Soviet Union has been only superficial. Even if a detente between the United States and China were to be more substantial, the outlook for peace would still be unpromising. However, the change in the postwar structure of international relations from bipolarity to multipolarization is going to force the three superpowers into seeking to establish more positively friendly and constructive relations with each other, because, from now on, each of them will be anxious to avert the danger of a coalition between the other two.

IKEDA: The situation of the Asian nations, caught between the superpowers, is precarious. Asian countries must assume a middle-of-the-road stand and form a buffer zone between China and the United States. But some nation must take the initiative in this delicate operation. That nation must have sufficient economic strength to be politically independent of both blocks. Japan meets this qualification. Therefore, I believe that Japan must accept the responsibility of leading other Asian nations in their effort to establish economic as well as political independence.

Japan and China have maintained cultural and social ties for fourteen hundred years. During this amazingly long period, good relations were severed only by the Sino-Japanese War of 1904 and by World War II. No other independent nation has been more profoundly related to China than Japan. One may safely assume that Japan's opinion of China will greatly influence other nations in shaping their views of the Asian giant. I believe that Japan has a leading role to play in promoting cooperation between China and many countries of both the East and the West.

If Japan and China become a center around which the other Asian nations can unite, they will naturally influence world politics. Since there is no sign of improvement in Sino-Soviet relations, Russia has stepped up attempts to form closer ties with Japan. The general opinion in Japan is that Asian unity centering on a China-Japan nucleus would contribute greatly to world peace.

TOYNBEE: In the diplomatic enterprise of helping the three atomic superpowers to improve their relations with each other, there is going to be an important role for Japan, which is already one of the world's great economic powers.

Japan's historic cultural and social ties with China are, I feel sure, of prime importance. The voluntary self-Sinicization of the Japanese people through their reception of the Chinese version of Buddhism began in the sixth century of the Christian era, about one generation earlier than the voluntary self-civilization of the English people through their reception of the Roman

229

version of Christianity. The part played by Chinese civilization in Japanese history is enormous, and its importance is not diminished by the Japanese people's success in molding it into something that is specifically Japanese.

Japan already had good relations with both the United States and the Soviet Union when the American impediment to good relations between Japan and China was removed. A Sino-Japanese reconciliation has followed, and, thanks to long-standing cultural intercourse, Sino-Japanese relations are likely to become more intimate than either American or Russian relations with China. On the diplomatic plane, these facts are going to put Japan in a unique position to act as "an honest broker" (Bismarck's phrase) between the three atomic superpowers. Japan's ability to play this role will be enhanced by her renunciation, in her present constitution, of the right to go to war and by the fact that she is not armed with nuclear weapons herself.

Japan's next role in international affairs is going to be that of "an honest broker," but I do not expect to see her role remain confined to this function, important though her mediatory services seem likely to be. I believe, as I have said, that Japan will eventually get together with China, Vietnam, and Korea to create an axis round which the unification of the whole world will be achieved.

IKEDA: In relation to the axis around which the world will be united, I am most deeply concerned with the nature of the contributions Japan can make to Asia and, in turn, with the nature of the contributions Asia can make to the building of peace and the development of a civilization worthy of humanity.

Much of Asia is threatened by starvation. Unfortunately, full-scale industrialization in Asia is still a long way in the future. In the fields of learning and culture, too, Asia is behind the Western nations.

But the undercurrent of Buddhist philosophy common to all the peoples of Eastern Asia deserves attention because its future influence can be great. Though its visible influence today is small, Buddhist thought has cultivated and enriched the spiritual life of East Asian peoples for centuries and has enveloped their histories in an aura of peace. East Asian culture, which was reared under the influence of Buddhist philosophy and which inspires repose and a sense of wonderful harmony between man and nature, has inspired in the peoples of this part of the world a mighty urge to live. It seems to me that philosophy and religion, especially Buddhism, will be the fields in which the peoples of Eastern Asia can make the greatest contributions to peace and civilization.

TOYNBEE: I expect that a major positive contribution to the establishment of peace and the advancement of human civilization is going to be made by Eastern Asia. I do not think that the rest of Asia (the Indo-Pakistani subcontinent and the Middle East) is likely to play a comparable positive part in the kind of stabilization of the world's affairs that is the only alternative to a worldwide catastrophe. India, Pakistan, and the Middle East are economically backward, in spite of the Middle East's vast reserves of petroleum. These regions are also politically chaotic. The feuds between Hindus and Muslims, between Arabs and Israelis, between Pakistan and Bangladesh, and between the politically conservative and the politically radical Arab states are counterparts, on a gigantic scale, of the feud between Protestant and Catholic Christians in Northern Ireland. The peoples of Western Asia will not help to solve mankind's problems; they present regional problems of their own that will have to be solved with other people's help.

What is the situation in Eastern Asia? China is not a superpower in the economic or the military sense at present. Even if she were to set herself to achieve parity with the United States and the Soviet Union on these planes, the prospect of her succeeding is remote. Yet the two present superpowers, Japan, and most other countries show by their actions that they consider China to be already a major force in the world. Anxiety about relations with China has moved the Soviet Union to become more conciliatory towards the West. Richard Nixon showed how much importance he attached to China by visiting Peking. Taken together, these are striking indications of China's present prestige. This prestige is out of all proportion to China's present and probable future material power. How, then, is it to be explained?

From the time of the Opium War till the communist takeover of China, the rest of the world treated China with contempt and bullied her with impunity. Even now, China is not much more powerful materially, by comparison with the Western countries, the Soviet Union, and Japan, than she was during that humiliating century of Chinese history. It looks as if the present high estimate of her importance is based, not on China's record during this relatively short period of her modern history, but on her performance during the preceding two millennia and on a recognition of the permanent virtues of the Chinese people—virtues that they continued to display during their country's century of humiliation, especially in the worldwide private activities of Chinese expatriates in the modern age.

Eastern Asia preserves a number of historical assets that may enable it to become the geographical and cultural axis for the unification of the whole world. These assets are, as I see them: (1) the Chinese people's experience, during the last twenty-one centuries, of maintaining an empire that is a

231

regional model for a literally worldwide world-state; (2) the ecumenical spirit with which the Chinese have been imbued during this long chapter of Chinese history; (3) the humanism of the Confucian Weltanschauung; (4) the rationalism of both Confucianism and Buddhism; (5) the sense of the mystery of the universe and the recognition that human attempts to dominate the universe are self-defeating (to me, the most precious intuitions of Taoism); (6) the conviction (shared with Buddhism and Shinto by Chinese philosophy of all schools, except perhaps the now extinct Legalist school) that, far from trying to dominate nonhuman nature, man's aim should be to live in harmony with it; (7) the demonstration, by the Japanese people, that it is possible for East Asian peoples to beat the Western peoples at the Westerners' own modern game of applying science to both civilian and military technology; (8) the courage shown by both the Japanese and the Vietnamese in daring to challenge the West. This courage will, I hope, survive but be dedicated, in the next chapter of mankind's history, to the constructive enterprise of helping mankind to put its affairs in order peacefully.

The modern world has learned by experience that the Chinese are extremely able in all kinds of business and that they also have a high standard of family life. The Chinese have continued to display these virtues even when their country has been weak or actually in chaos, but chaos is not China's usual condition. Though there have been bouts of turmoil in China before the one that began in 1911 and ended in 1949, China has been politically united and effectively administered for most of the time since her original political unification in 221 B.C. Before that date, China's political history resembled the political history of the west end of the Old World. China, too, had been divided among a number of warring local states. But, since 221 B.C., China has relapsed into political disruption and anarchy only occasionally and temporarily. On the whole, the history of the Chinese Empire, which still survives in the form of the present People's Republic, has been a political success story. It contrasts dramatically with the history of the Roman Empire, which tried and failed to give lasting political unity and peace to the West.

Since the collapse of the Roman Empire in the West, the Western world has never succeeded in regaining its lost political unity. It has developed enormous energy in all fields of human activity, and, within the last five hundred years, it has united the whole surface of the globe on the economic and technological planes and on the cultural plane to some extent. But the post-Roman West has not succeeded in giving political unity either to itself or to the rest of the world. Politically the influence of the West on the world has been divisive. The political regime that the West has propagated beyond its own borders has been the sovereign state; the post-Roman Western political tradition has been nationalistic, not ecumenical. It therefore seems improbable that the West will be able to give political unity to the world as a whole. Yet global unification on the political plane is demanded by the global unity on other planes that the worldwide expansion of Western peoples has already established.

It is conceivable that the future unifier of the world will not be a Western or a Westernized country but will be China. It is also conceivable that a premonition of the possible future political role of China is the cause of China's surprising present worldwide prestige. For nearly twenty-two centuries, with only occasional lapses, a unitary Chinese government has held hundreds of millions of people together politically. Moreover, unified China has been the Middle Kingdom, whose political suzerainty has been recognized by a circle of client states and whose cultural influence has radiated still farther afield. In fact, China, for most of the time since the third century B.C., has been the center of gravity for half the world. Within the last five hundred years, the whole world has been knit together by Western enterprise on all except the political plane. Perhaps it is China's destiny now to give political unity and peace not just to half but to all the world.

IKEDA: Of course, politically successful regimes, like the Chinese Empire or the Tokugawa shogunate in Japan, have brought peace to their nations. But under such systems the creativity and freedom of the people have been subjected to considerable restraint, and the regimes themselves have tended to be closed and fixed. Systems that suppressed individual creativity allowed Japan and China to stagnate. European peoples, who have advanced considerably because of the system of free enterprise, supplied the impulse that jolted China and Japan out of their peaceful drowsiness.

In the world today human beings demand stability and peace more than progress. For this reason, Chinese-style unity may have significance. Still, I very much doubt that a fixed society that suppresses individual freedom and the exercise of its talent can be permanent. We must give serious consideration to devising a system that provides stability and peace without infringing on the freedom and creative potential of the individual.

Although I realize that we do not see eye to eye on this matter, I nonetheless believe that a federation on equal footing—perhaps something like the European Economic Community—might meet both these requirements. In general, the world seems to be structured around a kind of tripolar arrangement composed of China, the Soviet Union, and the United States, with China having already announced that she has no intention of becoming a superpower. It is certain that China could not successfully resist the other two powers either militarily or economically, but her influence in cultural matters can be immeasurable. In terms of views of nationality, the world, and culture, China's outlook is entirely different from that of the Western nations. If she emerges in the future on the stage of international society, she is certain to set up wave-propagation patterns of great importance, especially for the nations of Asia and Africa. The most important immediate question involves the abolition of nuclear armament. If China begins to participate actively in the United Nations' disarmament committee, will she be able to force the United States and the Soviet Union to give up nuclear weaponry? Will China take the initiative in arms-reduction discussions and display a strong drive toward the establishment and maintenance of perpetual world peace? This point will deserve constant attention in the future.

In *The Present-day Experiment in Western Civilization*, you said, "A Chinese domination and colonization of the entire surface of this planet is one of the possibilities that the future may hold in store for us." May I ask on what grounds you base this statement? Do you still feel that this possibility exists?

I do not think that the Chinese are a people with aggressive ambitions. On the contrary, I regard them as essentially pacifists seeking peace and security for their own country. China was forced to engage in, but did not start, the Opium War, the Sino-Japanese War, and the Korean War. It seems to me that the Chinese participate in hostilities only when it is necessary to defend themselves. In my opinion, the Chinese people developed a nationalistic inclination as a natural reaction against the successive invasions by foreign countries—including Japan—that have occurred since the Opium War. This nationalistic attitude is only a disguise for diplomatic purposes; basically, the Chinese maintain a predominant cosmopolitanism combined with Chinese ethnocentrism. Communist China had persisted in its diplomatic isolationism because of the need to straighten out domestic affairs after the revolution and because of the venerable and proud tradition that China is the entire world.

TOYNBEE: Basically I agree with your diagnosis of the Chinese attitude. I have read somewhere that Napoleon said, apropos of China, "Do not waken the sleeping giant." The British had no sooner disposed of Napoleon than they did waken China by making the Opium War.

I agree that, since 1839, the Chinese have fought only in self-defense. I think they interpret self-defense as including the recovery of the frontiers that the Chinese Empire had attained when the Ch'ing dynasty was at its zenith, during the latter part of the reign of Ch'ien Lung. This accounts both for China's reconquest of Tibet—from the Tibetans' point of view, an act of aggressive colonialism—and for China's otherwise inexplicable breach with

234

India, which had previously been China's best friend. China broke with India over some strips of territory in the high Himalayas that, though worthless in themselves and strategically superfluous for China, had, I guess, symbolic importance, because India claimed a frontier line imposed by the British when China was too weak to object. I see no indication that China intends to expand beyond her frontiers of the year 1796, the year of Ch'ien Lung's death. Indeed, though recently the Chinese have clashed with the Russians along the Amur River, they do not seem to be seriously intending to try to recover the vast territories beyond the left bank of the Amur and the right bank of the Ussuri that China was compelled to cede to Russia in 1858–61. The Chinese element in the population of these territories was, and is, very small.

China's foreign relations since the Opium War, however, have been something new in Chinese history. Before 1839, China was in truth the Middle Kingdom of the East Asian half of the Old World, and she was even all that is under heaven in the sense that the Chinese civilization had been adopted by all China's neighbors, including Japan, though Japan has never been subject to China politically. China did not begin to make contact with the non-Chinese civilized peoples of the western end of the Old World until the latter part of the second century B.C. The only great foreign impact on China, before the modern Western one, was made by India, and the Indian impact took the peaceful form of the infiltration of Buddhism into China. Moreover, China Sinicized Buddhism when she adopted it, just as she Sinicized the northern barbarians, from the Hiongnu to the Manchus inclusive, who conquered China, or parts of China, at various times.

On the other hand, China has been unable to Sinicize the Russians, who replaced the barbarians in the seventeenth century as China's northern neighbors. Nor has China been able to Sinicize the Western peoples who impinged on China in the sixteenth century and temporarily dominated her in the nineteenth century. While this temporary Western domination is now over, Western influence persists. Like the older Indian influence, it has taken the form of the conversion of China to a non-Chinese religion. China Sinicized Buddhism; it now looks as if she is going to Sinicize communism in its turn. Yet Sinicized communism seems likely, like Sinicized Buddhism, to have a profound modifying effect on the Chinese Weltanschauung and way of life.

Down to 1839, China's relations with other parts of the civilized world were superficial and unimportant, with the one big exception of the impact of Indian civilization in the peaceful form of Buddhism. But, within the last five hundred years, the Western peoples have unified all mankind (on the technological and economic planes) by their worldwide expansion, and this process of unification, on Western initiative and originally in a Western framework, has drawn China, as it has drawn Japan, into the net of a new global civilization. Since 1839, China has been implicated, more and more deeply, in a worldwide system of international relations on all planes of human activity: military, economic, political, cultural, technological, religious. While China has now shaken off the West's temporary military, political, and economic domination, she cannot withdraw into isolation. China's world has been enlarged by the West's impact from the eastern half of the Old World to the entire surface of the globe. China can never again be the Middle Kingdom of an insulated Eastern Asia. It is in this sense that I see a possibility of Chinese domination of the world.

IKEDA: The United States and other members of the free world must accept much of the responsibility for China's earlier isolationist policies and for her tardiness in taking a place in the United Nations. Although the attitude is probably found in other peoples as well, I think that the Chinese are especially sensitive to the way in which people are prepared to accept them. By this I mean that, after having been unfairly treated throughout much of the postwar period, the Chinese put great importance on whether the position offered them now represents an accurate estimation of their standing in the world. China cannot tolerate the idea that the United States and the Soviet Union dominate the globe. Of course, France and Britain probably feel the same way, but at present their diplomatic technique is one of compromise on this point. The Chinese, on the other hand, are more strongly moved to stick to their demand for a fair evaluation of their status. If the world is unprepared to give them a place suited to what they feel is their just due, they prefer to wait in isolation from international society until things change to their liking.

Japan's Contribution to the Future

IKEDA: In the past, the Japanese people have shown a great talent for absorbing and assimilating alien civilizations and cultures. During the first ancient period of unification, Japan modeled her political and social order on that of China and learned production techniques and arts from both China and Korea. The culture of the Asuka and the Tempyo periods (sixth to eighth centuries) were strongly derivative, but by the Heian period (794–1192) Japan employed what she had assimilated from her neighbors to create an original and unique culture. During the Kamakura (1192–1333) and the Muromachi

(1392–1573) periods, as civil wars ravaged the land, importation and absorption were once again the main cultural currents, but under the isolationist policy of the Tokugawa shogunate during the Edo period (1603–1868), Japan once again settled down to the development of a truly Japanese culture, one which penetrated even to the level of the common people. After the Meiji Restoration of 1868, Japan embarked on a policy of rapid modernization, which involved a great deal of learning from European models. This learning has continued since World War II, with the influence of the United States gaining predominance. Until the nineteenth century, Japan's history was one of comparatively brief, widely spaced periods of cultural borrowing followed by long periods of assimilation and creativity.

TOYNBEE: Considering that the West has become a problem even for itself as a result of its having smothered the natural environment under an artificial environment conjured up by modern Western technology, it is not surprising that the Japanese should be confused by the influences of Western culture, which is evidently more difficult to cope with than the Chinese culture of the T'ang period. But the Japanese seem to me to have been the most successful of the non-Western peoples in dealing with the Western question. They have been more successful than the Russians, and far more successful than the Chinese, Hindus, and Muslims.

The Japanese have experimented with four different ways of dealing with the West's impact. In the sixteenth century, they were rather uncritically receptive to Western culture and religion. On closer acquaintance, they reversed their policy and went to extreme lengths in trying to isolate themselves. Then, when they perceived that the Tokugawa policy of isolationism was going to cease to be practicable, they made the Meiji Restoration and tried the experiment of living simultaneously in two worlds for different purposes: in the modern Western world for technology and economics and international relations including trade, diplomacy, war; and in the traditional Japanese world for the cultural and spiritual side of domestic life. This third essay in coping with Western civilization ended in a catastrophe for Japan in 1945. Since then, the Japanese people have made a fourth experiment. They have sought to offset their military defeat in World War II by beating the West, in the nonmilitary field, in the West's own game of technological virtuosity.

In this, the Japanese have been sensationally successful, but technology is only one department of human affairs and not the most important one. I believe that the spiritual component is more important than the physical component in the human psychosomatic organism, and I have the impression that this is also the Japanese people's belief.

237

IKEDA: Yes, that has been the traditional belief of the Japanese people. And they ought to live in accord with it now.

In terms of what Japan can contribute to the world of the future, I think we can mention two points. First, she can—as can all peoples—offer the fruits of her independent creativity. Second, Japan can serve as a model of how it is possible to live in a spirit of harmony and union with a culture other than one's own.

TOYNBEE: What you say is true, but I approach the issue from a different standpoint. My guess is that today the Japanese people are asking themselves: "Have we concentrated our efforts and attention so exclusively on the technological field that we have neglected the spiritual field? Has our postwar triumph perhaps been lopsided? Have we counterbalanced our technological victory by an equivalent spiritual victory? If we have not, ought not this now to be our main objective? And, if so, what is Japan's spiritual role in the present-day world to be?"

Only the Japanese themselves can answer these questions. It is hazardous for a foreigner to try, even if he has, as I have, an admiration and affection for the Japanese people. Nevertheless, I am going to hazard a suggestion. The Japanese have now demonstrated their capacity to excel in modern technology. But, everywhere, modern technology has been getting out of hand. In the process of producing material wealth, it has also been producing physical and spiritual pollution. Mankind now needs to call technology to order—not to reject it but to curb it. This means curbing human greed, which is much older than technology; it is as old as life itself.

The Japanese command the necessary spiritual resources. Their ancestral religions, Shinto and Buddhism, both stand for man's ethical obligation to cooperate with nonhuman nature. This is in contrast to the Judaic tradition of the West, which stands for man's alleged license to coerce and dominate nonhuman nature. The Western course is heading for disaster. I believe that the Japanese people can lead mankind into a safer and happier path. The Japanese have mastered modern Western technology without having lost their indigenous religious tradition. This tradition offers the right spiritual antidote to modern technology's pollution of nonhuman nature and dehumanization of human life. The Japanese tradition stands for the dignity of nonhuman nature as well as for the dignity of man.

From Bipolarity to Multipolarity

IKEDA: Though in recent years considerable improvement has taken place in relations between the Soviet Union and the United States, a basic antagonism still persists. The arms race between the two nations, especially in the field of nuclear weaponry, continues to pose a grave threat to the peace of the world. What are your feelings about future developments that are likely to occur in connection with the division of the world into capitalist and communist blocs?

TOYNBEE: As I see it, the antagonism between capitalism and communism is to a large extent a sham. It is a mask for conflicts of a much older kind between the competing national interests and ambitions of local states. In this conflict, militant-minded people on each side try to arouse the fanaticism of their fellow citizens by branding the rival state with an ideological epithet that excites fear and antipathy. At the western end of the Old World, this propaganda device has precedents. The so-called wars of religion between Christians and Muslims, between Sunnite and Shiite Muslims, and between Roman Catholic and Protestant Western Christians have masked rivalries of competing local states.

The proof of the superficiality and insincerity of so-called ideological and religious antagonism is that, within each of the two allegedly monolithic blocs, there are feuds that are as bitter as those between the two blocs themselves. There are also alliances that cut across the dividing lines between the blocs. Within the communist bloc, the feud between the Soviet Union and China is one of the most bitter of any in the present-day world. Within the capitalist bloc, France has challenged the hegemony of the United States. India and Pakistan are both capitalist, yet their feud, as bitter as that between the Soviet Union and China, has boiled over into warfare. In the earlier religious cleavages at the western end of the Old World, Shiite Muslim Iran allied itself with Christian Venice and the Habsburg monarchy against Sunnite Muslim Turkey, and Catholic Christian France allied herself with Muslim Turkey and with the Protestant Christian German states and Sweden against the Habsburgs. The Protestant Christian Hungarians welcomed the Muslim Turks as liberators from the Catholic Christian Habsburgs.

I conclude that even if their ideologies had been identical, the hostility between the United States and the Soviet Union would have arisen after their joint victory in World War II. Because they were the two surviving great powers in the world, they drifted, almost automatically, into competition with each other for worldwide dominion.

239

I agree, of course, that their competition and their consequent mutual hostility are an enormous threat to the peace of the world. It is a threat of unprecedented gravity because these two rival powers are now armed with weapons of unprecedented destructiveness. Their awareness that in a direct war between them each would annihilate the other and neither could win has deterred them from going to war with each other directly. But the proxy wars in the Middle East and in Southeast Asia, if they continue, might at any moment draw the two rival powers into direct confrontation against the wills of both.

Almost equally dangerous, and quite equally immoral, is their competitive arming of their respective satellites. This competitive arming is not limited to satellite nations engaged in active hostilities in proxy wars. Its effects, both military and economic, are bad. For instance, India and Pakistan, two poverty-stricken countries, have incurred expenditure, or at any rate indebtedness, that they cannot afford, in order to buy arms, which, if used, will be used only against each other and not for the furtherance of the policies of the powers by whom the arms have been supplied.

IKEDA: So far, there has been no direct conflict between the United States and the Soviet Union. Moreover, the leaderships of the two powers have weakened to such an extent that there is an increasing tendency to multi-polarization. The enmity between China and the Soviet Union and the Czechoslovakian uprising, both of which may be examples of the multipolarization phenomenon, could serve as a buffer to prevent a head-on clash between America and Russia. But the frictions, conflicts, and confrontations aroused by multipolarization are basically the result of hostility between the two camps. To make any headway in international affairs, the opposing blocs must resolve their antagonism.

TOYNBEE: The mutual frustration of the United States and the Soviet Union has loosened their grip on their respective satellites, and this has stimulated international mutlipolarization. France now defies the United States, and Israel dictates to her successfully. Czechoslovakia's attempt to defy the Soviet Union failed; but Romania, in defiance of the Soviet Union, has made friends with China. Revolts of satellites are minor events, however, compared to the change in China's position. When the communists made themselves masters of the whole of continental China, the nation still remained a satellite of the Soviet Union. Now China has not only thrown off the Soviet Union's hegemony but has also raised herself to the rank of a third great power and is recognized as one by the other two. This is a revolutionary change in the

240

postwar structure of international relations. The deadlock between the Soviet Union and the United States has now been broken by the new possiblity that any two of the present three powers may put pressure on the third by combining against it.

Moreover, Japan and West Germany have become great powers again on the economic plane; in the atomic age, in which a war between great powers would be suicidal, economic, not military, strength is the key to political power. If we measure power in economic terms, there are now five great powers —the United States, the Soviet Union, China, Japan, and West Germany— instead of only two. Thus the structure of international relations has become more like what it was at the outbreak of World War I, when the number of great powers was eight. While multipolarization is probably a less dangerous configuration than bipolarity, it is too dangerous to be tolerable.

IKEDA: The splitting of the world into antagonistic groups is essentially attributable to a lack of mutual understanding among peoples. The effect of this lack can be illustrated on a very homely level. As long as next-door neighbors refrain from associating with each other, it is impossible for one to know the other's mind. Under these conditions, even a well-meant action or speech may produce an unexpected misunderstanding. One such misunderstanding is invariably followed by another; as time passes, misconceptions turn into obstinate prejudices. Thus hostility between neighbors grows more and more difficult to dissipate.

I believe that the most crucial key to world peace is the promotion of understanding among peoples. When this understanding becomes a reality, Americans and Russians alike will see that they are similar in many respects and that each belongs to the same human race. When an overflowing stream of common feeling underlies the speech and actions of all people, the hostility of governments will become absurd.

Although this is not a question of the relations between the Soviet Union and the United States, it is certain that the so-called ping-pong diplomacy and previous private exchanges greatly facilitated the realization of Richard Nixon's trip to Peking in 1972.

Man cannot be completely free from prejudice. Increasing contact and interchange do not always lead to the promotion of goodwill. Nevertheless, disputes between peoples who are familiar with each other certainly cause less unnecessary fear and suspicion. Lack of mutual understanding, by creating an endless succession of hatred and fear, eventually leads to destructive consequences. To build mutual understanding as a sound foundation for international relations is the first prerequisite for lasting world peace.

241

Because the world is figuratively shrinking with unprecedented rapidity thanks to modern means of communication and transporation, it is no longer difficult to promote mutual understanding. Strengthening of intimate relations between governments may not be immediately feasible, but this is no cause for despair, because increased interchange among peoples is more effective in bringing about peace than intimacy on governmental levels. Do you agree with me on this point?

Do you believe a peaceful settlement of the problems between the two blocs is feasible? If you believe it is, on what grounds is your belief based, and in what way do you think the solution will be realized?

TOYNBEE: I see two grounds for hope. First, the annihilation of distance by modern technology has increased the volume of both business and tourist travel and the volume of information about foreign countries that can be obtained (without travel) by means of radio and television. There has been an increase in the realization that we are all members of one human family and that, as such, we have common interests and problems.

Second, huge international technological projects inspire a sense of unity among peoples. The exploration of outer space is, in one aspect, an expression of the rivalry and competition between the Soviet Union and the United States; yet, at the same time, the Russians, the Americans, and the rest of mankind feel that this is a common human enterprise. The Soviet Union and the United States governments congratulate each other on successes and condole with each other on failures.

Commercial traveling, tourism, radio, and television can cumulatively do much to overcome misunderstandings, prejudices, and suspicions. With this in mind, the Western Allies, at the Paris peace conference of 1946, proposed to the Russians that there should be large-scale exchanges, not only of tourists but also of students and of professional men and women, physicians, surgeons, and civil servants. Stalin refused, and his refusal was correctly diagnosed as signifying that he intended the relations between the ex-allies to be unfriendly. Stalin has been survived by the Iron Curtain, but now that bipolarity in the international field has been replaced by multipolarization, it seems likely that neither the Soviet Union nor any other of the three great powers will feel able to afford isolationism. Each power will be in competition with the others for winning goodwill, under stress of "the nightmare of hostile coalitions" (in Bismarck's phrase).

Increasing contact and interchange do not always lead to the promotion of goodwill. But, on the whole, I expect that the improvement in global means of communication, interacting with the aggravation of global social problems, is going to make mankind realize that it is a single family, and it is also going to make it behave like one.

World Unification

IKEDA: Regarding the process of world unification under a single government, you make several points, which I might summarize as follows. China is likely to play a leading role in this unification. The Chinese principle of rule will serve as an inspiring example. A dictator with outstanding leadership ability may be a necessity in the course of world unification. You expect to see the rise of a new world religion that will serve as a catalyst for the spiritual unity of all nations.

The thread of uniformity throughout these points seems to derive from the impression made on you by the Chinese Empire, which has almost always been ruled by a single emperor acting on the ethical and philosophical basis of Confucianism. But an important distinction must be made here. You consider the concentration of governing power in the hands of one man as part of the transition to a wider unification. I, on the other hand, do not believe that the idea of one-man rule will find universal welcome in the modern world. Many people would find such a government distasteful in the extreme. Furthermore, I believe that it would be still less likely to succeed if a dictatorship were tried as a countermeasure against the kind of social disturbances we are experiencing at present.

I feel that a precedent for future world unity may be found in the current European attempt to achieve an intracontinental federation of nations. This suggestion reflects my thought that the European formula (in which local sovereign states with varied historical backgrounds and characteristics form a federation maintaining independence and unique characteristics on equal terms) ought to be adopted as a basic way to achieve world unity.

To be sure, we need an integral system of religion or philosophy that will help to incorporate all nations into one body. The achievement of this religious or spiritual unity may require a personality capable of effective leadership. Even so, I do not think such a person should have political power; he must be a leader on the levels of religion and philosophy. I believe that the problem of political power must be settled through negotiations in which all concerned nations are justly and equally represented.

Division has been the karma of the European world. But if Europe achieves unity, the success may mean a breakaway from past karma. Am I wrong to think that such a federation would be more valid in our own times than the Chinese experience in the third century B.C.?

To follow the path of China may be effective in overcoming short-range dangers, but it may also lead to peril. The European formula will require long, patient efforts, but I see in it much less risk of danger.

The unification of Japan effected by Oda Nobunaga, Toyotomi Hideyoshi, and Tokugawa Ieyasu in the late sixteenth and early seventeenth centuries was based on an ancient tradition of national oneness. In the case of the Greek federation of the fifth century B.C., too, all of the participants were Hellenes with a sense of being part of a large group. The Italians in the nineteenth century had recollections of the Roman Empire to inspire them to unite. In other words, in all these cases force was merely the means; the motivating factor in the unification was a feeling of close relationship among the people. It may well be that, in these cases, force was the lesser evil, but today it is an absolute evil. The first thing we must concern ourselves with in connection with global unification of the modern world is the development of a feeling of spiritual oneness for all mankind. Once this feeling has been established, concrete methods for unification will emerge automatically.

TOYNBEE: I agree that, in the present age, any attempt to unify the world politically by force would result not in unification but in self-destruction. Guerrilla warfare at one extreme of the gamut and nuclear warfare at the other extreme make unification by military force no longer practicable.

However, I do not know of any past political unification—and none of these was worldwide—that was achieved without the use of force, though I agree that force, where it was successful, was aided by a widespread desire for political unity and that force alone might have failed to achieve unity if there had not been a widespread will for it.

As you note, the unifications of Japan in the sixteenth century and of Italy in the nineteenth century were brought about by a combination of public feeling and military force. But without the military force, could the political unification have been accomplished?

The case of ancient Greece is particularly pertinent. At least as early as the eighth century B.C., the Greeks had a strong sense of cultural unity, which found expression in such important nonpolitical institutions as Pan-Hellenic religious centers and periodical Pan-Hellenic festivals. Yet for three centuries, beginning in 480 B.C., when a few Greek states cooperated momentarily to save themselves from being incorporated in the Persian Empire, the Greeks tried again and again to achieve political unity among themselves, and they never succeeded. Eventually, political unity was imposed on—or was provided for—the Greeks through their being conquered militarily by Rome, a non-Greek power.

Greek history makes me pessimistic about the chances for a voluntary political unification of the present-day world. At the same time, I believe that the human race will be unable to survive unless it achieves political unification quickly. I am therefore pessimistic about mankind's prospects. A sudden widespread change of heart through a revolution on the religious plane is not impossible, and this might save the situation.

IKEDA: The problem is very difficult, and I am convinced that only religious fervor and ideals can help us overcome it. Confucianism and Taoism were the supports on which the unity of ancient China rested; today the thoughts of Mao Tse-tung are serving the same purpose. In the Middle Ages, Christianity succeeded, at least for a time, in creating a more unified Europe than we know at present. And such unity as the world of Islam has known has been based on the power of Mohammed and the teachings of the Koran.

Today, Christianity, Islam, Confucianism, and Taoism have fallen into a powerless state, and we face the question of finding a new religion to unite all the peoples of the world. Of course, a religion must not be enforced upon people; unless it is supported by a spontaneous human search for truth and the fervor of faith, it is meaningless.

The religion required for world unity must appear reasonable to man. Modern man's reasoning faculty forbids illogical doctrines. Such doctrines might appeal to a small group of people because of their very illogicality, but the majority will not believe in them. If the majority will not follow, no religion can hope to become the dominant trend of its time. Do you feel that a world-wide religion is necessary? If you do, what conditions must it satisfy?

TOYNBEE: In the partial unifications that have been achieved in the past, religion, as well as military conquest, has been a potent unifying force. In the Chinese and the Roman empires, religious unification followed military unification: Confucianism was adopted in the Chinese Empire, and Christianity in the Roman Empire. In Islamic history, religious propaganda and military conquest went hand in hand. But in the medieval Western world, religious unification was neither accompanied nor followed by political unification. In a future voluntary unification of mankind on a global scale, I suppose that an important part is likely to be played by the worldwide spread of some kind of common religion.

Man looks to religion for answers to his questions about the purpose, meaning, and destiny of human life. Human minds do not possess the knowledge

245

and understanding for giving verifiable answers to these fundamental questions. Our answers to them can be no more than tentative and provisional. The traditional religions have offered dogmatic answers, and this appearance of certainty was one of their original attractions. But modern man has perceived that this appearance of certainty is fallacious, and his disillusionment with religious dogma has discredited religion itself in his eyes.

I do not think that man will accept any dogmatic form of religion again. A religion that declares frankly that its answers to the fundamental questions are no more than guesses will, I believe, win his respect by its candidness. However, the answering of questions about the nature of the universe is not the only function of religion—indeed, is not its most important function. Besides providing a chart of the universe, religion gives guidance for human conduct. This function of religion fulfills one of the spiritual necessities of human life. Unlike their dogmas, which differ widely from each other, the precepts of traditional religions in the realm of conduct have been almost identical on a number of key points. The discrediting of the dogmas has left the validity of the precepts intact, and I imagine that the same precepts will be preached by any future religion that mankind may embrace.

The key precept of religion is that self-mastery is man's first task. We must master our greed and our pride. These two fatal human failings have perhaps never been so rife as they are in the modern age, when man has turned the tables on his natural environment as a result of his progress in technology. Man's recent victory over nature has inflated his pride and, at the same time, has increased his power to indulge his greed. Yet the achievements of science and technology, of which modern man is so proud, have solved some of man's old problems only at the cost of creating new ones. In the so-called developed countries, the price of material enrichment has been the pollution of the natural environment and a social conflict over the division of this newly made wealth among the participants in the production of it.

The present sequel to the Industrial Revolution is demonstrating that, in spite of his scientific and technological prowess, modern man, like primitive man, is not master of the situation in which he finds himself. He has failed to master it because he has failed to master himself. Self-mastery is the only means of avoiding self-frustration. This truth was proclaimed by the traditional religions; I believe it will be proclaimed by any serious future religion. To master oneself is the essence of religion as I see it, and I think a future religion that preaches this traditional religious precept will win the allegiance of mankind, because this precept is, I believe, the only effective response to the challenge of being human.

246

III

PHILOSOPHICAL

AND

RELIGIOUS LIFE

THE NATURE OF THINGS

Origin of Life

IKEDA: Regarding the origin of life, modern scientists seem to support the concept of abiogenesis. The Russian biochemist A. I. Oparin and the British biochemist J. D. Bernal assume that life emerged spontaneously in the course of terrestrial evolution. They see the generation of life as a succession of steps and generally agree that in the very beginning organic compounds were generated from inorganic substances. This step was followed by the development of proteins and later the appearance of life with its metabolic ability. These hypotheses have been substantiated by the discovery of fossil remains of the first primitive organisms and by recent successes in synthesizing simple organic compounds.

TOYNBEE: The scientists you mention understand life as a material phenomenon, and they try to discover what provided the opportunity for life to develop.

IKEDA: Oparin's doctrine involves some particular points that further study may modify, but I do not think he is mistaken in assuming that life began on earth itself. However, I think it is more important to attempt to discover *why* life was born in the world of inanimate materials than to be concerned with *how* this phenomenon occurred.

TOYNBEE: This topic basically concerns the nature of change in general and, in particular, the nature of the change from a universe that was apparently inanimate to a universe that, while remaining inanimate in part, came to contain animate beings, some of which are human and conscious.

IKEDA: Though the earth itself may have been inanimate when life first emerged, I believe that the tendency toward life was inherent in the earth. Life is obviously an active, not a passive, entity. But what is the source and motivating force of its activity? I suggest that life is inherent in inanimate matter. What we call the origin of life is actually no more than the point at which life manifests itself.

TOYNBEE: Perhaps that is so, but we cannot know at this stage. We can, however, intellectually analyze the idea of change, and this may bring us nearer an understanding of the origin of life, since that origin was in itself a momentous change.

There are two alternative possible explanations of change or novelty. It may be produced by creation—by the bringing into existence, or the coming into existence, of things that did not exist previously. Alternatively, novelty may be produced by evolution in the literal meaning of this word—that is, the unfolding of something that was contained in the package from the beginning. According to the evolutionary explanation, the appearance of change is really an illusion. Everything that exists or that is ever going to exist has been in existence from the start. All that happens is that some originally latent elements of reality are made manifest progressively.

IKEDA: I believe that the evolutionary explanation is correct. Perhaps I can express my meaning by saying that I consider life to be the product of its own creation. That is, from the time it first appeared on earth until the present, life has maintained the potential of manifesting and individualizing itself. The power—or energy—of life force, which gives activity to individualized life, was already inherent in the inanimate world.

TOYNBEE: You then give a verdict in favor of evolution, as against creation. I myself believe in the reality of creation.

IKEDA: It would seem that recent scientific successes in synthesizing life endorse your belief. I consider this not creation but an artificial way of allowing life to manifest itself. I do not believe it is possible for life to be created. The most that it is possible for human beings to do is to call forth life energy already existing in inanimate material things. I am not, of course, employing the word *energy* in the meaning used by physicists.

TOYNBEE: I am not denying that it is possible for scientists to trace, and even to repeat by contrivance, the physical change of structure from inorganic matter to the physical organism that is one facet of the indivisible psychosomatic entity (endowed with consciousness and will) that constitutes a human being. But the tracing and repeating of this physical evolution explains neither the difference between inanimate matter and a living organism nor the further difference between a nonconscious living organism and a conscious one.

Matter arranged organically may be the indispensable enabling condition for the existence of life, but it is not life itself. Live matter may be the indispensable enabling condition for the existence of consciousness, but it is not consciousness itself. I think that both life and consciousness are genuine novelties and that genuine novelty, in contrast to the evolution of what has been latently present from the start, is logically incomprehensible. I suspect that the reason why it is incomprehensible is that human thought is limited to thinking in terms of space-time, and space-time may be only phenomenal; it may be nonintrinsic to the unknowable nature of reality-in-itself.

IKEDA: I see your point, but I think there is a way of showing that we need not be disturbed about the logical incomprehensibility of genuine novelty. If the universe is interpreted in terms of no more than the concepts of nonbeing and being, one is forced to say that life was and still is being generated from nonbeing. Buddhism takes a different stand and posits the existence of a state of nonbeing that contains inherent possibilities of becoming being and thus transcends both the concept of being and the concept of nonbeing. Buddhist thought interprets this state as the true entity of the universe and calls it *Kū*. This *Kū* is a mysterious entity, of the kind you mention, that cannot be explained in the dimension of space and time. I believe that a person who understands the nature of *Kū* will have little trouble in understanding the nature of life itself.

The entire universe, including our earth, is a life entity: it is *Kū*, which contains life. When the conditions are right for the tendency for life to manifest itself, life can be generated anywhere and at anytime. Modern scientists suspect that there may be life on other planets. I interpret their suspicion as the first step toward the proof of the idea of the life-nature of the universe. I believe that the entire universe is a sea of life potentiality comprising infinite possibilities for manifestation.

Organic compounds are the basic conditions making possible the manifestation (as operating, individualized life) of the life that is inherently *Kū* because, in order for life to act consciously, complex and accurate physical compounds are required.

251

TOYNBEE: This is, of course, a fascinating and important topic that we must investigate further. I maintain, however, that life and reality-in-itself are, for me, a mystery that is not explicable in terms of evolution.

The Question of Eternal Life

IKEDA: Does life persist after death, or does it belong only to this world? If it does continue beyond death, is it eternal or finite, and in what state does it persist?

TOYNBEE: The possible eternal nature of life is an important question that arouses points insusceptible of actual proof.

IKEDA: Since the eternal continuance of life is ultimately related to the idea of death, knowledge of what happens after death is the necessary key to any solution to this question. There are two major approaches to this issue: the materialist idea that, upon death, the matter of the body reverts to an inorganic state and life itself vanishes, and the spiritual approach that life is immortal.

TOYNBEE: Buddhism, Hinduism, Zoroastrianism, and the three Judaic religions agree with each other in holding that physical death, after which the body of the person who has died reverts to inorganic matter, is not the end of life. They also agree that when life reappears after death, it presents itself in the form of a reembodiment. They hold that the personality that reappears is a psychosomatic unity, like the person who has previously died.

IKEDA: As you say, the so-called higher religions agree that life continues after death, but the doctrines concerning the nature of his life vary greatly among the religions.

TOYNBEE: That is true. According to Christian belief—as expounded in the Epistles of Saint Paul and in the accounts, in the Gospels, of Jesus' appearances after his alleged resurrection—the resurrected body of a dead person and the transformed body of a person who happens to be alive at the moment of the Last Judgment differ in kind from the physical body as we know it by direct observation in a living person. This new body is, in Saint Paul's parlance, a "spiritual" body; this is the kind of body in which Jesus is reported to have reappeared after his resurrection. He suddenly is present and he suddenly vanishes. He passes through doors that are closed and locked. He ascends from the surface of the earth till he is lost to view in a cloud. I have been told by Roman Catholic Christian contemporaries of mine that, according to the dogma of the Assumption into Heaven of Mary the mother of Jesus, her body—like Jesus' body, recorded to have ascended into Heaven—is deemed to be a spiritual body, not a physical body of the kind that is one of the phenomena of our human experience.

IKEDA: The Christian idea that the body of a resurrected person is a spiritual body in contrast to the ordinary physical body of actual human experience reflects the religious doctrine that the flesh is impure. Other religions hold similar doctrines. According to Southern Buddhism, it is imperative to destroy the body, which is viewed as a virtual hotbed of human desire, in order to attain the state called Nirvana.

TOYNBEE: Buddhists and Hindus hold that there can be, and usually is, more than one reincarnation; indeed, they hold that there may be, and probably already has been, an infinite number. This belief implies, I suppose, the further belief that the universe is eternal. The four Western religions all believe that the universe, at least in its present form, has had a beginning and is going to come to an end. They also believe that, after death, there is going to be one reincarnation only; but since they maintain that this reincarnation is to be everlasting, they, too, claim that the universe—though, in their view, it did have a beginning—is going to be everlasting in a form different from the present one.

IKEDA: Religious views of immortality may be divided into two general categories: transmigration, as taught by the Buddhist and Hindu religions; and the immortal soul, as taught by the Western religions centering on Christianity.

TOYNBEE: Yes. These two views agree in thinking of immortality as being a temporal extension of a human being's life in the time-dimension in which we live our brief lives in this world. Hindus hold (and some schools of Greek thought, also, held) that the soul has preexisted for an infinite length of time before birth (or a series of births) in this world in a body and that it will go on existing for an infinite length of time after death (or a series of deaths) in this world in a body. Southern Buddhists agree with the Hindu view, subject to the proviso that the series of rebirths can be brought to a close by spiritual endeavors during lives in this world. Christians hold that a soul is created by God at the moment of the conception of a body in a woman's womb but that, once created, a soul will continue to exist after death for an infinite length of time. The Christian conception of immortality seems to me to be less rational than the Hindu conception.

At the same time, I do not believe that a human being exists before his birth or continues to exist after his death in the time-dimension in which human beings live in this world. I suppose that what I call "the ultimate spiritual reality" is not in the time-dimension and that the effects of a human being's karma on the ultimate reality are not in the time-dimension either, though human life is lived in the time-dimension and human karma is created by human action in the time-dimension. Here I find myself at the limits of my human power of understanding.

IKEDA: Assuming that life is immortal, we still must answer the difficult question of its nature after the decomposition of the physical body. Does it merge with the ultimate spiritual reality behind and beyond the universe? If so, do all souls merge with that spiritual reality on a basis of complete equality without regard to the ethical consequences of the individual's acts during mortal life?

TOYNBEE: Since I am a human being, my human consciousness distinguishes between good and evil, and my human conscience tells me to try to do what seems to me to be good and to refrain from doing what seems to me to be evil. My human nature commits me, so I believe, to holding that a human being's acts during a lifetime in this world do have ethical consequences, that these consequences are important, and that they are important not only for the person himself but for the rest of mankind and for the whole of the universe. I believe that a human being's life in this world has an effect on the universe, for good or for evil, and that this effect gives a human life in this world a value, either positive or negative, and therefore a significance. Consequently, I believe that the ultimate spiritual reality is affected by the karma of every human being.

IKEDA: For me, the most arresting point in your discussion is your assertion that the actions—hence the fate—of each individual influence the ultimate spiritual reality. The higher religions often teach that the ultimate reality is absolute. It is not influenced by anything; indeed, it is itself the influencing force. Can I understand your interpretation as a reversal of this thought?

Further, I recognize the connection between your standpoint and the teachings of Buddhism. But if the ultimate spiritual reality is influenced by the fate of the individual human being, does it not then cease to be ultimate? Can you offer anything as proof of the existence of the ultimate spiritual reality?

TOYNBEE: I do not find any cogent evidence either for the immortality of the soul or for rebirth. I do not find any cogent evidence for the existence of the ultimate spiritual reality in which I myself believe. As I see it, the human mind has only a limited capacity for understanding the nature of the universe in which we find ourselves. Our verifiable knowledge does not supply us with the information and the guidance that we need for living a human life. The most important questions that confront us cannot be answered even by the most rational presentation that we can make of the information that we have. Therefore, we are bound to act on unverifiable hypotheses. We have to take these hypotheses on trust because we have to act, even though our knowledge is incomplete and our judgment of what is right and wrong is disputable.

IKEDA: You are correct in saying that the inadequacies of our spiritual abilities limit our theories about the universe and about the true nature of life to unverifiable hypotheses. Scientific theories are subject to and must be subjected to theoretical and experimental tests of validity. Ways of evaluating religious hypotheses, however, are different. First, religious hypotheses must be judged on how well they explain the phenomena of life that seem inexplicable to unaided human intelligence. Second, they must be judged on how effective they are in providing a foundation for human judgments and actions. In other words, we must ask whether scientific hypotheses are true, whereas we must ask whether religious hypotheses have value for the improvement of the qualities of humanity. I find the Buddhist hypothesis that life is eternal and constantly changing from one mode to another an effective explanation of the differences in the various fates of human beings born into this world. If we do not posit a former life for a person living in the present, the fate of that person must be ascribed either to an absolute, supernatural being or to pure chance. By avoiding a supernatural being governing the actions of man, the Buddhist explanation allows man to realize that he is himself responsible for his fate and in this way makes possible fundamental independence.

TOYNBEE: Immortality and rebirth are hypotheses which, if true, would answer some of the questions that we cannot evade but that we also cannot answer by drawing on our inadequate stock of verifiable knowledge.

The hypothesis of rebirth does offer, in combination with the verifiable experience of karma within a single lifetime, an explanation of the inequality of human beings' fortunes and fates. To accept the hypothesis of rebirth does not, I suppose, require one also to accept the hypothesis of immortality. In Southern Buddhism, so I understand, the purpose of an arhat's spiritual exercises is to bring the series of rebirths to a close as far as his own rebirths are concerned. He believes that he is threatened with being immortal, and he is trying to escape this fate.

IKEDA: Southern Buddhism teaches that we are bound to a karma of evil passions repeated in successive birth-death patterns and that breaking away from this pattern is the highest ideal. The arhat attempts to achieve the ideal of putting a stop to this transmigratory series.

TOYNBEE: The Hindu and the Christian conceptions of immortality seem to me to be vitiated by an identical misconception. They both conceive of the soul, when it is not living in a body in this world, as being, nevertheless, in the time-dimension in which bodily life is lived. But, if we guess that a human being's life is not confined to one, or alternatively to a series, of bodily lives in this world, we have no warrant for assuming that the unembodied state of life is in the time-dimension.

The only state of human life that is within our experience is the psycho-somatic state. The mental distinction between soul and body is a hypothesis, not a datum of experience. We do not have any sure evidence, derived from experience, of the existence of unembodied souls. We do have the experience of the existence of corpses. A corpse is an assemblage of matter that is no longer animated by the life that formerly made the now dead body a living organism. A human corpse is also no longer possessed of the consciousness that formerly made the now disorganized organism human. Indeed, a human being's consciousness does not have the same time span as his life. His consciousness awakens only gradually after birth, and it sometimes fades out before death. A human being may become senile before his physical death.

We know what happens to a corpse: it rapidly disintegrates into inorganic matter. Even if this assemblage of matter is artificially preserved, it has ceased to be organic when it has ceased to be alive. Since we have no experience of the existence of souls apart from bodies, it seems to me that we are bound to infer that, in terms of existence in the time-dimension, the soul ceases to exist at the moment of death. This conclusion suggests that there can be neither immortality nor rebirth in the time-dimension. Once a human being has died, his psychosomatic life in the time-dimension has come to an end, but death does not rule out the possibility that a human soul may have an existence outside the time-dimension. Nor does death rule out the possibility that karma, created by action in time during a psychosomatic life in this world, may have an effect, for good or for evil, on the ultimate reality, since we have no ground for supposing that this ultimate reality is in the time-dimension. The only state of conscious, living existence that we know, by experience, to be in the time-dimension is our psychosomatic life in this world.

IKEDA: Though each human exists as an individual being—in its profoundest parts—his life is at the same time one with the great all-embracing life of the universe. In this sense, I think I understand what you mean by the ultimate spiritual reality behind the universe. On the other hand, when you say that, at death, the soul, in contrast to the body, which reverts to inorganic matter, is absorbed into the ultimate spiritual reality, you seem to infer that spirit has an independent existence. There is no denying that after a certain fixed period most of the body's cells are renewed and that many physical changes take place during life. If we take the case of a hypothetical Mr. A, we see that though between the ages of three and thirty, his physical body undergoes many changes, he nonetheless maintains a certain basic nature of his own. That is to say, although the physical body seems independent, in its deepest parts it is not unrelated to the all-pervading life and its tendencies. Perhaps my meaning will be clearer put in reverse form: the inherent spiritual reality is imbued with tendencies toward physical life. Consequently, though the body dies and reverts to inorganic matter, the physical characteristics contained within the spiritual reality continue to exist. Furthermore, when motivated properly and given actualized form, they become part of another physical life body. Thus, from this standpoint, it is probably a mistake on the part of the intellect to think that death sunders the body and the spirit.

TOYNBEE: The dissection of a human being into a spiritual component and physical component is a mental operation. It is not a datum of experience; it is a conclusion from reflections on the data of experience, and it is neither the only possible conclusion nor the only one that has ever been drawn.

In our experience, we do not encounter unembodied souls or soulless living human bodies. In a mentally defective or senile person, the soul is eclipsed; in a physically defective or maimed person, the body is crippled. But I think these defects should be regarded as abnormalities, not as evidence that a soul and a living human body can exist independently of each other in objective reality, as distinct from our mental dissection of a human being into these two notional components.

IKEDA: Earlier you proposed the possibility that life, if it persists after death, does not exist in the time-dimension. I agree, but I go a step farther and insist that the basic nature of the very life we lead now in the present goes beyond the limits of the time-dimension. That is, life is in time but surpasses it. Certainly, if human lives take place within the framework of time, the human intellect is capable of understanding this. Bergson has stressed the concept of flowing time. In his view, temporal divisions into past, present, and future do not exist as such but have been produced because the flow of human consciousness is constantly aware of such internal divisions. But this kind of flow of consciousness is only a part of human life. If this is true, we can say that phenomenal temporal divisions—past, present, and future—do not exist in the basic nature of life but only manifest themselves when life is participating in concrete actions.

TOYNBEE: Kant has pointed out that the concepts of time and space are inescapable categories of human thought. Einstein has pointed out that the distinction between these two mental categories is only an intellectual operation and that, when we are making scientific observations, time can be measured only in terms of space, and space only in terms of time. But have we any warrant for assuming that the three mental categories—time, space, and time-space—have any objective existence? May they not be merely limitations of the human mind's capacity for comprehending the universe?

IKEDA: I too think that time and space are concepts created by the human mind and that if we attempt to find out what their true natures are, we are compelled to return to the nature of the greater life force. Furthermore, I believe that time and space, though characteristic traits of life, would cease to exist without life. Consequently, it is unreasonable to attempt to force all of life force into the spatial-temporal frame.

Time is a characteristic of human life, and we are made aware of it through the actions and changes in the universal life force. From our own daily experience we can see that time and its movements vary with activities performed in it. When we are happy, time seems to speed by; when we are sorrowful, the hands of the clock seem to move very slowly.

The state that in Buddhist teaching is described as *Kū*, a void imbued with potentiality, is an existing reality, though it is manifest in no phenomena. When life is in the state of *Kū*, it transcends both space and time. Since *Kū* cannot be seen with the human eyes, it might be thought to resemble nonbeing (*Mu*). But since, given an opportunity, it can become manifest in visible forms, it is different from nonbeing. In short, *Kū* is a state that cannot be

258

expressed as either being or nonbeing. The basic nature of the greater life force is to exist eternally outside of time while manifesting itself as life (or being) and death (or nonbeing).

TOYNBEE: From what you say, I suggest that a human personality's real existence is on the plane of *Kū.* I suppose that this is the meaning of the Hindu dictum *Tat tvam asi,* or "thou art that," an affirmation of the oneness of the individual and the universal. I conclude that the phenomenon of death, followed by the disorganization of the physical aspect of a personality that we encounter as a psychosomatic unity, is, in terms of reality-in-itself, an illusion arising from the limitations of the human mind's conceptual capacity and that a question about ultimate reality—*Kū*—cannot be answered when it is formulated in space-time terms.

I find both the Hindu-Buddhist concept of reincarnation and the Zoroastrian-Judaic concept of a single once-for-all resurrection intellectually incomprehensible. I am also unable to comprehend either the Hindu-Buddhist or the Zoroastrian-Judaic concept of the intermediate time interval between a personality's death and its resumption of psychosomatic life. In contrast to the time-and-space-bound phenomena that can be apprehended by the human intellect, may not reality-in-itself be both timeless and spaceless? I believe that reality itself is timeless and spaceless but that it does not exist in isolation from our time-and-space-bound world.

IKEDA: Northern Buddhism teaches that life and death are different time-and-space manifestations of life, which is itself a unity transcending time and space. I believe that the individual life is an actualized form of the all-embracing life force of which death is an inactive aspect. Inactivity, however, does not infer a return to nothingness. In Buddhist thought, this *Kū* state, though imperceptible to human senses, has its own awesome existence. The concept of *Kū* is one that falls outside unilateral determinations of existence or non-existence. Cosmic life force exists as *Kū.*

In contrast to *Kū, Ke* is that aspect of the all-embracing life force that assumes various actual and individual forms. The individualized life is a form of *Ke,* but at the same time it is impregnated with *Kū,* the inactive mode. In similar fashion, life force after death exists as *Kū* but is impregnated with fundamental characteristics and tendencies inherent in *Ke.* The all-embracing life that runs through both *Kū* and *Ke* is called *Chū.* Though sometimes assuming inactive form and sometimes actual form, *Chū* is the basic substance of the great life force and as such is a limitless continuum. Perhaps *Chū* can be represented by the basic idea of self as it is used in modern philosophy.

Buddhism further teaches that *Kū*, *Ke*, and *Chū* are a consolidated, harmonious entity that must be understood as a whole.

TOYNBEE: Is reality-in-itself the nature of *Kū*, "the great all-embracing life force of the universe," according to the Buddhist concept of *Kū* that you have described? If so, *Kū* would be the equivalent of the Zoroastrian-Judaic concept of eternity.

All six religions are confronted with the problem, discussed here in Buddhist terms, of envisaging the state of the personality during the single time-interval, or the series of successive time-intervals, during which, after a death and a dissolution of the personality in its physical aspect, the psychosomatic form of the personality's existence is in abeyance.

If I were to accept the six religions' common postulate of psychosomatic reappearance after death, I should find the Hindu-Buddhist account of this more convincing than the Zoroastrian-Judaic account of it. However, I am conscious of the intellectual difficulty that is brought to light in the discussion of the Buddhist concepts *Kū* and *Ke*. Therefore, I doubt whether this question can be answered when it is put, as all six religions do put it, in terms of time and space. Does life persist *after* death? And where does the soul go when the body goes back into the inorganic section of physical matter? To sum up, I believe that these questions can be answered in terms of *Kū* or of eternity, but not in terms of space-time.

The Universe

IKEDA: In roughly 3000 B.C., the Sumerians devised their own distinctive view of the universe. The ancient Greeks made full use of logic to give form to a number of interpretations of its nature. But it was not until the Renaissance that study of the heavenly bodies became an object of truly scientific research. With the invention of the telescope by Galileo, the science of astronomy entered an age of rapid development.

In the twentieth century, Einstein's work in the fields of relativity, quantum energy, and subatomic particles became the basis for a new growth in an astronomy that opened outward from the solar system, through the nearer galaxies to the whole universe itself. Development in this branch of study was immensely stimulated by the use of the radio telescope in the years following World War II. The 1930s and 1940s saw dramatic and fateful developments in atomic physics. The 1950s were a period of equally dramatic events in the field of biology. The 1960s and 1970s are the golden age of astronomy. This suggests that future histories of mankind will compare our time with the early seventeenth century, when Galileo first trained his telescope on the sky and when Kepler explained the movements of the planets.

Still, in astronomy, as in all other sciences, the wider the field of vision, the more numerous the difficulties. This is especially true when the objects of research cannot be directly examined and investigated at close range. Ultimately the two most important questions involved in astronomy are the size and the origin of the universe. These issues are as important for philosophy as for astronomy.

TOYNBEE: Today we have brought a much greater part of the physical cosmos within our ken than was known to the Babylonians and the Greeks in the last millennium B.C. We also know much more than they knew about the composition, temperature, metamorphoses, and movements of the stars that are within range of our observation. However, when we consider the question of the universe as a whole and attempt to understand its basic nature, we find ourselves as ignorant as our Babylonian and Greek predecessors. We, like them, are cognizant of only a minute fraction of the history and area of the physical cosmos. Our ideas about the whole of it are, like theirs, merely speculations, and our speculations, like theirs, conflict with each other inconclusively. We have no means of testing any of them; we do not have the necessary information.

IKEDA: You are quite right; we do lack the information. Still our curiosity draws us on to discuss such things as the size of the universe. Since the discovery of the Doppler effect in light waves from various heavenly bodies, it has been learned that the universe is expanding and that the nebulae within it are moving away from one another at startlingly high speeds. The farther they are away, the greater their speeds. For instance, nebulae that are approximately twenty billion light-years from our earth are receding farther and farther from us at a speed near that of light. Since even the most advanced methods of modern science cannot perceive what is happening in space beyond a radius of twenty billion light-years, our knowledge is effectively limited to that range. Anything beyond that physical limit becomes material for philosophical speculation. For instance, is the universe boundless? Does it simply extend on and on without end, or are there other universes outside the one we experience? Can it be that there is nothing at all beyond certain fixed limits? We can give no answers to these questions, but applying philosophical and rational investigation to them has great significance for humanity, because our interpretations of the universe profoundly influence our way of living.

One view in favor of an expanding universe is the explosion theory propounded by George Gamow and others. According to these scientists, the universe began expanding about twenty billion years ago when still in its original state, though already enormous. This theory leads to the assumption that the presently observable universe, while vast, is finite. The case would be different if the universe were infinitely large in its primitive stage, but this possibility is considered remote. Gamow and his disciples argue that there is but one finite universe, which is isolated, and complete emptiness lies beyond its boundaries. But there is another possibility. From a macroscopic viewpoint, there may exist another gigantic universe (and probably many such systems) outside ours.

Some scientists who posit the existence of another universe outside our own argue that the universe is not expanding but contracting. If they are correct, one may assume that what we call the universe is in fact only a small part of the true universe, which is boundless and eternally immutable.

TOYNBEE: The only infinite line that we can draw or can even visualize mentally is a line that has no open ends: a circle or an ellipse. The Hindus and the pre-Christian Greeks believed that the structure-motion of space-time is cyclic. In this view, every event and every entity recurs periodically an endless number of times. This conception of the physical cosmos corresponds to the phenomena of our own solar system, in which the planets move in unvarying orbits round the sun, and the planet earth rotates round its own axis once in every twenty-four hours. We have no evidence, however, that the present state of our own solar system is a fair sample of the structure and motion of the cosmos as a whole. Indeed, this is denied in the theory that the universe is constantly expanding. Moreover, the cyclic theory is incompatible with the possibility of there being such a phenomenon as irreversible change or as genuine novelty, yet change and novelty are data of our human experience, whether we believe or disbelieve that our experience of them is an authentic apprehension of reality.

IKEDA: In concrete terms, what do you mean by novelty?

TOYNBEE: The idea of novelty implies that it is possible for something to come into existence that has not been in existence previously. In other words, it implies the possibility of creation *ex nihilo*. This is logically inconceivable, yet novelty, like irreversible change, is a datum of human experience.

262

If irreversible change and genuine novelty are realities, the structure-movement of space-time cannot be infinite in the repetitive way of a circle or an ellipse. It must be finite, like a line that has two ends. An open-ended line is capable of being prolonged ad infinitum in either direction. If it is closed at two particular points, this limitation of the line's length must be the arbitrary act of a draughtsman who has chosen to set bounds to the line's potential infinity.

IKEDA: The natural world is not, as you say, describable without reference to irreversible change and novelty. But I do not agree that novelty is the creation of being out of nonbeing, because I support the Buddhist doctrine of a void that encompasses both being and nonbeing and that, when phenomenalized, gives the superficial impression of novelty.

The age of the universe too is a fascinating issue. The opinion held today by Gamow and others is that the universe began twenty billion years ago, but this beginning is not necessarily the only one. The present idea is only that the twenty-billion-year estimate falls within the range of physics and that discussing anything prior to that period is valueless from the scholarly view.

If it is true that the universe began twenty billion years ago, then we are compelled to admit that this system of energy and matter (being) was created suddenly from absolute nothingness (nonbeing) in that remote age. Presupposing that being cannot be produced from nonbeing, the very existence of our universe proves that it has had an infinite past. One may consider that, from a limitless past, the universe was contracting and that the processes of contracting and expanding recur in a limitless cycle. Similarly, on the premise that neither energy nor matter can be reduced to absolute nothingness, our existence proves that the universe has a boundless future.

TOYNBEE: Since at least as early as the rise of the oldest of the civilizations (about five or six thousand years ago), it has been recognized that the earth and the cosmos of which the earth is a part have undergone changes. Some thinkers have inferred that the earth, the whole cosmos, and all its contents must have had a beginning and must eventually cease to exist. Other thinkers have held that the cosmos is eternal. These two rival theories are still in dispute at the present day; so far, neither theory has been demonstrated to be either true or false.

A cosmos that is finite in space-time is logically inconceivable, for if space-time is not infinite, there must be further space-time before it and after it and beyond it and outside it. Yet this logical necessity is ruled out *a priori* by the conception of finiteness. A finite space-time must therefore be bounded by some power that is of a different order of being from space-time itself.

Thus, if we hold that the cosmos is finite, we seem to be compelled to conclude that it has been created and planned and is being directed towards a goal by a power that cannot be conceived of in space-time terms—in other words, God. The expansion theory of the cosmos looks like a depersonalized version of the Judaic myth of the creation of the universe out of nothing.

And what about the psychic aspect of the universe? If the physical cosmos did not contain conscious beings, there would be no awareness of the cosmos's existence and no possibility of speculations—let alone verifiable knowledge—about it. Human conscious beings are psychosomatic organisms. Our vision of the universe is incomplete and incorrect if we do not envisage it in its psychic as well as in its physical aspect. Do the concepts of finiteness and infinity have any meaning in the psychic realm of reality? My conclusion is that we have more knowledge of the universe than our predecessors had but that we have no more understanding of it than they had.

IKEDA: In other words, interpretations of the nature of the universe are ultimately the task of philosophy. No matter how much knowledge we have amassed, our understanding of the universe is no better than that of the peoples of ancient times.

But you have mentioned the monotheistic creation myths of the Judaic religions. Please elaborate on this point.

TOYNBEE: Human beings change things deliberately by the exercise of skill. For instance, we make pots out of clay. On this analogy, some thinkers have guessed that a being who is humanlike because intelligent and purposeful, but superhuman because omnipotent and immortal, has created the universe. In one view, he created it at a single stroke, constructing it so as to evolve according to the creator's initial plan. In another view, the creator is continually at work changing his plans in accordance with new ideas and is putting these new plans into execution.

The belief in the existence of an omnipotent creator god has been held by the adherents of the Judaic religions (Judaism, Christianity, Islam). These religions have supplanted the pre-Judaic religions at the western end of the Old World and in the Americas, but they, and their naive conception of an omnipotent creator god, have not made much impression on southern and eastern Asia. In modern Western society, since the nineteenth century, attempts have been made to dispense with the Judaic notion of a creator god and to find other explanations for the observed and inferred facts of change—particularly for the emergence of life on this planet—for the increasing differentiation of the forms of life, and for the superior complication and sub-tlety of some of the younger species of living creatures. I myself do not have the scientific knowledge that is needed for passing judgment on nontheistic theories of evolution. My impression is that they are either reproductions of the theistic theory in nontheistic terms or, alternatively, explanations that are no more satisfying intellectually than the theistic explanation.

The notions expressed in the words *change* and *novelty* are suggested by human experience. We do experience, and also do produce, change and no-velty; yet, logically, these notions are puzzling. They imply the notion of creation, but creation is a still more puzzling notion. It implies the production of something out of nothing, and it also implies a humanlike act of planning and execution, whether the agent is a transcendent god or an immanent impulse in nature. It is perhaps impossible for human thought to avoid thinking in anthropomorphic terms, yet we realize that it is most improbable that the ultimate reality in and behind and beyond the universe is really humanlike.

Intelligent Beings on Other Planets

IKEDA: Guesses and suppositions have been made about the possibility that living beings on a par with, or perhaps superior to, human beings exist on celestial bodies other than earth. Although no proof of any kind is available to substantiate such suppositions, I find them especially interesting because the Lotus Sutra of Sakyamuni teaches the premise that countless worlds with living beings exist in the universe. From the philosophical standpoint, what are your opinions of the likelihood of living beings existing on other celestial bodies?

TOYNBEE: In declaring that the existence of intelligent beings on other planets is probable, our scientists are making a justifiable guess on the basis of the amount of certain knowledge that they already possess. With the most far-reaching instruments that they have invented so far, the scientists have demonstrated two facts: the portion of the physical cosmos that they have brought within range of observation for observers on our own planet is almost inconceivably vast by comparison with the scale of our own planet, solar system, and galaxy; this known portion of the cosmos appears to be only a fraction of the whole; and there is no evidence that the whole cosmos has any limits.

265

Space-time, even if we believe it to be infinite in the sense of being endlessly recurrent, is so vast that it is improbable that our own planet is the only point-moment in the structure-history of the universe in which there is, has been, or will be life and consciousness.

Life, in the sense of life as we know it, can exist only under certain rather narrowly limited physical conditions. It is conceivable that other forms of life might be able to exist under different conditions. It is possible that our planet is the only one in our solar system that is capable of harboring life in any form. Possibly there is no other planet capable of harboring life in any of the other solar systems within our own galaxy. But the number of known galaxies, beyond ours, is immense, and there may be innumerable other galaxies beyond our present range of observation. It seems probable that there is somewhere at least one galaxy, besides ours, that contains at least one solar system that has at least one planet, capable of supporting life, which is actually inhabited by living beings, some of whom are intelligent in the sense in which we are. A chance that would be improbable in a finite cosmos is probable in a cosmos that appears to be virtually infinite.

Therefore, it seems likely that mankind is not unique. It is not only credible; it is probable that some other planet—or indeed a vast number of other planets—is inhabited by intelligent beings of approximately the same kind as ourselves.

It seems highly unlikely to me, however, that planets inhabited by intelligent beings will be accessible from earth. The great lesson to be learned from putting men on the moon is the immense difficulty of reaching another planet. In order to land a few human beings on the surface of the moon, which is far nearer the earth than any star, staggering outlays in money and technology were required. To reach a hypothetically habitable planet, even one within our own galaxy, we would have to invent spaceships in which people could live, die, and be born generation after generation.

IKEDA: If living beings do exist on other planets, they may be different from us in form, function, and chemical composition. For example, some scientists argue that, in contrast to the basically carbon-oriented organisms of earth, living creatures on other planets might be composed largely of silicon or that some might discharge ammonia instead of carbon dioxide. Do you think that such things are possible?

TOYNBEE: If life does exist elsewhere, it is likely to be psychosomatic as it is on earth, but the chemical composition and the functioning of the somatic aspect of living beings elsewhere may be quite different.

266

If there are living beings elsewhere, some may possess consciousness, and some of these hypothetical conscious living beings may be superior to mankind either intellectually, ethically, or in both respects. Does this guess commit us to assuming that life is latent in the physical cosmos as a whole and in every part of it?

IKEDA: The Buddhist philosophical interpretation leads us to assume that life is latent in the whole universe and in every part of it. Buddhism teaches that the universe itself constitutes a vast life entity and that even the seemingly inorganic celestial bodies contain a life potential assuming various manifestations that conform to diverse environmental conditions.

Universal life finds verbal expression in these Buddhist terms: the realm of the Buddhas ranges the ten directions of space and spans the three periods of time. The ten directions of space represent the total expanse of cosmological space. The three periods of time are the endless temporal span from the infinite past, through the fleeting present, into the eternal future. The countless realms of the Buddhas are ever present throughout the universe and are the dwelling places of the *shujō* (*sattva*). The term *shujō* means sentient beings and includes human beings.

As the above explanation implies, in the Buddhist sense, life entities are not limited to biological beings. Buddhism considers the entire universe to be the source of the generation of all entities. The universe itself is a vital being including the life potential that develops into all forms of life; it is, therefore, defined as the greatest life entity. All Buddhist theoretical thought develops from the idea that the whole universe is one vast life body. This being the case, the Buddhist should not find the idea of living, intelligent beings on other planets surprising in the least.

TOYNBEE: Whether the whole universe is one vast life body as Buddhism asserts depends on whether we admit or deny the reality of irreversible change and the reality of novelty. The ground for denying their reality is that they are logically inconceivable. The ground for admitting their reality is that they are data of our human experience. If we deny the reality of these data, we are bound to conclude that the phenomena that are apparent to the human mind are illusions that give us no idea of the nature of reality-in-itself.

IKEDA: I believe that irreversible change and novelty are concepts invented by man but are not part of reality. It is an error to assume the reality of irreversible change and novelty solely on the basis of phenomena suggesting that they are real.

If we assume that there are intelligent living beings beyond earth, we find ourselves confronted with the possibility of coming into contact with them and establishing some kind of exchange. If intelligent beings do exist on other planets, will it be possible for the inhabitants of earth to communicate with them?

TOYNBEE: So far we have no evidence for the existence of such beings anywhere else in that portion of the physical cosmos that is within the present range of observation from our planet. Probably our range of observation will expand, but possibly there are limits to its expansion. In any case, supposing that we were to discover the existence of intelligent beings somewhere else in the cosmos, we do not know whether we should ever be able to communicate with them. Nor, conversely, do we know whether they would be able to communicate with us if they were to discover our existence. I am skeptical about recent supposed indications that our planet is already being reconnoitered by beings from somewhere in what, from our standpoint, is outer space.

If such beings do exist elsewhere, their habitat may be hundreds of millions of light-years distant from our planet; moreover, the distance may be increasing at a prodigious pace, if the theory that the physical cosmos is expanding is correct.

In these circumstances, communication could be established only if both parties were intelligent to a high degree and were also technologically efficient in a corresponding measure. Therefore, if contact were to be established between mankind and other intelligent beings elsewhere, it is probable that these would prove to be at least as intelligent as ourselves, and it is possible that they might prove to be very much more intelligent.

IKEDA: If we do make contact, humanity will be forced to know what attitude to take toward these beings.

TOYNBEE: In the eventuality of contacts being established, our own attitude ought not to be like the inhuman attitude of modern Western Europeans to their fellow human beings after the discovery and colonization of the Americas. Towards intelligent beings on other planets we must be modest, tactful, and conciliatory. We should be anxious and cautious until we have taken the measure of the other party's intelligence. They might be so much more intelligent than we are that they might regard us as vermin. They might have no more compunction about exterminating us than Westerners have had about exterminating American Indians or than we all have about exterminating the anopheles mosquito. These hypothetical intelligent beings from other planets might choose to preserve some specimens of mankind as scientific curiosities, as we now preserve some rare nonhuman species of living beings on this planet. Of course, the other party might turn out to be inferior in intelligence to us. Intellectually he might be on the level of some of the now extinct primitive hominids. In that event, we ought to treat him with greater mercy than *Homo sapiens* (so-called) has treated hominids of other species that once competed with him for dominion on this planet.

Beyond Waves and Subatomic Particles

IKEDA: Until only recently it was believed that the subatomic particles are the ultimate basic unit of matter, but now attempts are being made to discover something still more fundamental. Heisenberg's uncertainty principle, the discovery of wave movements, and variable identities in elementary particles indicate that, in relation to the microscopic world, the analytical method of natural science has reached a limit. Current knowledge that wave activities accompany all matter and that matter is surrounded by what are called fields suggests that matter cannot be explained entirely on the basis of the theory of units of fixed sizes. That is to say, matter must be understood not only in terms of particles but also in terms of the natures and characteristics of waves and fields.

Science then must pursue the fundamental nature of matter from many angles, and to grasp the meaning of matter in a new and unified way, it must have an effective methodology. Until the present, the scientific method has been based on the analytical approach. Certainly, analysis has proved useful in many cases, but it is now time to adopt a more inclusive, deductive methodology.

TOYNBEE: I agree that a deductive method would be valuable. As you point out, scientists have reached the limits of scientific explanations—demonstrable and verifiable explanations—of the nature of the physical facets of the universe. They have discovered two different pictures of the ultimate nature of matter: subatomic particles and waves and fields. In addition, they have found that these two pictures cannot be observed simultaneously.

The limitedness of the capacity of science is a particular case of the limitedness of the capacity of human nature in general. *Homo sapiens* is a conscious psychosomatic organism that is physically feeble but is at the same time

269

physically handy enough to serve the purposes of a powerful mind. So far, *Homo sapiens* has proved capable of survival through the coordinated action of mind and body. He has exterminated all other species of hominids and has imposed his dominance on most of nonhuman nature, both animate and inanimate, almost everywhere on or near the surface of this planet. He also has a surplus capacity, over and above what is required for his survival, and he has used this surplus both for good (creating works of art and satisfying his intellectual curiosity) and for evil (making war and enabling an unfairly privileged minority to live frivolously and luxuriously).

However, this surplus capacity is limited. It is not great enough to enable *Homo sapiens* to know, to understand, and to control the universe as a whole. The universe remains a mystery to us, and this mystery still holds us at its mercy.

IKEDA: One of the reasons for the power the mystery of the universe has over us is certainly the nature of our abilities to perceive. Engel's assertion that the only real world is the one perceptible to the senses fails to convince. Although sensually perceptible elements are one of the aspects of matter, they are not the whole picture; there is a current beneath these elements that man cannot perceive with his senses.

TOYNBEE: What you have said about the limits of the perceptivity of the human senses is quite true. For example, we can observe the structure or the motion—not both simultaneously, however—of the material aspect of the universe on what appears to us to be its smallest scale, but we cannot prove that the smallest scale on which matter is observable by us is also the smallest in reality. It seems more likely that only a minute section of the spectrum of the universe is perceptible to human senses.

IKEDA: Our inability to perceive what can be convincingly called *ultimates* forces theoretical physics to take on a pronounced philosophical coloring. This is not surprising to me, since I am convinced that any conclusive answers we can obtain must be philosophical.

Whether space is truly void has been a point of argument from ancient times. In classical Greece, the problem of vacuum developed from discussions of existence and nonexistence. In his theory of atoms, Democritus recognized a vacuum that allows atoms to move freely. As modern science developed, the problem of the vacuum became very important, and heated argument raged between proponents of the opposing ideas of action through a medium and action at a distance.

Modern physics, which established the field theory, has disproved the notion that space is vacuum. Michael Faraday, who expounded the theory of electromagnetic fields, thought that the lines of magnetic and electric forces were space attributes that could be manifested by the use of a magnet and a charged body. Forces working between two physical objects belong to the attributes of space. J. C. Maxwell, who gave Faraday's field of force mathematical form, held that light is a form of electromagnetic force manifested in space. His theory has had great influence on the theory of elementary particles. Although Albert Einstein, who tried to integrate field theories, did not succeed in establishing a unified field for both gravity and electromagnetic force, he did develop clear ideas about space.

Even space that is empty of matter combines separated physical objects, transmits electromagnetic waves, and produces new matter. Mass and energy are equal and interchangeable, and, as Einstein pointed out, "Matter is where the concentration of energy is greatest." Therefore, it follows that matter and field space are not different in quality but are two forms of the same thing.

Field space is not mere empty space; it has attributes that influence physical objects contained in it. It also has the possibility of producing matter under certain conditions. Today progress is being made in the study of fields of nuclear forces and the related field of mesons. In their pursuit of the relationship between space-time and elementary particles, Dr. Hideki Yukawa and other scientists have hypothesized an element region (the elementary region of space).

All of these varying approaches to research on the ultimate nature of matter seem to me to be leading directly to the Buddhist concept of Void (Kū). The Buddhist Void transcends being and nonbeing because all things are essentially void. The Void includes, but is not, time and space. Since modern physicists cannot come closer to the ultimate nature of matter than two unreconcilable pictures—subatomic particles and waves—it may be that they will be forced to admit that matter is actually neither of these two and that perhaps it is a non-thing. Should they admit this, they would be approaching the Buddhist belief that matter and all things consist of Void.

TOYNBEE: My understanding of modern physics is so rudimentary that I cannot express any authoritative opinion about current tendencies in this field. Subject to this reservation, I do think that modern physics may be approaching the limits of what is understandable in terms of time and space. I therefore guess that physics may never begin to give us an understanding of the nonphysical—that is, spiritual—aspect of reality. Time and space are functions of the physical aspect of reality. But reality is spiritual as well as

271

physical, and its spiritual aspect is just as real as its physical aspect. The Buddhist concept of Void refers to the spiritual aspect of reality, and I believe that spiritual life can be described only in spiritual terms—though our vocabulary for spiritual things is derived, by analogy, from our vocabulary for physical things, because the human mind finds it relatively easy to grasp physical phenomena, whereas spiritual things are impalpable and elusive. While we cannot avoid using an analogical vocabulary for speaking about spiritual things, this vocabulary is not only inadequate, it can be positively misleading. It betrays us into misconstruing the nature of spiritual reality by thinking of it in the inappropriate physical terms that our vocabulary suggests.

Religious Approaches to Ultimate Reality

IKEDA: You say that religion leads man to seek union with the ultimate spiritual reality behind and beyond the universe and that such a religious experience is purely subjective and personal. Is that experience similar to the revelations and enlightenments of the Buddha, Jesus, Moses, and Mohammed?

TOYNBEE: I think the revelations received, or believed to have been received, by Moses (if Moses is a historical character) and by Jesus and by Mohammed were the same and that they were different from the enlightenment of the Buddha.

The founder, or founders, of Judaism, and Jesus and Mohammed as well, were theists who believed that the ultimate spiritual reality is a unique, omnipotent god. The prophets of Israel and Judah, and Jesus and Mohammed, believed that they had received their revelations from God. The form in which they sought union with God for themselves and for their followers was a communion between a human being and a humanlike divinity, two living beings who, in the Judaic view, were like each other in being persons in the human sense of the word, though they differed in respect of the vast superiority of God's power.

IKEDA: What do you consider the nature of Buddha's enlightenment to have been?

TOYNBEE: Sakyamuni was not a theist—or if he did believe in the existence of gods, he thought of their role as being a minor one. Sakyamuni believed that he had won his enlightenment by his own spiritual exertions. He believed that the ultimate spiritual reality is a state (Nirvana) in which desire—the component of human nature that generates karma—has been extinguished. The form in which he sought union with Nirvana was an exit into Nirvana out of his life as a human being. He believed that, in order to escape from human life, he must liquidate his karma account. He believed that he could liquidate it by extinguishing all his desires—*all* of them, including love as well as greed. The condition for passing out of human life into Nirvana was the achievement of complete psychological detachment.

IKEDA: That is the teaching according to Southern Buddhism.

TOYNBEE: As I understand it, the Southern Buddhist scriptures teach that the Buddha did not practice what he preached. When he himself had attained enlightenment, it was open to him to make his exit into Nirvana; he also believed that this was the goal that all sentient beings, including himself, ought to pursue. Nevertheless, he postponed his own exit until after his physical death in order to spend the rest of his life teaching other people what he had discovered for himself. His motive is said to have been compassion for other sentient beings.

There seems to me to be an unresolved contradiction here, for compassion is desire: it is desire in the loving, as opposed to the greedy, form. But this is still a form of desire; and if the Buddha did still feel compassion after his enlightenment, he had not yet detached himself completely and therefore had not yet attained the state that, in the Buddha's belief, must be attained in order to qualify a human being for making his exit into Nirvana.

IKEDA: In what way do you believe Buddhism resolves the contradiction inherent in that attitude?

TOYNBEE: Northern Buddhism, so I understand, preaches what the Buddha practiced. Northern Buddhism's heroes are bodhisattvas, who, like the Buddha, have postponed their own exit into Nirvana out of compassion for other sentient beings.

IKEDA: It is for this reason that I consider it impossible to understand the vast network of teachings of the Buddha or to grasp his true intentions unless one delves into the teachings of Northern, or Mahayana, Buddhism. Northern Buddhism teaches the possibility of entry into Nirvana as a consequence of repeated lives and births and does not advocate the extinction of desire. But how is it possible to enter Nirvana and remain within the stream of trans-migrations of life? Sakyamuni, in the Lotus Sutra, explained that this is possible through the awakening to the Buddhahood inherent in each human being. This awakening is brought about by means of the great Law. Upon awakening to one's inherent Buddhahood, one begins a course of action filled with boundless compassion for all beings. In other words, the Nirvana of Northern Buddhism is not the entry into a static state of void but a condition of limitless compassion created as a result of the individual's awareness of the Buddha nature within himself. It is true that this compassion is a kind of desire, and on the surface of things this would seem to result in the contradiction that you point out between what the Buddha preached and what he practiced. But Northern Buddhism resolves this contradiction. Instead of advocating the extinguishing of desire, Northern Buddhism teaches that it must be overcome by changing it from greedy desire to altruistic desire.

TOYNBEE: The Buddha, on the one hand, and the monotheists, on the other hand, had different visions of the nature of ultimate reality. Although their visions are incompatible with each other, it does not necessarily follow that one vision is correct and that the other is mistaken. It seems to me more probable that they saw different facets of reality.

IKEDA: But can reality have facets that are incompatible with each other?

TOYNBEE: Even in that fraction of the universe that the human mind can know by applying scientific reasoning to experience, matter, at the infinitesimal extremity of its gamut, is now said to have mutually incompatible properties.

Incompatibility that cannot be resolved by human thought is, I think, an indication that we have reached one of the limits of our capacity for understanding. It seems probable that the nature of ultimate reality is only partially comprehensible to human minds. I therefore think that the incompatibility between the Buddhist and the Judaic vision of ultimate reality does not indicate that either of these visions is false. It seems to me to indicate only that each vision, being human, is partial and imperfect. I think that the incompatibility of the visions actually increases our understanding of a reality that can, at most, be understood only partially by human minds.

IKEDA: Should people come to understand that it is the human vision and not the reality that contains contradictions, a unification of the higher religions might become possible. What form should the resultant religion take?

Should it center on one dominant religious philosophy, or should all the older elements blend to form something entirely new?

TOYNBEE: It looks to me as if a union of the higher religions is already beginning to take place. As I see it, this union is taking the form not of unification but of a mutual recognition that each of these religions has a distinctive and unique, though only partial, vision of ultimate reality and that all of them are valuable for mankind. Different human beings have different temperaments, besides having different experiences. Since there are different variations on our common human nature, it is fortunate that there should be more than one vision of ultimate reality to help us to catch a glimmer of understanding.

IKEDA: I too am of the opinion that, because ultimate reality is vast and profound and because our ability to understand it is shallow and limited, we can grasp only partial meanings of aspects of the whole.

Even though we are able to understand only aspects of the ultimate reality, there are cases in which potentialities exist for all people to put religious teachings into actual practice and other cases in which such practical application is limited to a small number of people. I believe that the Buddhist understanding can be put into application by all peoples, whereas the teachings of Judaism and Christianity are limited. This difference gives rise to another of a more profound nature. If God is a volitional being like man, then only those people in God's grace can come into contact with him and receive his revelations. Under these circumstances, human volition cannot be very important. Buddhism, on the other hand, teaches that the ultimate reality exists throughout the universe and to an equal extent in all living things. Consequently, all human beings enjoy equal possibilities of coming into contact with that reality. Even granted that between the two kinds of religions, recognition of the ultimate reality, basic attitudes, and ideals about human life and actions arising from these attitudes may share common points, the practical methods used for the sake of an understanding of the ultimate reality differ. Furthermore, the way we understand ultimate reality inevitably reflects deeply on the practical aspects of daily living.

TOYNBEE: The higher religions and philosophies all give the same practical counsels for human conduct. They all tell us that man's paramount objective ought to be to master himself, not to indulge his greed by trying to master the rest of the universe. They all tell us that the purpose of mastering ourselves is to make us capable of devoting ourselves to the service of something beyond

275

ourselves. The Buddha's compassion and Jesus' love are, it seems to me, reorientations of desire, which is, I believe, an ineradicable element in life. They are reorientations of desire from the self to the universe.

The Buddhist Approach

Epistemology: Santai Theory

IKEDA: Everything changes aspect according to the viewpoint of the observer. Even the universe, nature, and human life assume diverse aspects as approaches to them differ. No serious problem arises if the differences involve no more than human awareness, but this awareness of things does influence thinking and action. To give an extreme example, if one recognizes man as only an active mode of physical matter, one will be totally unconcerned with the dignity of human life. This being the case, I believe it is necessary—even if not possible in the strictest sense—to delineate and recognize the true aspects of things and phenomena exactly as they are. To grasp true aspects of things, both analysis and synthesis are indispensable. It is as necessary to keep an eye on the totality as it is to examine its parts closely. Furthermore, it is essential to realize the dynamic changes of things in the flow of time instead of observing them as fixed, static entities.

TOYNBEE: You have set forth two conditions as being requisite for grasping the true aspects of things. We need to take a bird's-eye view of the whole, besides taking a worm's-eye view of the parts. We also need to watch things on the move in the time-dimension. I am encouraged by the insistence on these two conditions, because I, too, have come to feel their importance as a result of my own reaction to the contemporary trend of thought in the Western world.

IKEDA: Why do you feel a need for both ways of looking at things?

TOYNBEE: In my view, present-day Western thought is vitiated by carrying specialization to extremes. The human mind's picture of a fragment of reality is distorted when this fragment is arbitrarily divorced from its setting and is studied as if it were a self-contained entity and not—as it truly is—an inseparable part of something that is more comprehensive. I also think that present-day Western sociological analysis loses touch with reality as a result of analyzing human affairs in unrealistic, instantaneous cross-sections divorced from both the past and the future, as if life were still-life. In reality, life is mobile, and it cannot be seen as it really is unless it is seen flowing in the stream of time.

IKEDA: In connection with suggesting ways in which it is possible to see things as they are, I should like to ask your opinion of a Buddhist epistemological principle called the *Santai* theory.

The *san* of *Santai* means three, and *tai* implies being clear or obvious. Therefore, *Santai* is frequently translated as the Three Truths. According to this theory, it is possible to grasp the realities of all things and phenomena if one observes their natures and aspects from three viewpoints: *Kū*, *Ke*, and *Chū*. Of these three, *Ke*, or *Ketai*, represents the images of surface phenomena of things perceptible to the human senses. Our physical bodies and the universe itself are in constant flux and change. The body, for example, undergoes metabolism and functions dynamically. The surface aspects of things are perceived by the human mind as images. But the images themselves are transitory.

Kū, or *Kūtai*, which signifies characteristics of things and phenomena, can be defined as neither existence nor nonexistence, because in it are inherent conditions permitting change into many kinds of phenomena. From the Buddhist viewpoint, reality and *Kū* are not identical, but *Kū* is essential to a correct awareness of the reality of things.

Chū, or *Chūtai*, the ultimate reality, embraces both *Ketai* and *Kūtai*. In other words, it is the ultimate life existence that is made manifest in forms and determines inherent natures and characteristics. *Chūtai* is immutable, but it reveals itself in *Ketai* and *Kūtai*; it does not exist outside them.

Kū, *Ke*, and *Chū* are one reality, and the true forms of all things are the products of the three ways in which this one reality manifests itself. Buddhism teaches that if one examines things from this standpoint, it is possible to perceive them, unmistakenly, as they are. I suggest that this epistemological theory could be an effective way of enabling us to make just such accurate perception.

TOYNBEE: *Santai* reminds me of the contrast, drawn by Plato, between the phenomena, which are in a constant flux (your *Ke*), and the unchanging forms, which are the ultimate reality that is reflected in the phenomena (your *Chū*). The Buddhist analysis links these two polar modes of existence by the middle terms *Kū*, which is neither phenomenal nor absolute but which nevertheless partakes of both modes.

IKEDA: The two theories are similar, with the exception you mention of the intermediary *Kū* mode.

TOYNBEE: But the thesis that the ultimate reality, *Chū*, reveals itself only through *Kū* and *Ke*, and never independently, corresponds, if I have interpreted it right, to Aristotle's, rather than to Plato's, conception of the relations between the permanent forms and the transient phenomena. In Aristotle's opinion, Plato undervalued the phenomena. Though these are transient, they give to human minds the only glimpse of ultimate reality that our finite intelligence is capable of obtaining. Aristotle likewise held that Plato was wrong in supposing that the unchanging forms, which are reflected in the phenomena, exist independently of the phenomena.

The ancient Greek school of philosophy is the one with which I am most familiar. The Buddhist *Santai* theory seems to me to agree closely with Aristotle's modification of Platonism. I think the addition of the middle term *Kū* makes the relations between particulars and universals more intelligible. The *Santai* theory seems to me to have some affinity with the modern Western philosopher Hegel's concept of the production of a synthesis through a confrontation between a thesis and an antithesis. At any rate, the Hegelian, like the Buddhist, three-term theory is dynamic. It sees reality on the move in the time-dimension. By contrast, both Plato's and Aristotle's two-term theory is static, like the present-day Western sociologists' analyses of human affairs in instantaneous cross-sections in which the time dimension is ignored. The dynamic theory that takes account of the time dimension seems to me more likely to correspond to reality.

Ten States of Life

IKEDA: Buddhist theory maintains that life manifests ten states or ten realms of being. One of these ten states dominates each individualized life, human and other, at every moment, and life changes into one or another of these ten states according to circumstances. The classification is completely different from that of the animal and the vegetable kingdoms, and it is different from that of sentient and insentient beings. The ten states are classified according to emotions.

This theory can be likened in some respects to the concept of hell, purgatory, and heaven described by Dante in the *Divine Comedy*. But there are differences. First, the number of categories are not the same. Second, in contrast to Dante's realms, which are worlds to be entered after death, the Buddhist states represent actual conditions of this life. For instance, in time of sorrow, the whole world is a source of suffering. By contrast, to a happy person every-thing looks bright.

In order of lessening agony and increasing happiness the Ten States of Life are these: *Jigoku* (Hell), *Gaki* (Rapacity), *Chikushō* (Animality), *Shura* (Anger), *Nin* (Tranquillity), *Ten* (Rapture), *Shōmon* (Learning), *Engaku* (Partial Enlightenment), *Bosatsu* (Bodhisattva) and *Butsu* (Buddhahood). *Jigoku* is the state of sufferings; *Gaki* is the state of being under the sway of desires; *Chikushō* is the state of fearing someone or something stronger than oneself; *Shura* is the state of constant competition or conflict in which one tries arrogantly to surpass others. The first three are called the Three Evil Paths, and these together with *Shura* comprise the Four Evils, signifying the varying conditions of unhappiness.

Nin is the common tranquil state one may sometimes observe in human society. *Ten* is the state of being overjoyed at the gratification of a desire. This feeling of happiness, brought about by the satisfaction of a physical desire or the fulfillment of ambition for fame or indulgence in pleasure, is fragile and temporary. The six states from *Jigoku* to *Ten* are collectively called the Six Paths. Because natural man's activities usually remain within these, Buddhism calls ordinary human life transmigration within the Six Paths.

TOYNBEE: And one of the practical aims of Buddhist teaching is to halt this transmigration within the Six Paths?

IKEDA: Yes. Transcending unhappy states of life and attaining permanent happiness is the essence of Buddhist practice. But since the Six Paths are inherent in life, there is neither a need nor an intention to eliminate them. Instead, Buddhism strives to find the way to permanent happiness by reform-ing human life. This is accomplished by preventing the Six Paths from gaining ascendance and by concentrating on higher human goals.

TOYNBEE: This practice, then, is based on actions in the actual world.

IKEDA: Yes. The next important stage, after the Six Paths, is that of *Shōmon*. The Chinese characters standing for *Shōmon* (literally, to hear voices) mean learning the philosophers' doctrines in order to realize truths. The state of life in which one feels joy in the pursuit of immortal truths is *Shōmon*.

The Chinese characters for *Engaku* literally mean to be enlightened by surrounding phenomena. This implies the state of life in which one finds joy in attaining a kind of enlightenment by observing universal or natural phe-nomena. But the joys of *Shōmon* and *Engaku* are self-centered. By contrast,

THE NATURE OF THINGS

Bosatsu is the state of altruism—the joy of helping others. In terms of practice, this state is like Christian love or Buddhist compassion.

Lastly, *Butsu* or Buddhahood is the state attained only as the result of practice as a bodhisattva. Buddhahood is defined as absolute happiness available only to the individual who penetrates to the ultimate truths underlying the universe and all-embracing life (the truths attained in *Shōmon* and *Engaku* being only partial) and who achieves identity with the universe and all-embracing life, thereby realizing the eternity of life. I believe that Buddhahood has much in common with your concept of happiness as "a satisfaction that is complete and permanent."

TOYNBEE: Buddhism has made a subtler psychological analysis than any that has been made, so far, in the West. *Shōmon* and *Engaku* seem to me to be the goals of Southern Buddhism. These are grand and difficult goals, but *Bosatsu* goes beyond them. The Southern Buddhist goals are perhaps the highest attainable by the individual self, but in *Bosatsu* the individual self opens its heart to expand itself spiritually into the universal self.

When I look for Christian equivalents of Northern Buddhist conceptions and ideals, I see an affinity between the bodhisattva, who voluntarily postpones his exit into Nirvana, and the second member of the Christian trinity, who emptied himself temporarily of his divinity in order to redeem his fellow human beings (the bodhisattvas redeem nonhuman sentient beings too). Like a bodhisattva, Christ incarnate suffered (according to the Christian story) by exposing himself to the painfulness of life, and his compelling motive was the same as a bodhisattva's: compassion.

IKEDA: The cases are similar and have much in common.

TOYNBEE: The bodhisattva phase of existence, like the incarnation of God in the Christian mythology, is, by definition, temporary; therefore, it cannot be complete or permanent. The complete and permanent satisfaction experienced by the Christian God, as represented in Christ, comes, I suppose, from his having temporarily made the altruistic, compassionate self-sacrifice of divesting himself of his divinity and suffering the worst spiritual and physical torments that are possible for a human being. Is the complete and permanent satisfaction that is attained in *Butsu* likewise retrospective? And does the *Butsu* state of a bodhisattva resemble Christ's state after his ascension?

IKEDA: I consider Christ, in his role as a savior, to be a manifestation of the bodhisattva state. In both instances, the aim is altruistic. In Southern Buddhism such altruism is limited to a postenlightenment state when the body and the intellect have been extinguished. It is, therefore, unrelated to the processes of practical activity.

You have asked whether the state of a bodhisattva who has made his exit into Nirvana resembles that of Christ after his ascension. Buddhism, in taking the Buddhist Law as its basis, differs from Christianity, which depends on a personality or, at any rate, a divine being. Insofar as Christianity takes the divinity incarnate in Christ as its foundation, it must seek its ultimate reality in a heaven that is removed from human life, society, and the world. In contrast, the Buddhist Law includes and is at the base of all phenomena in humanity, society, and the world. Consequently, the Buddha state is not removed from this world but resides always in individual human lives and in the universal life.

TOYNBEE: I think I understand what *Butsu* means for a Southern Buddhist. If I am right, early Buddhism, before it had adopted Greek iconography, represented the Buddha in Nirvana by a blank, and not by an anthropomorphic image inspired by the Greek image of the god Apollo. The blank symbolizes the extinguishedness of Nirvana.

IKEDA: Southern Buddhism strives to merge the individual self with the universal self by rejecting and destroying the individual self. This is certainly the highest thing possible of attainment within the limitations of the individual self. But such an achievement is of no value to others and therefore runs counter to the wish of the Buddha to bring salvation to humanity.

In contrast to this, Northern Buddhism teaches not that the individual self must be destroyed but that it must be expanded through altruistic acts. By becoming one with the Law, which is the basic nature of the universal self, the individual self can overcome desires, anger, and the instinct for self-preservation. In brief, Northern Buddhist teaching is that the individual self must be affirmed and expanded toward the universal self.

TOYNBEE: And what is the Northern Buddhist doctrine about *Butsu*? I infer, from what you say, that, for Northern Buddhists, *Butsu* means the completion of the expansion of the individual self into the universal self. But has not this goal been reached already at the bodhisattva stage? And is the subsequent *Butsu* stage a still higher form of satisfaction?

IKEDA: Bodhisattva is a stage in progress to the Buddha state. Within the Northern Buddhist teachings, the Lotus Sutra explains the aim of the Buddha

281

as the desire to bring all people to the same kind of enlightenment that he experienced. It further indicates the practical actions of the bodhisattvas as the process by means of which that enlightenment is attained. The Chinese Priest Chih-i (538–97), who founded T'ien-t'ai Buddhism, analyzed the bodhisattva world into fifty-two stages, the fifty-second of which is the enlightenment of the Buddha. If the bodhisattva were a being who had already merged the individual self with the universal self—in other words, one who had already become a Buddha—no process for the establishing of the universal self would remain to human beings, who are in the bondage of the individual self. In short, all ways would be closed to humanity.

As to why it is possible to call the Buddha state complete and eternal satisfaction, I might offer the following explanation. The Law exists as a reality behind the universe; this Law includes the universe—as you can see, this is related to your idea of the spiritual reality behind the universe. A personality who has been enlightened to that Law and who has become the universal self through fusion with the Law is a Buddha. No fixed or partial characteristics are used to define the life of the Buddha state. The only way to express it in words is to say that it is all inclusive on a horizontal (metaphorically speaking) plane and is therefore complete. On the temporal, or vertical (again metaphorically), plane it is eternal. Consequently, it can only be described as the state of complete and permanent satisfaction. The Buddha state is an inner state of perception of the true nature of life. Its surface manifestations occur in the other nine states of life: Bodhisattva, *Ten*, *Nin*, and so on. Southern Buddhist teachings end with the extinguishing of the individual self. Northern Buddhist doctrine teaches the expansion and employment of the individual self by means of the establishment of the universal self.

Northern Buddhist thought teaches that all life by nature includes the Ten States of Life. Consequently, all life, including human life of course, has concealed within it the supremely worthy universal life force. This means that all life deserves respect. All human beings, by practicing the Buddhist Law, can manifest the life of the Buddha state. This idea is the basis of the concept of the kind of human revolution that, I insist, is needed by all mankind. Furthermore, I think it is similar in essence to what you mean by self-mastery.

Life as Reality, Flow, and Entity

IKEDA: All kinds of life, while retaining individual characteristics, change from moment to moment in relation to the outer world. I have already introduced the theory according to which Buddhism divides all life into ten states depending on subjective emotional conditions. In addition to this approach to an analysis of life, Buddhism explains relations to the outer world, physical changes (or characteristics), and motion of each instant in life. The explanations are made from many vantage points, and treat all life motion in terms of the law called *Jū-nyoze* or Ten Life Factors.

In the second chapter of the Lotus Sutra, *Jū-nyoze* is described as consisting of these elements: *Nyoze-sō* (aspect), *Nyoze-shō* (nature), *Nyoze-tai* (entity), *Nyoze-riki* (power), *Nyoze-sa* (influence), *Nyoze-in* (cause), *Nyoze-en* (relation), *Nyoze-ka* (effect), *Nyoze-hō* (requital), and *Nyoze-honmatsu-kukyōtō* (consistency from beginning to end of all phenomena).

In this passage, *Nyoze-sō* (*nyoze* means true or real, and *sō* means an aspect) implies the outward aspect or appearance of life. (It corresponds to *Ketai* of *Santai*.) *Nyoze-shō* means nature originally inherent in life and, in human beings, refers to nature, mind, wisdom, and spirit. (It corresponds to *Kūtai*.) *Nyoze-tai* indicates the integral entity of life embracing both *Nyoze-sō* (the physical body) and *Nyoze-shō* (the mind or spirit). (It corresponds to *Chūtai*.) These three compose the reality of life. Buddhism teaches that life must be observed from three viewpoints: aspect, nature, and entity. *Nyoze-sō*, *Nyoze-shō*, and *Nyoze-tai* are the true nature of life force.

TOYNBEE: That is to say, the first three of the *Jū-nyoze* correspond to the *Kūtai*, *Ketai*, and *Chūtai* of the *Santai* discussed earlier, and they explain the true form of life force as a unity.

IKEDA: Yes, that is correct. These three interrelated factors compose a single life entity, the actions of which are controlled by a law pertaining to the seven other factors of *Jū-nyoze*.

Nyoze-riki means to develop and manifest the power inherent in life—the power to activate life itself. This power derives from the depths of life and influences the outer world. The influence is called *Nyoze-sa*. Buddhism recognizes a cause-and-effect law working in the depths of life that differs from similar laws of physics and chemistry in that it cannot be understood in terms of time and space. It exists in the ultimate reality of life and falls into the category of *Kū*. It transcends determinism bound by time and space. In the broad sense, the Buddhist causal law covers the cause and effect underlying your concept of ethical karma-account.

TOYNBEE: I think the law of life is karma. Actions produce consequences, and these consequences are inescapable. They are not, however, unalterable; they can be altered, for better or for worse, by further action. Every living being runs up a karma-account; and, if I understand the doctrine of the Lotus

283

school of Northern Buddhism rightly, a karma-account is never closed because the series of rebirths is endless.

I note that, in this realm, the relationships are conceived of as not being causal in the sense in which the concept of cause and effect is applicable to physical relationships.

IKEDA: In figurative terms, the law of cause and effect deep within life itself emerges into the world of phenomena by operating through physical and spiritual aspects of life activity. In terms of concepts of time and space, this manifestation of the law of cause and effect may be compared with what physics calls the statistical law of causation. Long-term observations make it possible to grasp life phenomena in terms of statistical laws of cause and effect that are inevitably accompanied by uncertainties. The degree of latitude of uncertainty is incomparably greater when one is dealing with human life than when one is concerned with inanimate beings or other forms of life. Nevertheless, life, maintaining its own directions of development, gradually emerges in clear phenomenal forms.

I must say here, however, that though I have used scientific terms in a figurative sense, the Buddhist law of cause and effect governing the very depths of life is in no way either spatial or temporal.

The cause in Buddhist terms, then, is called the *Nyoze-in*; it is evoked by a stimulus from the outside world called the *Nyoze-en*. Though the cause (*Nyoze-in*) may be latent in life itself, it requires the relation or stimulus (*Nyoze-en*) to activate it. Once the cause has been activated by the stimulus, however, it gives birth to the effect (*Nyoze-ka*); the effect is inherent in life itself. *Nyoze-hō* is the requital of causality manifested on the level of actual life activities. The only possible way to glimpse the Buddhist law of causation in terms of space-time-bound phenomena is to examine these requitals in detail. The last aspect of *Jū-nyoze*, the rather long term *Nyoze-honmatsu-kukyōtō*, signifies the integrity and harmony of life and is a summation of the other nine factors plus itself.

In summary, then, the reality of life is expressed by the first three elements of *Jū-nyoze*: aspect, nature, and entity. The active flow of life is represented by power, influence, cause, relation, effect, and requital. All these factors are integrated and fused into one unified life entity by the principle called *Honmatsu-kukyōtō*.

TOYNBEE: The Buddhist analysis of the dynamics of life, as you explain them, is more detailed and subtle than any modern Western analysis that I know of.

If I have interpreted you right, the Buddhist concept of *Jū-nyoze* is not unlike my own personal notion of challenge and response, in contrast to determined and unvarying cause and effect, as being the nature of relations in the field of reality in which the parties to a relationship are live beings and not inanimate objects.

IKEDA: If your challenge and response is a phenomenon occurring in the larger life itself, it may be a different way of expressing what is called the law of cause and effect in Buddhist terminology.

We can say that if there is a challenge, there must be a response. People may be aware that reprisal will follow an act contrary to national laws or regulations because they dimly perceive the existence of the larger law of life force. If a person is able to understand the nature of the law of life force, he can judge with clarity how he ought to live and act.

ROLES RELIGION PLAYS

11

Religion as the Source of Vitality

IKEDA: World history teaches that civilizations, like living organisms, go through recurrent cycles of genesis, growth, and decline. Egypt developed several civilizations and cultures during her ancient and modern history: the age of the pharaohs, when the Pyramids were built; the age of Roman rule, when the ancient Monophysite Christian church came into being; the Islamic period; and the modern republic. At various points in time, a civilization characteristic of a people achieves various stages of growth, but in the over-all current of time, each manifests the process of genesis, growth, and decline.

In this connection, two questions come to mind. First, what is the vitality that gives rise to a civilization? Second, what is the source of this vitality in the peoples who produce these civilizations? The answer to the first question is society, group living, and leisure. These three things are closely linked with increase in productivity, which, by creating a surplus of goods, fosters the birth and development of artists, architects, poets, theologians, and administrators. Organized groups (communities) are the supply source of the great concentrations of human power required for the accomplishment of the kinds of undertakings that result in historical monuments. Free time enables people to create.

TOYNBEE: The enabling condition of the establishment of a civilization has been the production of a surplus of food and other material commodities beyond the bare material necessities of life. The production of this surplus made possible the creation of noneconomic works—the tumuli in the

286

hinterland of Sakai in Japan, the Egyptian and Mexican pyramids, the Mayan and Khmer temples. The surplus also made possible the waging of wars and the maintenance of a minority that has been exempt from having to spend its time on producing the necessities of life and has therefore spent it partly on frivolity and luxury, but also partly on religious liturgy, theology, administration, architecture, visual art, literature, philosophy, and science.

The genesis, the growth, and the maintenance of each of the civilizations have been due to the creative work of a minority of the privileged minority. The cooperation of the masses has enabled this creative work to bear fruit. A common religious faith has been the spiritual bond that has made this cooperation possible, in spite of the unjust inequality of the distribution of the product of the joint efforts of all classes in a community and in spite of the misuse of the greater part of the surplus product for waging wars and for providing luxuries for a privileged minority that, for the most part, has not given the society any adequate service in return.

IKEDA: I do not think that it is surplus alone that gives birth to civilizations. Part of production activity is clearly based on the goal of creating an abundance of better daily-life commodities, but this does not explain the aim that stimulates man to try to put his surplus time and energy to meaningful use.

I believe that religion forms the basis of that aim. Though they may be the elements from which civilizations are built, surpluses of production power, social organizations, and human greed do not constitute the soul that must be breathed into a civilization to bring it to life. I am convinced that, to do this, the people creating the civilization must be aware of a purpose for their actions. The labors of the builders of the civilization and the plans of the designers must start at this awareness. The things that give people the ability to grasp the meaning of their aim and of the direction in which they must travel are philosophy and religion.

The Pyramids tell more than the mere fact that the Egypt of the time possessed human energy surpluses, social and economic organizations, and engineering technology sufficient to the feat of erecting them. They reveal the intensity of the Egyptian view of life and death that necessitated the raising of vast funeral monuments. In other words, it was this religious idea that supported the desire of the Egyptians to expend tremendous labor energy in these projects. Religious fervor has inspired the building of other of the world's monumental pieces of architecture, including the temples of the Mayas, the Aztecs, and the Incas.

TOYNBEE: I believe that a civilization's style is the expression of its religion.

I quite agree that religion has been the source of the vitality that has brought civilizations into being and has then kept them in being—for more than three thousand years in the cases of Pharaonic Egypt, and of China from the rise of the Shang to the fall of the Ch'ing in 1912.

The two earliest civilizations were established on the potentially rich soils of Egypt and southeastern Iraq. But these soils had to be made productive by drainage and irrigation on a grand scale. The transformation of a forbidding natural environment into a favorable artificial environment must have been achieved by the organized labor of masses of people working for distant returns. This implies the emergence of leadership and of a widespread willingness to follow the leaders' directives. The social vitality and harmony that made this cooperation possible must have sprung from a religious faith that was shared with the leaders by the led. This faith must have been the spiritual force that made possible the accomplishment of the basic economic public works that produced an economic surplus.

The two congenital social maladies of civilizations have been war and social injustice. Religion has been the spiritual force that has held each civilized society together for a time in spite of the drain on its vitality that has been caused by these two deadly social diseases.

By religion I mean an attitude to life that enables people to cope with the difficulty of being human by giving spiritually satisfying answers to the fundamental questions about the mystery of the universe and of man's role in it and by giving practical precepts for living in the universe. Each time a people has lost faith in its religion, its civilization has succumbed to domestic social disintegration and to foreign military attack. The civilization that has fallen as a result of the loss of faith has then been replaced by a new civilization inspired by a different religion.

Examples of this historical phenomenon are the downfall of the Confucian Chinese civilization since the Opium War and the rise of a new Chinese civilization in which Confucianism has been replaced by communism; the downfalls of the Pharaonic Egyptian civilization and the Greco-Roman civilization and their replacement by new civilizations inspired by Christianity and by Islam. The abandonment of the Mayan ceremonial centers in southern Guatemala is an unexplained enigma. We have no documentary evidence about it. The most convincing guess, however, is that the peasants eventually withdrew their economic support from the priests because they had lost faith in the priests' ability to make life tolerable.

IKEDA: There is still another point to discuss in connection with the vitality that enables a people to create a civilization. Some peoples have produced civilizations that soon declined and vanished; others absorbed and assimilated cultural elements from other civilizations to keep pace with the times and to revitalize their own cultures. Good examples of the former category are the Incas, Aztecs, and Mayans of America; the Khmers, whose culture reached its pinnacle at Angkor Wat; and the Indonesians who created the architectural wonder of Borobudur. The Egyptians and the Japanese, among others, belong to the second category. Although Europeans have not had this experience in the past, it may be one of the tests that they must undergo during the present period of their history.

TOYNBEE: I agree that there is high value and merit in the successful assimilation of elements from alien civilizations. Japan has met this challenge successfully twice in her history. In the sixth and seventh centuries of the Christian era, she assimilated the Chinese version of Indian Buddhism and, with it, the Chinese civilization itself. During the last hundred years, Japan has assimilated the modern Western civilization. The peoples of continental Southeast Asia and of Indonesia assimilated Hinduism and Buddhism. The Vietnamese assimilated the Chinese civilization, and the Indonesians, after they had assimilated Hinduism and Buddhism, the Islamic civilization. The pre-Columbian civilizations in the Americas and the civilizations of Africa south of the Sahara before the Arab and European impacts on this region, have, it is true, vanished. After having been insulated by geographical barriers, they were suddenly assaulted by aggressors equipped with irresistibly superior weapons. But they are exceptional cases.

IKEDA: The peoples of Indonesia, once they adopted Hinduism and Buddhism, were able to create a great civilization symbolized by the magnificent ruins at Borobudur. Later, the same peoples adopted Islam, but this did not enable them to produce anything comparable to their earlier achievements. I do not know what happened to the Khmers, though perhaps they exist today among the peoples of Indochina. Whatever they had that enabled them to build great temples like those at Angkor Wat, however, has long been lost.

In the latter half of the twentieth century the ancient traditions of these peoples have begun to revive, thanks to a growing awareness of national and racial sovereignty, intensified confrontations among advanced nations, and the end of colonialism. But the current revival of a few ancient customs in those long suppressed cultures does not signify a true cultural reawakening. In many instances such revivals are no more than manifestations of the protection policies of advanced nations, products of a growing interest in cultural anthropology, or merely shows for the sake of tourists. True creative prosperity, surging upward from the heart of a people, would be powerful enough to overthrow oppressors and to break free from trying circumstances.

TOYNBEE: As you said earlier, the Western peoples, who, during the last five hundred years, have taken the offensive against the rest of mankind, are now being thrown on the defensive and are going to have to meet the challenge that Japan has met twice. The Greeks and Romans had the same experience. Their military and political offensive against their eastern neighbors eventually provoked a religious counteroffensive. In the Mediterranean basin they were eventually converted to Christianity. The Greek conquerors of what are now Soviet Central Asia and Western Pakistan were converted to Buddhism. This episode of Greco-Roman history, in which we know how the story ended, gives us an inkling of one of the possibilities that may now be in store for the modern West.

IKEDA: Perhaps Western culture must face decline. If so, we will need to know more about the way new civilizations grow and prosper. We have agreed that religion inspires power enabling peoples to create civilizations. What is the cause of the weakness that prevents other peoples from making cultural revivals once their civilizations have fallen on evil days?

TOYNBEE: As I have already indicated, I think the success or failure of a culture is deeply related to the religion of the people. That is, a civilization is decided by the quality of the religion on which it is based.

Three Western Religions

IKEDA: If religion is interpreted in the conventional sense, modern Western civilization seems to have arisen as an outcome of the very act of rejecting religion. But in another light, the modern world has its own kinds of religions founded on aspirations for material wealth and faith in scientific progress.

TOYNBEE: I agree emphatically with the view that the modern West has not lost, but has changed, its religion. I believe that human beings cannot live without a religion or philosophy. There is no clear-cut distinction between these two forms of ideology.

IKEDA: Religion may be viewed in its traditional sense or in the sense of an

290

ideology guiding the actions of human life. In the traditional sense, religion today is practiced largely in the form of ritual and ceremonial. In the second sense, aspiration toward wealth and belief in the progress of science perform the religious function. This point is essential both to an understanding of the meaning of scientific-technological civilization, as it has developed to the present, and to attempts to forecast the ways in which the civilization will alter in the future. In other words, understanding the nature of modern religion will help us estimate how our civilization will alter when—as Pharaonic Egypt changed to Christianity and then to Islam and as Europe altered at the time of the Reformation—it too must inevitably give way.

TOYNBEE: Since Western civilization, in its modern form, has been propagated—partly by force and partly by choice—all over the world, it is important to identify and appraise the modern West's religion or religions. If it is true, as I believe it is, that a civilization's religion is the source of its vitality and that the loss of faith in this religion leads to the civilization's downfall and replacement, the Western peoples' modern religious history is the key to an understanding of the present condition and the future prospects of mankind as a whole, now that the whole world has become Westernized in some degree.

Western civilization supplanted the former Greco-Roman civilization when the religions and philosophies of the Greco-Roman world were superseded by Christianity. Christianity continued to be the major religion—indeed the exclusive religion—of the West until partway through the seventeenth century of the Christian era. Before the close of the seventeenth century, Christianity had begun to lose its long-maintained hold on the Western intelligentsia. In the course of the next three centuries, the recession of Christianity extended more and more widely through all classes of Western society. At the same time, the contemporaneous spread of modern Western institutions, ideas, and ideals—or loss of ideals—among the non-Western majority of mankind has loosened the hold on non-Western peoples of their own ancestral religions and philosophies—the Eastern Orthodox form of Christianity in Russia, Islam in Turkey, Confucianism in China.

According to my interpretation of Western history, the Western religious revolution in the seventeenth century has been by far the greatest and most significant break in the continuity of Western history since the conversion of the Roman Empire to Christianity in the fourth century. The seventeenth-century break is, as I see it, a far more important historical event than the previous split of the Western Christian Church into a Catholic and a Protestant camp and the previous rather superficial renaissance in the West of the pre-Christian Greco-Roman civilization.

291

IKEDA: Certainly the seventeenth century saw many revolutionary changes that shook the foundations of the Christian Church in relation to many fields of learning. In the first half of the century, with the conclusion of the Thirty Years' War, the last and biggest of a series of tragic religious conflicts, the idea was advanced that political power ought not to be used in controversies involving matters of faith. The theories of Galileo and Copernicus were brought before the Inquisition at about that time. Descartes created the foundations for modern rationalism. Equally important, Newton's active life falls in the period of the second half of the seventeenth and the first half of the eighteenth century.

Viewed in the light of the ideological developments occurring at the time, the seventeenth century has much greater significance than the Renaissance and the Reformation, which, because they took place within the limits of the Church, could not truly shake the grounds on which the Christian faith rested. Developments in the seventeenth century, on the other hand, stimulated revolutionary crises in the relations between politics and the Christian faith and between science and other fields of learning and Christian theology.

TOYNBEE: The religious change in the course of the seventeenth century has been mistakenly interpreted as having been merely a negative event, namely the recession of Christianity. It has not been recognized that human nature abhors a religious vacuum and that, consequently, when a society's ancestral religion recedes, it is bound to be replaced sooner or later by one or more other religions.

As I see it, the vacuum created in the West by the seventeenth-century recession of Christianity has been filled by the rise of three other religions: the belief in the inevitability of progress through the systematic application of science to technology, nationalism, and communism.

For Western minds, the coexistence of more than one religion in one society is difficult to comprehend because the West's ancestral religion, Christianity, has been the most intolerant of the three exclusive-minded Judaic religions. The Western peoples' conversion to the ideal and the practice of religious toleration, which was the negative aspect of their seventeenth-century reaction against the Catholic-Protestant wars of religion, dealt a mortal blow to Western Christianity, Catholic and Protestant alike. On the other hand, in most non-Christian countries the coexistence of more than one religion has been the normal state of affairs. Even Islam, which, like Christianity, has inherited Judaic monotheism's spirit of exclusiveness, is committed, in the Koran itself, to tolerating the two other Judaic religions, Judaism and Christianity, on condition that their adherents submit to the Muslims' political

292

dominance. In the pre-Christian Greco-Roman world, among the Hindus, and in Eastern Asia, the coexistence of several religions and philosophies has been taken as a matter of course. In precommunist China, the intrusive religion-philosophy of Buddhism coexisted amicably with the indigenous religion-philosophy of Taoism and even, except very occasionally, with the officially established philosophy of Confucianism. In Japan, Buddhism has coexisted not only amicably but cooperatively with Shinto, and, under the Tokugawa regime, neo-Confucianism enjoyed, if I am right, a status almost comparable to that of Buddhism and Shinto.

IKEDA: Indisputably many devout Buddhists and devout Shintoists have traditionally been most tolerant of the religious faiths of other peoples. In many cases, the Japanese have been able to reconcile comfortably the teachings of Buddhism, Shinto, and Confucianism.

Moreover, traditional Japanese religions have long maintained a remarkable relationship of coexistence with two of the three things that you describe as filling the blank space left by the recession of Christianity—nationalism and faith in scientific progress. The most obvious example of my meaning is the psychological support Shinto gave to the idea of Japanese imperialism from the late nineteenth century until the end of World War II. Though the official relations ended and the spiritual symbolism of Shinto lost most of its force after the Japanese defeat, its influence has not entirely vanished.

Shinto's relationship with modern technology is somewhat odd. Factories with the very latest technological equipment and high-rise buildings of the most up-to-date design not infrequently include small Shinto shrines. Before ground-breaking on the sites of new steel and concrete buildings, almost invariably an ancient Shinto ceremony to purify the land is held. What I am attempting to show is that, in Japan, faith in scientific progress, nationalism, and even communism, though part of the modern world in which the Japanese live and work, has not filled a vacuum caused by the recession of traditional religions. In this sense, our experience differs from that of the Europeans who resort to these things as a new spiritual support offering strength in time of internal spiritual conflict.

TOYNBEE: I agree that the situation does seem to be different. But for the sake of a fuller comparison, let me offer some details about the way faith in scientific progress, nationalism, and communism came to occupy an important place in the thinking and believing of European peoples. The conscious establishment of the modern Western faith in scientific progress may be equated with the foundation of the Royal Society in Britain in 1661.

The Royal Society was founded by members of the English intelligentsia who had been shocked by the seventeenth-century English civil war and had been disillusioned by its political sequel. They recognized that, in England, civil strife had been exacerbated by theological polemics. They rightly held that these polemics were discreditable to Christianity, harmful to secular society, and intellectually inconclusive, since the questions at issue could not be answered in rationally convincing terms. The Royal Society was designed to mitigate these evils by directing intellectual interest from theology to science and by diverting practical action from religious and political strife to the advancement of technology. The founders perceived that there was a possibility of achieving unprecedented advances in technology by applying science to technology systematically. They assumed that an advance in technology would necessarily be an advance in welfare as well. They did not perceive that power of all kinds, including power generated by scientifically advanced technology, is ethically neutral and that it can be used for evil as well as for good.

The religion based on their ideals was dealt a mortal blow in 1945, when the scientific discovery of the structure of the atom and the technological application of this discovery in the release of atomic energy through fission was immediately misused for the construction of the bombs that were dropped on Hiroshima and Nagasaki.

IKEDA: Scientists did not realize the dual nature of scientific progress until after two world wars, in which economic power and scientific skills, concentrated and put to maximum application, had brought misery and tragedy to mankind.

TOYNBEE: Nationalism, the second replacement of traditional Western religion, is the worship of the collective power of a local human community. Unlike the faith in progress through science, nationalism is not a new religion: it is a revival of an old one. This was the religion of the city-states of the pre-Christian Greco-Roman world. It was resuscitated in the West at the Renaissance, and this resuscitation of a Greco-Roman political religion has been far more effective than the resuscitation of the Greco-Roman style of literature, visual art, and architecture. Modern Western nationalism, inspired by Greco-Roman political ideals and institutions, has inherited the dynamism and fanaticism of Christianity. Translated into practice in the American and French revolutions, it proved to be highly infectious. Today, fanatical nationalism is perhaps 90 percent of the religion of perhaps 90 percent of mankind.

Communism, the third of the religions that have filled the vacuum caused by seventeenth-century thought, is a revolt against social injustice, which is as old as civilization itself. In theory, Christianity and all other precommunist religions and philosophies have condemned social injustice, but, on this point, their theory has not yet been put into practice. While communism has justly criticized all its predecessors, in concentrating its attention and efforts on the eradication of social injustice, it has fallen into the intolerance practiced by Christianity and into the exclusiveness that is characteristic of all the Judaic religions.

Communism is, in fact, a Christian heresy that, like previous heresies, has insisted on a particular Christian precept that the Christian establishment has neglected. The mythology of communism is Jewish and Christian mythology translated into a nontheistic vocabulary. The unique and omnipotent god Yahweh has been translated into historical necessity; the Chosen People has been translated into the Proletariat, which is predestined by historical necessity to triumph; the Millennium has been translated into the eventual fading away of the state. Communism has also inherited from Christianity the belief in a mission to convert all mankind. Christianity and communism are not, of course, the only missionary religions; Islam, Buddhism, and faith in progress through science are also religions of the missionary species.

IKEDA: I sense one common point distinguishing the new religions—faith in scientific progress, nationalism, and communism—from such older ones as Christianity, Buddhism, and Islam. Whereas the older religions strove to control and suppress human greed, the newer ones seem to have originated—or at least to be employed—for the sake of the liberation and fulfillment of that greed. I consider this to be the basic nature of the new religions, and in that nature I see the fundamental problem facing all three of them.

TOYNBEE: I think you are correct. Consequently, I feel the need for a new kind of religion. Mankind has been united, socially, for the first time in history, by the worldwide spread of modern (in origin, modern Western) civilization. The question of mankind's future religion arises because all the current religions have proved unsatisfactory.

The future religion need not necessarily be an entirely new religion. It might be a new version of one of the old religions, but if one of the old religions were to be revived in a form that answered to mankind's new needs, it seems probable that it would be transformed so radically that it would be almost unrecognizable. This is likely because the conditions of human life have changed radically in our time.

A future religion that is to bring into being, and to keep in being, a new civilization will have to be one that will enable mankind to contend with, and to overcome, the evils that are serious present threats to human survival. The most formidable of these evils are the oldest: greed, which is as old as life itself is, and war and social injustice, which are as old as civilization. A new evil that is hardly less formidable is the artificial environment that mankind has created through the application of science to technology in the service of greed.

IKEDA: My thinking on this topic is in complete agreement with yours. I too consider the major evils besetting our civilization to be greed, which is inherent in life itself; war and injustice, which are—as you say—as old as civilization; and the artificial destruction of the natural environment. Greed is a matter between the individual human being and himself, war and injustice are ills between human beings on the social plane, and environmental destruction involves relationships between man and nature.

According to Buddhist philosophy, these three factors are categorized as what are called Three Worlds: relations within the individual human being, relations among human beings (social relations), and relations with nature. All three sets of relations are indispensable to all life. Problems in any one are intertwined with the other two. To effect any kind of improvement in the world situation, each individual must improve—indeed revolutionize— himself from within. That is, we must take steps to set the first set of relations in order. Then and only then is it possible to do something about the upsets in our social organization and in the natural environment.

Returning to Pantheism

IKEDA: Judaism, Christianity, and Islam are monotheistic religions permitting no compromise with other divinities. When a man is converted to Christianity, he must abandon all past faiths and belong wholly to his new and only god. Religious exclusiveness seems to me to have been an important characteristic of the history of the development of Western civilization.

TOYNBEE: Buddhism resembles Christianity and Islam in being a missionary religion, but it does not resemble them in its effect on the regions in which it has been propagated. Buddhism has not supplanted the pre-Buddhist religions and philosophies of India and Eastern Asia. It has coexisted with them; consequently, its introduction has not led to the break in cultural continuity that the introduction of Christianity and Islam has caused in the regions to the west of India and also in the Indian subcontinent where Islam has succeeded in gaining a foothold. In Indonesia, the Hindu-Buddhist tradition has been so strong that Islam has been forced to come to terms with it.

For this reason, the break in cultural continuity has been extreme in India and Eastern Asia when—and only when—Judaic religion, carried by modern Western aggressors, hit these regions in the post-Christian forms of scientific faith, communism, and nationalism, carrying a charge of Christian fanaticism. Nationalism, which has also captured India and Eastern Asia, is a Western version of the pre-Christian Greco-Roman worship of the collective power of a local community. But nationalism, as well as communism and the scientific faith, has been keyed up by receiving a charge of Christian fanaticism as a result of its having been resuscitated in an ex-Christian environment.

IKEDA: In other words, though discontinuity was introduced by occidental elements, basic oriental continuity has remained unbroken; no fundamental conversion has been effected. In contrast, in the West, a basic change occurred in the foundation of the civilization itself, though the civilizational channels remained the same. The revolution in the West was a religious one.

TOYNBEE: In the West, the cultural revolution came in two separate stages at two different dates, and it was only in the first of these two stages (the conversion of the West to Christianity) that the break was caused by the impact of an alien religion. The second break, in which Christianity has been superseded by the three post-Christian Western religions, was not caused by the impact of anything from outside. The substitution of the three post-Christian religions for Christianity has been a purely domestic revolution, though this revolution, like the previous one, has been drastic.

In contrast to the civilizations at the western end of the Old World since the conversion of this region to Christianity and Islam, the cultures of India and Eastern Asia had been stable until the irruption of the western post-Christian religions. I agree that the difference between the cultures of India and Eastern Asia on the one hand and modern Western culture on the other hand is due to a difference in the character of their respective religions.

IKEDA: The difference between monotheism and pantheism is very telling in human civilization. Under conditions imposed by monotheistic faith, a great need to relate everything to an absolute being defines society and civilization and promotes the development of an all-pervasive uniformity. Because this makes the acceptance of alien elements difficult, when confronted with something foreign and new, a monotheistic society must undergo a win-or-lose, all-or-nothing transition. For this reason, changes in the historical current of the West have often been basic and far-reaching. In pantheistic societies, on the other hand, the value of alien ideas and things is recognized. The society is tolerant toward them; consequently, they can be introduced without the necessity of fundamental social alterations. No matter what new elements enter, the society remains basically unchanged.

TOYNBEE: The Judaic religions have concentrated the element of divinity in the universe into a unique, omnipotent, creator god outside the universe, and this restriction of divinity has deprived nature—including human nature—of its sanctity. By contrast, in India and Eastern Asia, before the impact of the modern West, the whole universe and everything in it, including nonhuman nature and man himself, was divine and, therefore, possessed, in human eyes, a sanctity and a dignity that have restrained man's impulse to indulge his greed by doing violence to nonhuman nature.

The Indian and East Asian attitude is pantheism, in contrast to Judaic monotheism. In the pantheistic view, divinity is immanent in the universe and is transfused throughout the universe. In the monotheistic view, divinity is withdrawn from the universe and is made external to it; that is to say, divinity is made transcendent.

At the western end of the Old World and in the Americas, the original local cultures—the Middle American, Peruvian, Sumerian, Greco-Roman, and Egyptian, and also the Canaanite culture that was the Israelites' culture before they became monotheists—were of the same species as the cultures of India and Eastern Asia before the modern Western impact. In all pre-Judaic cultures, everywhere, religion has been pantheistic, not monotheistic. The present adherents of the Judaic monotheistic religions and of the post-Christian substitutes for the Judaic religion of Christianity are, all of them, ex-pantheists. This historical fact suggests that there might be some hope of their reverting to the pantheistic attitude now that they have become aware of the badness of the consequences of the monotheistic lack of respect for nature.

IKEDA: Two things have affected modern man's religious views deeply: the ability to change natural conditions to the extent that they no longer limit production activities and the development of modern transportation to overcome distance. In the past, when man was forced to live and work under the limitations of natural conditions, he viewed anything surpassing his own strength as mystic. This view in turn gave rise to pantheism, the belief that divinity infuses the natural world. Now that man finds it within the power of the science and technology he has evolved to control and use the natural world, he is not likely to return to a pantheistic interpretation of the universe.

Man's pride over his abilities to deal with nature has led him to pollute and destroy the environment to the point that he is endangering his own existence. In spite of the fact that he is master of individual aspects of the world, man is utterly insignificant in the face of the life force that binds together all the constituent parts of total nature.

I think that a clear understanding of the aspects in which man is superior to and those in which he is infinitely inferior to the nonhuman natural world can be of great use in working out a truly meaningful religious faith for the future.

TOYNBEE: Like some of man's more recent endeavors, agriculture and animal husbandry are human interferences with nonhuman nature, but their action has been cooperative rather than coercive. Man's ability to coerce was limited so long as the physical power at his disposal was almost exclusively muscle power. But that ability became practically unlimited when, in the Industrial Revolution, he began to harness the immensely greater physical power of inanimate natural forces on the grand scale. This was the stage at which the license to exploit nonhuman nature, which has been given to man by God according to the doctrine of Judaic monotheism, began to have an important practical effect.

When Western man had won the upper hand over nature through the systematic application of science to technology, his belief that he was licensed to exploit nature gave him the green light to indulge his greed to the utmost of his now vast and ever-increasing technological capacity. His greed was not inhibited by the pantheists' belief that nonhuman nature is sacred and that it, like man himself, has a dignity that ought to be respected.

It is noteworthy that, in the seventeenth century, when the modern Westerners substituted the post-Christian faith in science for their ancestral Christianity, they discarded theism but retained the belief, derived from monotheism, in their right to exploit nonhuman nature. Under the previous Christian dispensation, they had believed themselves to be God's tenants divinely licensed to exploit nature on condition that they worshiped God and acknowledged his proprietary rights—his eminent domain, in legal language. In the seventeenth century the English cut off God's, as well as King Charles I's, head; they expropriated the universe and claimed to be no longer tenants of it, but freeholders—absolute owners. The religion of science, like nationalism, has now spread all round the globe. Communists and noncommunists alike are both nationalists and believers in the religion of scientific progress. It is these post-Christian religions of modern Western origin that have brought mankind into its present plight.

IKEDA: Perhaps for the sake of progress in the single limited field of scientific technology, the Western monotheistic attitude is valuable for the future material development of human civilization. On the other hand, from the standpoint of protecting the independence of all groups of people and of putting a stop to pollution and destruction of the natural environment, the Eastern approach is more important. But the two viewpoints ought to be combined in such a way as to compensate for the failings in each. I am convinced that only a new religion will be able to take the lead in a civilization on a high plane that combines both science and philosophy. But the religion that we need must inspire mankind's scientific and philosophical spirits and must be able to meet the needs of a new age. It must be a religion that can go beyond the differences between East and West and, binding all mankind into a unified body, save the Occident from its present crisis and the Orient from its current hardships. Discovering this kind of religion is the greatest task before mankind today.

TOYNBEE: We now need urgently to restabilize the relation between man and nonhuman nature that has been upset by the Industrial Revolution. The way for the technological and economic revolution was opened by a previous religious revolution at the western end of the Old World. This religious revolution was the substitution of monotheism for pantheism. I believe that mankind needs to revert to pantheism. We need to recover our original respect and consideration for the dignity of nonhuman nature. We need what we might call a right religion to help us do this.

A right religion is one that teaches respect for the dignity and sanctity of all nature. The wrong religion is one that licenses the indulgence of human greed at the expense of nonhuman nature. I conclude that the religion we need to embrace now is pantheism, as exemplified in Shinto, and that the religion we now need to discard is Judaic monotheism and the post-Christian nontheistic faith in scientific progress, which has inherited from Christianity the belief that mankind is morally entitled to exploit the rest of the universe for the indulgence of human greed.

IKEDA: I agree with your definition of right religion as one that teaches respect for the dignity of nonhuman nature and of wrong religion as one that licenses indulgence of human greed at the expense of nonhuman nature. I do not agree, however, with your evaluation of Shinto.

To be sure, originally Shinto posited the dignity of every entity in nature, but it lacks a philosophical body of concepts accounting for that dignity. Shintoism is based on an emotional attachment to the nature with which the ancestors of the Japanese people were familiar; ancestors become an intermediary between man and nature. The extreme manifestation of the Shinto ideology was belief in a so-called divine nation.

Shinto has two faces. Explicit on the obverse is a tendency towards reconciliation with nature; the tendency implicit on the reverse is isolation and exclusiveness. Probably these tendencies are not peculiar to Shinto alone but pertain to other pantheistic religious traditions as well.

TOYNBEE: Shinto, like many other similar religions, obviously has good and bad points. As I have seen it, in Shinto and in the pre-Christian religion of the Greeks and Romans one good point is that these religions consecrated the forces of nature and, by inculcating in man an awe of nature, to some extent restrained his greedy impulse to exploit nature. Shinto, as you say, has a weakness that is shared, as I recognize, by the pre-Christian religion of the Greeks and Romans.

Nature includes human nature. Man himself is inescapably a part of nature, even when he distinguishes himself from nonhuman nature in order to exploit it. At the stage in human development when man, who is by nature a social animal, comes to organize human society in large and efficiently constructed communities, collective human power becomes one of the most potent natural forces—as potent a force as a hurricane, a thunderstorm, an earthquake, or a flood. Therefore, at this stage of human development, the worship of collective human power—families, states, churches, and other networks of relations between human beings—overshadows the worship of other natural forces, and the gods who originally symbolized these forces are conscripted to serve as symbols of human institutions.

This new function was imposed on Shinto in the nineteenth century after the Meiji Restoration in Japan; about twenty-six centuries earlier, it was imposed on the gods of the Greek pantheon. These were made to serve as symbols of the collective power of a city-state when the Greek world came to be divided politically among a number of sovereign, vigorously competitive city-states.

I agree that this is a grave weakness of nature worship. This kind of religion, both in its original nonpolitical form and in its eventual political version, is inferior, spiritually, to higher religions.

IKEDA: In its original teachings and in its historical experience Buddhism has

301

worked out a sensible solution to this problem by surmounting the limits of pantheistic faith. Buddhism is founded upon laws of life—a system of laws universal to all forms of life. With this system of laws as first principle, Buddhism teaches a way of life that emphasizes the harmony and unity of humanity with nonhuman nature. In pantheistic faiths, the gods are regarded as only symbols of natural forces or of peoples. Buddhism, on the other hand, places these divinities within the system of the law of life. Since the life on which Buddhism is based is universal to all human beings and all living things, this system by nature transcends nationalism.

TOYNBEE: I see what you mean about the nature of Buddhism. And this brings me again to the nature of what I have called higher religions. By this term, I mean those religions that bring an individual human being into direct contact with ultimate spiritual reality, instead of giving him only indirect contact with it through the medium of either a nonhuman natural force or an institution embodying collective human power. Higher religions, as defined here, are the kind that modern man needs.

IKEDA: Without doubt a higher religion is urgently needed. It seems to me, however, that we must analyze the nature of such a religion in terms of the basis on which it rests. By this I mean that we must ask whether a higher religion ought to be based on a god or on a law. I believe that man today must rely on a religion based on a law, because such a religion is not only faithful to but also surpasses modern ideas of logicality and reason.

TOYNBEE: You are asking, then, which is more effective and more valuable, a theistic or a legalistic religion. Theism pictures the ultimate spiritual reality anthropomorphically. A god is a humanlike representation of ultimate reality. The Greek, Hindu, and Scandinavian gods were pictured as being humanlike even physically. The Israelite god Yahweh, who has been adopted by the Christians and the Muslims, is imagined as being noncorporeal and invisible, but, in the Israelite scriptures, Yahweh is debited with humanlike emotions—jealousy and anger—and he is supposed to have acted under the influence of these passions. That is to say, he is supposed to have acted in a way that is rightly condemned and censured in human beings.

Human beings crave for a humanlike ultimate reality, even in the form of a capricious tyrant, because, in human society, children need the help and guidance of human parents, while adults need leaders to whom they are bound not by ties of kinship but by reliance on a leader's superior wisdom or stronger willpower. Yet it is irrational to seek to satisfy this craving by depicting the ultimate spiritual reality anthropomorphically. There is no evidence that the ultimate reality is humanlike, and indeed it is most improbable that it does resemble man, for man is only one among the phenomena that are the constituents of nature. I agree that a universal system of laws of life, such as is presented in Buddhism, is likely to be a less misleading representation of ultimate spiritual reality than either a pantheon—Zeus, Athena, and Apollo—or a unique god—Yahweh.

GOOD AND EVIL 12

The Mixture of Good and Evil

IKEDA: The Chinese Confucian scholars Mencius and Hsün Tzu expounded two opposing doctrines about the nature of man: the former maintained the idea of original goodness, and the latter the concept of original evil. These two concepts can be found in the West as well. The Christian concept of original sin is close to the doctrine of innate evil. By comparison, Rousseau's idea of the noble savage represents something similar to the doctrine of innate goodness. Advocates of the theory of original evil insist that an outer force controls man, whereas supporters of the idea of original goodness deny such control and assign all responsibility to human nature. I believe that the nature of man is neither good nor evil, but that it partakes of both.

TOYNBEE: I agree that human nature is neither good nor evil originally and intrinsically. It is potentially both good and evil, and, in every specimen within our experience, human nature is a mixture of both. The proportions vary, but normally both good and evil are present in human nature in some degree. Possibly there has never been an actual human being who has been wholly good or one who has been wholly evil.

IKEDA: Buddhism teaches that all life—including the Buddha, who is possessed of the noblest possible character—includes both good and evil natures. Because human life includes both good and evil, it is necessary to stimulate the unlimited growth of the good sides of human nature and to attempt to control the bad sides. I must hasten to add, however, that social pressures will not control the bad sides. This end can only be achieved from within the individual human being.

TOYNBEE: This mixture in human nature of evil and good seems to me to be a consequence of the relation between a living being and the universe. A living being is partially detached from the rest of the universe but is also partially attached to it. This relation gives a human being a choice of attitudes and behavior.

Man may try to dominate the rest of the universe and to exploit it; that is, to make himself the whole universe's center and raison d'être. Insofar as a human being follows this greedy desire, his conduct will be evil. But alternatively he may try to devote himself to the universe and to serve its interests, not his own. Insofar as he follows this loving desire, his conduct will be good. The experience that each of us has of himself and of other people reveals a constant struggle between these two impulses in every human being. This struggle begins at the dawn of consciousness and is ended only by senility or by death.

IKEDA: Morality, ethics, and religion are the controls that are applied to enable the loving desire to triumph over greed in the complicated inner heart of man. But let us examine this issue by discussing a few more concrete questions.

Since everyone knows that murder is evil, why is it committed? To carry this simple, though widely pondered, question to a more general level, one might ask this: since immoral acts are generally condemned as wrong, why do people persist in perpetrating them? When young, most people acquire a certain degree of knowledge of morality through formal education, parental discipline, and reading; but it is not absolutely certain that this knowledge will become a criterion for action. In fact, it sometimes happens that people's behavior is quite contrary to their own moral training for the following reason. The effect emotion exerts on human actions is as strong as—perhaps stronger than—that of reason. Consequently, emotion can get the upper hand and suppress theoretical knowledge, which is dependent on reason. At the base of emotion is egoism, which prevents one from doing the thing one knows is good and allows one to commit the act one knows is evil. This self-love can extend to embrace family, fellow countrymen, nation, and race.

TOYNBEE: The individual living human being's source of psychic energy, and therefore of his higher spiritual energy, is, I believe, the ultimate spiritual reality. The energy that comes from the source is channeled through the separate life of the individual's ego and can be directed by the ego to either good or evil objectives. In this connection, we mean by *good* and *evil* what is good and evil for this particular living being's fellow men, for nonhuman living creatures, and for the universe as a whole.

The natural tendency of the ego is to try to dominate and exploit the rest of the universe. Alternatively, the ego can devote itself to other people and things, but this altruism, in contrast to egotism, is a tour de force.

IKEDA: Before the moral sense can be translated into action, the ego must be controlled. Social regulations can have only a limited effect, as is clear from the fact that, though all nations impose the maximum punishment on murder, homicide continues to take place.

TOYNBEE: Altruism can be achieved only by self-discipline, self-mastery, self-abnegation, and, if the need arises, self-sacrifice. To do evil, in spite of the contrary dictates of one's own conscience, is easy; it is perhaps impossible to totally extinguish desire except by self-annihilation, and it is very difficult to direct one's desire in a wholly loving and self-devoting way.

IKEDA: Human beings have made great efforts to overcome the ego, and some seem to have achieved their goal. To this end, some have resorted to the abnegation of all desires; others have sought to conquer the ego by means of universal love. I do not deny the achievements of people who have chosen these ways. But, though their methods have had effect, their lack of applicability to mankind in general casts some doubt on their total validity. As is the case with other aspects of morality, the assertion that mankind must seek universal love often stops short at mere knowledge, with the result that ego still holds sway.

TOYNBEE: As you point out, so far only a small minority of human beings has ever even tried either to extinguish desire totally or to dedicate itself to love totally. Consequently, so far, human society (the network of relations between human beings) has been tragically immoral and socially unsuccessful when judged by the standard of conduct set for all human beings by their consciences.

The average level of moral behavior has not improved. There is no evidence that so-called civilized societies are morally superior to so-called primitive societies; that is, those of the Lower Paleolithic Age and those that survive today at a virtually Paleolithic moral level. The progress that we call civilization is an improvement in technology, science, and the impersonal manipulation of power; it is not an improvement in morals—that is, in ethics.

Every improvement in technology brings with it an increase in power, and power can be used either for good or for evil. The most alarming feature of present-day society is that the power conferred by technology has recently increased to an unprecedented degree at an unprecedented rate, while the average level of the moral—or immoral—behavior of the human beings who now wield this vastly increased power has remained stationary, or may actually have declined.

IKEDA: Yes, as mankind has made technological progress, its standards of morality have tended to decline. The cause of this decline has been the foolish delusion that power won as a result of technological progress can take over the role of high moral standards. Breaking out of this delusion must be the starting point for the efforts to solve the dilemma in which man finds himself today, a dilemma which he has created himself.

TOYNBEE: We are aware of this widening gap between power and ethical standards of behavior. The gap has been dramatized in the discovery of the technique for atomic fission and in the immediate misuse of this discovery for dropping now archaic atomic bombs on Hiroshima and Nagasaki and for the subsequent stockpiling of improved—if the word can be used in this connection—atomic weapons on a scale that has put it within the power of human beings to destroy all life on this planet many times over.

It is hard to see how, in the atomic age, mankind can avoid committing mass-suicide if it does not raise the average level of its behavior to the level actually attained by the Buddha and by Saint Francis of Assisi. The founders and the later exponents of the higher religions and philosophies have spelled out, within the last twenty-five centuries, the standards of conduct that, in the atomic age, are required of everybody if mankind is to save itself from self-destruction. But these higher standards of behavior have been actually achieved in practice only by a tiny minority. The majority has recognized the validity of these standards, but it has treated them as "counsels of perfection," which ordinary people cannot reasonably be expected to follow.

IKEDA: While it is true that complete self-mastery is too difficult a goal for the majority, it seems unfair to say that the reason for the human inability to master the self is lack of will, since the obstruction to this mastery lies on a level deeper than desire or consciousness. In other words, in order to attain self-mastery one must devise a way of tapping power that lies deeper than consciousness. I am convinced that the power to make the effort to perform this admittedly difficult task is inherent in all people. The problem is finding ways to bring that power to light.

TOYNBEE: The "counsels of perfection" of which I spoke have become indispensable conditions for survival now that mankind, by concentrating its efforts on increasing the efficiency of technology, has thrust itself recklessly and prematurely into the atomic age. It is conceivable that every human being is capable of rising to the level of sainthood. Yet it seems improbable that the mass of mankind will make the arduous spiritual effort required, in spite of the widespread awareness that the price of failing to respond to the moral challenge of the atomic age may be the self-liquidation of our species.

I conclude that the survival of mankind is more precarious today than it has ever been at any time since mankind established its ascendancy over non-human nature. The threat to mankind's survival comes from mankind itself; human technology, misused to serve the diabolic purposes of human egoism and wickedness, is a more deadly danger than earthquakes, volcanic eruptions, storms, floods, droughts, viruses, microbes, sharks, and saber-toothed tigers.

IKEDA: I agree entirely both that man has created his present crisis and that he holds the key to its solution. The way to transform moral sense into moral action is not to abandon the ego but, always regarding it in the proper light, to put it to active use at some times and to suppress it at others. As a concrete method, simply teaching control as a kind of knowledge and attempting to propagate it in this way are meaningless. A total reformation of the individual from below the depths of consciousness is essential. Of course, this reformation cannot be imposed from without. Instead, the individual, in striving to better his own personality, must consciously strive to effect his own reformation. At the least, a philosophy propounding the need for such a reformation must give its followers strength sufficient to the task. It is this kind of reformation that I mean by the human revolution.

Dealing with Desires

IKEDA: Mankind has many desires: the instinctive will to survive as an organism, the thirst for glory and power, and longings for knowledge and beauty. In addition, the desire for human love or compassion is innate in life as manifest in man. In modern civilization instinctive desires and the thirst for power and possessions, though already immense, seem to be on the increase. As long as they remain unbridled, these desires give rise to conflicts among human beings and lead relentlessly to the destruction of the natural environment and of life.

TOYNBEE: I am very much concerned with the role of desires—especially greed—in the modern world.

IKEDA: I agree with your assertion that evil is the product of man's self-centeredness. You maintain that religious love is the way man can overcome his self-centeredness. I too believe that religion is the most fundamental and universal way to overcome egoism. If, however, we suppose that religious love can subjugate egoism, what psychological mechanism must it employ?

I believe in the existence of another kind of human desire on which all the ones enumerated above rest. I call it the basic desire, and I believe that it is the force that actively propels all other human desires in the direction of creativity. It is the source of all impelling energy inherent in life; it is also the longing to unite one's life with the life of the universe and to draw vital energy from the universe. This basic desire transmits the pulsation of universal life to all human emotions and thus elevates their natures. Consequently, the various human desires generated by human life stimulate creativity while maintaining contact with the basic desire.

TOYNBEE: Desire is another name for the psychic energy that generates and sustains life. The desire that animates a specimen of a species of living creatures and that impels it to try to keep itself alive and to keep its species in existence by reproducing itself is identical with the energy of the universe in this energy's psychic aspect. In other words, desire is identical with the ultimate reality, or at any rate with one of its facets.

IKEDA: On the other hand, in the depths of human life, the desires that originally exist for the sake of supporting life sometimes manifest themselves in the form of selfish lusts to subjugate and destroy both other people and nature. The will to power of Nietzsche and Adler and the instinctive death wish of Freud and Marcuse seem to me to have evolved from reflections on such deep inner workings as these. I call desire transformed into egocentric selfishness—those motives that lurk in the heart of life—diabolical desire.

TOYNBEE: The identity of each individual living being with the universe coexists with a separateness between the individual and the universe. This separateness may evoke in the separated being one or the other of two responses that are not only different from each other but are actually antithetical. One response is a loving desire for harmony with the whole of the universe; the other response is the diabolical desire to subjugate and exploit the rest of the universe. The loving desire does require self-renunciation, and in some cases it may require self-sacrifice. Love is an impulse to devote the self to the service of other living beings and of the universe.

IKEDA: Buddhist thought interprets the diabolical desire in this way. When they attempt to control others or to control and become the master of nature, human beings are bewitched by the diabolical desire. This desire itself strives to sever connections between all other desires and the basic desire in the attempt to bring all other desires under its own control.

TOYNBEE: The diabolical desire is more natural than the loving desire, for separate selfhood is of the essence of being alive. The diabolical desire seeks to carry this separate selfhood to its logical conclusion by aggrandizing the separate self into the center and raison d'être of the universe. Like the loving desire, the diabolical desire seeks to overcome the split in the wholeness and the unity of the universe that has been produced by the appearance of the separate self. But the two alternative ways of trying to reestablish unity are contrary to each other. Love seeks to reestablish unity by devoting itself; diabolism seeks to reestablish unity by asserting itself.

IKEDA: How can the diabolical desire be transformed into the loving desire?

TOYNBEE: Both responses are reactions to a tension set up by the fission of the universe into a number of separate selves. Either response exacts a price. The self-sacrifice that may be demanded by love may go to the extreme length of self-annihilation, and the lost unity will have been restored by the extinction of the life of the separated self. The diabolical response is an attempt by the separated self to maintain the life that is its essence. But the price of this aggressive reaction of a separate self is conflict and chaos. An aggressive self comes into conflict with innumerable other aggressive selves, and each aggressive self conflicts with the universe as a whole.

How is a separate living being to devote itself without extinguishing its life? And how is it to assert itself without coming into conflict with the life of other separate selves and with the life of the whole universe? These questions are forced upon us by our experience. We have to ask them, but we may find ourselves unable to answer them. The price of being alive may be a life-long struggle to solve an insoluble problem.

310

IKEDA: Undeniably life is a continual attempt to come to terms with the question of desire. I feel that man must constantly wage a struggle to suppress the diabolical desire and to reveal the basic desire. As part of human life, the diabolical desire cannot be eliminated, but it is man's fate to battle constantly to subject it and to weaken the power of its operations.

TOYNBEE: According to the Pali scriptures of Southern Buddhism, the Buddha practiced and recommended to his disciples the total extinction of desire of every kind, and his objective was to extinguish life—or, at any rate, to extinguish life as we know it in ourselves and in other psychosomatic living human beings on this planet—if this is the meaning of Nirvana. I believe that the Buddha made a correct psychological diagnosis in holding that *if* it were practicable to extinguish desire totally, this would be tantamount to extinguishing life itself; it would be an exit from life into the state of extinguishedness.

IKEDA: *Nirvana* means to blow out a light; that is, it means, as you say, extinguishedness. But Southern (or Hinayana) Buddhism and Northern (or Mahayana) Buddhism differ radically in dealing with this problem. Whereas Southern Buddhism seeks to repress human desire to the point of extinction, Northern Buddhism does not regard such repression as its main task. Northern Buddhism ultimately seeks social reform through individual enlightenment. It holds that, by translating the Buddhist spirit of compassion into action for this ultimate cause, the individual can not only control but also transform his desire into constructive spiritual forces.

Buddhist thought has made a detailed analysis of the manifestations of desires that have become subordinate to the diabolical nature and of their effects on life. On the basis of this analysis, Buddhism has attempted to find a practical method for subduing the diabolical desire. This method does not attempt to refute or diminish desires themselves; instead, it strives to subjugate the operation of their diabolical nature and to free them from bondage to that nature.

It is essential to control desire so that it can play a part in directing mankind, society, and the whole universe on the path of creative life. Control, not futile attempts at extinction, is the meaningful way to deal with desires. As psychoanalysts have shown, suppressing desires results in a backwash of energy into the world of the subconscious and becomes the cause of physical and mental disorders.

TOYNBEE: I agree that the total extinction of desire is impossible and would

311

be undesirable even if it were possible. It is impossible for the reasons you state. Desire cannot really be extinguished; it can either be suppressed from the conscious to the subconscious level of the psyche (with the injurious effects that you note), or alternatively it can be oriented deliberately to objectives that are right for oneself and are good for one's fellow human beings and for the universe as a whole. I believe that a human being should aim not at the unattainable objective of extinguishing desire but at the attainable and desirable objective of directing desire towards good objectives. Have I put my finger, here, on the difference of diagnosis and outlook and aim between Southern and Northern Buddhism?

IKEDA: Yes, I think you have, but, to amplify this point, let me go back to Buddhism as Sakyamuni taught it. In order to attain enlightenment, man must overcome his self-centered nature. Presumably in order to help him do so, Sakyamuni taught that all is vanity—indicating the vanity of a selfish life. The Buddhist concept of selflessness means that there is no eternal and unchanging substance in the ego. No conditions of our lives are immutable. We feel frustrated at one moment and satisfied the next. We strive for a high ideal for a while and in the next instant labor to satisfy an ugly desire. The impermanence of the phenomena of human life seems to substantiate the idea of selflessness or the nonexistence of an unchanging self. Yet even in this flux we cannot deny the existence of a certain consistency within the self. Awareness of the self is an essential part of human life. Let us assume that one can attain complete Nirvana, free from any suffering, if one succeeds in annihilating one's self. Nevertheless, the attainment of such Nirvana would be meaningless, because in such a state there would be no self that could sense freedom from suffering.

The concept of selflessness, orientated towards the extinction of desire, has no major part to play in Northern Buddhism—especially in the philosophy of the Lotus Sutra—which emphasizes harmony and unity of the self with the universe and which teaches that man can reach an ideal state of happiness in life integrated with universal life. The altruistic practice of compassion (in the Buddhist sense) leads naturally to the conquest of desire. In other words, by awakening to a greater (universal) self, man conquers his lesser (individual) self and the desires associated with it.

TOYNBEE: If I have interpreted your explanation correctly, according to the Lotus Sutra school of Northern Buddhism, Nirvana is not a cessation of rebirths. Rebirth continues endlessly. But if the self that is reborn succeeds in improving its karma, its life in the endless series of rebirths will become a state of happiness and not of torment, and happiness consists in the approximation of the individual self to the universal self. Is this doctrine identical with the doctrine of the school of Hinduism that believes the essence of the individual self to be identical with ultimate spiritual reality (*Tat tvam asi*)?

IKEDA: Though Hinduism is the traditional Indian religion and Buddhism the nontraditional one, their ideological bases are the same. While borrowing concepts from each other, the two have continued to assert their distinctive individuality. But Buddhism evolved its characteristic doctrines under the influence of Brahmanism, which, as you know, existed in India from an earlier time. Hinduism, which followed Buddhism in time, was influenced by Buddhist teachings.

The concept expressed in the words *Tat tvam asi* in the Upanishads became a central element in both Buddhism and Hinduism. Indeed, this concept in itself must be regarded as one of the greatest contributions to mankind of the Indian people. The difference between the teachings of Southern and of Northern Buddhism lies in the way the individual self comes into contact with the universal self. In contrast to the Southern Buddhist idea that the individual self must be destroyed to effect ultimate communion, Northern Buddhism, without rejecting the individual self, places emphasis on union of the individual self with the universal self.

TOYNBEE: Our judgment about what is the right attitude toward desire is decided by our conception of the nature of reality. As I see it, the ultimate reality is what is called here "universal life" and, alternatively, "universal self." The second of these descriptions is the more explicit of the two. It indicates the duality and ambivalence of the individual human self.

On the one hand, the individual self is (in terms of a simile from physical nature) a splinter of the universal self. It is a fragment of the whole that has detached itself from the whole and is trying—so long as it takes *its* line of least resistance—to assert itself against the rest of the whole. So long as the individual self acts in this egotistical way, it is rebelling against the universal self and is alienating itself from it.

This is a wrong relation between the individual self and the universal self. Unless and until a human being rectifies it, he cannot be good or happy. This truth is, I think, recognized by all people of good will, whether they are Southern Buddhists, Northern Buddhists, Christians, agnostics, or followers of some other way of spiritual life. The point on which they differ from each other is their particular prescription for attaining this common objective.

As far as my superficial knowledge goes, I have the impression that you explain correctly the Southern Buddhism prescription for overcoming the division, opposition, and tension between the individual self and the universal self. The arhat seeks to reestablish unity and harmony by extinguishing the individual self, which he correctly equates with the total extinction of desires of all kinds, without distinction or discrimination between desires of different kinds.

I agree that the Southern Buddhist prescription for reestablishing harmony and unity is impracticable. An individual who succeeds in extinguishing his individual self does not thereby reunite himself with the universal self. On the contrary, he cuts himself off from access to the universal self. You have pointed out this truth by saying that we cannot deny a certain consistency in the self, the awareness of which is an essential part of life.

This is the paradox and the difficulty of the self. Our only consciousness of, and access to, the universal self is through the individual self. It is also true that the individual self, so long as it follows the line of least resistance, is in revolt against the universal self. But, since both these truths are valid, the Southern Buddhist prescription is too simple—indeed, it is too simple-minded. We do have to master the individual self, but our objective ought to be not to extinguish it but to reorient it. This means that, in terms of the Southern Buddhist analysis of the individual self as being a hotbed of desires, we have to distinguish between different kinds of desire. We must subdue and subordinate our egotistic desires, but we must pursue—at however high a cost to the ego—our altruistic desires for harmony and unity with our universal self.

IKEDA: I suspect that the way of bringing about this fusion may be related to what you call self-mastery. To help me see whether I have interpreted your meaning correctly, please explain in more concrete terms what you mean by self-mastery.

TOYNBEE: What I mean by self-mastery is the conquest of desire pertaining to man's lesser self in the course of integrating the lesser self with universal life. Individual enlightenment is the indispensable means of social reform because, in the phenomenal world in which we human beings live and act, the agents are individual human beings. The concrete way of achieving this aim is to follow the lead of compassion, one of the desires that are innate in the individual self. Compassion is the desire that moves the individual self to widen the scope of its self-concern to embrace the whole of the universal self.

In this evidently very important point, it seems to me that Northern Buddhism is supported by the Judaic group of religions (Judaism, Christianity,

314

Islam). The Arabic word *Islam* means self-surrender or the surrender of the individual self to the service of the universal self, which, in the Judaic religions, is symbolized in the anthropomorphic term *God*. I find the nonanthropomorphic vocabulary of Buddhism a better expression of the ineffable truth about the self.

IKEDA: The universal self is, in my view, the universal life force. The Buddhist interpretation is that the life of individual human beings is connected at its profoundest depths with universal life, of which it is a particularization or individualization. The characteristic of individualized life is the ability to generate motion and action. But the fundamental reality that gives life this ability is the Law inherent in universal life force. This aspect of the teachings of Northern Buddhism sets it apart from the religions of the Judaic system. If a supernatural deity—God, Allah, or whatever form it may have—is presupposed, the power to generate motion and action in human life is not inherent in that life: it is bestowed by an outside entity. If this is the case, man becomes a kind of mechanism activated by power injected from without.

The Northern Buddhist Law that is the source of life is not a reality existing outside humanity; it pervades both universal and human life. Consequently, the essence of its teaching is the awakening to the knowledge of the Law within man himself or of the unity of individualized and universal life. Put in slightly different terms, the Northern Buddhist conceives of the ultimate reality not as a god—an anthropomorphic being—but as the universal life force and the Law operating at its profoundest level.

TOYNBEE: It does seem more convincing to interpret the universal self as a Law, instead of as a god. Furthermore, the Southern Buddhist method of conquering desire seems less easy to put into practice than the Northern Buddhist teaching.

The Northern Buddhist and the Judaic religions are, it seems to me, in agreement with each other, as against the Southern Buddhist prescription for human conduct.

All the higher religions call upon a human being to overcome his egotistic desires. This is a very difficult task.

IKEDA: Without doubt, overcoming them is difficult, but unless man strives to conquer his lower desires, the animalistic elements in his makeup gain the upper hand. In reflecting on the reason why conquering desires is difficult, I have come to think that it may be because some of the higher religions have not clearly understood the nature of the universal self and, as a consequence

315

of that failure, have created practical difficulties of method. Though aware of a need to master the self, they are not sure what the self is. While realizing that the self consists, to some extent, of desires and emotions, they fail to understand its full nature and to understand wherein it differs from the universal self.

Buddhism teaches that the individual self, which must be mastered, and the universal self are the same. Once a person has been enlightened to this knowledge, he sees that his own self is not an isolated fragment of the universal but *is* in fact the universal self. The attainment of this knowledge is the ultimate enlightenment to the Buddha world; it is internal spiritual realization. In terms of practical action, such knowledge must be imbued with the humility of the awareness that one is an integral part of the universal self.

The true role of religion is to supply man with the power to overcome desire and to develop the optimum aspects of his humanity. Religion must awaken man to an awareness of the life force deep within himself and inspire him with the strength to fuse that life force with the universal life force. I agree with you that a human being must constantly strive to devote himself to the universe.

TOYNBEE: In reality, the individual self and the universal self are identical. I believe that *Tat tvam asi* is the truth. However, *Tat tvam asi* is simply an intellectual proposition. It is therefore only potentially true unless and until it is made actually true by moral action—and this has to be taken by the individual self. The individual self is alienated from the universal self by greed. This greed is a desire to exploit the universe for the individual self's purposes; the converse of greed is compassion. By practicing compassion, the individual self can become the universal self actually.

The Meaning of Fate

IKEDA: There is a manifest inequality in the fortunes and fates of men. All human beings are not alike: some are richer, wiser, and more talented than others. Of course environmental factors contribute to the formation of each individual, but the environmental conditions into which a person is born differ from place to place, and the human being has no part in selecting them. This and the many hardships and vicissitudes that man encounters throughout life compel me to believe in the existence of fate.

Having arrived at this belief, I must try to discover what constitutes fate.

According to Buddhist thought, life flows through three time modes: past, present, and future. The actions of an individual in the past determine his fate in the present. Christianity, however, interprets fate as the will of an omniscient, omnipotent god.

TOYNBEE: Buddhism and Christianity agree with each other in holding that, in order to account for a human being's fortunes, we have to look beyond the limits of a single lifetime.

Buddhism holds that an individual's fortunes are determined by his own action (karma). If I understand the Buddhist concept of karma correctly, it is that our actions create for us a kind of ethical banking-account, in which the balance (it may be either a credit or a debit balance at a particular point) is constantly being changed by fresh entries in the credit and debit columns. This explanation of the inequality of fortunes requires the hypothesis that a personality has been formed before birth and is not extinguished by death. According to Buddhist belief, the personality, with its credit-and-debit account of karma still valid and still open, is reborn after death. Death and rebirth may recur any number of times.

Christianity holds that an individual's fortunes are determined by an omnipotent god, who has created the universe and is directing its course towards a goal set by him. This Christian explanation requires the hypothesis that an omnipotent god exists.

According to Christian belief, it is God who imposes on a human being his character and decides the time and place, and the social position within that time and place, in which a human being is born. Unlike Buddhists, Christians hold that a human being has only a single lifetime in this world. According to Christian belief, the date of his conception in his mother's womb is the date of the beginning of his spiritual as well as his physical existence. But Christians agree with Buddhists in holding that a human being's personality is not extinguished by death. Though Christians do not believe that man ever reappears in this world, they believe that he is immortal and that, after his death, his ultimate destination is either Heaven—perhaps via Purgatory—or Hell.

Christians who carry the Christian belief in the existence of an omnipotent god to its logical conclusion believe that a human being is predestined by God to go eventually to either Heaven or Hell. Other Christians believe that a human being's fate after death is decided, at least in part, by his karma, which, in the Christian view, is an account that is opened at birth and is closed at death within a single lifetime in this world. In the history of Christian theology, the controversy over the respective roles of God and of the human

317

being himself in the determination of a human being's fate has never been settled by any generally accepted agreement.

In the last three hundred years, more and more Westerners have ceased to believe the doctrines of Christianity. Many ex-Christians no longer believe in the existence of an omnipotent god or in the survival of a human being's personality after death. They agree with Christians in holding that a human being's appearance in this world is limited to a single lifetime. They argue that his fate during his lifetime is determined partly by the combination of genes that he has inherited from his ancestors, partly by his environment, and partly by his karma within the limits of a single lifetime.

It seems to me that these post-Christian Western beliefs are really the Christian beliefs expressed in other words. The individual's fortuitous actual heritage of genes is the equivalent of God's arbitrary act of predestination. The heritage of genes, too, is arbitrary because the number of possible combinations of genes is virtually infinite. The role of the environment is the equivalent of God's placing the individual in a particular time and place and social setting. Western post-Christians agree with nonpredestinarian Christians in holding that a human being's fate is partly decided by his karma, though, unlike Christians and Buddhists, they hold that his karma-account does not affect his fate after death; as ex-Christians see it, he has no post-mortem fate, because death is annihilation.

IKEDA: That is to say, views of fate differ widely depending on whether the individual believes that life is strictly a one-time thing or that it is eternal. If the individual's existence terminates completely at death, fate after death is not worth discussing. If one's fate begins at birth and ends at death, why are individual human beings all born different? If the omnipotent god were fair, he would give everybody an equal start, but he does not. Can you explain this? Does the ultimate spiritual reality behind the universe exercise volitional control over human fate?

TOYNBEE: Like other ex-Christian Westerners, I believe that differences of heredity and environment partly explain the differences in human fortunes. But I also believe that karma plays a greater part than is attributed to it by some of my more deterministic-minded fellow ex-Christian Westerners. I also differ from some of them who, unlike me, disbelieve in the existence of any ultimate spiritual reality beyond the spiritual aspect of human nature with which we are acquainted in our experience.

I have had direct experience of karma in my own life and in the lives of other people whom I know at first or second hand. I can also see that karma has operated in the histories of human communities and institutions. These are networks of relations between mortal human beings who replace their predecessors and are replaced, in their turn, by successors, so that a relations-network can, and often does, last for a far longer time than the duration of a single human lifetime. Thus the evidence for the operation of karma in the histories of communities and institutions does not require the hypothesis that a personality retains a continuous identity through a series of births and deaths. The continuity is maintained by the relations-network, not by the personalities of the human beings who are temporarily related through this network. Here are three examples, from British history, of what I mean by the operation of karma in the histories of communities and institutions.

In the fourteenth and fifteenth centuries, the English fought a hundred-year war with the objective of conquering France. They failed, and this led them to renounce permanently the ambition to conquer continental European territory and also led them to refrain from political and military intervention in European affairs except for the one purpose of preventing continental powers from conquering Britain. This was a successful cancellation of a debit entry in Britain's karma-account.

In the seventeenth century, the English people were politically violent. They fought a civil war, put their king to death, and brought on themselves a military government in place of an absolute monarch. This disillusioning experience led the English to become nonviolent in their politics. In this instance they were successful in converting a debit balance in their karma-account into a credit balance.

In the eighteenth and the early nineteenth centuries, the employers of industrial workers in Britain were merciless in exploiting the workers for the employers' profit. In the twentieth century, the British middle class repented of its past economic oppressiveness and voluntarily conceded greater economic justice to the industrial workers. But by that time the workers, in self-defense, had organized trades unions. These unions have now become powerful enough to take the offensive. Now that they have the power, they are behaving as mercilessly, for their own profit, as the employers behaved in the past. In this case, the British people have again tried to turn a debit karma-balance into a credit-balance, but this time they have failed. They have not succeeded in becoming merciful in their economic dealings with each other. In the relations between employers and employees, the tables have been turned, but the mercilessness of the behavior has not been eliminated.

IKEDA: I entirely agree with your understanding of karma in communities and nations. Since societies are aggregates of individual human beings, it is possible to consider them life bodies on a large scale. They have their own laws of operations, ways of growing and propagating, and abilities of self-regeneration. (I consider these functions to be the characteristic traits of a life body.) As large-scale life bodies, societies, institutions, and nations form their own karmas from within themselves. They are then influenced by these karmas and produce new karmas.

If this is true, the executives who lead nations and societies must think in terms of karma on a vast scale and must have an extensive awareness of things in order to keep the general karma balance sheet in order. No matter how skillful the leader may be in certain fields of politics or economics, if he allows karma to go from bad to worse and in this way upsets the balance sheet, he cannot avoid leading his people into misery. Japan during World War II was a clear case of a people who ignored the weight of karma, allowed it to run wild, and had to pay a bitter price at a later reckoning. Postwar Japan, too, has pursued profit-first economic policies that have created severe environmental pollution. As a debit entry in the karma balance sheet of the nation, pollution is resulting in violent public reprisals.

TOYNBEE: Your illustrations seem to substantiate my ideas about karma on a large scale. But earlier you asked about the nature of the ultimate spiritual reality.

I do not believe in the existence of a unique and omnipotent but otherwise humanlike male god of the kind in which the Jews, Christians, and Muslims believe. Nor do I believe in a plurality of humanlike gods, both male and female, like the Hindu pantheon and the pre-Christian Greek and Scandinavian pantheons. At the same time, I do not find it credible that human beings, or humanlike beings on other habitable planets in other solar systems, are the spiritually highest realities in the universe. Human beings are conscious of the difference between good and evil. Their consciences tell them that they ought always to do good, yet actually they do evil at least as often as not. Their experience of their own behavior and their condemnation of their own bad behavior imply a belief in the existence of something that is better than human nature.

IKEDA: You mean, then, that human humility before an ultimate reality transcending human knowledge makes possible ethical behavior. I suppose that reverence for this ultimate reality is religion.

TOYNBEE: Human nature does evil insofar as it fails to overcome its innate self-centeredness. But sometimes it does overcome this. Sometimes a human

320

being sacrifices himself for the sake of something beyond himself—some other human being or some group of human beings or all mankind or the whole universe. When he does that, he is trying to serve the universe instead of trying to make the universe serve his own selfish greed. The impulse that makes him sacrifice himself is love. Both love and greed are forms of desire, but they are desires with opposite objectives. Greed tries to subordinate the universe to a fragment of it; love tries to subordinate this fragment to the universe.

According to one of the Christian scriptures, "God is love." If a humanlike God did exist, he would hate as well as love and he would be bad as well as good. This is, in fact, how the Judaic God is presented, for the most part, in the Jewish, Christian, and Muslim scriptures. Though I do not believe that love is a person or that love is omnipotent, I do believe that love is the ultimate spiritual reality. This is an unverifiable hypothesis, like the belief in the existence of God and the belief in the rebirth of human beings.

IKEDA: But let us assume that love is the ultimate spiritual reality. Love exists in the human heart. Consequently, the ultimate spiritual reality existing in the universe exists at the same time in the human heart.

TOYNBEE: Love, as we know it in human beings, is a relation between persons, and persons hate as well as love and do evil as well as good. The ultimate reality cannot be a person like the god Yahweh or the god Vishnu. But I cannot conceive of the ultimate reality as being either subpersonal or suprapersonal. I can come closest to defining my idea if I put it in negative terms: man is not the spiritually highest reality, but the spiritually highest reality or ultimate reality, which is not man, is also neither God nor non-God.

IKEDA: In saying that the ultimate spiritual reality is not a god, you mean that it is not an anthropomorphic god of the kind worshipped in the Judaic religions. But in saying that it is also not non-God, you mean that it has no humanlike personality. Can we not say that the ultimate reality is the Law that is inherent in the universe? This Law is the cause of all phenomena and is the reality that becomes the basic principle maintaining strict harmony among all phenomena. I believe that the movement of the universe, which is based on Law, is compassion (*jihi* in Japanese Buddhist terminology)—or to use your word, love—which strives to build and preserve harmony among all things. When man manifests selfishness, he disrupts this harmony. On the other hand, to make the Law inherent in the universe the aim of one's actions is to act in accordance with universal harmony. On the basis of these con-

321

siderations, I suspect that what you call the ultimate spiritual reality is what I mean by the Law.

The ultimate reality is, as you say, neither subpersonal nor suprapersonal. When the individual human being strives for the ultimate spiritual reality and conquers his own greed, the ultimate reality becomes manifest in him. In other words, the Law that is inherent in the entire universe is latent in the human being, who is only a fragment of the universe.

It also seems to me that a human being's fate is determined by the way he maintains a relation with the ultimate spiritual reality. In other words, the ultimate spiritual reality in itself does not volitionally determine man's fate. Instead, man's attitudes and actions in relation to the ultimate spiritual reality determine his fate. In short, human actions and attitudes determine human karma.

Because it explains fate as the result of the causes and effects in individual human karma, Buddhism contains the key to the establishment of fundamental human responsibility and independence. In establishing this responsibility and independence, the individual is in effect taking the first step toward the transformation of his own fate and that of society and other institutions.

TOYNBEE: The presentation of karma in impersonal terms is, so it seems to me, one of Buddhism's great intellectual and moral achievements. Crude religions have tried to express the same truth in personal terms—"the Envy of the Gods" and "the Last Judgment." This imagery misrepresents the nature of karma by introducing an element of humanlike arbitrariness.

Defining True Progress

IKEDA: The idea of utopia has existed in many societies and races from ancient times. Sir Thomas More's *Utopia* has become a synonym for an ideal land, but there are several other works on similar subjects: *The New Atlantis* by Francis Bacon, *Civitas Solis* by Campanella, and *Modern Utopia* by H. G. Wells. In Japan, too, legends concerning *Shinsenkyō*, or a fairy land; *Hōraikoku*, or the island of eternal youth; and *Ryūgūjō*, or the palace of the dragon king, deal with utopias.

TOYNBEE: The earliest examples of this genre of literature are Greek, though the name *Utopia* was coined not by the Greeks but by Sir Thomas More. The Greek utopias—for instance those of Plato and Aristotle—are mostly retrospective. Their authors were conscious that, by their time, Greek civilization had passed its zenith. Their aim was to fix society or to freeze it, in the hope of saving it from declining further. These Greek utopias were never translated into realities in Greek history. On the other hand, in Japanese history, the Tokugawa regime was a political and social achievement in real life that Plato and Aristotle would have admired. I might add that the eventual failure of the Tokugawa regime to freeze Japanese society permanently shows that Plato's and Aristotle's utopias were, in a long-term view, unpractical.

IKEDA: The comparison between the utopian visions of Plato and Aristotle and the Tokugawa shogunate is fascinating. But as you say, even the Tokugawas ultimately failed to fix Japanese society.

In general, people look dimly on ideal worlds drawn as extensions of contemporary society. Aldous Huxley's *Brave New World* and George Orwell's *1984* illustrate the pessimistic outlook toward utopian versions of our world. The computer has become so pervasive in our times that some people have advanced the possibility of a "computopia." Still not even the people who suggest such a development are able to conceal a trace of scorn at what a "computopian" world must inevitably involve.

The pessimistic approach to utopian society springs from at least two causes. First, it is a reflection of man's critical comment on the fact that, though our civilization has ostensibly developed in the hope of a better world, human misery has only increased. Second, the very idea of utopia in its ancient form entails a peaceful society in which all human desires are fulfilled. People today are no longer sure that mere fulfillment of desires spells true happiness.

The dim view taken of utopia is connected with the sociological concept of progress. Obviously progress is a mainstay of the modern scientist, who finds great joy in adding something to truths already revealed or in advancing technology beyond its present level. Viewed solely within the framework of science, the achievements of progress are clear. But is scientific progress necessarily directly related to progress in human culture? Without doubt, seen from the scientific viewpoint, the development of nuclear energy is an epoch-making step forward, but do the hundreds of thousands of lives destroyed at Hiroshima and Nagasaki permit us to be happy at this kind of progress?

TOYNBEE: Most of the early modern Western utopias were optimistic, because they did not clearly draw the crucial distinction between scientific progress and spiritual progress. In some of them, at any rate, it is mistakenly assumed that cumulative scientific and technological progress automatically brings cumulative spiritual progress. This modern Western illusion was shaken by the outbreak of World War I and was shattered by the making and dropping of the atomic bombs at the end of World War II. H. G. Wells lived long enough to become disillusioned and embittered. Post-Wellsian utopias are satirical antiutopias. They are pessimistic in the extreme, in reaction against the excessive optimism of the utopias published during the four centuries ending in 1914.

IKEDA: The distinction between material and spiritual progress must be clearly drawn. Utopian literature has often failed to do this. Progress in fields of endeavor concerned with inorganic matter is clear. On the other hand, in fields related to living beings, especially perceptive, sensitive beings, it is inadvisable to make quick judgments about the progressive nature of any single invention or discovery. Human beings must be studied not only as physical beings but also as spiritual and mental beings. The reactions of such beings are never uniform in all cases. For instance, depending on the way it is received, a phenomenon may bring joy and happiness to one individual and sorrow and grief to another. The fulfillment of a certain social condition can be considered beneficial by a certain group and grievous in the extreme by another. Moreover, a given individual reacts with happiness to a certain phenomenon at one point in time, whereas the same phenomenon might later make him miserable.

As you pointed out in your comment on the shift from optimism to pessimism in connection with the utopian genre, subtle human reactions are reflected in attitudes toward utopias. Now that we no longer accept with unquestioning faith the idea that material progress is beneficial without qualification, we ought to attempt to reevaluate the significance of the very idea of progress and in that way discover to what extent it is worthy of our trust.

Examinations of progress ought to be made by the scientists as well. Instead of accepting progress blindly as the basis of their activities, men of science must examine their field of activity from the standpoint of its meaning for all mankind. In other words, in all his research, the scientist must be guided by a human conscience and by a strong ability to make value judgments. Probably scientists of the past would have violently opposed my idea as running counter to the liberty demanded by pure science. But, today, because it has the power to destroy us all, science and its motives must be scrutinized carefully and criticized honestly.

TOYNBEE: Progress in science, applied to technology, creates power for human beings over their fellow human beings and over nonhuman nature. Power is ethically neutral: it can be used for either good or evil. It merely increases the material magnitude of the effect of good and evil actions. Atomic power used for evil can kill millions of people in an instant, whereas human muscle-power, even armed with metal, could kill only one at a time in hand-to-hand fighting. Conversely, the power conferred on physicians by the progress of medical science can now save millions of lives that would once have fallen victim to bacteria or to viruses. On the other hand, the same science, applied to bacteriological warfare, can kill as many millions as atomic bombs can. Thus the effect on human life of power generated by scientific technology depends on the ethical level of the people who wield the power.

The progress of modern technology is the cumulative result of cooperative action. By contrast, karma, which determines ethical levels, is a running account in the spiritual life of an individual human being—whether we believe that a human being has a series of lives or that he has only one life in this phenomenal world. In a karma-account, neither the debit nor the credit entries are cumulative; the debit or the credit balance changes at each fresh entry in the ledger. The ethical level of a society at a particular moment depends on the state of the karma-account of each of the participants in the society and on the relative ethical influence—positive or negative—of each participant on his fellow participants. Thus the ethical level of a society, unlike its scientific and technological level, is fluctuating and precarious. Karma, not scientific and technological progress, is the factor in human life that produces welfare and happiness or, alternatively, misery and sorrow.

IKEDA: You have touched on a very deep point that is a matter of constant concern to me. I am convinced that it is the task of the individual to find a way to change his fate from one of an accumulation of miseries to one of happiness. It is this change that I mean when I speak of the human revolution.

TOYNBEE: The most important objective for a human being, both for his own sake and for the sake of society, is to improve his karma. The only way to improve it is for him to increase his self-mastery, and the struggle to master one's self is the personal action of an individual human being. Individual spiritual progress and regress fluctuate. In Hindu and Buddhist belief, this fluctuation may continue through a series of successive lives. But there is no such thing as cumulative, social, spiritual progress. The cumulative progress of science and technology has no counterpart in the ethical sphere.

IKEDA: The battle with fate demands unceasing effort. Though at a given moment, one may be conscious of elevated spiritual motives filling one's entire being, this does not mean that in the very next moment one cannot display the ugliest selfish ambition. Countless opportunities to give way to base desires and greed are an inevitable part of life. Consequently, it is of the greatest importance to refuse to lose the battles with them and to strive always to conquer our worse selves and live up to the best of which we are capable. Ceaseless effort to reach a higher plane is the only true spiritual progress for human beings. But, even in this field, the danger of satisfaction with progress for its own sake lies waiting to entrap us and to nullify whatever real progress we have made.

Love and Conscience

IKEDA: You have said that the evolution of living things is the process of the manifestation of love and conscience. But I do not agree completely, because love and conscience are always related to senses of value and the evolution of living things is unrelated to value. Comparisons of physical characteristics are the major elements behind studies of evolution, the whole issue being related to the structure of the brain and the spinal cord, which are the principal supports of spiritual functions. Cerebral physiologists claim that the frontal lobes of the brain are the seats of man's intellectual abilities. They further maintain that the development of these lobes is strikingly greater in man than in any other animal. But we must remember that if the frontal lobes of the brain are sometimes applied to creative effort, at other times they are the source of such actions as murder. In other words, whereas evolution in man—at any rate, as seen in the frontal lobes of the brain— can be called a manifestation of love and conscience when viewed in one light, viewed in another it has resulted in the development of malice and cunning. Your expression of evolution as the process of the manifestation of love and conscience must be a subjective hope and must therefore be different from an objective view of biological evolution.

TOYNBEE: Cerebral physiologists do seem to have shown that certain parts of the human brain are associated with certain emotions and impulses. But the enigmatic word *associated* indicates our inability to understand the nature of the relation between two different kinds of reality. Cerebral organic matter is physical, not psychic; and psychic activity is not physical activity, though it may be associated, in the enigmatic sense, with physical—electrical —events and may be impossible without the accompaniment of these physical events.

Perhaps the mystery of the association between psychic activity and physical events in an organic material medium is a product of the limitations of human thought. While human consciousness, life, and matter may in reality be a single indivisible whole, this indivisible wholeness is incomprehensible to us. We succeed in comprehending it partially by dissecting it mentally, but this comprehension by means of mental analysis is not complete, for we do not comprehend mentally the relation between the elements into which we have dissected human nature mentally. I agree that biological evolution produces evil as well as good and that it may produce more evil than good.

IKEDA: I am in accord with the idea that human life is a total, integrated reality and that, even when we can conceptually analyze it into the two different systems (physical and psychic), we cannot understand the inseparable unity of the two in this way.

In order to delve more deeply into the questions of biological evolution and love and conscience, let us examine some fundamental issues. You state that, without life, love could not have manifested itself. I agree that without human life there would be no love and no conscience. Perhaps, then, the important issue is finding out how human life, which manifests these two characteristics, came about in the first place. I understand that you do not believe in an anthropomorphic god, but do you assume that evolution itself is a kind of volitional and purposeful deity that is the ultimate reality of love and conscience?

TOYNBEE: I do not think of the spirit of love and goodness as a god in the sense of being a humanlike person that has plans and that tries to carry these plans out. The love and goodness that I know from direct experience manifest themselves in the feelings and actions of human persons and also of some kinds of nonhuman mammals and some kinds of birds. Goodness is the objective, or is at least partially the objective, of some human beings. It is also, I believe, the directive that every human being receives from his conscience, even when a human being is deliberately disobeying his conscience. Human action, good and bad, is teleological. But I do not think that biological evolution is teleological in the sense of being oriented, either immanently or by some transcendent external power, towards an ethical, or any other kind of, objective, except, possibly, the perpetuation of life.

IKEDA: I consider it an error to attach teleological significance to the evolution of living beings.

In your view, is there a part of the brain governing love and conscience or causing them to manifest themselves? If the manifestation of love and conscience truly constitutes the essential nature of the evolution of living things, man's physical characteristics must contain an inborn function responsible for such manifestation. Insofar as I know, no theory has ever proved that love and conscience are governed by a cerebral function. On the other hand, such qualities as desire, logical thinking, and memory are directly related to the brain. It seems to me that love and conscience materialize through interrelations among desire, thought, and memory and that, when some disorder occurs in these interrelations, love and conscience turn into hatred or an urge to kill. This leads me to believe that love and conscience are not the products of evolution but are qualities acquired through social or historical influences.

TOYNBEE: I disagree. Love and conscience have often led human beings to reject and to rebel against current codes of social conduct. But these rebellions cannot have been inspired by the social codes themselves. However, since man is a social animal who could not have become human and who could not remain human except in a social setting, it has been suggested by some thinkers that love and conscience have no absolute ethical validity but are psychic mechanisms for making social life practicable. It seems to me that this is another way of saying that love and conscience are products of evolution, at the stage at which evolution has generated the human social animal.

IKEDA: Although it may very well be that love and conscience are results of evolution, it is impossible that evolution should be a process acting teleologically toward the production of love and conscience. History shows that a great number of atrocities have been committed in the name of love or conscience. Europe, for instance, witnessed many heinous acts during the Crusades and the religious wars. Europeans in those days, I presume, committed such atrocious deeds because their consciences rationalized them away as something done for the love of God; they felt that they were carrying out just punishment on God's behalf. This indicates that neither love nor conscience is good in itself; they can be good or evil depending on the objects towards which love is directed and the principles on which conscience is based.

TOYNBEE: Of course I agree that love and conscience have often been misdirected. I believe that all human beings are conscious of the difference between right and wrong and feel a moral obligation to do what they believe to be right and to refrain from doing what they believe to be wrong. At the same time, different societies, and different individuals within the same society, hold different views about what is right and wrong in practice. The code of one society and of one individual may appear to be mistaken in the eyes of some other society or individual. Insofar as other people's love and conscience appear to us to be misdirected, they are likely to produce what will appear to us to be evil results, in spite of the fact that the intention of these other people is manifestly to produce good results. Thus the practical applications of the concepts of good and evil are diverse, and our judgments on other people's applications of the concepts are subjective. Yet we all agree in drawing the distinction between good and evil and in feeling an obligation to do good in accordance with our view of what is good.

IKEDA: Only when love is directed towards all mankind and all other forms of life on earth and only when conscience is based on an unbounded respect for the dignity of life, will both manifest good aspects. Even then, love and conscience as we understand them may prove to be evil insofar as creatures from outer space—if such exist—are concerned. It follows, then, that there can be no absolute good anywhere.

TOYNBEE: I agree that love and conscience will not produce wholly good results unless they are directed towards all mankind and towards all forms of life on earth and anywhere else in the universe and towards the whole of the universe itself. However, according to some codes of conduct, it is wrong not to work for one's own nation at the expense of the rest of mankind, and it is wrong not to work for one's own family at the expense of the rest of one's nation. Moreover, even if one believes that one ought to work for all mankind and for the whole universe, this is difficult, because a human being, like nonhuman living beings of every kind, is, by nature, self-centered. It is a tour de force for any living being to devote itself to the universe instead of trying to exploit the universe. In this sense, love and conscience are unnatural, and the unethical pursuit of our own interests is natural. Nevertheless, we feel that selfishness is wrong and bad and that self-sacrifice is right and good, and we cannot annul this ethical judgment, even when we are deliberately acting in contravention of it.

Love and conscience, like good and right, are relative terms. Good would be meaningless if it did not have an antithesis, namely evil. Right implies wrong. Similarly love implies hate, conscience implies sin, Nirvana implies *desire* and the suffering caused by desire, which are extinguished in Nirvana. In each of these pairs of opposites the two poles are complementary to each other and are, therefore, logically inseparable. Thus in logic they are on a par with each other, but in ethics they are not.

Ethically, we take sides with one of the two antithetical poles against the other. When we deliberately do evil and do wrong, we still feel that we ought to have done good and to have done right. We cannot make ourselves feel that good and evil are ethically indistinguishable, equivalent, or interchangeable. The English poet Milton makes Satan say: "Evil, be thou my good." It is, of course, possible to say these words, but it is not possible to reverse our feelings about good and evil.

The fact that the two poles in each of these pairs of opposites are logically complementary to each other and are at the same time ethically disparate suggests to me that there is a spirit in the universe that makes for love, conscience, good, right, Nirvana, but that this spirit is not omnipotent. It is always confronted by its antithesis. Good is not guaranteed to prevail by the fact that we cannot help taking sides with it and are unable to take sides with evil in our ethical judgments, even when we are doing evil deliberately. We cannot help feeling that we ought to do good, no matter what the cost, and we know that the cost may be high and that, insofar as we sacrifice ourselves for the sake of good, our self-sacrifice may, as far as we can see, fail entirely to make goodness prevail.

IKEDA: Conscience and greed, love and hate, exist in each of us in complicated relations of opposition. Nor is there ever any proof that conscience and love will come out triumphant. I believe that human beings find self-rejection and self-sacrifice for the sake of love and conscience extremely difficult.

TOYNBEE: My conclusion is that life is paradoxical, awkward, difficult, and painful. If this is the situation in which a human being finds himself, how is he to deal with it? Southern Buddhism advocates extinguishing life by extinguishing desire, and thus making one's exit into Nirvana. Northern Buddhism holds that the Buddha and the bodhisattvas have voluntarily postponed their exit into Nirvana when they have become capable of making their exit, and that they have done this in order to help other living beings to make the exit that the Buddha and the bodhisattvas have denied to themselves temporarily—perhaps for countless aeons in the bodhisattvas' case.

I find the ideals of Northern Buddhism more congenial than the ideals of Southern Buddhism. Perhaps this is because Northern Buddhist ideals are more like those of Christianity and I happen to have been brought up as a Christian.

IKEDA: Helping humanity find ways to understand the paramount problems of life is the point of origin of religion and philosophy. It ought to be the point they ultimately reach as well, though showing man the way in concrete terms is difficult.

Like you, I find the teachings of Northern Buddhism the more promising explanation of a way of life. The Northern Buddhist approach is to experience supreme joy through altruistic acts and in this way discover the true self.

Compassion as Practicable Love

IKEDA: In our world it is not uncommon for hatred to underlie what is strenuously asserted to be love or for egoism to hide behind a mask of love.

TOYNBEE: In modern Western languages the word *love* is used in two meanings that are not only different but are actually antithetical. In both meanings, love means desire, but in one meaning it means a desire to give and to help, while in the other meaning it means a desire to take and to exploit. Two different words are needed.

I agree that, in the modern world, even the kind of love that means giving, not taking, tends to evaporate through being made impersonal. *Impersonal love* seems to me to be a contradiction in terms, because self-devoting love, as we know it from experience, is a personal feeling. One person experiences it for another person, and that experience leads him to take action—if necessary at extreme cost to himself—to help the other person.

IKEDA: Perhaps today the giving love arising from personal human feelings is being lost or is being relegated to the activities of welfare and charity organizations. This, of course, is love not rooted in human emotions but institutionalized.

TOYNBEE: One reason why love today is in constant danger of evaporating into an impersonal relation is that the modern world operates on a very large scale and is organized impersonally, partly in order to make it possible to cope with huge present-day quantities and magnitudes and perhaps also partly because of the progressive secularization of life in Western countries since before the close of the seventeenth century of the Christian era. In the course of the last three centuries, the depersonalization of human relations has spread from the West into other parts of the world as one consequence of the West's temporary worldwide dominance.

The depersonalization of love in the modern West is illustrated by the modern evolution of the Western word *charity*. The original Latin word *caritas* means literally belovedness; the derivative English word *charity*, however, has come to mean not love but the handing out of a dole by the rich to the poor. *Charity* in the modern Western sense has been doled out with the sense of condescension that is the reverse of respect.

The giving and receiving of charity has carried with it the implication that the recipient is inferior to the giver either ethically or economically or in both ways, and, in this psychological setting, charity has been resented by the recipient. One frequent retort in the West to offers of help is, "I do not want charity." Of course, every human being does want charity in the word's original sense, namely love. It would hardly be possible to feel or to say, "I do not want charity," in this sense. It is, however, natural not to want charity in the sense of the word that implies a relation of inequality unaccompanied by genuine love.

IKEDA: Undeniably charity as a social act is good, but the psychological problems associated with it are difficult to unravel.

If the word *charity* has been stripped of its loftiness of meaning, the word *love* has been highly conceptualized and made very abstract. Just as charitable works without love can do harm, so abstracted love without practical application can be meaningless. I believe that the Buddhist concept of compassion (*jihi*), defined as removing sorrow and bringing happiness to others (*bakku-yōraku*), gives love substantial meaning.

The word *bakku* means to remove the fundamental cause of suffering hidden deep in human life. *Bakku* begins as empathy (*doku*), or feeling the suffering of another as if it were one's own and desiring to alleviate it. Without the feeling of *doku*, there would be no willingness to help others, and there would be no practical action to remove their suffering. *Doku* requires high-level intelligence and imagination because, in order to feel it, one must be able to empathize with the sufferer and imagine his suffering as vividly as if it were one's own. Beings whose intelligence is undeveloped remain indifferent to the suffering of other beings.

The feeling of *doku* is the basis from which has developed the distinctive human way of communal living. Group cooperative living is common in the world of living things, but only man maintains strong individuality while

332

consciously preserving groups for the purposes of daily living. Man is able to do this because he senses the sufferings of his fellow men and realizes the need for groups as protection against suffering. But *doku* must not degenerate into consolation unaccompanied by action. This is why we must move from empathy (*doku*) to *bakku*, the active removal of the cause of suffering.

TOYNBEE: Then you interpret the *bakku* (that is, the relief of suffering) of Buddhist compassion in terms of practical action.

IKEDA: Yes, I do. *Yōraku*—the second component of compassion in the Buddhist sense—means the giving of pleasure. The Buddhist term *raku*, which for present purposes is translated as "pleasure," is by no means transient, partial, or self-sufficient, nor is it an attempt to escape from reality. Instead it is the joy of living or what I have called elsewhere the ecstasy of life. It includes both material and spiritual pleasure. Without the deep feelings of fulfillment and the ecstasy generated by the emotions of life, pleasure in the truest sense is impossible. In brief, the Buddhist concept of *raku* involves the clean, strong joy that wells up from the profoundest depths of life.

Why is it that, in spite of the preachings of love spread all over the world by the great religions, bloody wars and conflicts continue? Surely it is not that love is weaker than hatred. The true reason is that love has not been given a practical form true to its nature: it has remained an abstraction. For this reason hatred has been able to overpower it.

TOYNBEE: As I have already mentioned, the word *love* as used today is vague. I find the Buddhist terms, at any rate their Japanese versions represented in words like *jihi*, more precise and therefore more realistic.

How is real love among human beings to be reimparted to human relations in a community in which these relations have become impersonal—partly because of the community's scale, and partly because of a prevalent tendency to rationalize the structure and operation of social life? While in principle rationalization is desirable, some of its effects on human relations are undesirable. Can the Buddhist tradition produce a solution for this problem in the present social circumstances of Japan and the other so-called developed countries? Has life in Japan been depersonalized, and have human relations been made loveless in the same way and to the same extent as in the Western countries, where the traditional religious background is not Buddhist but Christian? In the modern world, is computerization unavoidable? And can computerization and love coexist?

333

IKEDA: In Japan, as in the West, the increasing size and complexity of society have brought about loss of human individuality and spiritual desiccation. Though the Buddhist tradition persists in Japanese architecture and in some ceremonials, its spirit and content have largely been forgotten. In fact, the extent to which the Buddhist tradition has been lost in Japan may exceed that to which Christianity has departed from the mainstream of life in the West.

In reply to your questions about how we can restore love to human relations in an overrationalized society and about the possibility of Buddhism's working out a solution to the problem, I might make the following comments. Buddhist teachings and the ideal towards which they strive consist in the establishment of fundamental human independence; that is to say, independence in terms of the karma of the individual, of society, and of the natural environment. We find the manifestation of that independence in the concept of compassion (*jihi*). The independence of the individual is called the Buddha state (*Bukkai*), and its manifestation towards others in the form of compassion is called the bodhisattva state (*Bosatsu-kai*). Since, no matter how overrationalized and depersonalized it becomes, modern society is inevitably our social environment, Buddhism teaches the importance of establishing an independence into which depersonalized society can make no incursions and over which it cannot gain control. It is possible—indeed imperative—to expand the field of individual and human relations by resisting the forces of rationalization and depersonalization, no matter how strong they grow.

The ability to do this depends ultimately on the depth and tenacity of the independence of the individual.

Society is composed of individual human beings who manage it and put it into motion. In spite of the degree to which computers administer all kinds of affairs, it is nevertheless the individual human being who operates the computer. As long as man remains aware of his independence and does not forget to deal with society on the basis of that independence, it will remain possible to maintain and even expand compassion, or *jihi*, in human relations.

Expanding the Sphere of Love

IKEDA: Two of woman's outstanding characteristics are purity in regard to love and a tendency to be possessive. Of course, both of these traits occur in males as well; in fact, some men manifest them to a degree greater than do women.

TOYNBEE: I agree that normally love and possessiveness are stronger in women than in men. To these two feminine traits I would add patience, which, with possessiveness, is a corollary of love.

IKEDA: I believe that the kind of love that is characteristic of woman can become a great social force. You have said that possessiveness and patience are corollaries of love. Certainly patience is an unparalleled help in giving concrete expression to the emotion of love. Possessiveness, while intensifying the love for the beloved, can narrow that love. The important issue is not to allow love to narrow its field of operation to self or those immediately associated with self but to inspire it to seek ways to reflect on all of society. If men and women were to take this attitude toward the love that is an inherent part of their beings, they would find a starting point for creating a new image of humanity through their own independent action.

Women can help stimulate the development of this image if they refuse to confine their love to individuals and direct it instead to all things. If we ask ourselves why women love their husbands and children, I think we can answer that it is because women instinctively guard and protect life, the most valuable thing in the universe. Characteristically, since woman gives birth to newly phenomenalized life, she loves life more and hates any threats to it more than man. It is because this is the heart of woman's love for life that her capacity of love can grow to the universal scale.

TOYNBEE: I agree that love tends to be stronger, and pugnacity weaker, in women. This female virtue will be of prime importance in helping mankind to attain at least two of the objectives that must be attained in the near future: the abolition of war and the restraint of aggressive competitiveness.

It is well known that women are more averse to war than men. Though traditionally women themselves have been exempted from military service, their natural tendency is to feel that the killing or maiming of their husbands and sons in war is an atrocity that cannot be justified by any gains that victory may win for the state of which they are citizens. (Spartan mothers, who hounded their sons to death in war, are notorious because their attitude was repulsively unnatural.) There are also some indications that the wives of trades unionists are not as keen as their husbands on trying to extort increases in wages by strikes that impoverish the family temporarily and may impoverish it permanently by bankrupting the industry in which the husband earns a living. In these two fields, female possessiveness and female lovingness work together to cast women's votes in favor of peace instead of war and in favor of economic cooperation in place of economic strife.

IKEDA: The inherent female trait of cherishing life is of the utmost importance to all mankind and to all human society. By expanding their love from the personal to the universal level, women can become a great force against war and for peace. Their journey along this path may be slow, but it will also be sure. Living in accordance with this essential female mission is the way to true woman's liberation.

TOYNBEE: Yes, you are quite right. While female possessiveness tends to limit a woman's horizon to a concern for the members of her own family, female love is potentially universal, because universality is of the essence of love itself. Love means giving oneself, as opposed to taking for oneself. Love, like possessiveness, has no limits short of the limits of the universe.

In the history of Chinese philosophy, there has been a controversy over the question of what is the right allocation of a human being's love. The Confucian philosopher Mencius, citing Confucius as his authority, held that love should be allocated unequally. Love for members of one's own family should be given priority over love for human beings who are strangers and aliens. Mencius combated Mo Tzu, who held that a human being's love should be given in equal measure to all other human beings. This is one of the perennial basic ethical and social problems of human life.

It is a burning question today, when it is evident that mankind must learn to live together as a single family because this is the only alternative to mass suicide in this age in which distance has been annihilated and in which atomic power has been harnessed for weaponry. The problem is acute because current social tendencies are pulling mankind in the direction opposite to the one demanded by accomplished technological facts. Nationalism is becoming more fanatical; smaller and smaller fractions of mankind are now demanding separate local national sovereignty. Within each nation, the scope of family life is dwindling. The traditional human family held together under one roof not only parents and their nonadult children but grandparents, too. The urbanization of life is tending to reduce the scope of a family to a married couple and their nonadult children. There is no place in the family any longer for grandparents and no obligation for children towards their parents when the children are grown-up. Therefore, the Confucian school's insistence on the obligations inherent in family relationships has never been more apposite than it is today. At the same time, Mo Tzu's insistence on the obligation of universal love is still more to the point in a world that has been united technologically already but has not yet been united emotionally.

IKEDA: Although the viewpoints of Confucius, who advocated a graded love moving outward from the family and diminishing in intensity as it goes, and Mo Tzu, who insisted on universal love to all as intense as the love one has for oneself, differ, you are correct in saying that benevolent love of one or both of these kinds is extremely important in modern society. Lack of love is only too apparent in many cases today. People who do not love their parents, brothers, or sisters are not rare. Some parents do not love their own children. Lack of love is often reflected in the actions of people who come to regard their own lives so lightly that they attempt suicide. What can be the meaning of the admonition to love others as one loves oneself when there are people who hate themselves enough to terminate their existence?

I am convinced that the only way to regenerate love in our world is for people to come to understand the meaning of their own lives, of the life of the universe, and of the relation between the two kinds of life. This is true because it is possible to show understanding of the lives of other beings only when one has an understanding of one's own life.

In terms of international conditions, I agree that the universal love of Mo Tzu is entirely apposite in our world, afflicted as it is with hatred, prejudice, and lack of understanding. Mo Tzu's ideas harmonize well with ideals of abolition of war. His insistence that mankind must abandon selfish goals and pursue altruistic ideals leads directly to the kind of foreign policy that big nations ought to adopt. In other words, in keeping with the ideals of Mo Tzu, large, powerful nations are to be severely criticized if they attack small, weak nations for the sake of their own aggrandizement. Applied on a worldwide scale, Mo Tzu's ideals could exert a salutary effect on the modern world.

TOYNBEE: Confucius lived, like the present generation of mankind, in an age of militant nationalism. In his lifetime, the age of Chan Kuo (Warring States) had already set in, though the conventional date of its beginning is later than the date of Confucius's death. It is significant that Confucius drew an analogy between the family and the state, and held that a ruler's subjects ought to feel and to practice a devotion to the ruler of the kind that is due to a father from his children. After the political unification of China and the establishment of Confucianism as the official philosophy of the Chinese Empire, the Confucian concept of the ruler as the head of an expanded family was applied to the emperor. The love and loyalty that were owed primarily to the head of a family ought to be extended to the emperor, so it was held

337

by Confucians in the imperial age, because the emperor was the head of the greater family that was coextensive with all that is under heaven. In the modern age of mankind's history, all that is under heaven has expanded further to embrace the whole surface of the globe and all mankind, instead of remaining confined to the vast, yet less than global, section of mankind that was under Chinese sovereignty, suzerainty, or cultural influence during the twenty-one centuries ending in 1839.

The Confucians' advocacy of the grading of allocation of love in a series of concentric circles is, no doubt, more congenial to human nature than Mo Tzu's doctrine of the obligation of universal love. Every human being knows from his own experience that it is easier for him to love people with whom he is personally acquainted than to love strangers. Yet the paramount need in our own time is precisely the fulfillment of this difficult ethical demand on us to love strangers and to translate this universal love into practical conduct. Confucianism itself holds that the scope of love ought to be universal, even though, in the outermost ring or set of concentric circles, love may legitimately be less intense than within the innermost ring. Thus Confucianism is Mo Tzu-ist in principle.

It is also significant that although, in Chinese society hitherto, the Confucian kind of relative Mo Tzu-ism has prevailed over absolute Mo Tzu-ism, China has now adopted a missionary ideology, communism, which aims at uniting all mankind in a single fraternal communist society. Communism is a heretical version of an older missionary religion—Christianity—and Christianity is the source of Marxian universalism. The founders of the three principal precommunist missionary religions—Buddhism, Christianity, and Islam—all broke away from their families and from their native cities for the sake of teaching a way of salvation for all mankind. In this, Jesus was followed by Saint Francis, who had to break with his father in order to be free to practice the imitation of Christ.

IKEDA: It is impossible to achieve universality of love if one's emotions are narrow and prejudiced in their application. Moreover, love that is not universal but founded on prejudice is not love in the truest sense. In order for the great religious leaders to systematize true love, they found it essential to break away from love directed solely toward parents. But as a consequence of this act they were able to show their parents truer love.

TOYNBEE: After Buddhism had been adopted as one of the religions of China, the Neo-Confucian school of Chinese philosophers criticized the Buddha sharply, in the name of Confucian ethics, for having deserted his

338

family. In the present crisis in human affairs, in which universal love is mankind's one hope of self-salvation, I believe that we ought to be Confucians in the sense of insisting on the validity of the analogy between our obligation to all that is under heaven and our obligations to our intimate family circle. I also believe that we ought to go beyond the limits of even this latitudinarian interpretation of Confucianism. I believe that we ought to be Mo Tzu-ists. We ought to aim at achieving universal love without gradations or qualifications. Mo Tzu-ism is more difficult to practice than Confucianism. But Mo Tzu, rather than Confucius, is, it seems to me, the philosopher whose teaching is most to the point for mankind at the present day. At the western end of the Old World, Zeno, the founder of the Stoic school of Greek philosophy, taught that man is a citizen of the universe. Zeno was a Mo Tzu-ist in effect, though he was unaware that he had been anticipated by an East Asian philosopher.

IKEDA: I too believe that the universal love of Mo Tzu is more important to us today than the graded love of Confucius, but I find that Buddhism has gone even further than Mo Tzu, because it seeks as the source of universal love the universal life force inherent in all people. In other words, in contrast to Mo Tzu, who taught only the importance of universal love, Sakyamuni showed how it is possible for each individual human being to generate that love within himself. The reason for the veneration shown Sakyamuni by countless generations throughout time and over great expanses of space is the fact that, as an embodiment of universal love, he became a personality whose radiance has illuminated the spirit of man for ages and continues to shine undimmed today. Sakyamuni was a great religious leader in that he went beyond teaching theories and philosophy and manifested his religion in his own practical actions and in his life, which was an embodiment of his message. Christ, Mohammed, and Saint Francis, too, were what they taught.

The Highest Human Value

IKEDA: The standards of value upon which man bases his acts vary with the individual. Some assert that it is entirely a matter of taste. Some find criteria of action in values born of social systems—riches, status, and so on. Others stress love, thirst for knowledge, and the subjugation of avarice. Albert Schweitzer's concept of reverence for life is an instance of the latter approach. I think, perhaps in agreement with Schweitzer, that the highest value must be attached to the dignity of life as a universal standard. There can be no value greater than the dignity of life, and any attempt, whether religious or social, to rate something higher must ultimately bring oppression to humanity.

TOYNBEE: I agree that the dignity of life is a universal, absolute standard. But we must not confine the term *life* to the life of the separate—or semi-separate—living beings of whom we ourselves are specimens. The whole universe, and everything in it, is alive in the sense of having dignity. The so-called inanimate and inorganic parts of nature have dignity. There is dignity in the earth, air, water, rocks, springs, rivers, seas; if we human beings violate their dignity, we are violating our own dignity too.

This truth is, I am sure, patent to the Japanese people, who have an ancient tradition of respect for so-called inanimate nature, as well as for the vegetable and animal kingdoms and for human nature. This tradition has been institutionalized in Shinto, and it has been accompanied by a strong aesthetic sense—by a keen appreciation of beauty. However, the Japanese people have begun to violate the dignity of inanimate nature since their adoption of modern scientific technology from the West a century ago, and especially since the amazing explosion of technological expertise and productivity in Japan as a sequel to World War II.

Today there is a worldwide reaction against the pollution of nature through human technology. The present generation recognizes that, in violating nature's dignity, man is violating his own dignity. Such knowledge as I have of Japanese history and of the Japanese sense of dignity (a characteristic of Japanese life that makes a deep impression on foreigners) leads me to guess that the reaction in Japan against pollution is already, or is likely soon to be, especially strong.

IKEDA: Environmental pollution, already an urgent issue in Japan, has stimulated reactions that have taken the form of regional opposition movements by local citizens. Legal steps to do something about it, however, are still far from adequate.

The network of life force pervading all things, animate and inanimate, preserves a magnificent harmony throughout the natural world. Man himself is no more than one part of that world, and in doing it injury he injures himself. Buddhism interprets all of nature—in fact, all of the universe—as one great life force.

Kant says, "In the kingdom of ends everything has either value or dignity. Whatever has a value can be replaced by something else which is equivalent; whatever, on the other hand, is above all value, and therefore admits of no equivalent, has dignity." (*Fundamental Principles of the Metaphysic of Morals.*)

The dignity of life has no equivalent: nothing can be substituted for it. At present people demand a multitude of values; each man strives to develop his own value system. Though, because it may free the concept of value from such narrow confining frameworks as nationalism, this trend is welcome, it seems to me that, while admitting the merit of variety, we must also seek a view of value itself that can serve as a common foundation embracing many kinds of values. Without such a common foundation, human mutual trust and cooperation cannot come into being. In the final analysis, I believe that the worth of man and the dignity of life meet the requirements for this common foundation.

TOYNBEE: I agree again with your belief and with the Buddhist view of life. The distinction, quoted from a passage of Kant's works, between value and dignity is illuminating. Value is relative, and anything that has value can be exchanged for something of equal value (this is the function of money). By contrast, dignity (alias honor) is absolute, not relative; and there is nothing, however valuable, that can be exchanged for dignity or for honor. A human being is despised by others, and he despises himself, if he sells his dignity and honor to gain wealth or social status, or even to save his life. Loss of dignity and honor is the price of moral and physical cowardice. Dignity is irreplaceable; therefore, the loss of dignity is irreplaceable if dignity is lost irretrievably. I think this is the meaning of a passage in the Christian New Testament: "What is a man profited if he shall gain the whole world and lose his own soul? Or what shall a man give in exchange for his soul?" (Matthew 16, 26; Mark 8, 36–7.)

A human being loses his dignity if he sells it. He also loses his own dignity if he does not respect the dignity of other people. It is dishonorable to try to make a fellow human being behave dishonorably, either by persecuting him or by bribing him. The persecutor—and the tempter—forfeits his own dignity and honor, whether his victim preserves his dignity and honor or fails to preserve it under morally illegitimate pressure.

IKEDA: What you say is very true. The nature of the thing on which a man places greatest value characterizes that man's attitude toward all life.

TOYNBEE: I am in agreement with the thesis that dignity is a value that, unlike all other values, is absolute and is impossible to exchange for anything else. From this I conclude that our consciousness of human dignity ought to make us feel humble. Human nature does have dignity, but its dignity is precarious and never complete. A human being is dignified insofar as he is disinterested, altruistic, compassionate, loving, and devoted to other living beings and to the universe. He is undignified insofar as he is greedy and aggressive. The readiness with which we allow ourselves to be greedy and aggressive is humiliating, and the poorness of our ethical performance is made still more humiliating by its contrast with the brilliance of our technological performance.

IKEDA: Certainly, because it is irreplaceable, human life has dignity. But, as you have said, to make that life dignified in the truest and most actual sense requires ceaseless effort. Each human being must bear the responsibility for his own dignity. The dignity of human life has existed since man became capable of high-level consciousness, but man has walked a historical path filled with dissension, hatred, and injuries. The only way for men to give dignity to all aspects of their lives on a practical plane is to abandon hate and injury and to strive to act with beauty and love.

TOYNBEE: The level of man's ethical performance has been low, and it has not risen. The level of his technological performance has risen in an ascending curve, which has risen more rapidly in our time than in any previous time of which we have a record. Consequently the disparity between our technology and our ethics is greater today than it has ever been. This is not simply humiliating; it is mortally dangerous.

Our present situation ought to make us feel humble, and this sense of humility ought to spur us on to achieve the dignity without which our life has no value and without which our life cannot be happy. Human dignity cannot be achieved in the field of technology, in which human beings are so expert. It can be achieved only in the field of ethics, and ethical achievement is measured by the degree in which our actions are governed by compassion and love, not by greed and aggressiveness.

INDEX

Chikushō, 279
China, 42, 53, 95, 136, 164, 179, 229, 232, 241, 288, 336; imperial regime, 214
Ch'in Shih Huang-ti, 121, 214, 217
Christianity, 90, 112, 132, 154, 180, 230, 252, 264, 275, 280, 291, 294, 302, 314, 317, 320, 333, 338
Christian states, 131
Chū, (*Chūtai*), 259, 277, 283
Churchill, Winston, 63, 206
city-state, 81
Clausewitz, 186
communications, 31, 140–46
communism, 131, 164, 179, 181, 214, 220, 294, 297, 299; in China, 233, 235
compassion, 331
complacency, 33
Confucianism, 131, 180, 182, 232, 243, 291, 336, 339; Confucian morality, 66; Neo-Confucianism, 185
conscience, 326
conscious control, 26
consciousness, 26
conscious psychology, 28
conventions, 16
Copernicus, 292
counsels of perfection, 307
Crick, F. H. C., 20
currency, *see* finance

Dante, 72, 278
defense, 193
democracy, 215, 221; democratic leaders, 205, 210; Britain, Japan, 167–69
Democritus, 155, 270
depth psychology, 28
Descartes, 27, 292
desire, 306, 308, 314, 321, 328
dictatorship, 215
dignity of life, 154
diplomacy, Britain, Japan, 169–71
disarmament, 189, 195, 199
disasters, man-made, 43; natural, 42; worldwide, 54
Divinia Commedia, 73, 278
dōku, 332
Dostoevski, 71, 80, 212

East Asia, religions in, 293
economic affluence, 103
education, coeducation, 66–67; financing, 64–66. *See also* learning

egoism, *see* self-centeredness
Egypt, 42, 287
ehō, 37
Einstein, 33, 258, 260, 271
End, the, 54
Engaku, 279
Engel, 270
enlightenment, 314, 316
environment, 21, 37, 39, 43, 300
Epicurus, 81
epistemology, 276
Eshō Funi, 22, 37
ethics, 305
European Economic Community, 170
euthanasia, 151
evil, 56, 143, 325
eyes, the five kinds in Buddhism, 86

family, 132
Faraday, Michael, 271
fate, 316, 322
finance, 225–27
Four Evils, 279
Francis of Assisi, 40, 307, 338
freedom, 59; of literary expression, 69, 74; of the press, 145; restrictions on freedom of expression, 71
French Revolution, 136, 220
Freud, Sigmund, 27, 309
Fromm, Erich, 216

Gaki, 279
Galileo, 260, 292
Gamow, George, 262
genes, 20
genetics, 20, 23
Germany, 163; West, 241. *See also* National Socialist Party *and* Nazism
globalism, 214
God, 39, 54, 321
Goethe, 80
good, 44, 329
Greco-Roman, political religion, 294; religion, 301; world, 136, 290, 298
greed, 38, 43, 47, 58, 120, 295, 299, 305, 309, 321
Greek civilization, 323. *See also* Greco-Roman world
Greek federation, 244
gross national product, 106; welfare, 106

Han Liu Pang, 121, 208, 214

science, 35, 84; as a religion, 299; eye of, 83; importance of, 19; relation with religion, 35; role of, 112
scientific observation, 35; rationality, 35; research, 69; spirit, 19; technology, 44
self-centeredness, 23, 305
self-defense, 193–97
selfishness, 312
Selye, Hans, 95
sense perception, 16, 33, 86
senses (Indian Vijnanavada school), 27
sex, 15–17; education, 16, 144; liberation, 15; sexual behavior, 19; sexual relations, 18
Shih Huang-ti, *see* Ch'in Shih Huang-ti
Shikishin Funi, 24
Shinsenkyō, 322
Shinto, 38, 41, 232, 238, 293, 300
shōhō, 37
Shōmon, 279
Shujō, 267
Shura, 279
Siddartha Gautama, the Buddha, 40, 82, 307, 312, 339
sin, 329
Sino-Japanese War, 229, 234
Six Paths, 279
socialism, 100
social justice, 210
Socrates, 80
Solzhenitsyn, 70
South Africa, 165
sovereign states, *see* localism
Soviet Union, 70, 163, 229, 233, 236, 241
species, death of, 22
spiritualism, 24, 30
spiritual revolution, *see* human revolution
spiritual welfare, 106
state secrets, 145
state, the, 132
Stoic school, 81, 185
Strabo, 49
stress theory, 95
subconscious, 28, 33
suicide, 97, 153
Switzerland, 162

Taoism, 245
Tat tvam asi, 25, 259, 313, 316
teaching, 67
technology, 38, 41, 85, 140, 306, 342
telepathy, 30

television, 141
Ten, 279
Ten Life Factors, *see Jū-nyoze*
Ten States of Life, 278
theism, 302
Theodore of Tarsus, 63
Three Evil Paths, 279
Three Truths, *see Santai* theory
Three Worlds of Buddhism, 296
Tibet, 234
T'ien-t'ai Buddhism, 28, 282
Tokugawa Ieyasu, 121, 175, 214, 244
Tokugawa shogunate, 233, 323
Tokyo, 46
Tolstoy, 70, 76
Toyotomi Hideyoshi, 121, 175, 214, 244
trades union, 117–19, 319
traffic accidents, 50
transportation, 49
Turgenev, 81
Turkey, 180

ultimate spiritual reality, 254, 303, 313, 316, 320
unemployment, 125
United Nations, 130, 189, 236
United States, 161–63, 229, 233, 236, 241
universal life force, 28; love, 306
universe, 22, 261, 265
Upanishads, 313
Utopia, 322
utopia, 322–23

Vasubandhu, 27
Viet Cong, 142
Vietnam War, 19, 142, 161, 163, 177, 190
Vishnu, 321
Vita Nuova, 73
Void, the, 271

Wada, Juro, 90
war, 19, 148, 186, 190, 198, 201
war criminals, trials, 176–77
wasteful private consumption, 57
Watson, J. D., 20
weaponry, 187, 193; nuclear, 239
Weimar Republic, 209
welfare state, 102–5; in Britain, 102; in Japan, 104, 105
Weltanshauung, 37, 74, 232
women's liberation movement, 108

347